PARTY
LEADERSHIP AND
REVOLUTIONARY
POWER IN
CHINA

PARTY LEADERSHIP AND REVOLUTIONARY POWER IN CHINA

EDITED BY

JOHN WILSON LEWIS

Professor of Political Science
Stanford University, California

CAMBRIDGE
AT THE UNIVERSITY PRESS
1970

Published by the Syndics of the Cambridge University Press
Bentley House, 200 Euston Road, London N.W.1
American Branch: 32 East 57th Street, New York, N.Y. 10022

© Cambridge University Press 1970

Library of Congress Catalogue Card Number: 72–120056

Standard Book Numbers
521 07792 3 Clothbound
521 09614 6 Paperback

Set in Great Britain by Alden & Mowbray Ltd.
at the Alden Press, Oxford and
printed in the United States of America

CONTENTS

CONTENTS

PART IV

THE NEW VIEW OF POWER IN THE
CULTURAL REVOLUTION

PREFACE

STUART R. SCHRAM

This volume is the first in our series of Contemporary China Institute Publications. The Institute was set up in 1968 with the aim of furthering research on China since the May Fourth Movement, with particular emphasis on the period since 1949. It is linked to the School of Oriental and African Studies of the University of London, but enjoys a certain degree of autonomy, in keeping with its vocation of serving as a link between interested persons throughout the United Kingdom, both within and without the universities. The establishment of the Institute was made possible by an initial grant from the Ford Foundation.

In a sense, this first book constitutes a most atypical beginning for our series, which will have as its core the work of Research Fellows and other persons associated with the Institute. This volume of essays is the fruit of a conference planned before the Institute came into existence by the former Editor of *The China Quarterly*, Roderick MacFarquhar, and organized by Professor John Wilson Lewis of Stanford University. When control of *The China Quarterly* passed to the Contemporary China Institute in the spring of 1968, we assumed the sponsorship of the conference as well, Professor Lewis retaining full responsibility for the academic arrangements. This volume contains a selection of the papers presented at the conference, which was held at Ditchley Park, Oxfordshire, in July 1968.

Different as it is in origin from the works which will follow it in our series, this first title is, in another way, very much in its place, for one of the primary tasks which we have set ourselves is to encourage and facilitate contacts between those working on contemporary China in the United Kingdom, in Europe, and throughout the world. This volume, with contributions by scholars from many different institutions in England and the United States, can therefore be viewed as a step on the road to the still broader exchanges which we aim ultimately to foster. In particular, it is our hope that one day scholars from the Chinese People's Republic will agree to participate in the discussion of developments in their country.

Meanwhile, it is a pleasure to send forth this collection of essays, in the hope that it will be found interesting and useful by both specialists and non-specialists. It is likewise a particular pleasure to thank John Wilson Lewis for all the hard work and devotion which he has put into this undertaking, entirely without any reward save the excitement and satisfaction of contributing to the knowledge of an important and as yet inadequately explored phenomenon.

LEADERSHIP AND POWER IN CHINA

JOHN WILSON LEWIS

THE EMERGING POLITICAL SYSTEM IN CHINA

The convocation of the Ninth National Congress of the Chinese Communist Party from April 1 to 24, 1969 closed a four-decade era of political leadership in China. The revolutionaries who as youths joined ranks with Mao Tse-tung were held together by common bonds of ideological inspiration, personal loyalty and professional or conspiratorial dedication. In the Cultural Revolution these bases of brotherhood and their common world vision were shattered. Party members, once closely united, clashed over practical policy issues and then over the legitimacy of their Party adversaries to rule at all. Mao in the ensuing struggle deposed his former comrades and promoted the second political revolution of his lifetime.

While the Ninth Congress preserved the idea of a Chinese Communist Party, it also pronounced last rites for the national organization that had brought the revolutionary movement to victory in 1949. With its missions of mobilizing the Chinese people and constructing a powerful new China given to the People's Liberation Army and local "revolutionary committees", the Party had become just another Maoist tool for waging battle on sinister social influences and revisionist classes. The Communist organization, whatever its ultimate fate, had lost its special identity and its stature as the price of nominal existence in a Maoist world.

We are currently witnessing the emergence of a post-revolutionary political system on the Mainland. Nonetheless Mao still seeks in the name of revolution to revive chosen elements of the earlier Party-led system and to retain them as parts of China's political institutions. With the widely heralded republication of his "Report to the Second Session of the Seventh Central Committee" (March, 1949),[1]

[1] Reprinted in *Hung ch'i* [Red Flag], No. 5, 1968.

I

Mao seemed to be hoping to turn the clock back to this decree which shifted Chinese communism's "centre of gravity" from the rural bases to the cities and identified the social classes forming the new coalition of power. Much is made of the fact that Mao then warned his colleagues that the transitional years ahead could interrupt the revolution by weakening the class-based struggle and by causing individual Party members without class consciousness to succumb to corruption and the easy life. Mao is attempting, apparently, to erase from public memory much of what occurred in China from 1949 to 1969 and to fashion leadership techniques as if the seizure of power by revolutionary committees and the armed forces in the Cultural Revolution were a directed continuation of the Party's "Liberation" of China two decades ago. He would like the effects of his second revolution to be, simultaneously, conservative and progressive, which may account for some of the ambiguities in his thought and the lack of consensus in China on the revolution's results.

Mao has taken charge personally of the post-Congress rebuilding process. To insure his own dominance and that of his chosen associates, he presented a constitution to the Ninth Congress that defied Lenin's principles of organization, while invoking the Leninist symbols of democratic centralism.[1] The former vanguard apparatus had been composed of personally powerful cadres qualified to assume the responsibilities of leadership. Organized to determine priority tasks and get them done, cadres had acquired relevant skills in a bureaucratic and competitive process of training and indoctrination. Theoretically, a Communist cadre was so disciplined to abide by the Party line that he could be detached to function on his own. Now, however, the cadre's job assignment is secondary to his learning and transmitting the Maoist viewpoint of class struggle. All echo Chairman Mao, and even the word "cadre" has lost its former appeal and unique place in the Chinese political vocabulary. The current constitution also fails to give the political and administrative organs of the Central Committee final jurisdiction over policy determination. That power too now rests with Mao.

[1] For official English-language text, see *Peking Review*, No. 18 (April 30, 1969).

DIVERGENT ATTITUDES TOWARD THE
ORGANIZATION OF POWER

As the new Communist system begins to evolve it will be important for understanding it to compare its functions with those of the pre-1966 Communist Party. The authors in this volume based on papers presented to the Ditchley Conference on the Party have raised a series of questions concerning the Party from 1927 to 1969, and the answers to these questions may help facilitate this comparison. What role did Mao play in the crucial years of the Party's formation? What were the sources of his political strength? How did he and other leaders view the Party organization? What made his authority legitimate in the eyes of the membership? What limits were placed on that authority in practice? Within the top command, what were the personal relationships as well as institutional ties that could produce potential or actual cliques? To what extent were there clear boundary lines between the Party and the Army and between them and the society at large? What changes were wrought within the Communist organization after the take-over in 1949?

Perhaps the most elementary conclusion to be drawn from a consideration of these questions is that the Chinese Communists seek as an article of common faith to monopolize the full range of powers for eliciting compliance with their norms and directives and for inducing broad institutional change throughout China. Nevertheless, their writings on power provide contradictory interpretations of its proper domain, scope and coerciveness. Although it is only in the documents of the Cultural Revolution that Communist leaders openly acknowledge their lack of accord on how a Communist system of power should be constituted and for what purposes, the roots of these differences, I believe, can be found in the earlier history of the Party. While even the recent materials are vague concerning the precise definitions of power and its ultimate goals, they do indicate a fairly consistent range of views in the Communist hierarchy regarding the organization and exercise of power. This introduction is intended in part to summarize these differences and to examine their consequences.

Before proceeding to this task, however, I would caution against exaggerating the philosophical bases underlying different attitudes toward the organization of power. These bases, though certainly significant, must be weighed alongside the more personal preferences of key leaders and the way they perceive the stakes for which they are competing. The debate about the correct organization of power constitutes a serious component in the actual contest for power. Mao Tse-tung, for example, has characteristically opposed coercive or bureaucratic power within the Party, publicly considering it oppressive and self-defeating. A devaluation of this type of power, of course, would help diminish the influence of Party bureaucrats and lend support to Mao's allies outside the bureaucracy. Typical of his tactical usage of public contempt for the Organization Man was the introduction to his report of July, 1955 in which he deliberately sought to upset the established leaders blocking his policy for a "new upsurge in the socialist mass movement" in the countryside. He said in a reference directed toward that apparatus, "some of our comrades are tottering along like a woman with bound feet, always complaining that others are going too fast. They imagine that by picking on trifles, grumbling unnecessarily, worrying continuously and putting up countless taboos and commandments they are guiding the socialist mass movement..."[1] By discrediting the way these "comrades" approached power, Mao helped assure victory for his policies.

The practice of manipulating attitudes concerning the "correct" organization of power is not exclusive to Chairman Mao. In expressing a Utopian version of Mao's anti-bureaucratic bias, a local group in Hunan in 1968, the so-called *Sheng wu lien* (Provincial Proletarian Alliance), taunted the bureaucrats opposing them and rejoiced at their collapse: "People suddenly found that without the bureaucrats they not only could go on living, but could live better and develop quicker and with greater freedom."[2] Leadership without bureaucrats, they held, would not require coercion for it would elicit a more Confucian-like response to wise guidance and moral teaching.

[1] Mao Tse-tung, *The Question of Agricultural Co-operation* (Peking: Foreign Languages Press, 1956), p. 1.

[2] "Whither China?" *Kuang yin hung ch'i* [Canton Printing Red Flag], No. 5, March, 1968, in *Survey of China Mainland Press*, No. 4190, pp. 1–18.

4

Yet nationally the extreme Maoist position represented a challenge to the centre, and it never passed beyond the realm of wishful thinking as Peking's lieutenants smashed the *Sheng wu lien* group in the name of the Chairman.

The primacy of tactical considerations in debates about power has led to the promotion of concepts which cannot easily be put into practice. The organization of power in accordance with Mao's theory now that he reigns supreme has proved especially difficult because it has rarely been defined in positive, operational terms. Most of his recent views on the subject are found in denunciations of Liu Shao-ch'i, the former heir apparent charged with corrupting political leadership by the way he organized power in the Communist Party. Mao's persecution of the Liuist "group" is described officially as a pre-emptive strike against alleged trends in China toward a Soviet-style bureaucratic dictatorship. While it is probably true that the Chinese power structure under Liu could be fairly characterized as task-oriented, organization-minded and ruthless, the same labels could be attached to the actual Maoist alternative in current use.

Historically, power was never organized according to a strict "Liuist" or "Maoist" model, at least for very long. The deposed Liu's attitude towards the organization of power tolerated compromise for strategic gains and was not as fixed and consciously anti-Maoist as legend will hereafter have it. It is even debatable whether or not modern China had a single power system in the heyday of bureaucratic communism.[1] The politics of both Mao and Liu represented tendencies along a continuum, and according to complaints by the *Sheng wu lien* radicals in 1968, Mao in the course of the Cultural Revolution was compelled to stage a retreat which they called "unprecedented".[2] Substantiating this, a careful analysis of the outcome of the Cultural Revolution at the time of the Ninth Congress would indicate that Mao has not attained his stated objectives in the restructuring of power in China. Many top bureaucrats have been replaced, but others remain in positions of real

[1] For a contrary argument, see Tang Tsou, "The Cultural Revolution and the Chinese Political System", *The China Quarterly*, No. 38 (April–June, 1969), p. 63.

[2] "Whither China?", in *Survey of China Mainland Press*, No. 4190, p. 10.

authority, particularly at the local levels. Mao's efforts to rehabilitate and reform cadres as well as to "purify their class ranks" remain unfinished business.

THE CHANGING ROLES OF THE COMMUNIST PARTY IN THE REVOLUTIONARY STRUGGLE

None of the principal doctrines of power, when put into practice, has been able to escape the limits imposed by the requirements of making strategic choices over time or by the varied sociological and political conditions that differentiated one part of China from the other. The consequences of the changing and highly differentiated environments for the development of the Chinese Communist Party and its approaches to power are major themes in this volume.

Part I examines the history of the Chinese Communist movement with particular reference to the formation of the senior elite during the course of the pre-1949 revolution. This elite's ambiguous and uncertain role in the chaotic period following its near-destruction in 1927 is the subject of C. Martin Wilbur's essay. He discusses the makeup of the leadership cohort that outlasted the government's suppression campaigns of this period, and went on to guide the revolutionary movement. Both attracted and tested by the rigours of violent revolution, the youthful survivors gained command experience and self-confidence; success in combat bred a strong bond of comradeship among the Party leaders. In his careful, statistical account, Professor Wilbur recounts the burdens and the costs of the early struggle and explains the consequences of the conflict for the revolutionaries themselves. Characteristically, the survivors had proven leadership ability and extraordinary personal commitment to the Communist cause.

By assessing the impact of violence, frustration and defeat, the Wilbur chapter reveals that a steady transformation took place within the Party leadership after 1927. Raw, inexperienced young recruits were toughened and trained to become flexible, pragmatic and tough-minded. Party leaders either lost their fear and timid intellectualism or did not survive. The many geographical, institutional and psychological environments in which they operated taught them different lessons and each adapted in a slightly special way. In practice such adjustments to realities could involve the adoption of techniques from secret societies or other traditional institutions. The mini-circuit by which each Communist plugged in to the revolution could be quite unorthodox but the common language of Marxism tended to camouflage the uniqueness of individual experiences and to preserve the Communist's sense of revolutionary identity and correctness. For almost forty years leaders in the movement would help shape institutional practices and policies as if their unity of purpose were beyond doubt.

How it was that Mao emerged as the central figure in this movement is part of the story told by William F. Dorrill. His exhaustive inquiry into the actual part played by Mao in two key events in the Kiangsi Soviet raises doubts concerning the validity of Mao's public claim to legitimacy and highlights the competitive processes that underlay Mao's rise to power. The trial-and-error character of his leadership method stands out at the strategic Fourth Plenum of the Party Central Committee in January, 1931 and during the Fukien Rebellion of 1934. At these moments of critical decision, Mao was endowed with no special wisdom by which he could foresee the future and exhibited no unusual persuasiveness by which he could sway his colleagues. His position of authority, moreover, was subject to challenge by competitors in the base areas. Constrained by these intra-Party limits and the uncertainties of Moscow's mandate, Mao came to master the art of the possible. Tactically brilliant, he was usually able to manoeuvre his potential political rivals to commit themselves while he temporized and, as far as possible, let the situation work itself out elastically. Only later in the *ex post facto* reconstruction of Party history was the pure thread of ideological correctness woven into Mao's *ad hoc* and revocable decisions, and from the fictionalized version of events was to come the basis for Mao's claim to supreme leadership of the Communist revolution.

The problem of legitimacy raised by Professor Dorrill is a fundamental one.[1] The basis on which Chinese Communists accept

[1] For the attempts of two other scholars to deal with this problem, see Lucian Pye, *The Spirit of Chinese Politics: A Psychocultural Study of the Authority*

authority as legitimate must be ascertained before we can grapple with many of the concrete issues of power in Communist history. In large measure Mao's endowment with charisma was accomplished retroactively by a public relations campaign. This effort was restricted to an audience within the movement on the assumption that acceptance of Mao's charisma did not depend on external popular consent. Such an undertaking was not determined by the real issues of the past or by how they were resolved. The decision to establish Mao's legitimacy for the Kiangsi period was made in 1945, ten years after the period ended, and the Kiangsi history was written primarily with an eye to discrediting Mao's adversaries of 1945 and to give assurance to his supporters at that time that the failures of Kiangsi would not be repeated. As in the case of the Soviet effort to magnify Stalin's prestige, this rewriting of Chinese history was highly selective in that it skipped over those issues on which the memory was still too sensitive or where the issue itself was largely undecided. The act of legitimation would have the effect of giving assurances to the membership that the future would lead inevitably to Communist victory. This is particularly important in Communist organizations where in theory the leader must know where history is going and what the truth about history is. To the extent that the Party's voice is the voice of the leader, Mao had to be correct in his leadership from the beginning in order for the whole course of history associated with his name to have been correct. Such correctness is, it seems, necessary to preserve the element of faith in the movement.

This still leaves unresolved the question of how the Party leaders themselves think about history.[1] For those who had lived through the relevant events, the revision of history would mean something different than for those with no personal memory. For neither would

Crisis in Political Development (Cambridge, Mass.: M.I.T. Press, 1968); and Richard Solomon, "On Activism and Activists: Maoist Conceptions of Motivation and Political Role Linking State and Society", The China Quarterly, No. 39 (July–September, 1969). Professor Solomon participated in the Ditchley Conference and this section as well as many of the papers profited greatly from his insights.

[1] See Albert Feuerwerker, ed., History in Communist China (Cambridge, Mass.: M.I.T. Press, 1968).

a truthful account necessarily be important or desirable so long as the principal approach to the historical record was to obtain political advantage. The Communists appear to consider the current record of history as it legitimates or discredits, a useful device for silencing critics, teaching young recruits and authorizing new policies. All these uses can be seen in the history examined by Professor Dorrill.

The probing of orthodox history does more than explain policies and appearances. The extent of Mao's power and the accuracy of his analysis must be determined if we are to discover his own view of the Party not only in the Kiangsi Soviet but also in the successive decades of his leadership. Such a discovery helps us come to terms with the sources of Mao's power against such apparently strong organizations as the Army and the senior Party bureaucracy. In Kiangsi, Mao played the leading role in the Army and governmental apparatus, though others such as Chu Te also had great power. The Party high command had already repudiated him once, and during the turbulent Kiangsi years the men who ran the Central Committee came close to disgracing him again.[1] Mao's relationship with the Party was thus a strained one, and even as its Chairman he felt far from comfortable in leaving the interpretation of his will and the implementation of his policies to Party cadres.[2] His view of Party organization as revealed in the Cultural Revolution thus has roots that reach back to his experiences in the Kiangsi Soviet. Yet, in the optimism of his early leadership, he seems to have willingly tolerated great diversity in the movement, and only later did the traces of exclusivism in his thought become dominant.

The essay by Leonard Schapiro and John Lewis seeks to place Mao's relationship to the Party in comparative perspective. The roles of Communist and Fascist parties are examined in terms of the leader-party relationship as well as by contrasting the actual roles

[1] See John Rue, *Mao Tse-tung in Opposition: 1927–1935* (Stanford: Stanford Univ. Press, 1966), esp. chaps. x–xii.

[2] In the fifties Mao was often to declare before his comrades sentiments that harked back to mass, not Party, associations. On July 23, 1959, for example, he said: "...I would go to the countryside to lead the peasants to overthrow the government. If the Liberation Army won't follow me, I will then find the Red Army. I think the Liberation Army will follow me." "Speech at Lushan Conference", translated in *Chinese Law and Government*, I, No. 4 (Winter 1968–9), p. 35.

of the Chinese Communist organization that developed in territories under Mao and those under the immediate influence of partisan commanders. A review of totalitarian parties shows how different situations in the struggle for power imposed limits on the independent authority of individual leaders or, conversely, provided them with the opportunity for the exercise of greater authority. Totalitarian systems have exhibited no uniform pattern in respect to the relationship of the party apparatus to the leader. Variations in one-party government seem to depend especially on the strength of the party that exists at the time the leader comes to power and on his personality.

The institution of the Chinese Communist Party has changed drastically in response to the vision of the central leadership, the conditions of military and political combat, and beliefs about the Party stemming from Marxist–Leninist ideology. For a cadre capable of adapting Party mechanisms to his own local needs in the revolution, the Communist organization as he would know it would have a special meaning and utility. Generally speaking, however, in the thirties and forties, such adaptations divided roughly into two principal types, one associated with Mao's relatively secure base area in Yenan and one identifiable with those Communist guerrillas who operated behind enemy lines. Only the latter could truly appreciate the inadequacy of human courage when under a constant threat of death, and this *de facto* separation of the revolutionary movement into at least two types of areas, moreover, created a basic tension between ideologically determined norms of cadre behaviour emanating from the centre in Yenan and the demands on local guerrilla leaders to perform effectively. During the revolutionary war, the senior leadership elite concentrated on channelling this tension so as to maintain the Party's overall unity and to avoid "factionalism", a term often indicating excessive independence or localism. Informal steps taken to offset this pressure by seeking outside support were outlawed, and Party conflict was sealed within the organization itself. Up to the late civil war the Communist organization had concentrated so heavily on its own internal systems for cohesion and survival in revolution, that it had, despite the mythology, little direct relationship with Chinese outside the base area villages and few specific rules for the activist leadership role it was then called on to perform in the modern rural and urban sectors of society. Whereas the consequences of the Party's changing role were largely restricted to the Party itself and to the poorer rural areas of North China before the late forties, this exclusiveness was no longer possible after the Liberation. Thereafter inner-Party techniques were refurbished for use in the society at large, and a more uniform Party role was developed for national purposes. The one chosen was closely associated with the *apparatchiks* under Liu Shao-ch'i.

The essays in Part I could be summarized as the rise, temporary eclipse and crusading comeback of Mao Tse-tung. A recurrent theme in this section concerns Mao's relationship to the Party. This pertains not only to his own evolving role as Chairman within the Party but to his changing concept of Party morality. Thus this first part of the book helps identify the possible reasons why Mao attacked the Party in the Cultural Revolution. Did he do so because he was morally dissatisfied with the degeneration of Party institutions and with the self-seeking of its members? Is Mao a latter-day Lenin, revolted by greedy men who have wormed their way into an institution he considers essentially moral? Does Mao seek "revolutionary immortality", to use Robert Lifton's phrase, or is he more power-drunk than disgusted in his old age, obsessed more with the idea of smashing those who once wrenched power from him than with restoring the ideals of Yenan? Much of what we decide here depends on how Mao is viewed, and this section seeks to set forth, however tentatively, the range of issues which Mao considers decisive when discussing the Party. As will be evident from a comparison of the chapters in Part I, the several authors do not always agree on how Mao should be viewed or on the issues he regards as central.

THE POWER ELITE IN THEORY AND PRACTICE

The potential destructiveness of divisive forces within the senior elite assigned to different areas and responsibilities made critically important the maintaining of cohesion to insure the success of the

Chinese Communist revolution. One can see in the orthodox Maoist history of the Party a strong belief that disunity at the top was the principal factor for the revolution's major setbacks and errors. The attempt at unifying the Party still permitted the members some initiative even after the 1949 take-over, however, and some latent differences either were not perceived or were by-passed rather than openly confronted. The Maoists have now exaggerated these differences and fail to acknowledge that the previous unity of world outlook within the top command rendered tolerable sharp differences of opinion on policies and tactics.

What we are dealing with here is the inner world of the top command in China. Until it assumed power in 1949, this elite was in a state of constant motion, reacting to a hostile external world. Until its members retreated in their old age to reflection and mutual recriminations, the Communist leadership displayed remarkable toughness and self-assurance in the face of this hostility. The Chinese leadership—as is so often the fate of victors—then fell victim to internal disputes. When the relationships based on shared ideology and comradely affection weakened only more personal ties remained. During most of the period under review these personal bonds had served to produce strong loyalty and genuine comradeship. Common revolutionary experiences, intermarriage and friendship, once virtually ignored as politically significant, may now constitute the most important linkages in Chinese political life.

The three essays in Part II of this volume deal with just these problems from the viewpoint of ideology, intra-Party motivation and elite factionalism. The strains created by the changing roles of the Party over the past four decades gradually shifted the standards of correct behaviour for the senior Party member and upset the accepted bases for his authority and the content of his ideas. There was always a tendency to accentuate the sense of belonging to an impersonal system and these shifts merely accelerated the tendency until the Cultural Revolution. The integrative mechanisms in the power elite were meant to differ sharply from those in the society, and in fact the rule-book institutionalization of the elite was consciously directed to break down the old social relationships and to create acceptable alternatives. When Mao launched the

Cultural Revolution, he challenged the Party's independent identity in Chinese society and cast doubt on the need for a Party to sustain the Communist leadership.

The need for a Communist Party in Mao's China has thus ceased to depend on the uniqueness and utility of its organization. Its *raison d'être* is now ideological or nothing. The broad, comparative essay by Benjamin I. Schwartz portrays Mao as a deliberate wrecker of the Party organizations but still unprepared to jettison the sacred Party label. Many Communists and revolutionaries such as Fidel Castro, Schwartz states, are prepared to eliminate the Party as such because their revolutions succeeded without the Party. For Mao, however, communism's victory could not have come without the Party, making it almost sacred and a *sine qua non* of any revolutionary movement. He equates the role of the Party in the Chinese struggle with its role everywhere and thus has to rebuild the Party as a symbol of China's revolutionary authenticity. In China, perhaps more than in any other Communist country today, the Party is supposed to live up to, in a credible way, an intolerably heavy burden of moral and intellectual attributes.

According to Benjamin Schwartz this new Party is the tool of the supreme leader who bestows his mantle of authority on the organization rather than vice versa. The Party, moreover, is not the only body to receive his blessing as it competes with the Army, the revolutionary committees and even mass organs. The issue of leader versus institution finds its intellectual origins, Schwartz argues, in the political philosophy of Jean Jacques Rousseau. Rousseau like Mao was concerned with higher moral progress and put man's goodness above his economic development. Such goodness could only be achieved by a communal effort with the individual joining his will with that of the entire people. Since Rousseau, the Marxists and others have identified the general virtue with particular classes, institutions and eventually with a single charismatic leader. In China, Professor Schwartz says, Mao stands as the "fountainhead of all morality, standing high above all laws and institutions..." In theory, the moral leader assures the reign of virtue and the moral goodness of the Party institution.

Stuart R. Schram addresses his essay directly to the problem of the Party institution as it has been conceived by Mao and Liu Shao-ch'i. The central reality for Mao was that any structure could halt revolutionary momentum by inhibiting the struggle that was supposed to underlie all action. According to Professor Schram, Mao argued that only the leader could give the necessary orders and bring unity to the movement while Liu stressed the importance of Party organization and group discipline for promoting the revolutionary cause. Professor Schram's analysis shows why Mao finally decided to smash the Party hierarchy as a way of preserving the Party's spirit and mission and sets forth the historical steps by which Mao came to oppose Liu's concept of the Party as an independent, almost metaphysical entity. Although Mao came to believe that the Party bureaucracy precluded effective leadership by cutting the cadres off from the populace, his Yenan views of Communist organization closely approximated Liu's. Both held that the Party represented the interests of society as a whole.

Since the onset of the Cultural Revolution in the mid-sixties, Mao has set out to re-establish the subjective bases for his moral authority. In the process of upsetting the old order, ideology has been narrowly redefined as the thought of Mao Tse-tung, and a firm attachment to this thought has been fostered to create closer linkages between the political system and Chinese society. By ideological exhortation, leaders and led are induced to work together, and this sharing in labour, Mao holds, provides the proper moral basis for correct leadership. Mao uses ideology to insulate the revolutionary from the hollowness of routine and to enhance his ability to participate meaningfully. In this way the Maoist cadre in theory can adapt to the pressures from the centre above and the masses below. But in fact cadres in the recently created activist-based institutions have become victims of these increasingly powerful cross-pressures. The result has been a separatist and somewhat anomic reaction contrary to Mao's expectation that the restructuring of relationships would insure continuing high motivation and unified leader–mass relationships.

This raises the question of how the Chinese Communists value certain capabilities in the movement. Still hoping to maximize all skills, Mao has witnessed the way some skills cancel others out.

He has thus had to set priorities and his choice has fallen on ideological loyalty and personal dependence. It is not enough to say that subjective factors are crucial to revolutionary life for in every case it makes a marked difference which factors are approved. Mao has not been able to escape the organizational dilemma posed by having to choose between stability for effective rule in the short run and moral principle for the long run.

Mao's approach to leadership is a classic one wherein the personal authority of the leader at the top is supreme, and the members in the organization below simply provide him with extra pairs of hands to do his bidding. Mao's cadres are required to respond only to him, but his concept of leader requires little, if any, reciprocation on his own part. In such a one-sided system, the only sensible way out for the cadre is the formation of independent bases of support and personal factions. In the fifties, the Maoist concept of leadership coincided with bureaucratic tendencies towards localism and autonomy in the Party and state organizations where Communist rules stressed task completion and organizational stability.

How and why this happened is the subject of Philip Bridgham's chapter on factionalism in the Central Committee of the Communist Party. As Dr Bridgham's carefully researched paper shows, Mao's preoccupation with his own authority made him label any signs of opposition to that authority as "factional" even though the cadres so identified by him would not, at first, have considered themselves to be factionalists. What we have here is a failure to communicate. Bridgham's chapter describes how the men and women who survived the early battles of the revolution have reacted to more recent crises and problems in terms of their earlier perceptions. The three great factional struggles analysed by this chapter are examples of how differing perceptions can cause efforts at reform to escalate into full-scale power struggles. What Mao has failed to realize is that his own concept of leadership and power in China was as much to blame for factionalism as the bureaucratic tendencies linked to Liu Shao-ch'i.

Attaching weights to the sources of cohesion and cleavage in Chinese politics has always been an annoying problem. This is so in part because the bases for solidarity in the Chinese Communist system are difficult to perceive through the façade of official propaganda and the misleading aura of organizational unity that pervades the ideology. This is also the case because the formal command and mobility structures superimposed on Party operations make it difficult for the principal actors below the top echelon to understand the real politics involved and to make the requisite adjustments. These structures distort the analysis of leadership and power by making formal organizational patterns seem more important than they are. As seen in the rivalries exposed in the Cultural Revolution and also in the make-up of the Ninth Central Committee, informal groupings are crucial to the flow of decisions, indeed to the whole conduct of Chinese political life.

In the ongoing political combat in China, formal appearances of course can help camouflage positions of vulnerable officials and their emerging policies. Limited to the public media—now mostly newspapers and radio broadcasts—for our data, we cannot readily ascertain who has actual power in Peking or by what mechanisms national power is exercised. The old labels that helped provide some guidelines have also become blurred: Party, Army, cadre, Communist and revolutionary lack fixed or discrete meanings. It may well be that at present there is no single well-integrated political system for all China and that, as Mao has sometimes insisted, there are a number of different centres or even "independent kingdoms" within the power elite exercising autonomous authority. Some near the top may have greater access to the instruments of coercion as well as those of economic and normative power, and clearly China has long been a country in which experience in the highest echelons provides a decisive advantage over those lower down. For the period after 1965, however, we do not yet know what kinds of experience—comparable to participation in the revolution—provide the critical assets for surviving the internal power struggle at the top. We can conclude from the Bridgham study that those political combatants uninhibited by a rigid operational code and a genuine sense of discipline and loyalty to the Party have a decisive edge over adversaries who adhere to Communist rules and loyally obey the decisions of the centre.[1]

---

[1] This modifies somewhat the "general rule" that "Under conditions of political combat, those who have no firm values of their own become the

Mao exemplifies a man who wants others to do what he says, not what he does. Articles on unified centralism in early 1969 made this point with unusual force and candour. The newspaper *Wen hui pao* on January 5, for example, proclaimed the need for "correct" centralism in the power elite in order to achieve unified thinking, policies, plans, command and action. Correctness, in this definition, started with Mao's statements for only Mao is presumed to have the correct thinking. Others were required to imitate the lessons set forth in his verbal instructions. Those who do not are guilty of bourgeois factionalism and other evils. None dares examine Mao's actual practice. The Chairman is thus attempting to obviate the practical problems that may arise in the institutionalization of the elite by creating a written standard for all actions that becomes internalized and absolute. He also expects Party members to integrate themselves with the populace so that through them his message will be transmitted to the country without distortion and without question. In the name of activism Mao has deactivated many sectors of the power elite and neutralized the men of initiative who ran China for twenty years. Now more than ever before, leadership appears rehearsed; the political scenes are drawn from a Peking opera written and orchestrated by Mao.

THE COMMUNIST PARTY AND CHINESE SOCIETY
AFTER THE TAKE-OVER IN 1949

The essays in Part III describe the Party in Chinese society after 1949. The first two chapters, one by Thomas Bernstein and one by Merle Goldman, deal respectively with the operations of the Communist Party in villages and intellectual circles and attempt to show the degree to which various intra-Party techniques and skills equipped the Party cadres and members for leadership in various sectors of the society. Michel Oksenberg's essay at the end of this section makes the case that by virtue of its leadership position

instruments of the values of others." Philip Selznick, *The Organizational Weapon* (New York: Free Press, 1960), p. 308.

before the Cultural Revolution the Party increasingly provided the key to personal success. This adjustment occurred at all levels of the leadership and within the society itself.

Since a substantial portion of the elite structure had operated only at the local levels in the revolutionary base areas, many Party members and cadres had not had to shed their local biases or remould behaviour patterns that favoured secrecy and internal solidarity. There is a ring of truth in the recent accusations that Liu Shao-ch'i and others "maintained a curtain of secrecy" during the transitional years after Liberation. According to *Chieh fang jih pao* of January 10, 1969, "the result was that the Security Affairs Department wrote reports, public security organs made arrests, and the masses read announcements, while a large number of people remained totally ignorant". There were thus strong organizational solidarities stemming from the base area period and affecting the new institutions charged with running the society and state. The Party's penetration of rural levels only rarely brought villagers and townsfolk into an active political role for themselves.

As Thomas Bernstein analyses so well, however, political cadres did become more actively involved in village life after the take-over. As the Party bureaucracy expanded in the fifties, the individual cadre became part of a system that appeared from the outside to be more monolithic and authoritarian. Yet, in the countryside, many cadres were reverting to traditional practices and habits. Communist programmes—land reform is an example—in some localities reinforced conservative traditions generally by making the cadres of poor peasant origin who now received land more attractive as marriage partners. These cadres were thus committed as never before to the family way of life. No less active, peasant cadres pursued local and private interests at public expense. After the initial surge of ideological enthusiasm, local Communist officials became more status-conscious, more ambitious for personal power and less dedicated to continuing the revolution.

This relaxation of Communist zeal and the waning of discipline and motivation in the villages produced a bureaucratic response from middle-level officials particularly at the *hsien* (county) and provincial levels as they felt their sources of power slipping away.

This chain reaction of local independence and middle-level bureau-cratism created especially difficult policy problems for the central leadership in Peking. As one consequence the centre found itself launching campaigns to deal with excessive cadre commandism in the middle echelons that had resulted in many instances as a reaction to the lack of cadre political initiative in the villages. The campaign against the village cadres on the other hand reinforced the middle-level bureaucracy and its commandist style. The village cadres, who needed the Communist badge to remain in office, began acting out two different lives, one in their home villages and one in the Party branches for the benefit of their superiors in the towns.

The decisions to alternate between competing strategies against first this level and then the other produced a constant shifting in Party policies and a consequent cycling in the apparent (or pres-cribed) patterns of compliance elicited in society.[1] In order to create effective organizations the Party had to allow the development of substantial autonomy in local units but this in turn insulated the affected local organizations from central control. As is true at the village level, the Party relationship with other local institutions over the past twenty years illustrates a classic problem that arises when a powerful government seeks to decentralize to the level of local activity where things get done, but finds that in doing this it breaks down decision-making into so many hands that it loses the ability to regulate the sub-elites that can capture effective power at the local levels. As Mao has put it: "[A]fter entering the cities, we became scattered, each person attending to his own stall..."[2] The Party did indeed have to scatter its personnel into "stalls" in order to insinuate its apparatus into the Chinese populace and give it direct guidance, but many cadres assigned locally gained sufficient indigenous support to act without further recourse to higher-level

[1] For a somewhat different and more complex view of this phenomenon, see G. William Skinner and Edwin A. Winckler, "Compliance Succession in Rural Communist China: A Cyclical Theory", in Amitai Etzioni, ed., *Complex Organizations: A Sociological Reader* (2nd ed.; New York: Holt, Rinehart & Winston, 1969), pp. 410–38.

[2] "Speech at the Report Meeting" [October 24, 1966], translated in *Chinese Law and Government*, I, No. 4 (Winter 1968–9), p. 96.

sanction. In gaining alternative bases for their authority, these village officials became more responsive to local demands and more identified with particularistic peasant interests. In the first twenty years the trend of policy fluctuated between decentralism and re-asserted central control. Paradoxically, Mao has belittled those lower-level cadres for failure to follow the mass line when they empathized too closely with the peasantry but purged middle-level cadres for their separation from the masses.

The periodic demands by lower-level cadres for autonomy that have appeared in China indicate in addition to localism the degree to which Communist officials have been influenced by professional-ization. Peking has sought to regulate this process and thus to counter one of the most complex trends in modern political develop-ment. If it were feasible, the central leaders would like to divorce their policies from certain of their consequences by political fiat. To do this in practice they have had to engage in a dialectical process of giving leeway to the local authorities on a seasonal, annual, or task-completion basis only to reinstitute central control when local authority begins to deny initiative to the top. In the end this see-saw process has undermined the cadre role and helped break the cadre as the critical link holding together the many parts of society.

Merle Goldman has illustrated another of the consequences of growth of organizational autonomy in the highly prestigious sector of Chinese society associated with the intellectuals. This group draws on centuries of experience in employing intellectual and artistic talents to bolster its political influence and social standing. At times the intellectuals have appealed to the "authority" of foreign experts to back their positions and then again to China's own classical tradition. One of the most significant aspects of Mrs Goldman's essay is its comparison of the 1962 Hundred Flowers Campaign with its well-known predecessor of 1957. As a threat against Party cadres was mounted by the Maoists in the aftermath of the Great Leap Forward, some of these cadres, often the more senior ones, joined forces with the intellectuals to attack Mao, thus reversing the line-up in the 1956–7 Hundred Flowers. This new coalition caused Mao at the crucial working conference of the Central Committee of January,

1962 to repudiate this turn of events as tantamount to "revisionism".[1]

Mrs Goldman's investigation of campaigns relates directly to the problem of policy cycles discussed earlier. The alternation of "push" and "relaxation" phases involved in the campaign technique entails other regularities that deserve further investigation. The "push" is associated with anti-bureaucraticism, cadre participation in labour, mass mobilization, ideological orthodoxy, greater central control, a stress on national self-sufficiency, and a higher rate of investment in the countryside. Some campaigns have specific aims while, more generally, there is an unending "campaign" to manipulate social forces for national development and other political ends. Earlier campaigns against intellectuals contained consistently recurring goals for the push and relaxation phases—the first making the intelligentsia a target, the second an indispensable participant in the development of the society. The years 1961–2 were a unique period of relaxation in which the intellectuals made Mao the target and mobilized their artistic and literary talents against the most loathsome reminders of the previous push. When Mao retaliated, the intellectual lost his indispensability and politically privileged position.

Finally, in this section Michel Oksenberg examines the problems of the elite from the perspective of social mobility. His discussion deals with the structuring of career opportunities and choices facing China's young men and women in the pre-Cultural Revolutionary period. The leadership line of the Chinese Party had always stressed the closeness of the elite–mass relationship, and Professor Oksenberg makes a convincing case that access to higher social status was increasingly determined by the specific criteria for membership and advancement in the Party. The individual had to decide early in life whether to pursue a political or non-political career, and at later crucial stages he would have to calculate and adopt positions that would determine success in that career. So close were the measures of status in the Party and society that the one began to merge into the other in such a way that societal values could gradually shape

[1] See below for further discussion of this conference, pp. 222–6. See also Lin Piao, "Report to the Ninth National Congress...", *Peking Review*, special issue (April 28, 1969), p. 14.

Communist organizations. As the job market came to dictate the motives of young political aspirants, many problems emerged. Few cadres wished to retire. Choices made early could turn out to be foolish in the light of later changes in the political structure such as occurred in 1958 and 1966. Here is where policy cycling and political order clashed. Most important, in this process of adaptation to the job market of China the Party lost its revolutionary zeal and shifted from an active to a passive agent of change.

This process ran directly counter to the value prescriptions of Chairman Mao Tse-tung. The transformation of the elite apparatus into a bureaucratic and professional ladder of success brought Mao to realize that the members of the Party were using professional routines to shield themselves from criticism and to ameliorate the tension between the prescribed and actual systems of status. Communist Party members also came to abuse Party rules in much the same way that members of labour unions in the West have "worked to rule" as a safe method of slowdown and protest. They utilized regulations to protect themselves and to turn the system to their own advantage against the machinations of the higher echelons. Earlier we noted the importance of informal political arrangements and downgraded the significance of formal organizations. This should now be qualified, for the formal structures themselves often served the purposes of informal groups. This reached a point in the sixties where officials operating through the formal structures could no longer be trusted and top Party officials such as Mao and Liu had to send their wives and trusted friends on fact-finding missions. As in the Soviet Union, however, this growth of informal systems, though disapproved of officially, often helped make the otherwise rigid bureaucracy function effectively.

Recently Mao has blamed the flourishing of guild-like interests and personalistic politics on the growth of an impersonal and highly specialized bureaucratic environment. His response is reported in a recent *People's Daily* article, which noted that Liu Shao-ch'i's ideas of "minute division of labour" and professionalization made "everyone do only his own work".[1] Bureaucracies run according to these ideas, it said, "will have their own immediate superiors,

[1] *Jen min jih pao*, October 31, 1968.

22

their own plans, their own administration. They will do what they think is right." Professional bureaucrats under these conditions, the article added, "will be seriously divorced from reality, the masses and class struggle. Such division of labour will inevitably result in bringing practical work instead of politics to the fore." By "politics" Mao means essentially moral guidance toward the creation of an ethical culture, and he has concluded that only the morally-fit generalist can bear the responsibility for such guidance. The goal is a new Chinese political culture composed of "new men" on a mass scale who have internalized the values, norms and beliefs of Mao's version of Communist ideology. Fundamentally, the Chinese leader rejects the notion that reform of society can begin with, and be accomplished by, the reform of elite institutions alone. Unlike Lenin who concentrated on the reform of the elite and cadres, Mao seeks to universalize the conversion of all the "people" into good Communists.

THE NEW VIEW OF POWER IN THE GREAT CULTURAL REVOLUTION

While these general developments were taking place in the relationship of the Party to the society, there arose fundamental shifts in the mechanisms by which centralized power was exercised in China. From the beginning of the People's Republic in 1949, the centre had encouraged senior Party officials to double as specialists in the Central Committee's departments and in counterpart state organizations In the process of this *de facto* merging of power organizations, individuals were given practical, specialized training as a basic start in new top-level careers. Assignments, moreover, tended to be made within a single part of the bureaucracy, thereby identifying individual cadres with wider networks and tying together similar ministries, Party offices and sectors of the economy and society. Proximity over time bred personal relationships and trust, making possible informal influence and an increasing independence from centralized control.

The two essays in the final section of the book deal with just such problems of autonomy within the State Council and the People's Liberation Army. The political professional outside the Party carried with him more than the special expertise of his calling. Donald

Klein's careful analysis of personnel shifts in the State Council during the Cultural Revolution demonstrates how viable these extra-Party organizations could become. Within the state organs after 1949, powerful individuals appear, as in the Soviet Union, to have formed bureaucratic networks, and, as shown by other essays in this volume, these networks were reinforced by bonds of professional pride and common career. These organs gradually became indispensable for the daily operation of Chinese administration and, in the Cultural Revolution, one of the few lasting sources of order and stability. Mr Klein's statistics indicate that Party membership was a definite liability for State Councilmen threatened by the Red Guards, and that personnel in the state machinery managed to survive the Cultural Revolution at a higher rate than their counterparts who held positions in the Party alone.[1]

As was seen in Bernstein's essay on village-level Party organs, the growth of a bureaucratic spirit in the governmental administrative apparatus did not necessarily involve the concomitant separation of the government from the populace. Rather cadres in the highest organs of the State Council, Army and other state institutions sought to create independent bases of support among selected elements of Chinese society. This developed from 1949 to 1956 into a type of pork barrel politics—now pejoratively labelled "economism"—by which members of these organizations and their sub-components gained a popular foothold.[2] In the early fifties this type of politics was often encouraged officially as a "mass line" strategy of penetrating localities and production units. When the Great Leap line

[1] Premier Chou En-lai has tried to explain the reasons for different levels of purge in the various power organs. On April 20, 1968, he said that Liu Shao-ch'i and Teng Hsiao-p'ing "wanted to intervene and disturb both Party and government work. The armed forces were less interfered with and disturbed because they were under the direct jurisdiction of Vice Chairman Lin Piao. Our Party administration work with its forty years of tradition was under the direct control of Liu and Teng. They were on the first front, and the government, which was also under their direct control, was subjected to greater intervention. Therefore, it was quite natural that there was greater intervention on this side in the struggle between the two lines." Quoted in *Selections from China Mainland Magazines*, No. 631, p. 26.

[2] For evidence on "economism" in mass organizations, see Paul Harper, "The Party and the Unions in Communist China", *The China Quarterly*, No. 37 (January–March 1969), pp. 84–119.

of "politics in command" reversed the official attitude towards "economism" in government, however, the cadres naturally felt a loss of power and prestige, and many appear to have felt self-contempt for having to perform their jobs below the previous professional standards. Later Mao, wounded by failure and criticism, appears to have used their frustrations against his Party opponents. He directed their anger as if the Party as a whole had been responsible for the Great Leap slogans of "politics in command" and "red and expert" associated with their frustrations.

In the purge that followed, key leaders of the People's Liberation Army (PLA) did not survive to the same extent as leaders in the State Council. John Gittings makes clear, however, that high-level Army officers fell from power while the Army as an institution was being given a more significant role in the running of China. His study shows how in the early fifties inter-personal harmony between high-level members of the Army and Party coexisted with rivalry between the two organizations as institutional systems. This incongruence between the relationships of individuals and systems, which was to develop into hostility on both levels in the Cultural Revolution, helps explain the Army's inability to acquire sufficient institutional power to prevent its periodic decline. What seems to have occurred in the Army is that many senior officers in the fifties became acutely sensitive to the possibilities of autonomy arising from excessive professionalism as the armed forces were being modernized and self-consciously campaigned as good Communists to ensure that the Maoist political leadership could continue to control the gun. While creating a reasonably disciplined apparatus, this effort had the effect of dividing the Army leadership and reducing its sense of professional élan. In this way, the politically weakened army could be manipulated not only from Peking but by lower (usually provincial) Party committees. The strong military figures who might have competed for power were also those who would have given the Army real stature and a sense of national purpose and greatness. As was true of other instruments of coercion in China—such as the police and courts[1]—the Army could not protect its members from dismis-

[1] See the excellent article by Jerome A. Cohen, "The Party and the Courts: 1949–1959", *The China Quarterly*, No. 38 (April–June 1969), pp. 120–57.

sal because it had never developed the organizational mechanisms for the entire military body to operate as a cohesive and national political force.

The Army—as is true of the Party and other organizations in China—contains many different elements, and the use of shorthand labels may introduce a serious distortion in the analysis. One problem in defining the exact content of the term "Army" involves the question discussed above of the fuzzy boundary line between the military and political domains. How do Army officers on the Central Committee look at their identity? In what areas of political life do they reveal the workings of a "military mind"? How much has the attitude of any individual varied over time and why? Added to such difficult questions are uncertainties about the fluctuating role of the Military Affairs Committee (MAC), the military's official voice within the Central Committee. The MAC hardly entered the news in the first nine years of the People's Republic, and its apparent rise in the power structure in the early sixties was paralleled by the movement of Party men into the position of political commissar in the Army. Thus, the Army as a national organization was gaining influence and expanding its mandate, but its subordinate echelons were coming under greater Party control. The use of the term military, moreover, contains a number of other pitfalls, particularly since "Maoist" militia and the regional forces turned out to have localist and even anti-Mao, anti-PLA sentiments during the political crisis of the past few years. Finally, although Mao purportedly relies more heavily on the Army since 1966, there is no doubt that many of its senior members have been tarred by the sins of his opponents. As the Hunan *Sheng wu lien* put it in 1968:

Since a Red capitalist class is already formed in China, the Army of course cannot detach itself from this reality... It was necessary to carry out the Cultural Revolution from the lower level upward in the Army and rely on the people's revolution—the locomotive of progress in history —in order to change the state of opposition between the military and the civilian population brought about by the control of the Army by the bureaucrats.[1]

[1] "Whither China?", in *Survey of China Mainland Press*, No. 4190, pp. 5, 7.

In the literature on developing countries much has been said about the role of specialists in violence. The military in China as elsewhere has helped provide order in some places, but no special power seems to grow out of the barrel of a Chinese gun. Many military leaders have been stripped of rank or otherwise disgraced unless protected by powerful political supporters, either nationally or locally. Some localities have shown signs of military warlordism, but generally the power of individual PLA commanders derives from their identity with local interests.[1]

What then is the new view of power in the Cultural Revolution? Clearly the view held in Peking, at least as it is reported, is a mixture of a Maoist emphasis on mass spontaneity and ideological uniformity combined with enforced order and organizational control. As Professor Schram argues, Mao wished to destroy a Party linking a well-defined structure, the principle of working-class leadership and the role of technical expertise and to replace it with a revolution of the "poor and blank". This wish was not fulfilled. To a certain extent this means that Mao has had to compromise, but it also means that he has succeeded in reversing certain trends that would have moved China in even more bureaucratic directions. The present mood of experimentation and tentativeness does not mean that Mao has failed completely in imposing aspects of his view on the government and Party of China. By attaining even partial success he has broken the concentration of power at the top and in the hands of bureaucratically oriented cadres. When Mao decided that senior-level Communist institutions were undermining the Communist virtues as he defined them, he was able to upset their autonomy and their professional code of conduct.

As a result, it is no longer possible to hold a simple view of power and leadership in which the actions at the top ramify neatly to the base, nor can the actions of the "base" in any one part of the country be considered typical of those in any other. While it is necessary to consider this power situation as transitional, we should also note that the fragmentation of power has produced a *de facto* system of

[1] The percentage of military men on the Central Committee jumped from 30% in 1956 to 40% in 1969. Military figures are particularly prominent on the Political Bureau of the Ninth Central Committee.

checks and balances, in which decisive movement in any direction is now far less likely. The transition to a fundamentally different political system will thus take years if not decades. Even the death of Mao Tse-tung will probably not change, basically, the fact that power resides in many hands and that doctrine has innumerable interpreters.

PARTY LEADERSHIP IN PERSPECTIVE

A great deal of attention in this volume is given to different kinds of organizations that have arisen in Communist China and the types of organizations that different leaders would like to employ as models for the Chinese Communist Party. Some favouring hierarchical organizations would like to reduce the dichotomy between the individual and the organization and insulate the Party from its social environment by stressing the internal mechanisms by which the individual becomes absorbed into the apparatus. Mao, however, emphasizes the dichotomy ("contradiction") between individual and organization because he does not want the individual to be cut off from the society by slipping behind an organizational curtain nor organizations to lose their dynamic qualities by becoming planned and fixed. His concept of the mass line stresses the activation and mobilization of the populace in contrast to Liu Shao-ch'i's view of a mass line for channelling the populace in support of the elite and its programmes.[1] In this sense, Mao deliberately raises a philosophical question concerning the future of organization in an ordered society.

Aside from the obvious campaign mentality of the regime, it is difficult to characterize how power is actually organized and how leadership is carried out in today's China. The relatively small number of names and activities by which social and political groups or roles could be categorized in the past has now been replaced by a vast array of confusing labels and descriptions. One is tempted to characterize the system of power at one and the same time

[1] For a discussion of the mass line prior to the Cultural Revolution, see John W. Lewis, *Leadership in Communist China* (Ithaca, N.Y.: Cornell Univ. Press, 1963), chap. iii.

28

as confederal and dictatorial. The very emphasis on the cult of Mao and on ideological conformity helps offset the high degree of fragmentation in Chinese politics.

As one result of the Cultural Revolution, the exercise of leadership and the achievement of compliance involve a much more complex process of negotiation than in the fifties. A substantial amount of bargaining goes on to settle the balance of power on an *ad hoc* basis between cadres and informal leaders at the village and city levels, and this in turn has made lower-level political cadres less responsive to central authority. In August, 1967, after a period of severe upheaval, Lin Piao, among others at the centre, reacted to this loss and commanded his subordinates in the provinces not to wander too far from Peking's lead. He said:

One must report to and ask instructions from Chairman Mao, the Central Committee and the Cultural Revolution Group. One must not think that you yourself have understood and need not report to the centre; you must not think that it is clear and that you can deal with it yourself. You must not think that you yourself are intelligent and do not need to report and ask for instructions. You need not fear that you are causing trouble to the centre. No matter whether it is a big or small affair, everything must be reported and instructions sought for. The Premier and the Cultural Revolution Group comrades are working day and night ...You can also fly and come here and be here in a couple of hours. You must not adopt the attitude of this must be so, assume yourself to be clever and act according to your own light.[1]

Lin could not accept the diminution of central power as the price for creating mass participation and local initiative. As so many other Maoist prescriptions, his call for responsive compliance was assumed,

[1] Text of speech in *Chu ying tung fang hung* [Pearl River East is Red], September 13, 1967. Article 5 of the 1969 Party Constitution states in part: "If a Party member holds different views with regard to the decisions or directives of the Party organizations, he is allowed to reserve his views and has the right to bypass the immediate leadership and report to higher levels, up to and including the Central Committee and the Chairman of the Central Committee...The organs of the dictatorship of the proletariat, the People's Liberation Army, and the Communist Youth League and other revolutionary mass organizations, such as those of the workers, the poor and lower-middle peasants and the Red Guards, must all accept the leadership of the Party."

despite the evidence, to be compatible with Mao's concurrent demand for flexibility and spontaneity.

The evidence is that Mao cannot have it both ways. Right down to the present, societal constraints have forced a choice between competing designs of political power.[1] More than ever before, China needs a mediator-type leader to deal with the powerful interests organized for political combat in the provinces and cities.

A great deal of political activity crucial to the life of the nation now is determined by decisions made locally, in urban centres and even in more rural areas. As the national-level bureaucracy has contracted,[2] power at the local levels has reverted to those who have managed to establish contacts with the centre as well as those who have strong bases of power in their own local spheres. Previously such local power had been constrained by the fact that the governmental and Party administration was ubiquitous; contacts with officials were normal and overlapping and thus less capable of being manipulated by a few. What seems to be resulting in some cities and towns is the development of bossism and political machines around those having access to the far smaller number of official contacts. These political machines, though always called "revolutionary committees", are reminiscent of the kinds of political organizations found in urban places throughout the world.

The future of local power in China is, of course, not the subject of this volume of essays, but, to the extent that it now becomes more crucial to the analysis of Chinese politics more generally, it provides a useful way to discuss the strengths and weaknesses of the system that developed under the Chinese Communists from 1927 to the Cultural Revolution in 1966. At the beginning of the period after the near collapse of the Party in 1927, there was a repudiation of the degree of administrative centralism under the Central Committee that was held responsible by Mao and others for the debacle.

[1] On the more general problems raised here, see John W. Lewis, "The Social Limits of Politically Induced Change", in Chandler Morse, ed., *Modernization by Design* (Ithaca, N.Y.: Cornell Univ. Press, 1969), pp. 1–33.

[2] One piece of evidence for this contracting at the national level is the disappearance of the Party Secretariat during the Cultural Revolution and the failure to reconstitute it at the Ninth Party Congress. This body had been responsible for the central administration of Party affairs.

In its stead, Mao experimented with, and finally established, a base area system where power could be adapted to local conditions and central authority would be assumed to exist in the common ideology and in the spirit of the wartime cause. After the war and with the rise of the Chinese Communist state in 1949, administrative centralism again gradually became the way of organizational life in China. Not only did it carry with it the problems that we have reviewed in this brief introduction and bring into power those individuals Mao has labelled "revisionists", but it also created a system that proved to be remarkably brittle and weak. Mao's case against the former centralized system as an inadequate instrument for the transformation of China towards his version of modernity has substantial merit.

As of now this circularity of systems, this return to the old base area concept in the search for new political form, makes one realize just how much the current discourse about politics in China is influenced by Mao Tse-tung. By his writings and periodic "latest instructions" Mao sets the tone and the limits for political life without actually controlling much of the conduct of political affairs outside Peking. Mao's greatest asset is his ability to think in large historic terms and to adjust to new situations without losing his nerve or his image of being in command. By "standing at the helm" at this time in China's history Mao has sanctioned but not caused substantial institutional change. What the causes of these changes are we can now see only dimly. It may well be that by understanding what is going on at present we may be better prepared to grasp the full implications of how the Chinese Communist Party came into being in the first place and how Communist leadership and revolutionary power will develop in the future.

ACKNOWLEDGEMENTS

An undertaking that involves scholars around the world depends on their cooperation over many months. As the editor of this volume, I wish to thank my co-authors and David Wilson of *The China Quarterly* for their patient cooperation and constant encouragement. It is also my pleasure to acknowledge with gratitude the generous assistance that I received during the editorial stages. Alexander L. George, Roderick MacFarquhar, Michel Oksenberg, Dorothy Solinger and D. Gordon White commented on drafts of the Introduction and on the organization of the entire manuscript. The burden of preparing the manuscript for publication fell on Marion Bieber and Gerry Bowman, both of the Center for East Asian Studies at Stanford University. Finally, I wish to express my gratitude to the Center for Research in International Studies at Stanford for its financial contribution toward the cost of preparing the manuscript.

J.W.L.

PART I

THE CHANGING ROLE
OF THE COMMUNIST PARTY
IN THE REVOLUTIONARY
STRUGGLE

I

THE INFLUENCE OF THE PAST: HOW THE EARLY YEARS HELPED TO SHAPE THE FUTURE OF THE CHINESE COMMUNIST PARTY

C. MARTIN WILBUR

Early in 1928 the Chinese Communist Party was in crisis. It might have disintegrated and disappeared. Yet in fact it persisted, constantly refashioned itself, and ultimately became the political system of the country. The broad questions we may ask about this historical fact are: What was the nature of the Party in 1928? What had been the experience of the leadership? And what was the relationship between the Party, with its distinctive ideology, and the Chinese social environment? Thus the object of this paper is to analyse the Chinese Communist Party as a system that had developed during its first eight years, and to appraise its potentialities in 1928 for adapting to, and manipulating, the Chinese environment.

THE CHINESE COMMUNIST PARTY AS A SYSTEM

During its early years the Chinese Communist Party was a patriotic, revolutionary organization which provided a psychological sanctuary for a displaced potential elite. It was patriotic in that its leaders were dedicated to "saving" China, and it was revolutionary in that their goal was to reshape Chinese society rapidly. Many of its members found in the Party the emotional security and the intellectual reassurance which they could not find in the society that was crumbling about them. The organization depended upon Soviet Russia for its ideology, strategy and important financial support. One of the greatest changes that took place in the years following 1928 was the Party's gradual emancipation from this dependency. The analogy to a maturing person is intriguing.

The Chinese Communist Party, as conceived in Shanghai during the spring and summer of 1920, with the advice of Gregory Voitinsky, was a direct product of the "May 4th Movement"—that patriotic, searching, reformist tide which arose from the frustrations of intellectuals with China's apparently stagnating society, corrupt and chaotic governments, and intolerable international position. Its forerunners were Professor Li Ta-chao and his group of student admirers in Peking. All the organizers of the Party were intellectuals —professors, editors and college students. In Shanghai some ten radical reformers participated in the discussions with Voitinsky, a scout for the newly created Communist International; they ranged in age from 40 down to 20. At least six were Returned Students from Japan, some had participated in the revolution which overthrew the Manchu dynasty, and a few were still followers of Sun Yat-sen, who was then in Shanghai. They had absorbed a variety of radical ideologies, but now had a common interest in Marxism and the Russian Revolution. They knew almost nothing about how a Communist Party should be organized and led. The Shanghai group agreed upon a draft constitution—now lost—and established a provisional central organization. Some then set about establishing Communist groups in other Chinese cities. Voitinsky and his assistant, I. K. Mamaev, helped in this, while Mme Voitinsky and the Chinese interpreter, Yang Ming-chai, taught Russian to a small group of students destined for Moscow. Within a year there were six centres of Party activity in China, with a membership of perhaps sixty when the first Congress was held in Shanghai in July, 1921.[1]

[1] Chow Tse-tsung, *The May Fourth Movement: Intellectual Revolution in Modern China* (Cambridge, Mass.: Harvard Univ. Press, 1960), p. 248. Dr Chow lists the founding members in Shanghai as Ch'en Tu-hsiu, Tai Chi-t'ao, Li Han-chün, Shen T'ing-i, Shao Li-tzu, Ch'en Wang-tao, Li Ta, Shih Ts'un-t'ung, Yü Hsiu-sung and Yüan [Juan] Hsiao-hsien; his account is unsourced but appears in substantial accord with other accounts I have read. Two followers of Sun Yat-sen, Tai Chi-t'ao and Shao Li-tzu, soon separated themselves from the Communist Party, and Li Han-chün was expelled. Five of the ten were natives of Chekiang. "A Brief History of the Communist Party", a Communist source in Russian, written about September, 1926 lists seven of these men, omitting Shao Li-tzu, Li Ta, and Yü Hsiu-sung, and noting that only three of the seven were still in the Party. C. Martin Wilbur and Julie Lien-ying How, *Documents on Communism, Nationalism, and Soviet Advisers in China, 1918–1927* (New

The first centres were in the very cities which had long traditions of reformist and revolutionary activity among intellectuals; such cities as Canton, Shanghai, Peking, Changsha and Wuhan; and the same may be said of the two foreign countries, Japan and France, where Chinese Communist nuclei were formed. Through the lives of its first recruits, the Chinese Communist movement was intertwined with the reformist and revolutionary traditions of the period beginning about 1895—a point which could be richly elaborated through biographical evidence.

Up until about 1925 most recruits were middle school and college students. This implies that most of the first thousand members came from a narrow sector of society, from families able to give them a better than elementary education at however great a financial sacrifice in some case. These early members were not sons and daughters of the proletariat nor from poor "peasant" families. Typically they were young men and women of "modern education", who had already rejected many of China's cultural norms. Most of them were living the students' life in a provincial capital or a metropolis such as Peking, Shanghai or Canton. They were members of discussion societies, eagerly read *The New Youth* and other progressive journals, participated in patriotic demonstrations and contributed articles to student magazines which echoed the *mélange* of ideas injected into the Chinese intellectual world by such writers as Liang Ch'i-ch'ao, Ts'ai Yüan-p'ei, Wu Chih-hui, Ch'en Tu-hsiu, Hu Shih, and a host of others influenced by late nineteenth- and early twentieth-century currents of Western thought. Some were students in Japan or in France, and a few had studied in Russia. They were young idealists, the members of a student generation that provided the political and intellectual leadership for China throughout the 1930's and 1940's. Whether individuals from that generation moved into the Communist Party, the Kuomintang, the Young China Party, or none of them, was a matter of chance

York: Columbia Univ. Press, 1956), p. 48. For an account of Li Ta-chao as a forerunner, see Maurice Meisner, *Li Ta-chao and the Origins of Chinese Marxism* (Cambridge, Mass.: Harvard Univ. Press, 1967), pp. 114 ff. On the First Congress see Ch'en Kung-po, *The Communist Movement in China: An Essay Written in 1924...Edited with an Introduction by C. Martin Wilbur* (New York: Octagon Books, Inc., 1966), pp. 18–31, 79–82, 102–5.

and temperament. To join a political movement was fashionable. To work among the masses and be part of a world revolution against imperialism were attractive ideas to young intellectuals psychologically at war with themselves and with the older society from which they came.[1]

Like many institutions created by man, the Communist Party had two essential ingredients: the ideational and the human. Its ideology was, of course, Marxism–Leninism, which defined the Party's goals and prescribed the methods for achieving them. Ideology provided a vision and a myth. The vision was an ideal society—a classless society with social democracy. The myth was that such a society could be achieved through revolution directed by a tightly organized and disciplined Party supported by the Chinese proletariat and the vast peasantry. There was no way to test the validity of the vision, but the myth could be tested against social realities through the revolutionary effort. During its early years the Party learned a great deal about the limits society imposed upon revolution. It learned to adjust strategy and tactics to the social environment, and had enough success that it was not compelled to abandon the myth that revolution would succeed.

Another ideational element lay in the norms of Party life. This refers to a conceptualized structure and hierarchical arrangements of parts that made up a system on paper and in the minds of its members. The structure was defined in a constitution which codified the idea of "democratic centralism". Authority descended from a small decision-making group through a pyramidal organization, while support and information ascended from as wide a base as possible. The norms demanded an ethic of "inner Party discipline". Ideally, the units and members within the system carried out the decisions arrived at within a formally recognized process.

Potential leaders were schooled to give themselves to the Party completely. A guide for training[2] drawn up by the Moscow branch

---

[1] I am indebted to Robert J. Lifton, *Thought Reform and the Psychology of Totalism: a Study of "Brainwashing" in China* (New York: Norton, 1961) for the concept of a student generation in which the individuals were "at war" with themselves and society.

[2] Wilbur and How, *Documents*, pp. 135–7.

of the Chinese Communist Party in the early 1920's contained 34 injunctions of which the following are a sample:

> . . . cultivate a pure revolutionary philosophy of life and selfconscious training. . .stand firmly on class grounds. . .absolutely oppose anarchist tendencies. If we oppose iron discipline, we would be. . .helping the bourgeoisie to destroy the proletariat's revolutionary organization. We must cultivate the habit of perseverance—Communists are always willing to "lie on faggots and taste gall" in order to struggle for the interests of the proletariat. . .[W]e should absolutely collectivize and adapt our own lives and will to the masses. There is absolutely no such thing as individual life or individual free will. We must strictly criticize our comrades' errors and humbly accept our comrades' criticism. The organization's work is our only work. Aside from revolution, Communist members have no other profession—we are professional revolutionaries.

Though we speak of a Party, this is an abstraction. The Party existed in the minds of its members. They were scattered geographically, some in China and some in Russia. Those in China lived in many different cities and some in rural areas. They could not communicate easily. By early 1928 the "Party" had met only five times, and these were meetings of only a few selected individuals, ranging in number from 13 at the First Congress in 1921 to about 80 who met for the Fifth Congress in 1927. Thus the Party's communication system was crucial. One may visualize the Party as a policy-forming, decision-implementing organization unified and operated by means of a communication system. The system consisted of meetings for reports, discussion, and resolutions on policy and strategy. Decisions were then disseminated through further meetings, directives on paper and a variety of publications. There was also an upward channel of communication through written reports, appraisals of concrete situations and objections to instructions. All this was verbal.

These major ideational components of the Party as a system— the vision and the myth, the norms of Party life, and the conceptualized structure—were taken over from Soviet Russia and adapted and internalized by the membership during the first eight years.

Two major policy decisions shaped the Chinese Communist Party during its early years. The first was inherent; by its very nature the Party should be *the* independent party of the proletariat, and should also seek to lead the peasantry. The determination to be the only party of the proletariat, voiced in the resolutions of the First and Second Party Congresses in July, 1921 and July, 1922, would lead Communist activists into immediate competition with anarchists, socialists, Christians, and Kuomintang members for control of the nascent modern labour movement, and more concretely for control of unions organized by them. The credo that the proletariat should lead the peasantry would cause conflict with the Kuomintang, which was also encouraged by its Russian advisers to lead China's vast farm population into the national revolution.

The second major policy was for Communist leaders to join the Kuomintang. This strategy was dictated by the Comintern when Dr Sun Yat-sen rejected a proposed alliance between the Kuomintang and the Communist Party but agreed to admit individual Communists into his party. Sun was eager for Russian aid when he made this agreement in August, 1922. Nor was it a strange decision in view of Dr Sun's self-confidence, his interest in socialism and admiration for the Russian Revolution, his determination to revitalize the Kuomintang, and his previous experience of heading multi-group revolutionary coalitions. The Comintern strategy was based upon Lenin's analysis of the possibilities for revolution in colonial and semi-colonial countries, which he articulated in "Theses on the National and Colonial Questions" at the Second Comintern Congress, July–August, 1920. Briefly, Lenin believed that national liberation movements—essentially under bourgeois leadership—must precede second-stage socialist revolutions. Lenin did not conceal the inevitable conflict that would occur when the proletarian component in the national revolution turned against the national bourgeoisie in the struggle to lead the revolution from capitalism to socialism. This predicted struggle was an additional reason why the proletarian Communist Party must maintain its autonomy during the stage of revolutionary cooperation. Cooperate but prepare to fight: this was the Comintern's prescription. The moral ambiguities involved in joining another party in order ultimately to seize control of it or, to put it more creditably, to lead it into the second stage of revolution, required feats of rationalization. A number of the early

Chinese Communist leaders resisted accepting this Comintern strategy; it was decided upon by the barest of margins at the Third Party Congress in June, 1923; and it caused the Party's main leader, Ch'en Tu-hsiu, much anguish.[1]

[1] On Lenin's theses, see Xenia Joukoff Eudin and Robert C. North, *Soviet Russia and the East, 1920–1927: A Documentary Survey* (Stanford: Stanford Univ. Press, 1957), pp. 63–5; and Allen S. Whiting, *Soviet Policies in China, 1917–1924* (New York: Columbia Univ. Press, 1954), pp. 42–58. Perhaps the bluntest statement on record by a Chinese Communist of the implications of the policy of joining the Kuomintang was that of Liu Jen-ching, made at the Fourth Comintern Congress in November 1922:

"Starting from the premise that in order to exterminate imperialism in China an anti-imperialistic united front will have to be erected, our party has decided to form a united front with the national-revolutionary party, the Kuomintang. The nature of this united front will be expressed in the fact that we, under our own names and as single individuals, will join the party. The reason for it is twofold. In the first place, we want to propagandize many organized workers in the national-revolutionary party and win them over for us. In the second place, we can only fight imperialism if we combine our forces, the forces of the petty bourgeoisie and the proletariat. We intend to compete with this party in regard to the winning of the masses by means of organization and propaganda. If we do not join this party we shall remain isolated, and we shall preach a Communism which holds great and noble ideas, but one which the masses do not follow. The masses would rather follow the bourgeois party, and this party would use the masses for its own purposes. If we join the party, we shall be able to show the masses that we too are for revolutionary democracy, but that for us revolutionary democracy is only a means to an end. Furthermore, we shall be able to point out that although we are for this distant goal, we nevertheless do not forget the daily needs of the masses. We shall be able to gather the masses around us and split the Kuomintang."

Quoted from Eudin and North, cited, p. 151, as translated from *Protokoll des Vierten Kongresses der Kommunistischen Internationale, Petrograd-Moskau vom 5 November bis 5 Dezember, 1922* (Hamburg: C. Hoym Nachf. L. Cahnbley 1923), p. 615. Conrad Brandt, *Stalin's Failure in China, 1924–1927* (Cambridge, Mass.: Harvard Univ. Press, 1958), pp. 18–42, describes the steps leading towards this marriage of convenience. Ch'en Tu-hsiu's anguish is revealed, after the fact, in his *Kao ch'üan tang t'ung chih shu* [A Letter to all Comrades of the Party], December 10, 1929, 17 pp. Reprinted in *Kung fei huo kuo shih liao hui pien* [A Compilation of Historical Materials on the Communist Bandits' Calamity to the Nation], which is a secret supplement to the series *Chung hua min kuo k'ai kuo wu shih nien wen hsien* [Documents Collected on the Fiftieth Anniversary of the Founding of the Chinese Republic] (Taipei: Chung hua min kuo k'ai kuo wu shih nien wen hsien pien tsuan wei yüan hui, 1964), I, 427–41. See Wilbur and How, *Documents*, p. 570 for bibliographic reference to an English translation of Ch'en's letter in *The Militant*, 1930–1.

We turn now to the human component of the Party. Its membership had grown from about ten in 1920 to nearly 58,000 in May 1927, and then had fallen to less than 20,000 in November, of whom only one-fifth were reportedly active.[1] The essence of the Party in its human component, however, was not membership but leadership. The Party could exist with very few members, as it did from 1920 to 1925 with less than a thousand. It could lose the majority of its cadres by defection, executions and sheer disappearance, as it did between May and November, 1927, and yet survive in its remaining leadership. Lenin said, "cadres are everything". On the contrary, "leaders were everything". The persistence of the leadership echelon is a striking characteristic of the Party's history in spite of some defections and staggering losses in combat. One may look on the Party's history up to 1928—and equally thereafter —as a screening process within its leadership.

During the period from 1920 onwards, Chinese society was presenting a large number of "demands" for change. It was the ability of the intellectuals to perceive, sort out, articulate, and act upon these demands that to some extent determined the viability of the Party. Some examples of these demands, at the abstract level, were that "imperialism" and "warlordism" must be overthrown or that "socialism" be introduced; on the concrete level, that farm rents be reduced and rural taxes be allocated more equitably. The leaders perceived such demands partly as a result of their acquaintanceship with various sectors of society and partly as a result of the Marxist ideology which postulated that such demands ought to exist. An important part of the screening process was the ability of some leaders to sort out actual demands from those which ideology alone postulated.

A gradually assembled leadership gained invaluable experience in creating institutions and coping with the Chinese social environment. Examples of institution-building were the Youth Corps,

[1] "Tang ti tsu chih wen t'i chüeh i an" [Resolution on the Question of Party Organization], November 9, 1927, quoted in Wang Chien-min, *Chung kuo kung ch'an tang shih kao* [A Draft History of the Chinese Communist Party] (Taipei: privately printed, 1965), I, 529. Of the approximately 4,000 active members, "most are engaged in unplanned, unorganized, and individual heroic struggles".

labour unions and farmers' associations. Such institutions were important sources of power and were recruiting grounds for future leaders. But the particular institutions could be scattered and nearly destroyed, as were the farmers' associations in Kwangtung and Hunan in 1927, and the Communist-dominated labour unions between 1927 and 1932. What had continuous value was the leaders' experience in institution-building and in stirring men to action. The leaders had learned to create symbols of nationalism, anti-imperialism, anti-warlordism, and class struggle, and to use them effectively to arouse the energies of large numbers of Chinese. Through symbol-manipulation the leaders tried to concentrate this energy in support of the Party's revolutionary goals. This experience, too, had important carry-over value.

This rather abstract discussion is meant to outline the general nature of the Party as a system. Now let us look more directly at its leadership.

EARLY LEADERSHIP OF THE PARTY:
THE INSISTENT NEED FOR DIRECTING PERSONNEL

When the membership of the Communist Party began to grow rapidly after the May 30th Incident in 1925, there was an acute shortage of leadership personnel. By this is meant a shortage of reliable and trained members who could devote most of their time to directional work in the Party itself, in the Youth Corps, and in mass movements under Party control. In July, 1926, the Central Committee noted the need for 355 directing personnel for regional work, local and sectional committee work, and for special or Party cell work. In fact there were barely 120 responsible persons. "We must train more personnel in order to save the situation", the Plenum recorded.[1]

All Party members were supposed to be leaders, at least potentially, but they needed guidance. The membership, as in any Communist Party of that period, was organized in cells within factories villages, schools, or city streets; big cells had smaller units and cells

[1] Wilbur and How, *Documents*, p. 115.

were grouped into sections. There were also Communist factions in a variety of other organizations. All these units required secretaries who could devote much time to training cell members and leading agitation among the masses. There were local committees and provincial and regional committees. The latter had functional departments, ran training classes for cadres, and published newspapers and journals. The Central Committee had commissioners to supervise the work of regional and local committees; it ran short-term schools and a sophisticated propaganda programme. The Party placed great emphasis upon face-to-face contact and persuasion within the membership and between members and the masses. It feared bureaucratization, although this was inevitable. As membership swelled the cells multiplied; as the Party began to run mass organizations with thousands and hundreds of thousands of members the problem of competent leadership became acute.[1]

We may illustrate the need for reliable leaders by the case of the farmers' movement. The Farmers' Movement Training Institute, a Communist-controlled school in the Kuomintang central organization in Canton, had produced 453 graduates plus 25 auditors from its first five classes, from July, 1924 to December, 1925. Of these, 386 were from Kwangtung and not all of them served in the Kwantung farmers' movement. In a resolution prepared for a meeting of special deputies of the Kuomintang Farmers' Bureau to be held on August 15, 1926, the Communist drafter, probably Lo Ch'i-yüan, complained that there were only 600 Communist Party members working among some 800,000 Kwangtung farmers who were enrolled in more than 10,000 village associations. Approximately thirty-five upper-level comrades in six regional offices in the province were swamped in trying to handle all sorts of emergencies which arose.[2] During the first stage of the Northern Expedition

[1] This summarizes a discussion, based upon contemporary CCP documents, *ibid.* pp. 95–9.

[2] Lists of graduates and auditors in the first five classes are given in Lo Ch'i-yüan, "Pen pu i nien lai kung tso pao kao kai yao" [Short Report of the Past Year's Work of This (i.e. the Kuomintang Farmers) Bureau], *Chung kuo nung min* [Chinese Farmer], No. 2 (February, 1926), pp. 147–203. The information is brought together in Eto Shinkichi, "Hai-lu-feng—The First Chinese Soviet Government (Part I)", *The China Quarterly*, No. 8 (October–December, 1961),

when mass organizations grew and the Party and Youth Corps expanded rapidly, the question of leadership must have become ever more critical.

Another implication of the above examples, however, is that a few leaders had been able to build a large party and, in three years between mid-1924 and mid-1927, to organize a large labour union movement and a vast network of farmers' associations. It did not take many specializers to "mobilize the masses". To give another example, the Nanchang Uprising of August 1, 1927, was engineered by about twenty-five Communist leaders, and there were only 180 comrades among the thousands of troops which marched south to Swatow.[1]

Who were the leaders of the Chinese Communist Party before 1928?

I know of no roster of Party leadership or table of organization that dates from 1927 or 1928. Even the membership of the Central Committee elected at the Fifth Congress in May, 1927 is in doubt, though 21 of its 29 full members can be identified. I have tried to construct a list of Communist "leaders" as of April 1, 1927, just before disaster struck the Party. Those who have ploughed this biographical field know how difficult it is to distinguish between members of the Communist Party and leftists within the Kuomintang. To complicate the search there are the pitfalls of pseudonyms, alternate names and multiple literary names. My criteria for listing were: membership in the Party by 1925, and positions of leadership within the central offices or regional, provincial and metropolitan branches of the Party and its Youth Corps; positions of responsibility within the Kuomintang even though these may have been lost during the reshuffle of May, 1926; and leadership positions in mass organizations.[2]

pp. 160–83, esp. p. 182. The Resolution describing the shortage of Communists in the farmers' movement appears in *Kwangtung nung min yün tung pao kao* [Report on the Kwangtung Farmers' Movement] (n.p., October, 1926), pp. 165–89, esp. pp. 170 and 188. This work is on microfilm at Hoover Library, Stanford, "*Ex libris* Taihoku Imperial University."

[1] C. Martin Wilbur, "The Ashes of Defeat", *The China Quarterly*, No. 18 (April–June, 1964), pp. 3–54, esp. pp. 6 and 22.

[2] The list was built up from a variety of sources and cannot be exhaustive, objectively balanced, or free from errors.

SOME CHARACTERISTICS OF THE PARTY LEADERSHIP

First consider table 1 (pp. 63–4), a list of 120 persons who had already distinguished themselves and were leaders in the Chinese Communist Party by early April, 1927. Before discussing their provincial origins, ages and education, it may be well to repeat that

I wish to express my appreciation to Mr Donald Klein for making available many biographies in the forthcoming volume, Donald W. Klein and Anne B. Clark, *A Biographical Dictionary of Chinese Communism*, and the files of the Chinese Communist Leadership Project of the East Asian Institute, Columbia University. Because of this help my present list is somewhat different from that published in *The China Quarterly*, No. 36 (October–December, 1968) and some details going into the numerical data have been corrected.

I began with a purge list drawn up in early 1927 and appended to the records of a meeting of the Kuomintang Central Supervisory Committee on April 2. This listed 196 alleged Communists in the Kuomintang Central Executive Committee, Central Supervisory Committee, and various provincial committees. *Ko ming wen hsien* [Documents of the Revolution] (Taipei: Chungkuo Kuomintang Central Executive Committee's Commission for Compiling Historical Documents of the Party, 1957), XVII, 3091–2. A similar list appears in *ibid*. XVI, 2826–7. Many of the persons named were Kuomintang leftists and not members of the Communist Party, so far as I can discover. On the basis of other evidence 60 entered my list of 120. (Many more might have entered the list had there been more evidence of their leadership in the CCP.) Another source is two Chinese collections of biographies of Communist martyrs, one printed in Russia in 1936, the other compiled by Hua Ying-shen (Hong Kong: Hsin min, 1949), which together contain 33 different names. I searched the following biographical dictionaries: Howard L. Boorman, ed., *Biographical Dictionary of Republican China*, Vols. 1 and 2 (New York: Columbia Univ. Press, 1967, 1968); Union Research Institute, *Who's Who in Communist China* (Hong Kong: Union Research Institute, 1965); and Japan Foreign Office, *Gendai chūgoku jinmei jiten* [Biographical Dictionary of Contemporary China] (Tokyo: Gaikō jihōsha, 1962). I also consulted four Chinese studies: Li Yün-han, *Ts'ung jung kung tao ch'ing tang* [From the Admission of the Communists to the Purification of the (Nationalist) Party] (Taipei: China Committee for Publication Aid and Prize Awards, 1966); Chiang Yung-ching, *Paolot'ing yü Wuhan cheng ch'üan* [Borodin and the Wuhan Regime] (Taipei: China Committee for Publication Aid and Prize Awards, 1963); *Wang Chien-min, Chung kuo kung ch'an tang shih kao, op. cit.*; and *Chung kuo kung ch'an tang chih t'ou shih* [Perspectives on the Chinese Communist Party] (Taipei: Wen hsing Bookstore, 1962). (This is reprinted photographically from a study of the Investigation Section of the Organization Department of the Kuomintang, 1935, and is Part 3, Vol. 1 in the series *Chung kuo hsien tai shih liao ts'ung shu*.) Two sources useful for capture lists are: U. T. Hsu (Hsü En-tseng), *The Invisible Conflict* (Hong Kong: China Viewpoints, 1958) and Warren Kuo, *Analytical History of the Chinese Communist Party*, Vol. 2 (Taipei: Institute of International Relations, 1968).

the list inevitably has a subjective quality even though the attempt was made to apply objective standards for inclusion and exclusion.

It was a young group. At the present stage of research, I can give the ages in April, 1927 of 68, something better than half of them. The average age was 30·33 years and the median age was 29. Nearly half of them (32 persons) were in the age group 25–29, while 55 (80%) were 35 or younger. This means they were from two or three student generations. These young leaders looked out on the world with a common experience and, so far as historical events had impinged upon them, presumably with rather similar reactions. Only eleven of the leaders were "elders", ranging in age from 35 to 53. This youthfulness of the leadership was an asset for the future. Most of the men and women were just entering their prime years. Those who stayed with the Party and who survived the executions and wars of the next nine years could still look forward to long careers directing the Party.

When we consider province of origin (see table II, pp. 64–65), 102 can be identified. The rank order of provinces is as follows: Hunan—29, Kwangtung—16, Hupeh—15, Szechwan—8, Kiangsu —7, and Chekiang—5, the remaining 22 persons coming from 11 different provinces. The majority of the leadership came from central China, the band of provinces near the Yangtze, from Szechwan eastward to Kiangsu and Chekiang. These seven provinces account for 72 leaders, or 70% of the identified cases. South China produced 20 and North China 10. Most of the leaders were natives of inland provinces. China's four most urbanized and westernized coastal provinces—Chihli (Hopeh), Kiangsu, Chekiang and Kwangtung—produced 32 of the leaders, or about 31%; the three west-central provinces of Hunan, Hupeh and Szechwan produced 52, or just over half. This striking concentration persists in the next period also. A tabulation by *hsien* probably would show an even more striking concentration within the three focal provinces.

Most of the leaders were educated persons. Of the 88 for which it was possible to gather information on education or to deduce it from positions held, it appears that only 8 of the leaders had little or no education. They were from among proletarians whom the Party eagerly recruited. All the rest apparently had had a proper

47

old-style education or had entered schools beyond the higher primary level. At least 19 had attended colleges in China. Forty-one had studied abroad, which is nearly half. It does not surprise us that Japan, France and Russia were the countries which turned students towards Marxism and the Communist Party. Many of the leaders had had professional careers as intellectuals—as professors, teachers, editors or journalists. Only two had had military careers before joining the Party in 1925 or earlier (one of the criteria for listing). Nine others received military training at Whampoa or other revolutionary academies.

In respect to education and occupation, the Communist Party leaders were much like the leaders of the Kuomintang. They were younger and as a group less well educated, and they counted a smaller number of military men. The main difference between the two groups, it seems, is that most of the "pure" Kuomintang leaders had been drawn from an earlier student generation. There seems little to distinguish the two groups in their social origins. The youthfulness of the Communist intellectuals, and hence their closeness in age to oncoming student generations, probably was an asset in the revolutionary struggle between the parties after 1927.

Some Communist leaders had been members of the Kuomintang or its antecedent organizations before joining the other Party, and from 1923 onwards most Communist leaders joined the Kuomintang and worked under its banner. Although the process of separation in 1927 was traumatic, the earlier commingling of leaderships had provided valuable experience for those Communists who survived the purges. They knew the Kuomintang system of operations, both at the centre and in many provinces and cities. They had an insight into the personalities of their enemies. The reverse also was true, but apparently to a lesser extent because membership in the Communist Party was often kept secret and the Party's inner operations were carefully concealed. In April, 1927 Right Wing leaders of the Kuomintang made up a list of important "Communists" to be driven out of the Nationalist Party, but it seems they were ill-informed.[1]

[1] *Ko ming wen hsien*, XVII, 3091–2. While many of the 196 persons named were Communists holding important positions in the Kuomintang, some apparently

The Chinese Communist Party suffered a great blood-letting in the year of purges and insurrections beginning in April, 1927. Table III gives a list of the men and women among the 120 leaders who are known to have been lost to the Party during that year.

There were, of course, hundreds of Communist activists of lesser stature, who were executed during the purges or who lost their lives in futile uprisings. Among those not on our list but of some prominence, there were 20 executed and 23 probably executed, and 4 others who may have been Communists. It was a dangerous time for leftists; many who were not members of the Communist Party had to flee or withdraw from political life. For example, Chan Ta-pei, a veteran of the 1911 Revolution, an alternate member of the Kuomintang Central Executive Committee, and a member of the Hupeh Provincial Government was captured and executed on December 16, 1927. Li Han-chün was captured with him and executed the next day.

Finally, we must mention Ch'en Tu-hsiu, who withdrew from the Secretary-Generalship of the Party in July, 1927 and gradually moved into the opposition. Probably no one suffered more anguish than he, with the Comintern policies he had tried to carry out now in tatters, and two sons executed.

There is also the curious role of happenstance. Two of the Communists' most eminent later leaders were arrested, but escaped execution—Chou En-lai and Mao Tse-tung.

By the spring of 1928 when a few leaders started off to Moscow to hold the Sixth Congress, the Party had suffered a series of disasters. Collaboration with the Kuomintang, extremely valuable during the course of Party-building, had proved an utter failure as the route to control of the National Revolution. The Nanchang Uprising, the Autumn Harvest Uprisings, the Canton Commune, and the Hai-feng Soviet had all been drowned in blood. The Party was even more scattered than before and its communications system scarcely existed. The life of the Party lay in the groups of determined leaders who had survived and stayed with the organization, together

were not Communists, e.g. Teng Yen-ta, Hsü Ch'ien, Ku Meng-yü, Kuo Mo-jo (though he may have joined soon after), Liu Ya-tzu, Shen Yen-ping, Ch'en Ch'i-yüan, and Li Han-chün (a founder of the Chinese Communist Party, but expelled).

with more recent recruits who continued the struggle against
seemingly hopeless odds.

I prepared a second list of newly emerging leaders in 1928
(table IV, pp. 66–7). The determining criteria for this selection
were that they be Party members by mid-1928, that they participate
and achieve note in the Party's struggles in China, whether rural
or urban, and that they *survive* into the relative calm of late 1936.
In short, this is the group which, together with the surviving
seniors, brought the Party through to the Sino-Japanese war
period. There were 94 in the new group.[1]

The second group was naturally younger than the first. Out of 92
for whom I can find ages, the average in 1928 was 24·8 years and the
median age lay between 23 and 24. The largest five-year category
was the years 20–24, in which there were 48, over half. Here was a
group that would move through time to positions of power. Only
seven of the newly emergent group were over 35 years old.

Provincial origin shows interesting similarities with and differences from the earlier list. The provinces in rank order show Hunan
again far in the lead with 27, followed by Shensi—9, Hupeh and
Kwangtung—each 8, Fukien and Shansi—each 7, Anhwei and
Szechwan—each 6. The remaining 16 were scattered in eight
provinces. Again the central China provinces along the Yangtze
predominate with 56 out of 94 (60%). Now the north exceeds the
south by 20 to 17 in new leaders. The three west-central provinces
of Hunan, Hupeh and Szechwan produced 41, as against 16 from
the four modernized coastal provinces of Chihli (Hopeh), Chekiang,
Kiangsu and Kwangtung.

The new leaders were less well educated than their seniors,
as we should expect from their youthfulness. But that is not the

[1] For the second group, Mr Klein's files, the Union Research Institute,
Who's Who in Communist China and the above cited Japanese biographical
dictionary were most useful, as were the works of Edgar Snow and Helen Foster
Snow (Nym Wales). Some later prominent leaders joined the Party after 1928
but were active in it during this period; I have excluded them. Examples
are Lo Ping-hui, Sung Shih-lun and Wang En-mao. Others had joined by 1928
and made important contributions, but did not survive through the period, e.g.
Huang Kung-lüeh, Mao Tse-t'an, and Shen Tse-min. Yet others were apparently
not active in China during the period 1928–36; for example, Chi Chao-t'ing,
Jao Shu-shih, Wang P'ing-nan, and Yeh T'ing.

only factor for now more "proletarians" with little or no education appear, 16 as compared with 8 on the previous list. Comparing the 87 new leaders on which there is educational information with the similar 88 on the senior list, it is clear that in each educational category beyond primary school there were fewer newcomers with corresponding education, except in the category of military education. There are now 24 newcomers with formal military training, compared with 11 on the earlier list: at Whampoa 17 as compared with the previous 7. Soviet Russia was, naturally, the place for study abroad; but only 16 of the 94 are known to have studied abroad as against 41 in the earlier list.

About 90 of the senior leaders were available in mid-1928 to carry on the Party's struggles if they chose to do so. I was curious to know how many of them could stand the criteria applied to the newer leaders—participation in the Party's struggles in China and survival into 1936. There is another list of martyrs and also a few defectors shown in table V (pp. 67–8).

The underground war between the Kuomintang and the Chinese Communist Party in Shanghai and in other Chinese cities was as brutal as the guerrilla war in the countryside. The remaining early leadership was riven by factions. Some moved into the Third Party, some followed Ch'en Tu-hsiu into a separate Marxist Party, while others fought it out in inter-clique struggles between Li Li-san, the Moscow "Returned Students", and the Ho Meng-hsiung–Lo Chang-lung faction. There were betrayals and defections. It was these internecine struggles as well as open warfare between Communists and Nationalists which reduced the potential leadership of 1927 to a mere 36 who made it through to the calmer days of 1936 as members of the Party.

If we add the 36 veterans to the 94 rising stars we have a profile (shown in table VI, p. 68) in mid-1928 at the time of the Party's Sixth Congress held in the security of Moscow.

TYPES OF VALUABLE EXPERIENCE

Collectively the Communist leadership had gained invaluable experience by mid-1927. All but a few of them entered the Party as bookish individuals only narrowly acquainted with Chinese social realities, especially the realities of the life of the masses they aspired to lead. A process of transformation occurred. Considered analytically, this transformation within the leadership may be separated into cognitive and cathetic elements. The first involved acquiring knowledge, such as learning organizational and propaganda techniques and discovering how such techniques might be applied, or must be adapted, for use among particular groups within Chinese society. In this process some leaders became specialists in propaganda, others in work with youth, labour, women, or farmers. A few learned military arts and how to operate under conditions of increasing revolutionary violence. This tended to make specialists of men and women most of whom had had very little practical experience when they entered the Party; and it helped to shape their future careers. The cathectic element relates to personality and psychological needs, a much more subtle field of inquiry. Basic personality apparently is very little altered by adult experience and acquisition of knowledge. Persons of certain personality types may have been drawn into the Party because of psychological needs. If Party work helped to meet these needs, anxieties and frustrations may have been overcome. Experience may have intensified certain fundamental psychological traits. Aggressive impulses, for example, had opportunities for relatively uninhibited development. Li Li-san and Mao Tse-tung come to mind. Generalization seems risky in the absence of many intensive biographical studies. At the present stage of the art it seems more productive to concentrate upon the knowledge and experience acquired by the leadership.

By 1927 the Party had published many journals. A group of editors had learned to appeal effectively to educated youth and women, as well as to a broader public. They had also experimented with publications written in simple, earthy language directed to labourers, farmers and soldiers. Others had proved their ability at haranguing the masses in public meetings, and in leading demonstrations. In revolutionary China where propaganda played a vital role in recruitment and in mobilization of support or sympathy, the collective talents and experience of these writers and speakers were a great asset.

A related line of experience was in manipulating multi-class movements, essentially patriotic movements. By manipulation, I mean the effort to convert patriotic movements to the Party's other goals. Certainly the Party leaders were patriots, and a major goal of the Party was to liberate China from all aspects of foreign control—except for the delicate and somewhat remote matters of Russian control of Outer Mongolia and of the Chinese Eastern Railway. The Party used multi-class patriotic movements to promote solidarity between educated youths, workers, farmers and soldiers. This they constantly stressed. They used demonstrations to discover activists, and then cultivated them and brought the most ardent into the Party or Youth Corps. Patriotic movements brought the leaders closer to the masses, at least temporarily. They also opened the door to other leadership groups.

Working in the United Front with the Kuomintang for common nationalistic goals, Party leaders gained experience in organizing multi-group committees made up of representatives of existing organizations. Such committees provided guidance in policy and strategy for bursts of patriotic activity. A good example is the Joint Committee formed shortly after the May 30th Incident in 1925. The Joint Committee of Workers, Merchants and Students had equal representation from the newly created and Communist-controlled Shanghai General Labour Union, the National and the Shanghai Federation of Students' Associations (in both of which the Communist Youth Corps was influential), and the Federation of Street Merchants' Associations. The inner core of the Joint Committee was a group of Communists, but there was broad enough representation of other radical patriots for the Committee to exert influence in the constituent organizations, in whose name it operated, and outwardly on the general public. Working in the Committee, the Communist leaders improved a skill in directing but not domineering, and of compromising on inessentials.[1]

[1] Based upon my recent research into the May 30th Movement. Teng Chung-hsia stated it was the strategy of the Party to make the Joint Committee the focal point of the United Front; to have the General Labour Union make connection with the Left Wing of the Students' Association to repress its Right Wing; to use the Students' Association to make connections with the Left Wing of the Federation of Street Merchants' Associations to repress its Right Wing; and

Communists created many such joint committees during the next two years, such as relief committees, federations of women's organizations, committees of workers, farmers and soldiers, *hsien* (county) civic committees and similar bodies. Communist leaders became intimately acquainted with outstanding leaders in various occupations and localities, and gained an understanding of interest groups. Most importantly, they learned to channel the abilities of others when there was a common purpose.

The last effort of this sort before the purge was a municipal committee for Shanghai which the Communist leaders hoped might govern the city after its take-over in 1927. This gambit was stillborn; Right Wing Kuomintang leaders would have none of it. Communist leaders had little opportunity to use their skill in organizing front groups during most of the period between 1928 and 1936, although some used it in the League of Left Wing Writers and in the patriotic student movement of December, 1935. As soon as the Communist Party made the decisive strategic turn to a United Front Against Japan—rather than against the National Government and the Kuomintang—experience in "united front work" once more was useful. It continued useful into the 1950's.

In the field of labour, a group of experts emerged who had mastered the difficult art of coming "close" to the real proletariat, winning its confidence, and organizing its energies both to struggle for economic concessions and to strike and demonstrate for the more abstract causes the Party espoused. To come close to labour was not easy for educated, middle-class youths to do. Most of the Chinese proletariat, particularly in its main centre in Shanghai, was illiterate and spoke dialects unintelligible to most *Kuo-yü* speakers. Occupationally, it was fractured by localities of origin. The workers were dominated by labour bosses and contractors, and by secret societies such as the *Ch'ing Pang*. The influence of speech-group fraternities and old-style guilds was pervasive. Furthermore, the proletariat

to use the Federation to make connections with the Left Wing of the General Chamber of Commerce to repress its Right Wing. *Chung kuo chih kung yün tung chien shih* [A Brief History of the Chinese Labour Movement] (many editions since 1930; I have used one published by Hua chung hsin Hua shu tien in 1949), p. 160.

was difficult to organize for strikes because of four main obstacles: a great reservoir of labour from villages always ready to compete for jobs; the high proportion of impermanent female labour; speech-group rivalries within various occupations; and pitifully low wages which left almost no margin for loss of income in strikes.

How the two sides came together—the modern-oriented, middle-class, educated youths and the tradition-bound, fractionalized and vulnerable proletariat—is one of the fascinating subjects of the Communist Party's early years.[1] To generalize the matter most simply, each side could help the other when they had learned how to do so. The keys which unlocked the passageway were the school/club and the strike. The young activist intellectuals established spare-time schools for workers, as in the railway town of Chang-hsin-tien, the mining town of An-yüan, or the workers' quarter in Cha-pei. In these school/clubs they became acquainted with ambitious workers whom they cultivated and indoctrinated, and from whom they learned the workers' real grievances. The worker-activists were inside the yards, the mines and the factories; they were known to their fellows, spoke their dialects, and could recruit other activists.

Together the school/club organizers and the inside activists planned a strike against such grievances as the pay rake-off of labour contractors, brutality of foremen or foreign guards, or the lag of wages behind the rising cost of rice. An intense, brief struggle for a worthy cause knit a psychological bond, reinforcing the teacher–student or master–disciple relationship.

To be effective, the strike required organization, élan, coercion, some financing, and public support. The intellectuals with their broader horizons influenced the outer world. They explained the workers' demands, justified their cause in street lectures and publications, raised subscriptions and, finally, acted as the workers' advocates in the inevitable negotiations conducted by arbitrating bodies. Arbitration was usually done by chambers of commerce, street

[1] Jean Chesneaux, *Le Mouvement Ouvrier Chinois de 1919 à 1927* (Paris: Mouton, 1962), pp. 85–218; English translation *The Chinese Labor Movement, 1919–1927* (Stanford: Stanford Univ. Press, 1968), pp. 48–148; and my study of the May 30th Movement on how unions were formed.

merchants' associations, distinguished elders or government officials These were educated, middle- or upper-class people and the workers needed advocates of the same background to negotiate with them. The inside activists, organized in ten-man teams, provided the discipline and coercion to hold the strike together. They manned the picket-corps that prevented workers from going back to the job until a concession was won, and that drove off scabs. Strike pay was controlled by the leaders: enrolment for pay meant enrolment into unions. Out of the strike emerged the effective worker-leaders. The Party recruited and organized them as Communist cells in shop or work crews. Concessions won in the strike solidified the union.

The local strike was essential as a recruiting and training field, but it was a slow way of building unions. The anti-imperialist movement provided the dynamo for rapid growth, as was evident during the May 30th Movement in Shanghai, the Hong Kong strike and boycott of 1925-6, and the unionization movement in Wuhan after the arrival of the Northern Expeditionary armies. The students' organizers found their outside support, both public and financial, and their large-scale following within the ranks of labour when they could link anti-foreign passions with worker grievances. In this they proved adept.

The Chinese Communist Party, having unions in Soviet Russia as a model, attempted to organize the entire proletariat into a network of industrial unions—railwaymen, seamen, miners, factory workers —linked in functional and metropolitan federations and all tied together in a national General Labour Union controlled by the Party itself. In a few years of intense work a score of young intellectuals had succeeded, amazingly it must seem, in creating, or in penetrating and taking over, hundreds of unions, several large federations, and a national organization which claimed some three million members in mid-1927. This was the accomplishment of such young intellectuals as Teng Chung-hsia, Chang Kuo-t'ao, Ho Meng-hsiung, Li Ch'i-han, Pao Hui-seng, Li Li-san, Liu Shao-ch'i and Ts'ai Ch'ang, aided by the natural leaders among labour whom they drew into the Party. Among the latter were the seamen, Su Chao-cheng, Lin Wei-min, Ch'en Yü, Teng Fa, and Yang Yin; dockyard workers such as Hsiang Chung-fa and Lo Teng-hsien; railway workers, Hsü Pai-hao and Wang Ho-po; mill hands such as Sun Liang-huai and Hsiang Ying; the mechanic, Ku Shun-chang and the printer, Ch'en Yün. There were, of course, many other intellectuals who tried their hands at labour movement work and turned to other tasks, and an uncounted number of lesser leaders from among the proletariat.

The Party's success in its chosen field was partly due to the cover it enjoyed in the Kuomintang and partly due to the great anti-imperialist tide that was created by nationalists and that swept China in the early 1920's. The success had a built-in danger, however. It had been too rapid, and the labour unions and federations were very fragile. An illusion of strength and power, together with the dogma of a revolution in which the proletariat must be the leading force, brought the Communist Party nearly to extinction in the cities between 1928 and 1932, when the Kuomintang cover was gone and the anti-imperialist movement had receded.

The same danger existed in the apparently successful farmers' movement that counted millions of members early in 1927. Under the Kuomintang's banner and with the benevolent assistance of Liao Chung-k'ai until his assassination in August, 1925, a group of young intellectuals organized farmers' associations in Kwangtung, linked them together in county units, federated them provincially, and spread the movement into Hunan, Hupeh and Kiangsi. Among some of the specialists in this work were P'eng Pai, Lo Ch'i-yüan, Juan Hsiao-hsien, T'an Chih-t'ang, Liu Kuo-chen, Wu Chen-min, Mao Tse-tung and Fang Chih-min. The Farmers' Movement Training Institute was a device to prepare young activists, either students or farmers, to serve as organizers. The most effective among the graduates were kept on as Special Deputies of the Kuomintang Farmers' Bureau; they formed the web of the organization. Coercive power lay in the Farmers' Guards, but actually they were only a local instrument of very limited power unless backed up by the Revolutionary Army.

One special feature of the organization of farmers' associations merits comment. Although farmers' associations were organized under Kuomintang auspices, the young Communists in the Kuomintang who were the actual organizers vehemently insisted that the entire system of associations be completely autonomous. This stipulation was written into the first and subsequent charters. The Farmers' Association was not to be under the control of the National Government nor of the Kuomintang. The Communist Party intended to control the system itself. Despite its apparent success in enrolling a vast number of farmers in associations, and despite an organizational structure which looked impressive on paper, the Party could not control the movement it set in motion. The village was the very seat of conservatism, with a social structure that was nearly impervious to reorganization from the outside. Doctrines based upon European conditions were irrelevant. The evils of imperialism were not the problems which farmers could understand. Most importantly, the tensions in rural life could not be unleashed and then manipulated by a few leaders in the interest of larger aims such as continued cooperation with the Left Wing of the Kuomintang. During a few months the farmers' movement in Hunan and Hupeh exploded in violence which was beyond the Party's control, and then was crushed, county by county. Farmers' associations scattered like dust.

Few of the early stars of the farmers' movement survived the wars up to 1936. Yet many men and some women had gained invaluable experience which they carried over for work in the central Yangtze provinces. They had learned the complexities of the rural social structure and the facts of local power. They knew the intensity of inter-group hostility which lay beneath the apparently placid surface of village life. After the failure of the Autumn Harvest Uprisings of September, 1927 and the crushing of the Hai-Lu-feng Soviet early in 1928—to mention only two better known instances[1]— some of them gathered together small bands of insurgent farmers and commenced to create rural guerrilla bases. It took these leaders years of experimentation, however, and years of vacillation concerning land revolution before they constructed new rural organizations,

[1] Roy Hofheinz, Jr., "The Autumn Harvest Insurrection", *The China Quarterly*, No. 32 (October–December, 1967), pp. 37–87; Eto Shinkichi, "Hai-lu-feng—The First Chinese Soviet Government (Part 2)", *The China Quarterly*, No. 9 (January–March, 1962), pp. 149–81, esp. pp. 177–81.

village by village and county by county, which supported guerrilla armies and which the Party actually controlled.

Another line of indispensable experience was military work. Among the group of senior leaders—those who had joined the Party by 1925—there were very few with military training and command experience. Chu Te and Yeh T'ing are the best-known examples. Another group worked as political instructors in the Whampoa Military Academy and thus had the opportunity to recruit cadets into the Communist Party. Among such instructors were Chou En-lai, Nieh Jung-chen, Ch'en I and Yün Tai-ying. Other early leaders worked in the political departments of armies in the National Revolutionary Army (Lin Tsu-han and Li Fu-ch'un are examples) or in the Kuominchün (Wang Jo-fei and Teng Hsiao-p'ing). How many cadets from Whampoa or its branch in Wuhan joined the Communist Party is unclear; there may have been hundreds. At least twenty helped to lead it through the guerrilla wars into 1936. Chang Yün-i, Ho Lung, Liu Po-ch'eng, and Yeh Chien-ying were among the experienced commanders who had joined the Party by 1927; P'eng Te-huai had joined by March, 1928. Some of their subordinate officers and troops were the basis for the formation of Red Armies. Thus the military experience of a few leaders and the opportunity of others to indoctrinate officers and soldiers were valuable after the Party began its insurrectionary course in August, 1927. It is difficult to conceive the history of the Communist Party thereafter without the contributions of its military men.

The women's emancipation movement was another training ground. Feminine leaders were important to the Party because doors were open to them which men could not enter. They could recruit female students who were exceptionally militant in patriotic movements. They could work with women in textile factories, a group that it was difficult for male organizers to approach. The Communist role in the women's emancipation movement is a subject which has not been given much systematic attention, but the Party became well aware of women's revolutionary potential and tried to exploit it just as the Kuomintang did. Yet the Communist Party was dominated by men. Whether my lists reflect the historical realities or not is difficult to say, but only five women are in the first list and six in the combined list of those who brought the Party into 1936: Hsia Chih-hsü, Teng Ying-ch'ao, Ts'ai Ch'ang, Yang Chih-hua, Li Chen and Li Chien-chen.

Finally, one should mention experience with training schools. Many of the Communist leaders from both groups had studied in the University of the Toilers of the East, or Sun Yat-sen University as it was later named. Others taught or studied in Shanghai University, a radical school set up jointly by the Kuomintang and the Communist Party in the summer of 1923. Whampoa Military Academy and the Farmers' Movement Training Institute have already been mentioned. In all these schools, indoctrination was an essential part of the curriculum. During its entire later history the Communist Party has created academies to train its future leaders and specialists in many lines of revolutionary work. This was a debt to the past.

By mid-1928 the Communist leadership was accustomed to violence. It is doubtful that the founders of the Party and its early student recruits had a clear conception of revolutionary struggle. They were idealists, but through experience many became practical and tough. The toughening was gradual. They learned violence in the farmers' movement, where they met repression by counter-violence and came to condone the killing of "evil gentry and local bullies". They learned it in labour movement work in which picket corps moved from rough stuff to assassination of obstructive foremen. Middle-school students flocked from all parts of China to enrol in the Whampoa Academy to be trained in warfare. Intellectuals planned and led the Nanchang Uprising and the Canton Commune. Thereafter they were fully committed to warfare both for survival and for the revolutionary cause. This transformation occurred during the Party's early years.

Another transformation which I think was under way, but is difficult to prove, was a shift from dependency upon ideology to empiricism. While it was still necessary for men and women who had studied their Marxism to clothe decisions of policy in class categories and stages of history, still in practical matters of revolutionary strategy some adjusted theory to Chinese social realities. The Party's abandonment of the proletarian illusion did not come until about 1931, but guerrilla leaders had given it up long before.

To sum up this section, during its first eight years the Chinese Communist Party developed a vigorous leadership with many talents, wide contacts with various strata of society, and much useful experience in revolutionary work. A screening process removed the faint-hearted and, unfortunately for the Party, many of its most talented leaders by execution or death in insurrections. The Party lived on in the determination of the leaders and recruits that remained, some in Moscow but most of them scattered in the cities and mountains of the Yangtze provinces.

THE THRUST OF THE PAST

In 1928 the Party existed in the minds of hundreds of leaders and potential leaders. Many of them had known no other adult occupation than revolutionary work within the Party. This band strove continuously to rebuild the shattered structure. They formed and reformed Central Committees, Political Bureaus, regional and provincial committees and Party cells in mass organizations. The individuals in these organs changed; some were killed and others defected or formed opposition factions. Yet through the years there remained a vital core. The Chinese nation, in a state of nearly chaotic disorganization, provided ample numbers of fresh recruits from among its student cohorts and its rural and urban poor.

In fact, the recruitment among workers and peasants during the first period began to pay off after 1928 as men of humble background, little education, but natural talent began to rise to positions of leadership. Some fifteen or twenty from the third list—active leaders who survived into the period after 1936—were men of this sort: farm hands, miners, seamen, potters, textile factory workers and the like. Only a small proportion, it is true, for the leadership of the Party has continued to be manned largely by people with at least a middle-school education—far beyond the reach of the proletariat in China of those days. Also among the Party leaders were a number of military men commanding small contingents which became the nuclei of armies yet to be formed. Men with the experience of Chu Te, Ho Lung, Liu Po-ch'eng, P'eng Te-huai and a few others were well prepared to begin that process. There were also scores of Whampoa graduates and other officers from the National Revolutionary Army and the Kuominchün who had joined the Party and possessed a martial temperament and military skills to contribute to guerrilla warfare. A few others, by chance and vision, started on that road; Mao Tse-tung and Fang Chih-min, are examples. Inland China, with its mixed mountains and plains in the Yangtze provinces, its reservoirs of under-employed and discontented men, and its fractured military–political structure, was ideal for guerrilla warfare. Yet this situation provided only the opportunity for leaders who could learn to exploit it. Five years of collaboration with the Kuomintang taught these men that geographical bases and armies controlled by a party were essential for revolution in China. These they set out to create. Until the victory on the Mainland, armies and bases sustained the Party. They were never negotiable.

In 1928, however, the official leadership was still committed to the fundamental belief that the Party was proletarian and that the urban proletariat must be the leading force in the revolution. Compelled by this belief and still under the dictate of the Comintern in strategy, most of the leaders concentrated on trying to rebuild an urban labour movement under Party control. It took four years of fruitless effort and fearful repression in the cities before the Party adjusted itself to realities and abandoned the proletarian illusion, in fact if not by admission.

Dependency upon Soviet Russia for ideology, policy guidance, finance and cadre training were still a part of the thrust from the past. Gradually the Party emancipated itself. It adjusted "the universal truths of Marxism–Leninism" to Chinese realities. Party leaders—some sooner, some later—developed their own strategies for coping with their environment. Cadres were still being trained in Moscow till the early thirties. It would be difficult to demonstrate that the Chinese leaders trained in Russia were better prepared to lead a Chinese revolution than those in the Party who were not; the weight of the evidence probably would fall on the side of those who had not undergone such schooling. Whatever the case, the Party's psychological and material dependency on Soviet Russia were gradually replaced by self-confidence and independence won through victories in the Chinese countryside. The disengagement was, however, a two-sided process as Soviet Russia became absorbed in building socialism in one country and as the Chinese Party went deep into the wilderness.

The thrust from the past was thus the essential moulding influence, but it guaranteed nothing. Survival and ultimate victory were the product of determined leaders who gradually understood their real world and hammered out a strategy that successfully harnessed two dynamic forces, rural discontent and Chinese nationalism.

Table 1. *List of 120 Communist Party leaders in April, 1927*

Name		Name	
An T'i-ch'eng	安體誠	*Ho Ch'ang-kung	何長工
Chang Ch'iu-jen	張秋人	Ho Meng-hsiung	何孟雄
*Chang Kuo-t'ao	張國燾	Ho Shu-heng	何叔衡
Chang Po-chien	張伯簡	Hou Shao-ch'iu	侯紹裘
Chang T'ai-lai (lei)	張泰來	*Hsia Chih-hsü	夏之栩
Chao Shih-yen	趙世炎	Hsia Hsi	夏曦
Ch'en Ch'i-hsiu	陳啓修	Hsiang Ching-yü	向警予
Ch'en Ch'iao-nien	陳喬年	Hsiang Chung-fa	向忠發
*Ch'en I	陳毅	*Hsiang Ying	項英
*Ch'en T'an-ch'iu	陳潭秋	*Hsiao Ching-kuang	蕭勁光
Ch'en Tu-hsiu	陳獨秀	Hsiao Ch'u-nü	蕭楚女
Ch'en Yen-nien	陳延年	*Hsieh Chüeh-tsai	謝覺哉
*Ch'en Yü	陳郁	Hsiung Hsiung	熊雄
*Ch'en Yün	陳雲	Hsü Chih-chen	許之楨
*Cheng Wei-shan	鄭唯善	Hsü Pai-hao	許白昊
Chiang Hsien-yün	蔣先雲	Hsü Su-hun	許蘇魂
Chiang Tung-ch'in	江董琴	Hsüan Chung-hua	宣中華
*Chou En-lai	周恩來	Huang Jih-k'uei	黃日葵
Chou I-ch'ün	周逸羣	Huang P'ing	黃平
*Chou Shih-ti	周士第	Jen Cho-hsüan	任卓宣
Chu Chi-hsün	朱季恂	*Jen Pi-shih	任弼時
*Chu Teh	朱德	Juan[Yüan]Hsiao-hsien	阮[袁]嘯仙
Ch'ü Ch'iu-pai	瞿秋白	*K'ang Sheng	康生
Fang Chih-min	方志敏	Kao Yü-han	高語罕
Feng Chü-p'o	馮菊坡	Ku Shun-chang	顧順章
*Fu Chung	傅鍾	*Kuan Hsiang-ying	關向應
Han Lin-fu	韓麟符	Kuo Liang	郭亮
Ho Ch'ang	賀昌	Li Ch'i-han	李啓漢

Name		Name	
Li Chih-lung	李之龍	Pao Hui-seng	鮑慧僧
Li Ch'iu-shih	李求實	P'eng P'ai	彭湃
*Li Fu-ch'un	李富春	P'eng Shu-chih	彭述之
Li Kuo-chen	李國珍	P'eng Tse-hsiang	彭澤湘
Li Li-san	李立三	Shih Ts'un-t'ung	施存統
Li Ta	李達	Su Chao-cheng	蘇兆徵
Li Ta-chao	李大釗	Sun Liang-hui	孫良惠
*Li Wei-han	李維漢	T'an Chih-t'ang	譚植棠
Liao Ch'ien-wu	廖乾五	T'an P'ing-shan	譚平山
Lin Chün	林鈞	Teng Chung-hsia	鄧中夏
*Lin Tsu-han	林祖涵	*Teng Fa	鄧發
Lin Wei-min	林偉民	*Teng Hsiao-p'ing	鄧小平
Lin Yü-nan	林育南	*Teng Ying-ch'ao	鄧穎超
*Lin Yü-ying	林育英	*Ts'ai Ch'ang	蔡暢
Liu Chih-hsün	柳直荀	Ts'ai Ho-shen	蔡和森
*Liu Chih-tan	劉志丹	*Tung Pi-wu	董必武
Liu Erh-sung	劉爾崧	Wang Ho-po	王荷波
Liu Fen	劉芬	Wang I-fei	王一飛
Liu Jen-ching	劉仁靜	*Wang Jo-fei	王若飛
Liu Po-chien	劉伯堅	Wang Shou-hua	汪壽華
Liu Po-lun	劉伯倫	Wu Chen-min	吳振民
*Liu Shao-ch'i	劉少奇	*Wu Yü-chang	吳玉章
Lo Chang-lung	羅章龍	*Yang Chih-hua	楊之華
Lo Ch'i-yüan	羅綺園	Yang Hsien-chiang	楊賢江
Lo I-nung	羅亦農	Yang P'ao-an	楊匏安
Lo Teng-hsien	羅登賢	Yang Yin	楊殷
Lu Ch'en	陸沉	Yeh T'ing	葉挺
*Lu Ting-i	陸定一	Yü Fang-chou	于方舟
Lung Ta-tao	龍大道	Yü Hsiu-sung	俞秀松
*Mao Tse-min	毛澤民	Yü Shu-te	于樹德
*Mao Tse-tung	毛澤東	Yüan Ta-shih	袁達時
*Nieh Jung-chen	聶榮臻	Yün Tai-ying	惲代英

* Among the 36 who led the Party through to 1936

Table II. *Provincial origins, age groups, and education of early Chinese Communist leaders**

	Group				Group		
	I	II	III		I	II	III
Province				Education			
Anhwei	4	6	6	In China (Highest known)†			
Chekiang	5	2	3	Little or none	8	16	19

64

	I	II	III
Chihli (Hopeh)	4	3	3
Fukien	—	7	7
Heilungkiang	—	1	1
Honan	1	1	2
Hunan	29	27	38
Hupeh	15	8	13
Kiangsi	4	4	5
Kiangsu	7	3	6
Kwangsi	1	1	1
Kwangtung	16	9	11
Kweichow	2	—	1
Liaoning	1	—	1
Shansi	1	7	7
Shantung	2	—	1
Shensi	1	9	10
Szechwan	8	6	12
Yunnan	1	1	1
Total	102	94	129
Don't know	18	—	1
Total	120	94	130

Age group

	I	II	III
Under 20	—	8	8
20–24	7	48	51
25–29	32	20	35
30–34	17	9	18
35–39	3	4	4
40–44	6	2	4
45–49	2	—	3
50–54	1	1	1
Total	68	92	124
Don't know	52	2	6
Total	120	94	130

	I	II	III
Classical or probably	3	2	5
Middle school or probably	28	16	25
Normal or technical	19	13	22
College	19	16	23
Military	11	24	28
Whampoa Military academy	7	17	20
Other revolutionary academy	2	2	2
Other academies	2	5	6
Total	88	87	122
Don't know	32	7	8
Total	120	94	130

Abroad‡

	I	II	III
Japan	14	3	8
France	22	1	14
Russia	22	12	18
Other European	3	1	3
Total	51	17	43
Double counts	10	1	6
Persons involved	41	16	37

---

* Basis for selection by group:

GROUP I. Up to April, 1927. Had joined CCP by 1925, held positions of leadership in central offices, or regional, provincial and metropolitan branches of the Party and its Youth Corps; or positions of responsibility within KMT, civil or military, even though replaced in reshuffle of May, 1926, or leadership positions in mass organizations.

GROUP II. Up to July, 1928. Had joined the Party, would participate and achieve note in the Party's struggles in China, whether rural or urban, and survived into 1936.

GROUP III. Up to July, 1928. Made up of Group II plus survivors from Group I who participated in the struggles in China and lasted through to 1936 with the Party. Ages calculated as of July, 1928.

† Enrolled, not necessarily graduated.

‡ At least one year and presumably enrolled for education.

Table III.   *Communist leaders lost from first list*

Executed by mid-1928

An T'i-ch'eng	–May, 1927
Chao Shih-yen	–July 3, 1927
Ch'en Ch'iao-nien	–January 19, 1928
Ch'en Yen-nien	–June 27, 1927
Hou Shao-ch'iu	–April, 1927
Hsiang Ching-yü	–May 1, 1928
Hsiao Ch'u-nü	–April 18, 1927
Hsü Pai-hao	–January 19, 1928 (probably)
Hsüan Chung-hua	–April, 1927
Hsiung Hsiung	–April, 1927
Li Ch'i-han	–April 15, 1927
Li Chih-lung	–April ?, 1927
Li Kuo-chen	–Early 1928
Li Ta-chao	–April 29, 1927
Lin Tao-wen	–February, 1928
Liu Erh-sung	–April 15, 1927
Lo I-nung	–April 21, 1928
Wang Shou-hua	–April 11, 1927
Wu Chen-min	–Early 1928

Died in battle by mid-1928

Chiang Hsien-yün	–May, 1927
Chang T'ai-lai[lei]	–December 12, 1927

Withdrew from Party

Li Ta	
Shih Ts'un-t'ung	–May, 1927
T'an P'ing-shan	–November, 1927
Yü Shu-te	–Late 1927

Defected to the Kuomintang

Jen Cho-hsüan	–Late 1927
Pao Hui-seng	–Late 1927
Yüan Ta-shih	–Late 1927

Table IV.   *List of 94 Communist Party members in 1928 who led the Party into 1936*

Chang Chi-ch'un	張	際	春	Chia T'o-fu	買	拓	夫
Chang Ch'i-lung	張	啓	龍	Ch'in Pang-hsien	秦	邦	憲
Chang Kuo-chien	張	國	堅	Chou Hsing	周	與	中
Chang Ting-ch'eng	張	鼎	承	Chaou Pao-chung	周	保	駒
Chang Tsung-hsün	張	宗	遜	Fang Fang	方	方	彬
Chang Wei-chen	張	維	楨	Feng Pai-chü	馮	白	勳
Chang Wen-t'ien	張	聞	天	Feng Wen-pin	馮	文	龍
Chang Yün-i	張	雲	逸	Ho Lung	賀	龍	
Ch'en Ch'ang-hao	陳	昌	浩	Hsi Chung-hsün	習	仲	勛
Ch'en Cheng-jen	陳	正	人	Hsiao K'e	蕭	克	民
Ch'en Ch'i-han	陳	奇	涵	Hsieh Fu-min	謝	扶	東
Ch'en Keng	陳	賡		Hsü Hai-tung	徐	海	謙
Ch'en Po-chün	陳	伯	鈞	Hsü Hsiang-ch'ien	徐	象	達
Ch'en Po-ta	陳	伯	達	Hsü Kuang-ta	許	光	
Ch'en Shao-yü	陳	紹	禹	Hsü Meng-ch'iu		?	
Ch'eng Fang-wu	成	仿	吾	Hsü Ping	徐	冰	
Ch'eng Tzu-hua	程	子	華	Hsü T'e-li	徐	特	立

Hsü Ti-hsin	許 滌 新
Huang Huo-ch'ing	黃 火 青
Huang K'o-ch'eng	黃 克 誠
Kan Szu-ch'i	甘 泗 淇
Kao Kang	高 崗
Kao Wen-hua	高 文 華
K'o Ch'ing-shih	柯 慶 施
Ku Ta-ts'un	古 大 存
Kuo Hua-jo	郭 化 若
Li Chen	李 貞
Li Chien-chen	李 堅 真
Li Hsien-nien	李 先 念
Li K'o-nung	李 克 農
Li Ta (a different person)	李 達
Liao Ch'eng-chih	廖 承 志
Lin Feng	林 楓
Lin Piao	林 彪
Liu Hsiao	劉 曉
Liu Hsiu-feng	劉 秀 峯
Liu Jui-lung	劉 瑞 龍
Liu Lan-t'ao	劉 瀾 濤
Liu Ning-i	劉 寧 一
Liu Po-ch'eng	劉 伯 承
Lo Jui-ch'ing	羅 瑞 卿
Lo Jung-huan	羅 榮 桓
Ma Ming-fang	馬 明 方
Nan Han-chen	南 漢 宸
Nieh Ho-t'ing	聶 鶴 亭
P'an Tzu-li	潘 自 力
P'eng Chen	彭 真

P'eng Hsüeh-feng	彭 雪 楓
P'eng Te-huai	彭 德 懷
Po I-po	薄 一 波
Shao Shih-p'ing	邵 式 平
Su Yü	粟 裕
Sung Jen-ch'iung	宋 任 窮
T'an Chen-lin	譚 震 林
T'an Cheng	譚 政
T'ao Chu	陶 鑄
Teng Tzu-hui	鄧 子 恢
T'eng Tai-yüan	滕 代 遠
Ts'ai Shu-fan	蔡 樹 藩
Ts'ao Ping-san	?
Tseng Hsi-sheng	曾 希 聖
Tseng Shan	曾 山
Tso Ch'üan	左 權
Wang Chen	王 震
Wang Chia-hsiang	王 稼 祥
Wang Shang-jung	王 尚 榮
Wang Shou-tao	王 首 道
Wang Shu-sheng	王 樹 聲
Wang Wei-chou	王 維 舟
Wu Hsiu-ch'üan	伍 修 權
Wu Liang-p'ing	吳 亮 平
Yang Han-sheng	陽 翰 笙
Yang Shang-k'un	楊 尚 昆
Yang Te-chih	楊 得 志
Yeh Chien-ying	葉 劍 英
Yeh Fei	葉 飛
Yen Hung-yen	閻 紅 彥

Table v. *Further losses of early Communist leaders*

Executed, 1929–1935

Ch'ü Ch'iu-pai	–June, 1935
Fang Chih-min	–July, 1935
Ho Meng-hsiung	–February, 1931
Hsiang Chung-fa	–June, 1931
Kuo Liang	–Sometime 1930
Li Ch'iu-shih	–February 7, 1931
Lin Yü-nan	–February, 1931
Lo Ch'i-yüan	–July, 1931
Lo Teng-hsien	–July, 1933
Lung Ta-tao	–February, 1931

Died or killed, 1929–35

Chou I-ch'ün	–1931
Ho Shu-heng	–February 26, 1929
Hsia Hsi	–Autumn ?, 1934
Juan [Yüan] Hsiao-hsien	–1935
Yü Hsiu-sung	–1930?

Defected to the Kuomintang

Huang P'ing	–Autumn, 1934
Ku Shun-chang	–April, 1931

P'eng P'ai   –August, 1929
Teng Chung-hsia–May, 1933
Ts'ai Ho-shen   –Autumn, 1931
Yang P'ao-an   –July, 1931
Yang Yin   –August, 1929
Yün Tai-ying   –June, 1931

     Many others, about whom facts are unclear.

Table VI.   *Profile of 130 Chinese Communist leaders in 1928*

Average age: 26·3 years	Largest age group 20–24:	51
Median age: 26	Under 35:	112
Youngest: 16	Over 35:	12
Oldest: 53	Total known:	124

Provinces of origin in rank order

Hunan	38	Shansi	7	Honan	2
Hupeh	13	Anhwei	6	Heilungkiang	1
Szechwan	12	Kiangsu	6	Kwangsi	1
Kwangtung	11	Kiangsi	5	Kweichow	1
Shensi	10	Chekiang	3	Liaoning	1
Fukien	7	Chihli (Hopeh)	3	Shantung	1
				Yunnan	1

Central Yangtze provinces:	83, or 64%
Northern provinces:	25, or 19%
Southern provinces:	21, or 16%
Total known:	129 99%
Three west-central provinces:	63, or 49%
(Hunan, Hupeh, Szechwan)	
Four modernized coastal provinces:	23, or 18%
(Chihli [Hopeh], Kiangsu, Chekiang, Kwangtung)	

Education in China		*Education abroad*	
Little or none	19	Japan	8
Old-style classical	5	Russia	18
Middle school	25	France	14
Normal or technical	22	Other Europe	3
College	23		
Military	28	Total	43
Whampoa Military Academy	20	Double count	6
Other revolutionary academies	2	Persons	37
Other academies	6		
Total known	122		

2

TRANSFER OF LEGITIMACY IN THE CHINESE COMMUNIST PARTY: ORIGINS OF THE MAOIST MYTH

WILLIAM F. DORRILL

INTRODUCTION

In January, 1935 the weary, decimated main forces of the Chinese Communist movement paused during their epic Long March from the shattered Kiangsi Soviet to rest and regroup at Tsunyi in the hills of northern Kweichow. During their brief occupation of this remote, provincial town, the top political and military leaders present held a conference which has come to be regarded as the major turning point in the history of the Chinese Communist Party (CCP). At the time, however, no such significance was attached to the stop-over in Tsunyi and, indeed, the very fact that an important political meeting had convened there was not revealed for several years.

When the official interpretation of Party history was laid down in 1945, following the *cheng-feng* campaign for "ideological rectification", the successes and failures of the CCP were invariably linked to the presence or absence of Mao Tse-tung's leadership.[1] It was claimed that Mao's authority had not been decisively established over the Party and Army until the Tsunyi Conference of January, 1935. Thus, previous setbacks, culminating in the loss of the Central Soviet base in Kiangsi and the disastrous first leg of the Long March, were attributed to the "errors" and ideological deviations of other CCP leaders—in particular to the "Left opportunist line" of Wang Ming (Ch'en Shao-yü) and Po Ku (Ch'in

[1] See the Central Committee's "Resolution on Some Questions in the History of Our Party" in Mao Tse-tung, *Selected Works* (New York: International Publishers, 1956), IV, 171–218. All subsequent historical writings have conformed to this interpretation, although many have elaborated on it and added details.

Pang-hsien), said to have dominated the Party after the Fourth Plenum of the Central Committee in 1931. At Tsunyi, according to this account, the erroneous "Left" line was rectified and the Party, under Mao's new leadership, was set on the correct path towards successful completion of the Long March and eventual victory in the Chinese revolution.

This interpretation has been reiterated over the years and is stressed today in the Cultural Revolution.[1] For example, a polemic against Liu Shao-ch'i avers:

From the day our Party was founded, all its victories have been won under the guidance of Chairman Mao and are victories of Mao Tse-tung's thought. The Tsunyi Conference in 1935 unequivocally established Chairman Mao's leading position in the whole Party and saved the Chinese revolution at this turning point in its history. Since then, our Party has marched from victory to victory under the leadership of Chairman Mao.[2]

Indeed, the significance of this historical watershed has been magnified in the Cultural Revolution as increasing emphasis was placed on the role of "the leader" in the entire revolutionary process. As the above article declares: "Without a great leader and unifying thought it is impossible to win revolutionary victory and fulfil the great tasks that history has assigned the proletariat, namely, the liberation of all mankind."

The CCP's remarkable recovery after 1935 lent strong plausibility to this Mao-centred version of Party history—which was confidently, if belatedly, formulated in the safety of a decade of hindsight. Nevertheless, in recent years historical scholarship has done much to restore perspective, challenging the simplistic Communist

[1] While there have been sporadic calls in Red Guard media to revise the 1945 Party History Resolution so as to delete favourable references to Liu Shao-ch'i's leadership, nothing has come of these thus far—perhaps because the original proponents included the subsequently disgraced ultra-Leftists, Wang Li and Kuan Feng. In any event, such revision would not affect the Resolution's interpretation of Mao's rise to power in the Kiangsi and Long March periods.

[2] See excerpts from the second in a series of articles entitled "Thoroughly Criticise and Repudiate China's Khrushchev", published originally in *Chieh fang chün pao* and released by the *New China News Agency* [NCNA] on September 23, 1967.

interpretation of the Chinese Revolution and, without neglecting Mao's singular contribution, pointing out the vital importance of fortuitous external circumstances (e.g., the Japanese invasion) in the CCP's eventual victory. Unfortunately, the official version of Mao's role in the successes and defeats of the Kiangsi period leading up to the Long March and Tsunyi has only just begun to receive a similar critical evaluation. A fresh inquiry is needed into the origins and validity of the official myth of Mao's invariably correct and victorious leadership.[1] In particular, such an investigation should re-examine the manner in which the Maoist legend grew and was used to justify—or legitimize—his rule after the debacle of Kiangsi.

In political theory, the concept of "legitimacy" is associated with "rightfulness" and involves the leader's cultivation of acceptance among those subject to his rule.[2] Legitimacy thus conveys authority,[3] a property of immense importance in Chinese political culture. Belief in "the absoluteness of authority", according to Lucian Pye, is one of the "enduring characteristics" of Chinese politics (along with concern for hierarchy and the need for ideology).[4] Traditionally

[1] The use of the term "myth" in this study is not intended to be pejorative but seeks to convey the idea of a political legend, a saga containing elements both of historical fact and fictional elaboration and distortion. In this sense "myth" involves an objectification of individual and collective wishes which are personified in a "leader" believed able to fulfil them. As Ruth Benedict has pointed out: "Myth like secular folklore is an articulate vehicle of a people's wishful thinking. Secular heroes portray the ideal man of the culture, and myth remodels the universe to its dominant desire...Man in all his mythologies has expressed his discomfort at a mechanistic universe and his pleasure in substituting a world that is humanly motivated and directed." Thus, in secular mythology, the experiences and achievements of a people are often seen as "The outcome of human acts of the culture hero." See Ruth Benedict, "Myth", *Encyclopedia of the Social Sciences* (New York: Macmillan, 1949), XI, 181.

[2] See Carl J. Friedrich, *Man and His Government: An Empirical Theory of Politics* (New York: McGraw-Hill, 1963), pp. 233–41, *passim*.

[3] As Robert Dahl has observed: "When the influence of a leader is clothed with legitimacy it is usually referred to as authority. Authority, then, is a kind of influence, legitimate influence." Robert Dahl, *Modern Political Analysis* (Englewood Cliffs, N.J.: Prentice-Hall, 1963), p. 19. For further discussion of the relationship between legitimacy and authority see Young C. Kim, "Authority: Some Conceptual and Empirical Notes", *Western Political Quarterly*, XIX (June, 1966), 223–8.

[4] Although Pye's notion of the role of authority in Chinese politics may be somewhat overstated, his analysis provides many provocative and useful insights.

in China the idea of legitimacy has been related to the leader's performance, dynasties rising or falling as they were seen, through natural and social phenomena, to possess or lose the "mandate of heaven". More recently, leaders operating in the Marxist–Leninist context have had the further requirement of justifying their right to lead by demonstrating that they were carrying out the laws of history in accordance with the dialectical process. Thus, in the CCP it has been an important matter for leaders in power to be able to identify themselves with the successes of the Party and, above all, to be able to absolve themselves of any responsibility for failures that are encountered.

The defeat of the Kiangsi Soviet in Chiang Kai-shek's Fifth Encirclement Campaign in 1934 and the terrible losses subsequently sustained in the first segment of the Long March created an authority crisis in the CCP. It called into serious question the "scientific" wisdom and effectiveness of the constituted leadership and its strategy, including even the rural Soviet system. During the Long March and afterwards, as there was time to reflect on past experiences, the principal Party and military figures found it necessary to explain the reasons for the great loss, rationalize their own role in it, and particularly to legitimize the Maoist leadership which survived the ordeal and was now called upon to deal with an equally serious threat of Japanese invasion. At Tsunyi these assessments were probably limited to a venting of criticism against those responsible in the military failure—or, if all were guilty, those who could be made to appear most culpable—and to some reshuffling of posts and personalities in accordance with the censure. Later, however, after the Red Army had reached its new base in northern Shensi, the historical reassessments became more and more elaborate. The military defeat in Kiangsi was ascribed to basic errors of political leadership in the CCP over the entire four years from 1931 to

He views the Chinese concept as tending to be total and undivided, the expectation being that "authority should be monopolistic, diffuse, and capable of handling a wide range of matters without interference". He also notes that traditionally "government and family" in China have "conspired together to insure that young Chinese were overwhelmingly impressed with the sacredness of authority". Lucian W. Pye, *The Authority Crisis in Chinese Politics* (Chicago: Univ. of Chicago Center for Policy Study, 1967), pp. 16, 19.

1934, this despite the fact that the personnel changes after Tsunyi in no sense resembled a purge of convicted "opportunist" leaders. In this way the criticism of Po Ku, who among the CCP leaders appears to have incurred the most blame at the time for the military failure, was extended to Wang Ming who was not even in China for most of the period.[1]

It is the aim of this chapter to contribute to a re-examination of the Maoist claim to legitimacy in the aftermath of the Kiangsi defeat—the rationale for the transfer of rightful leadership to him in 1935. Since limitations of space prevent a comprehensive evaluation here of the numerous strands woven into the official legend, consideration will be given to two key episodes—one at the beginning and the other towards the end. The first concerns the rise of the Returned Student leadership under Wang Ming and origins of the so-called "third 'Left' line". In analysing it we shall look initially at the setting of power relations within the Communist movement (especially Mao's position *vis-à-vis* the Party leaders in Shanghai), consider the Central Committee's Fourth Plenum as the alleged starting point of the erroneous "Left" line, and examine Mao's later use of revised historical interpretations on this theme to support his claim to legitimacy. The second episode to be considered is the Fukien Rebellion of late 1933 and early 1934, in which it is said the misguided CCP leadership overruled tactical proposals by Mao that could have averted defeat in the fifth Encirclement Campaign. In this case we shall investigate the nature of the rebellion, evaluate the Communist policy response, and examine Mao's later reassessment of these events to enhance his claim to rightful leadership.

The results of this inquiry will, of course, be suggestive rather than definitive. The hope is that by re-examining the official interpretation at selected key points we may gain a better basis for evalu-

[1] As CCP delegate to the Comintern in Moscow after 1932, Wang was far removed from the scene of military decision in Kiangsi. Ironically, the indictment of him began as a criticism of alleged "Rightist" errors in the early United Front period *after* 1935, and gained real momentum only after his return to China (with Stalin's blessing) in 1937 put him in a position to challenge Mao's power over the Party apparatus.

ating the entire legend of Mao's rise to supreme CCP leadership and a clearer understanding of the manner in which his position was legitimized.

THE SETTING OF POWER RELATIONS
IN THE EARLY KIANGSI PERIOD

By the late summer of 1930 successive failures of the Li Li-san line of urban uprisings, highlighted by two disastrous attacks on the city of Changsha, had clearly demonstrated the need for fundamental changes in the CCP's strategy and leadership. However, the response of the Central Committee at its Third Plenum in September was indecisive and compromising. Afterwards the Comintern, loath to accept a tepid reform and apparently determined to reassert its control over the CCP, exerted increasingly strong pressure for a sweeping change in the leadership. Pavel Mif, the Comintern delegate to China, used his considerable influence to promote the careers of several trusted young protégés who had recently completed courses of study in the Soviet Union. Thus, despite their youth and inexperience Wang Ming, Po Ku, Lo Fu (Chang Wen-t'ien), Wang Chia-hsiang, Shen Tse-min, and others rose rapidly to places of power towards the end of 1930. In January of the following year, these so-called Returned Students and their allies won control of the Central Committee at its Fourth Plenum. Subsequently they were able to maintain this position despite a determined "Rightist" revolt led by veteran cadres such as Ho Meng-hsiung, Lo Chang-lung, and Wang K'o-ch'üan.

In assessing the real strength of the Returned Students, however, it is important to remember both their dependence on the Comintern and the existing pattern of power within the Chinese Communist movement. Possessing no indigenous power base and thoroughly disliked by many veteran cadres for their brash and bookish ways, these revolutionary apprentices were utterly dependent on the Comintern for elevation to and continued tenure in high Party office. However, there soon were ominous signs that Moscow's preoccupation with building "socialism in one country" and fear of provoking Japanese reaction were lessening the Comintern's interest in a programme of vigorous, direct action in China.[1]

Meanwhile, the centre of gravity in the Chinese Communist movement had long since shifted to the rural hinterland, although CCP's central leading organs continued to function in Shanghai. Years of failure and repression had eroded virtually all important urban strength and the Ho-Lo "Rightist" revolt had further reduced whatever support remained in the labour movement. At the time of the Fourth Plenum the CCP apparently had fewer than 6,000 members in its major strongholds in KMT territory— with only 500 of these in Shanghai.[2] As late as March, 1931, the Central Committee noted that while total CCP membership remained above 120,000, "the greatest majority" of these were in the Soviet areas and not more than 2,000 Party members in all were from the proletariat.[3]

The disproportionately large rural strength of the CCP, plus the extremely small percentage of authentic proletarian workers enrolled in the Party, suggest the distinct possibility that local Soviet military and administrative institutions in the countryside actually commanded a greater focus of loyalties—even from professed CCP members—than did the Party hierarchy in Shanghai. The latter, far removed from the peasant movement and guerrilla warfare of the Soviet areas, had little opportunity to play an active role in decision-making or to supervise operations. The Shanghai leaders would have found it very difficult to exercise firm control in the rural Soviets even if they had been able to rely on an ideologically sophisticated, highly disciplined Party apparatus there to do their bidding. In fact, such an organization simply was not available to them. Moreover,

[1] On the Comintern's "retreat" from China after 1930 see Charles B. McLane, *Soviet Policy and the Chinese Communists, 1931–1946* (New York: Columbia Univ. Press, 1958), pp. 9–13.

[2] Kang Sen [K'ang Sheng], "The Organizational Advance of the C.P. in Kuomintang China", *International Press Correspondence* [hereafter cited as *Inprecor*], XIII (December 29, 1933), 1309.

[3] Chung kung chung yang kuan yü fa chan tang ti tsu chih chüeh i an" [Resolution of the CCP Central in Regard to Expanding the Party Organization], (n.p., n.d. [passed March 5, 1931]), p. 1 [Bureau of Investigation Collection, Taiwan]. Similar figures had been presented by Chou En-lai at the Third Plenum in September, 1930.

local particularism and "lumpenproletarian" influence remained strong in the peasant-dominated Soviets and Red Armies.

Given the peculiar balance of forces in the Communist movement, perhaps the most significant limitation on the power of the Returned Students was the growing strength of Mao Tse-tung in the countryside. He had often shown a streak of independence and unorthodoxy that had put him at odds with more doctrinaire superiors and checked his rise in the Party hierarchy. During Li Li-san's tenure, Mao had demonstrated that it was possible for the Kiangsi leadership to exercise considerable independence in carrying out Shanghai's orders. Directives from the Central Committee which were regarded as dangerous or disagreeable were ignored, very broadly interpreted (since most were stated in general terms), or sabotaged in a variety of ways such as delay in implementation, *pro forma* acceptance, or even open flouting of minor provisions—without resulting in major disciplinary action or loss of power.[1] The Li Li-san debacle and ensuing vacuum in the Shanghai leadership provided Mao with a golden opportunity to consolidate his power base in Kiangsi and to demonstrate the superiority of his rural-oriented strategy. In the Fut'ien Incident of December, 1930 he eliminated his last significant local opposition. Afterwards, the Red Army's smashing victory in the First Encirclement Campaign added lustre to his reputation. When the Fourth Plenum convened in Shanghai in January, 1931, Mao enjoyed a position of unrivalled supremacy in the Kiangsi Soviet heartland and was the most prominent Communist leader in rural China.

Moreover, the Comintern—creator and sustainer of the Returned Student leadership—began after the Fourth Plenum to reduce its operational role in China and to lessen its interference in the affairs

[1] Thus, Mao and Chu Teh delayed by nearly 3 months responding to Li Li-san's order of April 3, 1930 to redeploy their forces northwards immediately to attack Kiukiang; Mao ignored several pressing invitations to attend a conference of delegates from the Soviet areas held at Shanghai in May, 1930; and afterwards he refused to implement the agrarian policy it had adopted although this led him into serious factional strife with the pro-Li Li-san Southwest Kiangsi Provincial CCP Committee. See Hsiao Tso-liang, *Power Relations Within the Chinese Communist Movement, 1930–34* (Seattle: Univ. of Washington Press, 1961), pp. 14–17, 21, 106–7; also Benjamin Schwartz, *Chinese Communism and the Rise of Mao* (Cambridge, Mass.: Harvard Univ. Press, 1952), p. 181.

of the CCP. While continuing perfunctorily to publish estimates of a "revolutionary upsurge" in China, Moscow began both to reduce its material support for revolutionary activities and to move towards a normalization of relations with Nanking. Following the arrest of the Noulens, a Belgian couple, at Shanghai in June, 1931, the Comintern's covert Far Eastern Bureau (Dalburo) was reportedly disbanded.[1] Police records introduced at their trial revealed that total disbursements for operations in the Far East at that time were not running more than the equivalent of U.S. $15,000 per month and much of even this probably was for trade-union work.[2] Thus the CCP apparatus in Shanghai became increasingly dependent upon the Soviet areas for financial support, the latter soon providing most of its operating funds, according to an ex-Communist source.[3] Meanwhile, the U.S.S.R., increasingly fearful of Japanese aggression after the invasion of Manchuria, began to move towards a *rapprochement* with Nanking.[4] In late 1932 diplomatic relations, severed in 1929, were formally re-established.

Along with these developments, there was a growing appreciation in Moscow of the primary importance of the Chinese Soviet movement and of Mao Tse-tung's key role in it. This is not to say that the Comintern ever abandoned its deep concern that the CCP develop a stronger proletarian membership and policy orientation or that it shared to the same degree Mao's emphasis on a rural-based revolutionary strategy. However, it is significant that after 1930 Russian

[1] T'ang Leang-li, *Suppressing Communist-Banditry in China* (Shanghai: China United Press, 1934), p. 71.

[2] Edgar Snow, *Red Star Over China* (New York: Random House, 1944), p. 183.

[3] Li Ang [pseud.?], *Hung se wu t'ai* [The Red Stage] (Ch'u-chiang, Kwangtung: Sheng li ch'u pan she, 1942), p. 156. In contrast with many dubious points in Li's embittered account, this assessment seems entirely plausible. In January, 1934, Mao told the Second All-China Soviet Congress that in the 1932 anti-Japanese strike of West Shanghai textile workers alone the Soviet Government had provided $16,000 (Chinese currency). See Conrad Brandt, Benjamin Schwartz, and John K. Fairbank, *A Documentary History of Chinese Communism* (Cambridge, Mass.: Harvard Univ. Press, 1952), p. 228.

[4] According to Chiang Kai-shek, "...after the Mukden Incident Moscow repeatedly expressed to [the KMT] Government its desire to resume diplomatic relations". Chiang Chung-cheng, *Soviet Russia in China* (New York: Farrar, Straus & Cudahy, Inc., 1957), p. 69.

and Comintern press media devoted considerably more attention to China's rural Soviets than to her urban labour movement.[1] Far from lavishing attention on the Returned Students to build up their power or authority, Comintern publications after the Fourth Plenum showed no greater honour or deference to any Chinese leader than to Mao Tse-tung.

THE FOURTH PLENUM: ORIGIN OF A "THIRD 'LEFT' LINE?"

While it may be seen from the previous discussion that potential sources of intra-Party tension existed at the time of the Fourth Plenum in January, 1931, contemporaneous documents fail to show that Mao differed from the Returned Students on any important issue that arose during the period of their ascent to power. He justified his bloody suppression of the Fut'ien revolt in December, 1930 on grounds that the rebels had been guilty of Li Li-san-ism—as manifested in a "rich peasant policy" and a doctrine of military adventurism. This paralleled the anti-Li attack being waged by the new leaders in Shanghai. Moreover, Mao sent delegates to Shanghai to attend the Fourth Plenum and there is no evidence that they opposed the Returned Students' accession to power, although a sizeable number of other delegates did. Rather, Chu Te recalled with satisfaction—as late as 1937—that the Fourth Plenum had "repudiated the Li Li-san line and affirmed ours" (i.e., the Mao-Chu line).[2]

Insofar as can be determined from authenticated contemporary evidence, statements by responsible CCP and Comintern leaders throughout the 1930's—and probably well into the following decade—continued to view the Fourth Plenum in a favourable light.[3]

[1] For a more detailed content analysis of relevant Comintern publications see McLane, *Soviet Policy*, pp. 21–2, 29–33.

[2] Quoted in Agnes Smedley, *The Great Road* (New York: Monthly Review Press, 1956), p. 294. Although Chu is quoted (in translation) as using the term "Fourth Delegates' Congress of our party", the context leaves no doubt that he was referring to the Fourth Plenum of the Central Committee.

[3] For example, see Wang Ming's speech before the Seventh Comintern Congress on August 7, 1935 in *Inprecor*, xv (November 11, 1935), 1491; Shee Pin, "A Heroic Trek", *The Communist International*, xiii, Special Number (February, 1936), 144; Pavel Mif, *Heroic China* (New York: Workers Library Publisher, January, 1937), p. 69.

They certainly showed no indication that anyone seriously believed that a new "Left" opportunist line had come to dominate the Party with the rise of the Returned Students in January, 1931.[1] Until late 1938—and, perhaps, much later—available statements by Mao and his lieutenants agreed with those of Wang Ming and the Comintern in their view both of the Fourth Plenum and the nature of previous deviations in Party History.[2] At the Sixth Plenum in October, 1938, long after Mao had disposed of Chang Kuo-t'ao and gained

[1] Thus, in June, 1937, a detailed survey of the past decade of CCP history by Lo Fu deplored the errors of Ch'en Tu-hsiu and Li Li-san but mentioned none by the 1931-4 leadership. Lo Fu, *Kuan yü shih nien lai ti Chung kuo kung ch'an-tang* [Concerning the CCP of the Last Ten Years] (n.p.: Chen li ch'u pan she, 1938), pp. 7, 12. A similar inventory of past intra-Party deviations, omitting any hint of "Left" errors in the Kiangsi period, was presented by Chang Hao (Lin Yü-ying) in lectures at the Anti-Japanese University in Yenan in 1937. Chang Hao, *Chung kuo kung ch'an tang ti ts'e lüeh lu hsien* [The Tactical Line of the CCP], (n.p., n.d.), p. 9. Likewise, a secret CCP cadre training handbook in use in the late 1930's, while reviewing the past record of intra-Party discipline and struggle, made no mention of leadership deviations in the Kiangsi years. *Tang ti chien she* [Party Reconstruction], (n.p.: reprint, July, 1938), pp. 37, 40, 44.

[2] During lengthy interviews with Edgar Snow in the summer of 1936 Mao freely discussed the sins of Ch'en Tu-hsiu and Li Li-san, but said nothing about a dominant "Left" line after 1931—nor did any of Snow's other informants (*Red Star Over China*, pp. 162-3, 178-83). Nor was Mao's disagreement with Chang Kuo-t'ao hidden from Snow in 1936, although Chang was not formally "tried" and disciplined for his offences until the spring of 1937. See Snow's *Random Notes on Red China (1936-45)* (Cambridge, Mass.: Harvard Univ. Press, 1957), p. 78. It is possible that Mao, in his military lectures of December, 1936, referred to a "Left" opportunism of 1932 (*not* 1931), but the authenticity of this passage is open to question because of the lack of any pre-*cheng-feng* period text for comparison, plus the fact that subsequent statements by Mao either ignored or contradicted such a view. See Mao Tse-tung, *Chung kuo ko ming chan cheng ti chan lüeh wen t'i* [Strategic Problems of China's Revolutionary War], (n.p.: Pa lu chün chün cheng tsa chih she, 1943), pp. 12, 21. Later revised editions, of course, date the period of "Left" errors as beginning in 1931 (Mao, *Selected Works*, I, 190, 201, 203). Mao's philosophical lectures "On Practice" and "On Contradiction" delivered in the summer of 1937 did not specifically refer to deviations in the Kiangsi period, although the latter work vaguely mentioned "mistakes of adventurism" in the CCP after 1927 which had been rectified "since 1935" (Mao, *Selected Works*, II, 31, 40). The only deviationists identified were Ch'en Tu-hsiu and Chang Kuo-t'ao. Again, the authenticity of available texts of these documents is open to serious question. See Arthur A. Cohen, *The Communism of Mao Tse-tung* (Chicago: Univ. of Chicago Press, 1964), pp. 23-7.

unchallenged control over the CCP, he referred vaguely to "opportunism" that had caused serious errors "during the Fifth Annihilation Campaign" (late 1933–4).[1] However, contemporary evidence indicates that for several years afterwards neither he nor other official critics of the Kiangsi period went beyond attemping to rationalize defeat in the Fifth Campaign to condemn the Fourth Plenum or the Returned Student leadership.[2]

If Mao actually intended to censure the Fourth Plenum as early as the autumn of 1938, it is strange that subsequent official CCP sources ignored his criticism and continued to regard the January 1931 session as necessary and correct. For example, a cadre handbook compiled in 1939 reiterated that the Third Plenum had been completely unable to rectify the Li Li-san line and actually set the stage for its transformation into the Rightist deviation of Lo Chang-lung.[3] Mao himself, writing in a secret Party periodical in October, 1939, described the Fourth Plenum as having played a positive role in vanquishing the Li Li-san line—although revised editions of his article have conveniently omitted this reference.[4] To judge from authenticated contemporaneous evidence, it was not until 1944 or 1945 that CCP spokesmen repudiated the historical role of the Fourth Plenum and condemned the Returned Student leadership for policies predating the Fifth Campaign.

As was noted above, in the 1940's after Mao had gained absolute control over the Party apparatus, the entire Kiangsi historical record was radically revised. During the *cheng-feng* movement (1942–4),

[1] Mao Tse-tung, *The New Stage* (Chungking: New China Information Committee, n.d. [probably 1939]), p. 72. The Chinese text appeared in *Chieh fang* [Liberation], No. 57 (November 25, 1938), pp. 3–34.

[2] To be sure, Mao is now quoted as criticizing the Fourth Plenum in his final speech at the Sixth Plenum in November, 1938—the earliest specific criticism that appears even in his revised *Selected Works*, II, 273–4, 276. However, the authenticity of this criticism is questionable since it conflicts with the position Mao took a year later (as we shall see below) and because no text of this speech appeared until after 1950, although the Sixth Plenum received detailed coverage in contemporaneous open and secret Party journals.

[3] CCP Central Propaganda Bureau, ed., *Kung ch'an chu i yü kung ch'an tang* [Communism and the Communist Party] (n.p., n.d. [probably 1939]), p. 198.

[4] Mao Tse-tung, "Fa k'an tz'u" [Foreword], *Kung ch'an tang jen* [The Communist], No. 1 (October, 1939), p. 8.

which was designed to rectify "erroneous tendencies" in the CCP, detailed discussions were held by the top leadership on the Party's history, purportedly to assess the causes of past failures. Following this, in April, 1945, the Central Committee adopted a resolution on questions of Party history which embodied the revised Maoist historical line. It paid particular attention to the period 1931–4 and to the rise of the Returned Student group, giving an account of intra-Party factional disputes never before published and no more than hinted—if that—in CCP documents (even secret ones) dating from the 1930's.[1] Subsequent historical writings, while occasionally furnishing new details, have rigorously conformed to the main lines of this interpretation.

According to the 1945 resolution, which was personally drafted by Mao, the Fourth Plenum

accomplishing nothing positive or constructive, accepted the new "Left" line [advanced by Wang Ming], which triumphed in the central leading body; thus began, for the third time during the Agrarian Revolutionary War, the domination of a "Left" line in the Party. The session itself put into effect two interrelated erroneous tenets of the new "Left" line, namely, the fight against "the Right deviation as the immediate main danger in the Party", and the "reform and replenishment of the leading bodies at all levels".[2]

Interestingly, however, Mao went on to admit that the session actually had "made no analysis of the current political situation or provisions for the concrete political tasks of the Party". Also, it gave only "vague opposition" to the "Right deviation" and to

[1] Thus, while in the original version of his "Foreword" to *The Communist* (*ibid.*), Mao declared that the "Left" opportunism of Li Li-san and that of "another time" (unspecified but likely that of the Fifth Encirclement Campaign) had been "thoroughly conquered at two historic conferences, the Party's Fourth Plenum and its Tsunyi Conference", this approving reference to the Fourth Plenum—placing it on a par historically with the Tsunyi meeting—was deleted in the revised edition of the text published in 1952 (*Mao Tse-tung hsüan chi* [Selected Works] (Peking: Jen min ch'u pan she, 1952), II, 602). To have allowed Mao's words to stand, crediting the Fourth Plenum with effectively combating "Left" opportunism, would of course, have undermined the post-*cheng-feng* contention that the January, 1931 meeting had ushered in the "third Left line".

[2] *Mao Tse-tung hsüan chi*, III, 965–6; Mao, *Selected Works*, IV, 182.

"opportunism in practical work". Indeed the only specific programmatic error committed by the session was to "approve" Wang Ming's as yet unpublished treatise, *The Two Lines*.[1] Organizationally, however, the Fourth Plenum allegedly erred by dealing "excessively severe blows" at followers of Li Li-san, "misdirecting" blows at Ch'ü Ch'iu-pai and other Third Plenum "conciliators" and promoting doctrinaire–sectarian "Leftists" to leading positions in the Party hierarchy.

Except for its reference to organizational changes, the revised Maoist account of the Fourth Plenum differs considerably from that revealed in earlier sources. Critical examination of Mao's indictment also suggests serious questions as to the timing and sequential relationship of specific charges. Did the plenary session, meeting in January, actually endorse the text of *The Two Lines* as we know it today—a treatise that was not published until the following month? Was the alleged preoccupation with "Right deviation" simply a bugbear invented by the Returned Students for their own purposes —a trumped-up threat to the Party with no basis in fact?

Contemporaneous documents established that Ho Meng-hsiung, Lo Chang-lung and other disaffected Party leaders did indeed form a serious and undisciplined opposition to the Party organization before and during the Fourth Plenum. Though sharing the Returned Students' militant rejection of Li Li-san and Third Plenum temporizing, they were equally determined to thwart Pavel Mif's intervention to impose a reform of the Central Committee from the top downwards. Arguing that the Third Plenum leadership was too tainted to reform itself, they pressed for an emergency CCP Conference (like that of August 7, 1927) to effect a thorough housecleaning "from the ground upward". After failing to prevent the calling of a Fourth Plenum, they proceeded to challenge Mif's authority to speak for the Comintern and to oppose his slate of

---

[1] Originally published at Shanghai in February, 1931 under the title *Liang t'iao lu hsien* [The Two Lines], Wang's booklet was substantially enlarged and republished in March, 1932 and in March, 1940 under a new title, *Wei chung kung keng chia pu erh se wei k'o hua erh tou cheng* [Struggle for the Further Bolshevization of the Chinese Communist Party], (third edition; Yenan: Chieh fang she, 1940), 218 pages. Many of the criticisms later raised against this treatise applied only to the enlarged second or third editions.

Returned Student candidates for Party office. Overridden at the session, they withdrew, rejected its decisions, and requested Mif's recall to Moscow. On January 17, Ho Meng-hsiung and others were arrested during a secret meeting in Shanghai which had been called to found a rival Central Emergency Committee and separate Party organizations in Kiangsu and the National Labour Federation. Finally, after exercising what would appear to have been remarkable restraint, the newly elevated CCP Politburo passed a resolution condemning the remaining dissidents and demanding that they cease their separatist activities.

MAO VS. THE THIRD "LEFT" LEADERSHIP:
LEGITIMACY THROUGH HISTORICAL REVISION

If, as seems likely from the above, there was reason for concern over the danger of Right deviation around the time of the Fourth Plenum, we may ask why Mao chose to attack Wang Ming and his coterie in the 1940's for having conjured up a false threat. Was he primarily interested in setting the historical record straight? Had he been unable to do so earlier?

If the Fourth Plenum was so distasteful to Mao and his followers, it is curious that they apparently made no serious efforts to frustrate the proceedings, as did Ho Meng-hsiung—whose righteousness they seem not to have discovered for the next decade. If genuinely unhappy about developments in Shanghai, but unwilling to risk their power in a test of strength at that distance, it seems strange that the Kiangsi leaders not only failed to manifest a minimal, subtle displeasure—which might have been registered within the still flexible limits of Party discipline—but went well beyond passive acceptance to voice positive enthusiasm for many years thereafter. Even with Pavel Mif's backing, the Returned Students hardly constituted a political juggernaut.[1] In fact, these eager young veterans of the classroom enjoyed considerably less standing with the CCP

[1] The term "Returned Students" is not used in official CCP analyses to denote the "Leftists" allegedly led by Wang Ming and Po Ku—the only leaders ever identified. Similarly, the term "twenty-eight Bolsheviks" has no official standing in Communist literature, having been popularized initially in anti-Communist writings of the late 1930's and early 1940's.

rank-and-file than had Li Li-san, whose "erroneous" orders Mao and Chu had found effective means to defy, sabotage, and delay in the spring of 1930. Even assuming a sudden radical change in Mao's behaviour towards the Shanghai leadership in 1931—a newly developed deference to "democratic centralism" in its most servile interpretation—if such terrible mistakes were committed by the Fourth Plenum leadership before the beginning of the Fifth Encirclement Campaign, it is difficult to understand why these were not exposed immediately after Mao's claimed victory over the "Left" leaders at Tsunyi in January, 1935. Instead, the latter retained high positions in the Party and apparently did not even incur blame for their actions during the Fifth Campaign until Mao's vague criticism at the Sixth Plenum (October, 1938).

It would seem unrealistic to assume that Mao, with god-like patience, simply refrained from criticizing Wang Ming and Po Ku until the *cheng-feng* movement (1942-4) in order to give them ample time to see the error of their ways and confess—meanwhile allowing them to damage themselves and the Party with Rightist deviations in the early United Front period. Certainly, he spared Chang Kuo-t'ao no such criticism, although Chang was later apparently given a chance to rehabilitate himself (under supervision) after the Yenan Conference of March, 1937. In any event, I am unable to locate any confession of wrongdoing by either Wang Ming or Po Ku, although they undoubtedly had to make their peace with Mao during the *cheng-feng* campaign.

It can be argued, of course, that Mao's long delay in finding fault with the Fourth Plenum was due to the fact that it enjoyed Moscow's stamp of approval; that criticism of the session would have been tantamount to flouting Comintern authority. While such considerations might have made Mao reluctant to speak out categorically and forcefully against the meeting at the time, they would not seem sufficient to explain his positive endorsement of the session in confidential internal communications as late as October, 1939 (later edited out) or his failure for many years even to hint at the existence of deviationist errors in the CCP leadership following the Fourth Plenum. Moreover, the argument that Mao refrained from criticism for fear of offending the Comintern fails either to account for the changed circumstances between Moscow and the CCP after 1931 or to explain his contrary handling of other sensitive issues in the middle and late 1930's.[1] If Mao and his lieutenants were too wary of offending the Comintern to speak out against the Fourth Plenum until the 1940's, one wonders how they were able to summon up the courage in 1936 to blame their Kiangsi defeat on its military representative, Li T'e, or in 1937–8 to criticize and virtually purge Wang Ming for his enthusiastic literal espousal of the Comintern-dictated "United Front from above". Or, assuming that these latter criticisms were somehow less sensitive or offensive to the Comintern than outright condemnation of the plenary session would have been why did Mao fail until the 1940's even to suggest the existence of "Left" deviationism in the Party leadership *after* the Fourth Plenum or to condemn the alleged "errors" of Wang Ming and Po Ku? Given Moscow's preoccupations in 1937–8 wouldn't it have been less offensive to have purged Wang Ming for previous sins of "Left" sectarianism than to have criticized him for currently having a "Rightist" United Front bias?

Rather than being delayed by internal or external constraints, it would seem more likely that Mao's *cheng-feng* attack on the third "Leftists" reflected a new consciousness or determination of their guilt. Moreover this new awareness may not have arisen so much from a desire to set the historical record straight as from a determination to manipulate and use it to establish Mao's claim to supreme leadership. In short, Mao appears to have employed the device of historical revision to create an aura of legitimacy about his rule. Thus, the revised account of the Fourth Plenum and the rise of the Returned Student leadership, drafted in 1945, can be explained

---

[1] Such an argument would imply, in the first instance, a continuing strong Comintern leverage or hold over Mao and the CCP all through the 1930's. However, as shown above, Moscow's interest and involvement in the Chinese revolution (and, hence, leverage over it) had markedly receded after 1931 as Russian national interests dictated a shift to *rapprochement* with Nanking, and as the Encirclement Campaigns in Kiangsi and subsequent Long March all but isolated the Chinese Communists from contact with the U.S.S.R. Even the remaining Chinese ideological loyalties must have been greatly eroded by the repeated instances of Moscow's willingness to sacrifice CCP interests for those of the Soviet Union, as well as by the increasingly independent and demonstrably self-sufficient leadership and strategy furnished by Mao Tse-tung.

as an attempt to remove any chance that at war's end Wang Ming and his friends, trading on previous close association with Moscow, might rise again to challenge Mao's supremacy in the CCP or thwart his postwar plans for the Chinese Revolution—not necessarily identical with those of Stalin.[1] It may be that Mao's belated attack on the Returned Students was really intended as a warning against any postwar intervention by the U.S.S.R. in CCP affairs. At the same time it served to disarm any potential rivals of Mao who might be effectively used by Moscow in such a gambit.

Finally, the delayed indictment possessed the necessary elements of credibility and feasibility. It was unlikely that anyone could or would venture to challenge the reliability of his reinterpretation. By the early 1940's, death and political attrition (e.g., the Lo Chang-lung split) had removed many if not most of the actual participants at the Fourth Plenum who might have raised embarrassing factual questions. Powerful figures other than Mao also stood to benefit by a rewriting of Party history. Chou En-lai, who had been forced into a grovelling confession of "compromisism" at the plenary session, probably had no objection to being vindicated—even at the cost of historical accuracy. Moreover, Mao's attack on Wang Ming and his associates, coming in the radically different atmosphere of the war-time United Front, was a message likely to receive easy acceptance by the Party rank-and-file. Long-nurtured memories of Li Li-san's "Left" opportunism in 1930 would have made it difficult even for the theoretically sophisticated to understand how the Fourth Plenum leadership could have complained of a Right deviationist threat in 1931. Also, the hapless Wang Ming and Po Ku—both deprived of any significant local following by 1942—presented a nearly perfect image of the bookish, doctrinaire theoretician, unable to relate Marxist learning to practical work and actually hampering the Party's growth and effectiveness by engendering a spirit of narrow

[1] By 1938 or 1939 Wang Ming, despite his early Comintern backing, had slipped from a position of real power in the Party hierarchy to the demeaning task of supervising the Yenan Girls' School. As noted above, his political demise appears to have resulted not from the Kiangsi "errors" later trumpeted in the *cheng-feng* campaign, but from his ardent advocacy of cooperation with the KMT in the early United Front period (an idea apparently not uncongenial to Stalin for several years thereafter).

sectarianism. What better scapegoats were available to blame for the devastating failure which had ultimately occurred in Kiangsi? What more convincing means to absolve Mao of all guilt in the disaster—thereby rallying popular support for him as a sincere, long-time proponent of the United Front and, particularly among the Party faithful, creating the illusion of an infallible, invariably successful leader who could show the way to victory over both Japan and Chiang Kai-shek.

The origins of Mao's legitimating myth can also be seen in a second case of historical revision—that pertaining to the Fukien Rebellion.

THE FUKIEN REBELLION: A LOST OPPORTUNITY?

The outbreak of the Fukien Rebellion on November 20, 1933 brought to a halt the first phase of Chiang Kai-shek's Fifth Encircle-ment Campaign against the Central Soviet area. Just as the Kuo-mintang (KMT) economic blockade was becoming effective and Nationalist troops were inflicting significant losses on the Red Army, Chiang was forced to curtail operations and divert sizeable units eastwards to defend against a possible rebel invasion from Fukien. For the beleaguered Red armies defending the Kiangsi Soviet base, this allowed a much-needed rest and a chance to turn with safety from the Fukien front to regroup for action in more critical sectors. The rebellion broke the KMT encirclement in the east, at least temporarily, and seemingly gave the Communist leadership at Juichin grounds for hope that an alliance could be formed with the rebel regime in Foochow which would open up new channels for supply of food and munitions.

The ultimate failure of the alliance hope has been called by Mao and his followers one of the greatest blunders of leadership in the history of the CCP and one of the principal causes for its defeat in Kiangsi. There is little doubt that a working alliance of Red and rebel forces would have had a serious impact on Nanking's programme for suppressing Communism and, possibly, also its plan for dealing with Japan. The following discussion will attempt to set out the main facts in the Fukien episode and assess its relation to the general

Communist defeat in the Fifth Campaign—paying particular attention to the consequence of alleged errors in CCP policy.

Although ruled in name by a National Government in 1933, China was far from united politically. Warlordism and regionalism were still powerful forces and the frail Nanking regime, barely five years old, was in direct control of less than a half dozen provinces in the lower Yangtze Valley. The Communists with strong bases in Kiangsi and Fukien further complicated the power structure. Clearly, if part or all of these regional forces could be united, the future of the Nationalist Government could be placed in grave jeopardy. In the autumn of 1933, the opportunity must have seemed ripe. Chiang's forces were deeply committed in the Kiangsi encirclement campaign and seemed to be relatively immobile. His policy of "internal pacification" before resistance to external aggression was becoming increasingly unpopular among all sections of the people including the military.

The Nineteenth Route Army, stationed in Fukien, formed the east wall of Chiang's anti-Communist encirclement. This army, famous for its heroic defence of Shanghai in 1932, had retained a militantly anti-Japanese spirit even after its subsequent reorganization and transfer to resume operations against the Red Army. Chiang's insistence on fighting the Communists first increasingly antagonized the veterans of the Shanghai war, particularly in view of the CCP's widely publicized policy of immediate resistance to Japan.[1] Moreover, in August and early September of 1933 the reluctant Nineteenth Route Army suffered a series of demoralizing defeats by Communist forces and the Red Army continued to threaten its flank.

On the other hand, the Communists operating in northeastern Kiangsi had more recently sustained severe reverses at Li-ch'uan and Hsiao-shih, and badly needed to free their forces tied down on the Fukien front to relieve the more threatened sector. Worse still,

[1] In April, 1932, the Chinese Soviet Government had issued a Declaration of War Against Japan—reiterating, however, the need to destroy KMT rule first. In January, 1933, the Soviet Government and Red Army offered to unite with any military organization to resist Japan and the KMT under three conditions: cessation of attacks on the Soviet areas, the granting of civil liberties (freedom of speech, assembly, strike, etc.) in areas under their control, and the arming of volunteer forces.

with Chiang's resumption of the Fifth Campaign in late September, a virtually impenetrable wall of fortified roads and blockhouses advanced determinedly on the horizon, offering the prospect of slow strangulation for the Central Soviet Area—unless some means could be found to break the blockade.

While the Nineteenth Route Army wavered and the Communists worried, a motley assortment of dissident KMT elements in Foochow began to discover a strong common interest in their opposition to Chiang Kai-shek and his policy of temporizing with Japan. This group included: (1) unemployed generals, such as Ch'en Ming-shu (ex-Governor of Kwangtung, commander of an army in the Third Anti-Communist Campaign, recently returned from Europe after scandal-forced resignation as Minister of Communications, self-styled leader of Social Democrats) and Li Chi-shen (Kwangsi militarist and member of the KMT Central Executive Committee, former inspector-general of military training and suppressor of the Canton Commune); (2) active civil and military officials, such as Chiang Kuang-nai (Chairman of the Fukien Provincial Government) and Ts'ai T'ing-k'ai (commander of the Nineteenth Route Army); and (3) assorted Left Wing politicians and political exiles, most of them associated with the Third Party (*Ti san tang*), such as Chang Pai-chün, Eugene Ch'en (Ch'en Yu-jen) and George Hsu Ch'ien. Several unsuccessful attempts were made to draw into the group, or at least neutralize the Kwangtung warlord, Ch'en Chi-t'ang, and influential politicians of the Southwest Political Council, such as Hu Han-min. There were reports of similar attempts to sway the Kwangsi leaders, Li Tsung-jen and and Pai Ch'ung-hsi.

Given Chiang Kai-shek's vulnerabilities and the relentless pressure of Japanese aggression against China, it was apparent that a new alliance of southern rebels offered the prospect of a fast ride to power on the rising wave of Chinese nationalism and anti-imperialism—much as the onward surge of the Northern Expedition in 1926–7. However, to strike a fast, dramatic blow at Chiang (which hopefully would lead others to join the revolt) the would-be rebels in Foochow needed to remove the military threat posed by the Red Army.

At some point, by mid-October, 1933 if not earlier, the coincidence of rebel and Communist interests led the two sides into direct contact. The more sober-minded Communist leaders probably realized that, beyond the immediate shared interest in survival against KMT attacks and opposition to Japan, there was little to cement a positive alliance. True, some of the rebel leaders had called for sweeping social and economic reforms, but so had many of the "reactionaries" in Nanking in times past. In recent memory CCP leaders had been purged for the "adventurism" of regarding factional anti-KMT rebellions as deep-seated conflicts that could be quickly transformed into class war. Even if the Leftist reformers in Foochow could be trusted, were they powerful enough to offset the conservative influence of the numerous militarists who were involved (with their armies) in the plot? The Communist leadership in 1927 had learned a tragic lesson on the unpredictability and decisive power of Generals not subject to Party control. Li Chi-shen, at Canton in April and December that year, had helped to teach it. Subsequently, Ch'en Ming-shu, Chiang Kuang-nai, and Ts'ai T'ing-k'ai had all participated in anti-Communist campaigns, some as late as September 1933. Had these leopards suddenly lost their spots? In a coalition-led rebellion there was always the danger that the non-Communist faction, if hard-pressed or bribed, would make a separate peace with the enemy, then turn on the exposed flank of its former ally.

Whatever the motives or misgivings on both sides, a rebel emissary was eventually sent from Foochow to offer cooperation, a man named Hsü Ming-hung. The Communists responded by calling a conference at Juichin to consider the rebel offer. While evidence for the positions taken in this debate is far from conclusive, two former Communist officials now recall that a split developed in the leadership between those favouring cooperation and those opposing it—and that the latter included Mao Tse-tung.[1] According to the

[1] See Warren Kuo (quoting Ch'en Jan), "The Campaign to Check Up Land Distribution and the 5th Plenum of the 6th CCP CC", (Part II), *Issues and Studies*, IV (October, 1967), 42; and Kung Ch'u, *Wo yü hung chün* [The Red Army and I] (Hong Kong: Nan feng ch'u pan she, 1954), p. 364. The reader should be cautioned that the quality of Kung Ch'u's account is very uneven, the product of hasty writing and imperfect recollection some twenty years later. A widely quoted secondary source, which the author finds much less impressive,

erstwhile Red Army officer, Kung Ch'u, the "conservatives" (*pao shou p'ai*), who were led by Mao, distrusted the rebels and proposed sending an unimportant representative to Foochow to test their intentions further before negotiating a definite commitment. In contrast the "activists" (*chi chi p'ai*), led by Chou En-lai, took the rebel offer seriously and advocated the immediate dispatch of an important official to Foochow to conclude formal arrangements. Mao's cautious faction finally won, according to Kung, and it was decided to send P'an Han-nien (P'an Chien-hsing) and Chang Yün-i back to Foochow with Hsü Ming-hung.[1]

A "Preliminary Agreement" to resist Japan and Chiang Kai-shek was signed on October 26, 1933 by representatives of the Chinese Soviet Republic and Red Army, on one side, and the Fukien Provincial Government and Nineteenth Route Army, on the other.[2] Unfortunately, the only available texts of the agreement were published by the Communist side and, because of a secrecy clause, none

unaccountably centres the rebel–Communist negotiations in Shanghai and has the CCP dutifully sending to Moscow for instructions, the subsequent reply forbidding more than limited military cooperation. This story, besides lacking corroboration elsewhere, would seem to exaggerate the importance of the remaining CCP operations in Shanghai as well as the Party's dependence on Comintern guidance. See Lei Hsiao-ch'en, *San shih nien tung luan Chung kuo* [Thirty Years' Turbulence in China] (Hong Kong: Asia Press, 1955), pp. 213–15.

[1] In a later statement (dated February 11, 1934), Mao and Chu Te, while acknowledging that they had never trusted the sincerity of the rebels, justified Communist negotiations with them on grounds that (1) general CCP policy at the time was to aid all anti-imperialist, anti-KMT movements, and that (2) the talks were only undertaken on condition that the rebel representative "assent to and accept all demands and conditions which we proposed", *Hung se Chung hua* [Red China], No. 149 (February 14, 1934), p. 3.

[2] The full title of the agreement was "The Anti-Japanese, Anti-Chiang Preliminary Agreement" ["Fan Jih fan Chiang ti ch'u pu hsieh ting"]. Texts of it appear in *Hung se Chung hua*, No. 149 (February 14, 1934), p. 4; and (from Communist documentation) in Sheng Lu, "Fu chou yü Jui chin" ["Foochow and Juichin"], *Kuo wen chou pao* [Kuowen Weekly], XII (March 11, 1935), 11. An incomplete version was published in 1951 in Hu Hua, *et al.*, ed., *Chung kuo hsin min chu chu i ko ming shih ts'an k'ao tzu liao* [Reference Materials for China's New Democratic Revolutionary History] (Shanghai: Shang wu yin shu kuan, 1951), pp. 259–60. This edition, which contains only the preamble and first four articles of the agreement, somewhat deceptively entitles the selection an "Anti-Japanese Fighting Agreement" [*K'ang Jih tso chan hsieh ting*]. However, even here the text of the preamble clearly refers to it as a "Preliminary Agreement" [*Ch'u pu hsieh ting*].

91

appeared until after the rebellion had been crushed. Subsequent accounts, however, have greatly exaggerated its binding strength and importance.

The two sides agreed to cease military operations against each other, restore trade, and exchange representatives. Most of the obligations assumed under the agreement were to be shouldered by the Fukien Government and Nineteenth Route Army, who were to release all political prisoners, permit the activities of all revolutionary organizations (including "all armed organizations of the revolutionary masses"), and grant civil rights such as freedom of speech, assembly and strike. Moreover, they were to issue an anti-Chiang Kai-shek declaration immediately after signing the agreement and begin preparations forthwith for military operations against Chiang and Japan. The key provision of the agreement was Article 9: "*After* [emphasis added] fulfilment of the above-mentioned conditions, both sides shall in the shortest time, separately conclude a concrete agreement for military operations against Japan and Chiang" (...*fan Jih fan Chiang chü t'i tso chan hsieh ting*). The Preliminary Agreement was to come into force immediately after being signed by plenipotentiaries of both sides, but it was to remain secret until joint approval of publication.

It will be seen that the agreement promised little more in practice than a military truce under existing conditions plus a vague intention of the parties to conclude further concrete arrangements for military and economic cooperation whenever they could work these out. Lacking any substantial basis of reciprocal advantage, the cement of most treaties, the Preliminary Agreement was so obviously one-sided as to suggest its being more a temporary device to halt Communist attacks on the Nineteenth Route Army than a durable covenant of equals sharing the same sentiments and objectives.[1] Had it wished legal grounds for repudiating any part of the treaty, Foochow could have made a plausible argument that the entire contract was negotiated under duress. Even this would have been unnecessary, however, in view of the very flimsy concrete obligations undertaken.

[1] This interpretation was supported in the Chu-Mao statement (para. 2) of February 11, 1934 after the collapse of the revolt. *Hung se Chung hua*, No. 149 (February 14, 1934), p. 3; Sheng Lu, "Fu chou yü...", p. 10.

Moreover, the agreement was negotiated and signed by representatives who apparently did not hold important positions in their respective governments or military organizations. Finally, any propaganda advantage which the Communists might have derived from the document was neutralized by the secrecy clause.

Despite the weaknesses of the agreement as an instrument of military cooperation, it was of considerable indirect value to the Communist side in the short term because it encouraged the conspirators in Foochow to proceed with their plans for revolt. Standing alone as they did against Nanking, with no support from Kwangtung or Kwangsi, the would-be rebel leaders needed at least some feeling of assurance that they would not fall prey to attack from the Soviet areas which had begun to starve for blockaded foods and war materials. By the same token, the Red Army could safely turn its back on Fukien and concentrate forces for action in more critical areas.

On November 20 a National People's Provisional Congress was hastily convened in Foochow. After a day of oratory, featuring denunciations of Chiang Kai-shek for not resisting Japan, the delegates proclaimed the establishment of a new regime for the nation— the People's Revolutionary Government of the Chinese Republic. Li Chi-shen was named Chairman, but real power was divided among at least a half dozen of the most prominent rebel leaders. The government was organized into several committees, the most powerful being the Executive Committee, headed by Ch'en Ming-shu,[1] and the Military Committee under Ts'ai T'ing-k'ai.

The new regime announced a programme which was decidedly social revolutionary in tone and militantly nationalistic. It called for complete tariff autonomy for China, abolition of unequal treaties, freedom of labour to organize and strike, religious liberty, state ownership of lands, forests, and mines, "readjustment" of domestic and foreign loans, abolition of exorbitant taxes, land reform, etc.

---

[1] Members of the Executive Committee included: Ch'en Ming-shu (Chairman), Li Chi-shen, Chiang Kuang-nai, Ts'ai T'ing-k'ai, Tai Chi, Eugene Ch'en Fang Chen-wu, George Hsü, and Huang Ch'i-hsiang. See *China Weekly Review*, LXVI (November 25, 1933), 510; and *The China Yearbook, 1934* (Shanghai: North China Daily News and Herald, 1934), pp. 373–4.

There was also—at first—talk of waging a prolonged war against Japan. However, Ch'en Ming-shu soon made it clear that his government had no serious intention of assuming an anti-Japanese posture, much less of taking any positive action along this line. In an interview with a correspondent of *Osaka Mainichi* on December 2, he declared that while the new regime was "determined to fight General Chiang Kai-shek to the last", he hoped that no one would misconstrue this militant stance as directed against Japan. Though "regretting" that Japan had oppressed China, he gave assurances that "we will not start any movement to oppose Japan". He also denied that his government was Communistic, but admitted it had arranged to cooperate with the Communists in Kiangsi to oppose Nanking.[1] Less than a week before this interview Chinese officials in Canton privately told U.S. Minister Nelson T. Johnson that they had evidence of intrigue between the Fukien leaders, especially Ch'en Ming-shu and the Japanese.[2]

In the area of social and economic reform the performance of the People's Government was also considerably below its stated objectives. To be sure, local newspapers dropped such terms as "Communist-bandit" and "Communist suppression" and printed slogans of agrarian reform now and then, but the leadership apparently had no intention of effecting revolutionary changes. Consider, for example, the announced goal of agrarian reform which was to be achieved through per-capita division of land. In framing a programme to carry out this reform the regime eschewed any notion of confiscation and merely revived the old, impotent KMT formula of government bond issues to finance state purchases of land for redistribution. Considering Fukien's impoverished condition, there was no realistic prospect of undertaking a significant programme along these lines. Even more indicative of the regime's basically unrevolu-

---

[1] Quoted in *China Weekly Review*, LXVII (December 9, 1933), 47.

[2] See Johnson's memorandum in *Foreign Relations of the United States: Diplomatic Papers, 1933*, (Washington, D.C.: U.S. Government Printing Office, 1949), III, 469–70. According to an American Communist-front source, on November 29 the garrison commander at Amoy publicly promised to protect the interests of foreign powers, including foreign concessions, and declared that he would put a ban on Communist activities. "Analysis of the Fukien Rebellion in China", *China Today*, I [Old Series] (January, 1934), 4.

tionary nature were the restrictions placed on the freedoms so lavishly announced at the start of the rebellion. The Left Wing reformers were forbidden to make speeches or publish articles expressing their views on social and economic programmes, innocuous and mild as those apparently were. Under the pretext of military necessity, martial law was imposed, civil liberties restricted, and the regular armed forces left in absolute control with no thought of arming the masses.

After a ten-day visit to Foochow in early December, Harold Isaacs was shocked by the ineffectiveness of the Left Wing leadership and the wide gap between the regime's professed goals and its actual accomplishments. Indeed, he claimed to have evidence that at a series of conferences held at Changchow prior to the rebellion, the Leftists had bowed to the dictates of Ch'en Ming-she [sic] and the militarists, agreeing that "the movement was to proceed on a purely anti-Chiang basis". By the terms of this understanding "phrases could be spilled at will through the manifesto, but it was to be made perfectly clear that nothing more was to be done about them".[1]

COMMUNIST POLICY IN THE REBELLION

The CCP finally took a public position on the rebellion on December 5 in a statement by the Central Committee.[2] Beyond expressing the Communist attitude towards the rebellion, it attempted to influence the new regime to make necessary changes to avoid the dire consequences forecast for its present course. Although nearly a month had passed, the Communists charged, the People's Government had done nothing to prove that it was either "people's" or revolutionary. Unless it took concrete action to restore civil rights, improve the people's livelihood, and prepare for war against Japan and Chiang (including the arming of workers and peasants), it would be no

[1] Harold Isaacs, "Radicalism and Realities: A Fukien Close-Up", *China Forum*, III (December 21, 1933), 5.

[2] "Chung kuo kung ch'an tang chung yang wei yüan hui wei Fu chien shih pien kao ch'üan kuo min chung" [Statement of the CCP Central Committee to the People of the Entire Nation on the Fukien Incident], *Tou cheng* [Struggle], Kiangsi edition, No. 38 (December 12, 1933), pp. 1–3. The statement was reprinted in Sheng Lu, "Fu-chou yü...", pp. 6–7.

different than the "counter-revolutionary" regime it had rebelled against. Accordingly, the Central Committee appealed directly to the people of Fukien to respond to the "successive" Soviet appeals for a united front against Japan and the KMT. (In deference to the secrecy clause, no mention was made of the "Preliminary Agreement" or the failure to follow up with concrete economic and military pacts.) The Communists urged the Fukien masses to take immediate, spontaneous action to organize labour unions, peasant committees, anti-Japanese associations, partisan bands, and an anti-Japanese/anti-Chiang People's Revolutionary Volunteer Army. In conclusion, a warning was voiced that only two paths were open to the Chinese people: "the colonial path of the imperialist KMT" or the "national liberation path or opposition to imperialism and the KMT". Third paths were doomed to defeat, and those who tried them would become tools of the counter-revolution.

The December 5 statement was strong language indeed, but before concluding that it alienated a potentially friendly rebel leadership one should recall the equally provocative statements emanating from Foochow earlier. So far as we know, the rebel government had evinced no desire for closer relations with Juichin, had ignored the "Preliminary Agreement", and had done little if anything to honour its own pledges of November 20. Nor was it a matter of being unable to do so. Up to this point, the rebels had engaged in no serious fighting against the KMT, were not threatened by external intervention, and were in no danger from civil disturbances in Fukien. However, because the CCP statement failed to induce the desired modifications in Foochow, it is often viewed as an intemperate, doctrinaire outburst which ruined any hope of future cooperation. Perhaps it would be more accurate to regard it as a delayed, calculated gamble—or, had it succeeded, "an imaginative, bold, stroke": to force the hand of the disunited, indecisive rebel leadership.[1]

---

[1] The statement's concluding reference to an inevitable choice between two paths has often been misinterpreted as a doctrinaire outright rejection of the possibility of alliance with the Fukien rebels. Bearing in mind that the "two-path" theory was standard Communist line at the time, one should note that its formulation in the December 5 statement was a relatively mild one. The choice posed was between colonialism, on one hand, and "opposition" to imperialism

Certainly, at the time, there was no intimation that the Communist Government or military officials in the Soviet areas doubted the wisdom of this CCP statement or that Party and non-Party leaders were then disunited in their approach to Foochow. On December 20 Mao Tse-tung and Chu Te, in the name of the Soviet Government and Red Army, sent an urgent telegram to the "leaders of the Fukien People's Revolutionary Government and the People's Revolutionary Army".[1] Observing that well over a month had elapsed since the signing of the "Preliminary Agreement", they charged that the rebels still had shown no signs of undertaking active operations against Chiang and Japan or even mobilized and armed the masses to fight. This, despite the fact that three large KMT detachments were now poised for attack against the cities of Foochow and Yenping (which could furnish the Japanese a pretext for intervention). Accordingly, the Soviet leaders issued a "demand" [yao ch'iu] that the rebels immediately take "positive action" in keeping with the "Anti-Japanese Anti-Chiang Draft Treaty" to concentrate their forces for a "decisive battle [chüeh chan] of resistance to Chiang". Mao and Chu went on to demand the arming of the masses, the development of mass struggle against Chiang

on the other. Although the latter implied a "revolutionary victory" of the masses' the statement did not specify that this must be led by the Soviets or CCP. Mao Tse-tung had drawn the alternatives more starkly as recently as the summer of 1933, declaring "the road to power of the Soviets is the only road to victory, the salvation of the Chinese masses." *Inprecor*, XII (December 8, 1933), 1230. Thus, it is not entirely accurate to say, as does Prof. Hsiao Tso-liang (*op. cit.*, p. 251) that the December 5 statement only offered a choice between a China "*Soviet* or colonial—leaving no room for a third road". Likewise, the CCP statement does not warrant the conclusion that: "The argument used...by the Central Committee against support for the Fukien revolt was that only two roads existed, that there was no middle way." Robert North, *Moscow and Chinese Communists* (Stanford: Stanford Univ. Press, 1963), p. 162. As has been shown above, opposition to the rebel regime was based on its refusal to honour previous pledges both to the people of Fukien and to the Communists. The December 5 statement continued to offer support to the rebels provided they would mend their ways.

[1] This telegram was later published under the title: "Chung hua su wei ai lin shih chung yang cheng fu chih Fu chien jen min ko ming cheng fu yü shih chiu lu chün ti ti i tien" [First Telegram from the Chinese Soviet Provisional Government to the Fukien People's Revolutionary Government and Nineteenth Route Army], in *Hung se Chung hua*, No. 149 (February 14, 1934), p. 4.

and Japan, the organization of a "genuine People's Revolutionary Army and Volunteer Army", and the granting of freedom of speech, press, assembly, association and strike. Meanwhile as a final taste of sweetness after all the vinegar, they stood ready "at any time" to unite in drawing up a military agreement for making war to overthrow the common enemy—Japanese imperialism and Chiang Kai-shek's KMT Government. The message ended: "We hope you swiftly notify us of your decision."[1]

So far as we know, there was no message in reply from Foochow. Instead, on December 22 Li Chi-shen and Eugene Ch'en went to pains to deny Shanghai newspaper allegations that the Nineteenth Route Army had entered into any alliance with the Kiangsi Communists.[2] By this time, the chances of an effective military alliance between the Red Army and Nineteenth Route Army to save the Fukien rebellion were becoming remote indeed.

After making several futile attempts to head off the revolt by political negotiations, Chiang Kai-shek had moved swiftly to strike a decisive military blow. Within three days after the People's Government was proclaimed in Foochow on November 20, Chiang's crack Eighty-eighth Division under Sun Yuan-liang was speeding south to the Chekiang–Fukien border area and by mid-December the government build-up there and in adjacent northern Kiangsi had reached a strength of 150,000–200,000 troops. To oppose them the Nineteenth Route Army could muster only 40,000—plus whatever support the Red Army might be able to provide. Taking advantage

[1] John Rue, in his *Mao Tse-tung in Opposition, 1927–1935* (Stanford: Stanford Univ. Press, 1966), p. 261, argues that Mao and Chu took a position during the Fukien revolt essentially in opposition to that of the CCP leadership, expressing "cautious hope" that "a genuine basis for cooperation" could be worked out while the Party chiefs in contrast only attacked the rebels. In light of the general substantive agreement between the December 20 telegram discussed above and the Central Committee's December 5 statement analysed previously, it would seem that Rue's interpretation is exceedingly strained and questionable. His contention that the Soviet Government and CCP failed to issue any joint statements on the revolt would appear, at most, irrelevant. Finally, Rue's assertion that Mao turned to "denouncing the rebels" only after the opportunity to form a united front had passed is contradicted by the available evidence cited above that to the extent any internal Communist division arose during the preliminary negotiations it found Mao squarely on the side of those resisting cooperation.

[2] *China Weekly Review*, LXVII (December 30, 1933), 181.

of newly improved railroads and highways, the attacking government forces advanced rapidly on Fukien along three routes: an eastern column marching from Chekiang south, a western column driving down the mountainous Kiangsi–Fukien border to split the Nineteenth Route Army from the Red Army, and a central column deploying for a decisive offensive down the Min River Valley to Foochow. The first significant clashes broke out on December 17 and 18, along the Chekiang–Fukien frontier. Soon the fighting had spread along a front nearly 150 miles in length.

To hold out against the overwhelming might of the KMT attack, the rebels desperately needed help from the Red Army in the west. Mao Tse-tung and Chu Te had again offered such help in their telegram of December 20 but, so far as we know, the rebel leaders remained unable or unwilling to satisfy the conditions of this offer (i.e., to carry out their promises of October 26 and November 20) On the contrary, they continued publicly to deny and repudiate any association with the Communists. This forced upon Juichin the very difficult question of whether to go ahead with support unilaterally despite the repeated rebuffs from Foochow. By this time the Communists had reaped the main short-term benefits of the rebellion—diversion of KMT armies from Kiangsi and relaxation of the Fifth Encirclement Campaign. They now had to decide whether it would be militarily more advantageous to throw their strength into a costly and unpredictable support effort for the Nineteenth Route Army in the northern Kiangsi–Fukien border area, or alternatively, to deploy their main combat units to reinforce other sectors of the Soviet defence perimeter and, perhaps, counterattack the KMT encirclement wall in places recently weakened by troop withdrawals.

Some sources indicate that this necessity for choice again divided the Communist leaders, some favouring immediate, all-out assistance while others advocated a continued policy of "watchful waiting"—using the rebellion without risking positive support. Thus, Kung Ch'u declares that, despite the acid language of the December 5 Central Committee telegram, Po Ku (Secretary-General), Chou En-lai, and Lo Fu urged swift dispatch of the Red First and Third Army Groups to Fukien to strengthen the Nineteenth Route Army and assist it to liquidate the vacillating elements within.

Mao Tse-tung, on the contrary, advocated caution and not rushing into action. He proposed first to invite the Nineteenth Route Army to cooperate in attacking a KMT unit under Liu Ho-ting in north-west Fukien. Failing this, Mao thought the Communists should wait for some further rebel demonstration of resolute action before extending assistance.[1]

Whatever may be the true story of inner-Party debates or secret last-minute communications with the rebels, it is clear that the Communists did not provide significant military support for the rebellion during the critical period before the end of December, when it might have been effective in slowing the KMT drive from Chekiang. Indeed, they appear to have withdrawn detachments initially from the Kiangsi–Fukien border sector of the Soviet area, transferring them south and west to threaten the rear of the deploy-ing KMT armies.[2] Later, however, there is some evidence that they belatedly attempted to send military support to Fukien. Lin Piao, then in command of the Red First Army Corps, subsequently told Edgar Snow that early in 1934 Communist forces had begun to move east to help the Fukien rebels—"but it was too late".[3] Kung Ch'u also mentions belated efforts of the First and Third Red Army Corps in Fukien which proved fruitless.[4] Immediately after the defeat of the rebellion Mao Tse-tung and Chu Te declared that the

[1] Kung Ch'u, *Wo yü hung chün*, p. 397. Warren Kuo (*op. cit.* pp. 33–4, 42), elaborates on the intra-Party debate, quoting the mysterious, ubiquitous Ch'en Jan. According to his account (which tends to conflict with the evidence given below on page 102) the increasingly desperate rebels eventually sent an emergency appeal to Juichin requesting that main force Red Army units be sent quickly—by the end of December—to Sha-hsien (southwest of Nan-p'ing and east of the Soviet area) to participate in joint operations with the Nineteenth Route Army against the attacking KMT columns. Although the Communists subsequently wired consent and appointed P'eng Te-huai to lead the expeditionary force, Ch'en declares that Mao was opposed and succeeded in delaying its deployment with the slogan "Let us sit idly to watch the tigers fight". Slow to get started, the force halted entirely at the frontier of the Soviet area and only continued east-ward to occupy Sha-hsien ("without firing a shot") in late January after the rebels had been routed.

[2] Wan Min [Wang Ming], "Discussion on the Report of Comrade Dimitrov", *Inprecor*, xv (November 11, 1935), 1489.

[3] Edgar Snow, *Random Notes on Red China*, p. 28.

[4] Kung Ch'u, *Wo yü hung chün*, pp. 366–98.

Red Army had "acted positively in North Fukien—from the occupation of Sha-hsien to the fall of Yu-ch'i'', to cooperate with the rebels in fighting against Chiang Kai-shek.[1]

With the occupation of Amoy and Foochow, on January 10 and 15 respectively, the People's Government ceased to function and many of its political leaders fled to Hong Kong. It had lasted less than sixty days. There was no general surrender of the Nineteenth Route Army; its commanders either fled the country or went over to the government. The last rebel strongholds fell with little actual fighting in late January, although mopping-up operations against small bands continued into the first part of February.

There were many reasons, as we have seen, for the defeat of the rebellion: fundamental differences of interest and intention among the disparate rebel leadership, failure to generate the expected support of either Left or Right Wing groups outside Fukien, and the surprisingly swift and effective military response by Chiang Kai-shek. The revolt failed to capture the popular imagination or even to rally an important following. Despite growing resentment of Japanese aggression and KMT inaction, the national mood was still predominantly opposed to a resumption of the old warlord pattern of civil wars and general instability. In these circumstances perhaps the only thing that might have saved the rebellion was timely, direct, unreciprocal, military aid by the Red Army. It is extremely doubtful that even this could have more than temporarily delayed its final defeat. However, since at least the opportunity to extend assistance was presented to the Communist leaders, their failure to exercise it and the subsequent defeat of the rebellion inevitably led to a re-examination of CCP policy in an effort to justify or condemn.

MAOIST REASSESSMENTS:
LEGITIMACY THROUGH ABSOLUTION

On January 26, after the collapse of the rebellion, the CCP Central

[1] See the Mao–Chu statement of February 11, 1934. *Hung se Chung hua*, No. 149 (February 14, 1934), p. 3; also Sheng Lu, "Fu chou yü...", p. 11.

Committee issued a second statement.[1] Shortly before this, on January 18, it had met in a Fifth Plenary Session and now the Second National Soviet Congress was in progress. The new statement unsurprisingly concluded that the previous policy, as originally set forth on December 5, had been correct and that the failure of the rebellion only proved the impossibility of trying to resist imperialism and feudalism by reformist methods. From the first, it declared, the rebel leaders had adopted a passive attitude, watching Chiang's redeployment without taking counter-measures, then turning tail and surrendering in droves when the KMT finally attacked.

Statements of Mao Tse-tung and Chu Te immediately after the collapse of the rebellion were in substantial agreement with the Central Committee's analysis and found nothing wrong with previous Communist policy. In speeches before the Second Soviet Congress Mao reiterated that the rebellion had originated in a desperate move by reactionary civil and military leaders in Fukien to preserve their rule. Realizing the bankruptcy of the oppressive, traitorous KMT regime and perceiving the growing popular admiration for the Soviet movement, they attempted to find a third path between the two in order to retain their power. However, the masses had seen that the rebel leaders, like the KMT, had no real concern for the interests of workers and peasants, and even refused to accept sincerely the three basic conditions proposed by the CCP as the basis for an anti-Japanese, anti-KMT agreement.[2] In his closing speech to the Congress on January 27, Mao repeated this analysis of rebel insincerity and attempted deception of the masses with a "third path", concluding that the entire episode "had not the slightest revolutionary significance".[3]

[1] "Chung kuo kung ch'an tang chung yang wei yüan hui wei Fu chien shih pien ti erh tz'u hsüan yen" [Second Statement of the CCP Central Committee on the Fukien Incident], *Hung se Chung hua*, Second National Soviet Congress Special Edition, No. 4 (January, 28, 1934), p. 2; text also in Sheng Lu, "Fu chou yü...", pp. 8–10.

[2] *Hung se Chung hua*, Second National Soviet Congress Special Edition, No. 3 (January 26, 1934), p. 3.

[3] *Hung se Chung hua*, Second National Soviet Congress Special Edition, No. 5 (January 31, 1934), p. 1. As Prof. Hsiao Tso-liang has pointed out (*op. cit.* p. 273), Mao's remarks on the Fukien Rebellion were omitted in the later Chinese and English editions of this speech (e.g., see Mao Tse-tung, *Selected Works*, I, 147–52).

On February 11 the Soviet Government issued a final post-mortem statement on the rebellion under the signatures of Mao Tse-tung and Chu Te.[1] It blamed the defeat entirely on the rebel leadership, which allegedly had solicited imperialist support from Japan and America, without democratic rights and refused to arm the masses on the pretext of military necessity, prohibited strikes and peasant struggles for land, and, finally, adopted a completely defeatist military line—failing to make the slightest preparation for defence and then surrendering without a fight. Professing to have seen through the rebels' tricks all along, Mao and Chu stressed that they had only acceded to the "Preliminary Agreement" subject to Foochow's fulfilment of certain conditions and had drafted the entire text "in accordance with our own basic revolutionary standpoint". Subsequent rebel non-performance had evoked warnings but to no avail. This again showed that "reformist factions" were counter-revolutionary and that only the Soviet Government and Red Army ("the anti-imperialist vanguard") and "only the Soviet path" could achieve national and social liberation.

Available evidence indicates that criticism of the Communist leadership for failure to provide timely military assistance to the rebels did not arise until after the general withdrawal from Kiangsi at the end of 1934. Ironically, the earliest documentation of such criticism comes from the former CCP Secretary-General, Wang Ming, in Moscow. Writing in *Communist Internatioual* in January, 1935, Wang described the rebellion as having presented a "most favorable situation" for the beleaguered Soviet Government and Red Army. However, "the Communist Party lost the opportune moment," he concluded, "due to mistakes committed both by us and on the part of the Nineteenth Army."[2] Addressing the Seventh Congress of the Communist International in Moscow in August,

[1] "Chung hua su wei ai kung ho kuo chung yang cheng fu wei Fu chien shih pien hsüan yen" [Statement of the Central Government of the Chinese Soviet Republic on the Fukien Incident], *Hung se Chung hua*, No. 149 (February 14, 1934), p. 3.

[2] Wan Ming, "The Struggle of the Chinese Red Army Against Chiang Kai-shek's 6th Drive", *Communist International*, XII (January 5, 1935), 17–18, 21–2. It should be noted that Wang's criticism was published *before* the Tsunyi Conference, when Mao is supposed to have rectified the previous "erroneous" Russian Returned Student leadership.

Wang charged more pointedly that some Party leaders had mechanically opposed "attempts to find a third path" and underestimated the significance of the events in Fukien. This had led to the tactical error of withdrawing Red Army detachments from the Fukien front, transferring them south and west to attack the KMT rear rather than going to the assistance of the Nineteenth Route Army, which consequently was defeated.[1]

It should be pointed out that Wang Ming's gradually changing interpretation of the CCP role in the Fukien Rebellion closely paralleled shifts that were taking place in the general Comintern line on United Front tactics. The Twelfth Plenum of the Comintern Executive Committee ECCI in September, 1932 had still called only for United Fronts "from below" (i.e., alliances with sympathetic non-Communist individuals, under overall Communist Party leadership to overthrow a local regime). The primary intention was to "convert imperialist war into civil war and overthrow capitalism".[2] However, the rise of Hitler, assisted by divisions among Germany's Left Wing parties, and the growing international menace of Japanese and Italian fascism, gradually forced in Moscow a thorough reappraisal of the radical and sectarian tactics which had characterized Comintern policy since 1928. At the Thirteenth Plenum of the ECCI in December, 1933, there were hints of a shift towards the "liberal" or "popular-front" line. In fact, K'ang Sheng, in commenting on the Chinese situation, asserted that after a strong "United Front from below" had been established, the CCP might supplement this "to a certain extent, in a certain measure, and in the proper form" with the tactics of a "United Front from above... by means of concluding fighting agreements for concrete operations".[3] Finally, in the summer of 1935 the Seventh Comintern Congress responded to the mounting worldwide Fascist threat with a formal

[1] *Inprecor*, XV (November 11, 1935), 1489; also Wang Ming, "The Revolutionary Movement in the Colonial and Semi-Colonial Countries and the Tactics of the Communist parties", *Communist International*, XII (September 20, 1935), 1326.

[2] See "Resolution of the 12th Plenum E.C.C.I. on the Report of Comrade Okano", *Inprecor*, XII (October 20, 1932), 1005–6.

[3] See Wang Ming and Kang Sin [K'ang Sheng], *Revolutionary China Today* (Moscow: Cooperative Publishing of Workers in the U.S.S.R., 1934), pp. 106–7.

shift in tactics to the broad "anti-Fascist popular front" or, in Asia the "anti-imperialist national United Front". This meant a wide alliance with all patriotic non-Communist parties, including those in power, directed primarily against a foreign aggressor. Wang Ming's speech at the Congress in which he criticized CCP policy during the Fukien Rebellion was thus part of a more general attack on the CCP's implementation of United Front tactics.

Within the Chinese Communist movement, criticism of the previous policy toward Fukien apparently developed more slowly, perhaps from a greater reticence to accept fully the change to a "United Front from above". The earliest available documentation of CCP criticism is to be found in a Politburo resolution adopted on December 25, 1935 at Wayaopao in northern Shensi.[1] Although this statement came several months after the Seventh Comintern Congress, it still envisioned a United Front directed against the dual enemy of Japan and Chiang Kai-shek. It repeated the old offer of the Soviet Government and Red Army to draw up an agreement with any armed force willing to join in resistance of the two enemies —like the one negotiated earlier with the Nineteenth Route Army. While admitting that in the latter case the Red Army's failure to provide timely assistance was incorrect (*pu tui*), the Politburo also insisted, parenthetically, that the Nineteenth Route Army had not made a positive request for it. This division of the blame between Juichin and Foochow was similar to the mildly critical analysis of Wang Ming almost a year earlier (January, 1935).

It was not until 1936 that leaders of the CCP and Comintern appear to have shifted to a categorical criticism of Juichin's policy toward the rebellion. In the summer of that year the Comintern's Far Eastern expert, Pavel Mif, declared that a "serious mistake" had been committed in failing to provide "the necessary active

---

[1] Moreover, the earliest available text of it was not published until 1938. "Chung kuo kung ch'an tang chung yang kuan yü mu ch'ien cheng chih hsing shih yu tang ti jen wu chüeh i" [Resolution of the Chinese Communist Party Centre on the Present Political Situation and the Party's Tasks], in Lo Fu *et al.*, ed., *Shih nien lai ti Chung kuo kung ch'an tang* [*The Chinese Communist Party in the Last 10 Years*] ([Hankow?]: Chen li ch'u pan she, 1938), pp. 27–51. (Note: The brief excerpts in Mao's *Selected Works*, I, 328–30 omit entirely the passage on the Fukien Rebellion.)

support to the 19th Army". According to Mif, the Chinese Communists had put too narrow an interpretation on their agreement with the rebels, failed to render aid, and lost a golden opportunity.[1] Through misinformation or deliberate slanting he considerably exaggerated the good intentions of the rebel side, even making it appear that the revolt had sprung from the Nineteenth Route Army's refusal to obey orders to attack the Soviet area. From this point on, a growing criticism of CCP's Fukien policy was to rely heavily on such distortions.

Meanwhile, in the summer and early autumn of 1936 Edgar Snow penetrated the wall of isolation which had surrounded the Chinese Communists since their defeat in Kiangsi and interviewed most of the top officials of the Party and Army in Shensi and Kansu. The Red Army had just failed in a serious attempt (February–May) to invade Shansi. However, events were moving rapidly toward a Communist *rapprochement* with Chang Hsüeh-liang's old Northeastern Army troops, then chafing under Nanking's order to suppress the Communists and avoid the Japanese. From this vantage point the Communist leaders reflected on their past history and suddenly the Fukien Rebellion loomed large in their explanations for the Soviet defeat in Kiangsi. Mao Tse-tung told Snow that "the failure to unite with Ts'ai T'ing-k'ai's army in 1933" during the revolt was one of the "two important errors" which had caused the debacle.[2] Others agreed and Snow concluded that "most of the leaders" of the Chinese Soviets and Red Army had been "quite sympathetic with the 19th Route Army", at the time of the rebellion. In fact, he reported, "they were prepared to move their main forces into Fukien, develop a strong flank attack on Nanking's troops, and in general, give the 19th Route Army full military and political support".[3]

This new revelation of strategic plans and assumption of CCP guilt for "erroneously" failing to extend aid (which, by implication, caused the defeat of the rebellion) had obvious advantages for Mao and his followers in the setting of 1936. First, it helped rationalize the earlier defeat in Kiangsi and assisted the Party to build a con-

[1] Pavel Mif, *Heroic China: Fifteen Years of the Communist Party of China* (New York: Worker's Library Publishers, 1937), pp. 77–88.

[2] Edgar Snow, *Red Star Over China*, p. 186.   [3] *Ibid.* p. 418.

fident, new image of strength and invincibility, important for restoring internal morale and attracting non-Communist support. By openly condemning alleged sectarian behaviour towards the Nineteenth Route Army the CCP leaders helped erase any lingering suspicions about the sincerity of their current United Front appeal and paved the way for cooperation with Chang Hsüeh-liang's troops. Coming on the heels of the Red Army's abortive attack on Shansi, this was a gesture of some importance. However, it also had the potential for raising other difficult questions. Who had been responsible for the "error" of non-cooperation? Were the culprits still in control of the CCP?

Completely ignoring Juichin's many vain attempts to secure a working arrangement with Foochow, and forgetting the various statements they had made both during and after the rebellion, the Communist leaders who talked to Snow in north Shensi in 1936 declared that the "mistake" had been primarily the fault of a foreign military adviser, known as Li T'e (romanized "Li Teh" by Snow).[1] Although unnamed others were said to have been involved in the "error", Li T'e alone was identified and was clearly regarded as the villain of the episode. Chou En-lai ruefully told Snow, "We could have successfully cooperated with Fukien but due to the advice of Li Teh...and the advisory group in Shanghai we withdrew instead."[2] In fairness, he might have added that statements of Mao and other Chinese Communist leaders at the time had manifested something less than enthusiasm over the prospect of cooperation.

By December, 1936, however, Mao was ready to go beyond mere negative criticism to reveal, in hindsight, his own preferred alternative strategy. In lectures at the Red Army Academy in northern Shensi (if we may assume the authenticity of the available revised texts), he declared:

When the Fukien Incident took place, the main force of the Red Army

[1] *Ibid.* Li T'e, a non-Chinese-speaking German Communist (variously identified as Otto Braun or Albert List), was an experienced military officer whom the Comintern had sent to advise the CCP. He arrived in Kiangsi some time in 1933.

[2] Edgar Snow, *Random Notes on Red China*, p. 60. It is a little difficult to believe the embattled Red Army in Kiangsi was taking tactical orders from an "advisory group in Shanghai".

should undoubtedly have moved speedily to the Kiangsu–Chekiang–Anhwei–Kiangsi region, with Chekiang as the center, to sweep over the length and breadth of the area of Hangchow, Soochow, Nanking, Wuhu, Nanchang and Foochow, transforming the strategic defensive into a strategic offensive by menacing the vital positions of the enemy and challenging him to battles in the vast zones that were devoid of blockhouses.[1]

Unfortunately, Mao neglected to point out that in getting to Chekiang the Red Army would have had to break past strong KMT armies moving eastwards towards Fukien from the area of Nan-ch'eng and Li'ch'uan in Kiangsi (where the Communists had suffered serious defeats in September, 1933). Also, he did not mention that the Red Army, moving north, would have run head-on into very strong KMT armies rushing south from the Nanking–Shanghai–Hangchow area toward the Chekiang–Fukien border. Why would it have been easier to break through these rapidly converging KMT spearheads into new and largely unfamiliar territory, than to have remained in the north Kiangsi–Fukien border area (to coordinate the timing of operations with the Nineteenth Route Army on the east) or than to have moved quickly to the west to attack Chiang Kai-shek's rear? While the area Mao wished to enter was mostly "devoid of blockhouses", it was not lightly defended, being geographically closer to the main centres of KMT power than the Kiangsi Soviet area. In general, it contained fewer wide stretches of rugged terrain suitable for guerrilla fighting. Moreover, to have withdrawn "the main force of the Red Army" from Kiangsi, as he advocated, would have left the Central Soviet area largely unprotected. Nevertheless, Mao insisted that:

by such means we would have been able to compel the enemy forces attacking southern Kiangsi and western Fukien to turn back to defend their vital positions [what about the troops defending the Nanking–Shanghai–Hangchow area?], to smash their attack on the base area in Kiangsi [which meanwhile had been left largely undefended], and to render aid to the people's government in Fukien.

Because of failing to adopt this strategem, he concluded, not only

[1] Mao, *Selected Works*, I, 251; *Mao Tse-tung hsüan chi*, I, 230.

did the Fukien Rebellion collapse, but the Fifth KMT Encirclement Campaign could not be broken.

As Mao consolidated his control over the CCP after 1937, comments on the rebellion dealt less and less with the military aspects and were increasingly put into a political framework. The "erroneous" CCP policy had resulted from the evil influence of the so-called third "Left" line, foisted on the Party by Po Ku, Wang Ming, and the Fourth Plenum leadership. By implication Li T'e, the Comintern's military representative, was also responsible and, perhaps, others who had sought to advise and influence the CCP, such as Pavel Mif. The Maoist interpretation, finally crystallized in the Central Committee's historical resolution of 1945, said little specifically about the Fukien Rebellion except to commend the "Preliminary Agreement" and imply that the third "Left" leadership had intervened with sectarianism to spoil things.[1] Subsequent histories have continued to ignore the very tentative and conditional nature of the agreement and the failings of the rebel regime. Rather, they treat the former as if it had been a concrete military alliance and the latter as if it had been genuinely revolutionary. The few distorted fragments which they present are forced into a preselected pattern: although the CCP acted correctly in some situations (i.e. signing an agreement with the rebels), the non-Maoist leadership inevitably intervened with "erroneous" policies to turn a success into failure.

The successive historical revisions, contradictory statements of leaders then and now, and fragmentary, polemical nature of current official histories make it extremely difficult to draw an intelligible picture of the Fukien Rebellion and the Communist role in it. Was Communist policy really in error? And was this the main reason why the rebellion failed? Did Mao and others favour unilateral, unconditional assistance to the rebels? Was this "correct" advice thrust aside by more powerful Left-line leaders in Juichin?

While it may not be possible to answer all these questions finally and completely, the evidence presented above—with all its inadequacies—casts serious doubt on the official Maoist interpretation. In fact, Mao Tse-tung and Chu Te appear to have been deeply involved in the formulation and implementation of Juichin's policy

[1] Mao, *Selected Works*, IV, 192–3.

towards Foochow, despite their attempts since 1935–6 to pin the responsibility on others. Regardless of who made the policy, it is questionable to term it "erroneous". From the standpoint of military strategy it was not demonstrably unsound. Moreover, it adhered closely to the conception of United Front tactics which was accepted at the time.[1]

Why, then, did Mao and his followers later criticize the Communist policy towards Fukien, contradicting their own statements of the rebellion period? There were probably several reasons. Having sustained a terrible defeat in Kiangsi in the fall of 1934, Mao ultimately needed to assure the Party faithful that this would never happen again. Believing history to be always on the side of the Revolution, he sought an explanation for the defeat in subjective "error": the alleged failure to unite with the rebels. To account for this—and remove any taint from themselves—Mao and his friends needed a scapegoat. Po Ku and the Returned Students, who possessed titular control of the Party centre, were perfect candidates. They were bookish, had little popular following and had arrived in the Soviet area comparatively late to build up an organization that could rival Mao's. Although originally installed in power by the Comintern, the latter had begun to indicate as early as 1934 that it had serious misgivings about the Fukien policy. In Kiangsi, Po Ku and his group, to judge from their public pronouncements, had been inclined to offer advice in terms of abstract theoretical analysis rather than take practical concrete positions—which later could be categorically attacked *or* defended. On the other hand, by 1936 Mao and his supporters might have reasonably supposed that any really demanding evidence against them either had been lost in the final chaos of the Kiangsi defeat and Long March, or else would be concealed or censored out by pro-United Front editors at the publishing houses in Moscow.

[1] Unless Juichin had been prepared to violate the "United Front from below" tactics ordered by the Comintern in 1932, and to abandon the three basic conditions for support of anti-Japanese armed forces adopted by the CCP in January, 1933, no other policy alternative was open to it in view of rebel behaviour. The fact that United Front tactics were substantially modified later—first by the Comintern, then by the CCP—only served to confuse the story of the rebellion.

It is also possible that the belated Fukien policy exposé was related to the CCP's difficult tactical shift to the "United Front from above" after August, 1935. Thus, on one hand, it might have been intended to help rationalize the shift *within* the Party—in particular, to alleviate persistent uncertainties and doubts as to the wisdom of the new line by suggesting a past situation which its application might have turned to advantage. On the other hand, externally, in order to convince an ever-widening circle of potential allies that the CCP now sincerely wished to cooperate in a liberal United Front, the Maoist leadership might have felt it necessary to drag the Fukien skeleton out of the cupboard so as to be able to pin the responsibility for it conspicuously on others—e.g. foreign elements such as Li T'e or "former" leaders no longer in power.

Whatever the motive, criticism of the Fukien policy not only helped to rationalize the defeat in Kiangsi, but also assisted Mao to consolidate his leadership over the Communist movement. Unquestionably, when the "Preliminary Agreement" was signed and the rebellion later broke out, the war-weary, blockade-starved Communist leaders and soldiers must have entertained high hopes for a working alliance with the rebels and a dramatic reversal of their military situation. These expectations had been ruthlessly dashed by the rapid collapse of the rebel regime, but in the bitter days of the Long March they could have easily been drawn from memory and given new credibility. By criticizing the "Left" leaders for failing to make the dream come true Mao was able to discredit for all time Po Ku and Wang Ming as potential rivals for power. At the same time he began building an image of himself as the "new", unique, and infallible leader who could guide the Party to ultimate victory.

CONCLUSION

In this brief analysis of two key episodes from the annals of the CCP in Kiangsi—the rise of the Returned Student leadership under Wang Ming and the Fukien Rebellion—we have attempted both to gain a better understanding of what actually happened and to explain why the historical record was later substantially revised. It has been suggested that the subsequent alterations and reinterpretations were part of a more general effort to legitimize Mao Tse-tung's leadership of the Party following the disastrous loss of the Central Soviet Area. The immediate need to regain self-confidence and bolster authority led Mao and his closest allies, first, to rationalize their role in the Fifth Encirclement Campaign so as to absolve themselves of any responsibility and shift the blame to others. Later these explanations became more involved—and charged with political implications—as CCP authority was further tested by bewildering changes in United Front policy and intensified demands of the hostile wartime environment. Finally, in the *cheng-feng* movement of the early 1940's, the revision of past history began to be blended into a myth of Mao's omniscient, infallible leadership—a legend officially endorsed in the Central Committee's 1945 resolution on Party history.

This rewriting of Party history in the decade after Tsunyi created an aura of unquestioned rightfulness about Mao's leadership despite the earlier defeat. As noted earlier, the ability to establish such a sense of legitimacy is a highly important matter in both the Chinese political context and the Marxist–Leninist frame of reference. In each it is essential that "the leader" be able to identify himself with his organization's successes and, at the least, avoid being associated with its failures.[1] Beyond legitimizing his claim to Party leadership, however, the device of historical revision helped endow Mao with a charisma important in eliciting broad popular support outside the Communist movement. His image and legend were to become a significant factor in Communist success not only in the civil war, soon to be resumed in earnest, but also in the years after the seizure of power in 1949 as the Peking regime began the process of stabilizing its authority.[2]

[1] Lucian Pye argues that, while Chinese political culture has generally been conducive to the notion of authority and leaders of organizations such as the CCP have had considerable freedom to make substantive policy changes on their own, the rank-and-file's "readiness to have complete faith in the wisdom and judgements of the leadership" depends heavily on its ability to demonstrate success. In modern times "the few men who have achieved [national] popularity have quickly lost their appeal as soon as they were confronted with difficulties and setbacks." Lucian W. Pye, *The Spirit of Chinese Politics* (Cambridge, Mass.: M.I.T. Press, 1968) pp. 27, 123, 192.

[2] Alfred Meyer observes that revolutionary charisma arising out of acute social anomie is capable of engendering power, but that its transformation into a more

Despite these successes, Mao's manipulation of history to his own ends may have involved costs and potential dangers which have not been fully appreciated. Certainly, a price was paid in historical accuracy. If our analysis of the Fourth Plenum and Fukien Rebellion is correct—or even partially so, it brings into question the reliability of the whole official account of Mao's role in Kiangsi and suggests the need for a thorough reassessment of causes and responsibility for the CCP's defeat. In a larger sense, we may ponder whether Mao's tampering with the historical record revealed, at a comparatively early stage, significant weaknesses as well as strengths in his character as a leader. To be sure, he may well have exercised acute political foresight in finally demolishing Wang Ming's reputation and career. In building up the myth of his own infallibility, Mao may even have made a positive contribution to the eventual success of the Communist movement. However, we may question whether this attempt to rewrite history did not also betray a potentially dangerous blindness in evaluating his own subjective limitations and an inability to learn from his defeats. Does one hear echoes of the past today in the Cultural Revolution as an older Mao, denying any possibility of error in another major CCP disaster—the Great Leap Forward—insists with utopian unrealism that human willpower alone can dramatically reverse the circumstances of history if properly inspired and led?

stable basis of social control depends upon a "primitive accumulation of authority," a legitimation of the new ruling elite by means of persuasion as well as organization, rewards, and coercion. A. G. Meyer, "Authority in Communist Political Systems", in Lewis Edinger, ed., *Political Leadership in Industrialized Societies* (New York: John Wiley & Sons, 1967), pp. 88–91.

3

THE ROLES OF THE MONOLITHIC PARTY
UNDER THE TOTALITARIAN LEADER

LEONARD SCHAPIRO AND JOHN WILSON LEWIS

INTRODUCTION

In 1961 Robert C. Tucker argued, contrary to the then-prevailing assumption of the uniform nature of totalitarian systems, that such systems could be classified into several different types for purposes of analysis.[1] Subsequently H. Gordon Skilling applied interest group theory to his study of Communist politics and, by doing so, also called into question the case for regarding totalitarian governments as a single category of states possessing unique attributes.[2] Skilling asserted that Communist states cannot be considered "conflictless", as is sometimes assumed, but can be more adequately understood in terms of the competing social forces commonly found in non-Communist societies. Because of the special, but varying, limits imposed by a central leadership elite on the public expression of conflict in the several Communist-run countries, he added, Communist political parties could play special and quite diverse roles. His thesis contrasts with that of Carl J. Friedrich, which stresses the uniformity of the party's role under totalitarianism. According to Professor Friedrich in his discussion of "the unique character of totalitarian society", the presence of a single mass party is a common feature of all totalitarian politics, and is "typically either superior to, or completely commingled with, the bureaucratic organization".[3] While Friedrich in his later work, written jointly

[1] Robert C. Tucker, "Towards a Comparative Politics of Movement-Regimes", *American Political Science Review*, LV (June, 1961), 281–9, reprinted in *The Soviet Political Mind* (New York: Praeger, 1963), as chap. 1.

[2] H. Gordon Skilling, "Interest Groups and Communist Politics", *World Politics*, XVIII (April, 1966), 435–51. His thesis contrasts with that of Carl J. Friedrich, ed., *Totalitarianism* (Cambridge, Mass.: Harvard Univ. Press, 1954), p. 47.   [3] Friedrich, *Totalitarianism*, p. 53.

with Zbigniew K. Brzezinski, acknowledges that "within the broad pattern of similarities, there are many significant variations" in totalitarian dictatorships,[1] the authors' emphasis is on the novelty and uniqueness of these dictatorships. They state:[2] "...it is our contention in this volume that totalitarian dictatorship is historically unique and *sui generis*. It is also our contention from all the facts available to us that fascist and Communist totalitarian dictatorships are basically alike..." In this paper, the purpose of a comparison of several totalitarian systems is to challenge the view that with respect to parties under such systems a uniform or unique pattern can be discerned.

In his 1961 paper Tucker noted the historical existence of at least two polar types of Communist Party, as determined by the Party's relationship to the leader.[3] The first could be described as a *Bolshevik* party wherein a disciplined elite would be connected with a mass-following through an elaborate network of party cells. The other, the *führerist* type, would find the Party reduced to "the role of an important cog in the apparatus of the State" under the supreme leadership of a single leader. The distinction between these two types—when applied to the Soviet case—led Tucker to suggest:[4]

Very real and important issues affecting the understanding and interpretation of the political changes in Russia since Stalin's death are involved in what may seem to be a problem of merely historical interest. On the postulate of continuity of the Bolshevik movement-regime from 1917–1953, "significant change" will logically mean *away* from Bolshevism or Communism. This assumption results in a tendency to deprecate the significance of the post-Stalinist changes in Soviet political processes and policies. If, on the other hand, we operate on the premise that Stalin's political revolution from above transformed the original Bolshevik movement-regime into a new one that was fuehrerist in its inner dynamism and political tendency, we shall reason that when Stalin died in 1953 Bolshevism had been moribund in Russia for fifteen years, and that the main issue was whether it would revive and if so to what extent.

[1] Carl J. Friedrich and Zbigniew K. Brzezinski, *Totalitarian Dictatorship and Autocracy* (Cambridge, Mass.: Harvard Univ. Press, 1956), p. 10.

[2] *Ibid.* p. 5. See also *ibid.* pp. 27–39 on "The Nature and Role of the Party".

[3] Tucker, "Movement-Regimes", pp. 284, 288–9 (italics in original).

[4] *Ibid.* p. 389.

Though highly suggestive, this thesis has remained substantially unexplored. Nor has anyone seriously examined its implication that a totalitarian leader seeking supremacy may have to emasculate or even at times by-pass the party if he is to solidify his personal rule and bend the system to his will. Rather than serving as an instrument of the leader, this thesis suggests that a strong monolithic party may constitute an autonomous and competing power base with independent strengths that undermine rather than reinforce the power of the central leader.

HITLER, MUSSOLINI AND LENIN

Some attempt will now be made in the following few pages to examine some aspects of the usefulness of these terms *Bolshevism*, *führerism*, *monolithic* and *movement-regime* in the light of the experience of the main dictators of our generation—Lenin, Mussolini, Stalin, Hitler and Mao.

Leaving Stalin and Mao for later consideration, let us look at the contrasts in political origins of Lenin, Mussolini and Hitler. It was certainly the case that all three came to power as leaders of what should more properly be described as a "movement" than as a "party". At all events, the term "movement" seems more appropriate to those who accept the idea that the party as a political institution is designed to *compete* for power within a pluralist political system, and that what it seeks is inevitably and invariably a *share* of power, even if it be the predominant share. The Bolsheviks and the Nazis certainly competed within parliamentary regimes (Duma, Reichstag) for a share of power in the formal sense. But this was merely a step to the totality of power, in each case undertaken as a deliberate act of deception. Thus, Lenin prepared for the seizure of power by the Bolsheviks under the guise of an electoral victory which was to result in a coalition of all the Left-Wing parties. This was the firm belief of the overwhelming majority of delegates to the Second All-Russian Congress of Soviets.[1]

[1] See Ya. A. Yakovlev, ed., *Vtoroi vserossiisky syezd sovetov rabochikh i soldatskikh deputatov* (Leningrad, 1928), p. 107.

He kept up the pretence of forming a coalition as a temporizing device after the seizure of power to give the Bolsheviks time to consolidate their hold over the country a little more firmly;[1] and used the uneasy and quite unworkable coalition with the Left-Socialist Revolutionaries, which was doomed from the start, for the same end.[2] Hitler's scrupulous insistence on observing constitutional forms as a means of getting to power, before assuming full personal powers, is well known. Mussolini maintained the form of a multi-party system for two and a half years before eliminating all the opposition parties in January, 1925. The first use by Mussolini of the term "totalitario" (which Hitler, incidentally, only used pejoratively, and Lenin never used at all) only dates from a speech of June 22, 1925—i.e., some six months after the abolition of all opposition parties on January 3, 1925—in which he spoke of "la nostra feroce volontà totalitaria".[3]

"Movement" therefore seems quite properly applicable to the following built up by all three dictators. However, there was a fundamental distinction between the aims of Mussolini and Hitler on the one hand and of Lenin on the other, which was reflected in subsequent developments. Mussolini and Hitler were both concerned to impose the rule of their movements on an existing state structure, which they modified and dominated, but did not or could not destroy. Lenin, in contrast, inherited a political machine which had virtually disintegrated before he came to power. The Provisional Government in effect destroyed the entire administrative machine of the Imperial regime without ever succeeding in creating, let alone establishing, the new institutions which they were planning on

[1] See the Central Committee Minute of November, 1917, reprinted in *Proletarskaia Revoliutsiia*, No. 10 (1922), pp. 465–70. The discussion on coalition then in progress, according to Lenin, "should have been treated merely as diplomatic cover for military action".

[2] See Leonard Schapiro, *The Origin of the Communist Autocracy; Political Opposition in the Soviet State First Phase: 1917–1922* (London: Bell, for the London School of Economics and Political Science [University of London], 1955), chap. VII.

[3] Text in Edoardo e Duilio Susmel, ed., *Opera omnia di Benito Mussolini* (Florence: La Fenice, 1951–63), XXI, 357–64. The term was apparently coined by Mussolini. We are indebted for this information on the first use of "totalitario" to Dr Meir Michaelis.

paper.[1] This is one reason why it is possible to apply the term *führerism* to the form of leadership set up by Mussolini and Hitler, but not to that set up by Lenin. The first two dictators were primarily concerned to assert domination by their own corps of followers at all vital points in the state and social machinery— even if Mussolini's success in this respect in practice was far from complete. Their parties, or movements, were designed not so much for administration, as for bending the existing institutions of the administration, political and economic, to their will. Lenin, on the contrary, used his Bolshevik following in order to create and improvise new, rough and ready, *institutions* which were only allowed to exist and to function under the control and guidance of their Bolshevik elements—whether Soviets, trade unions or industrial enterprises.

But there is also a second reason why *führerism* cannot be applied to Lenin as it can to Mussolini and Hitler. The principle of leadership, obedience and personal devotion to the leader was an integral, open and avowed characteristic of both the Fascist and the National Socialist movements. This was not in any sense true of Bolshevism as built up by Lenin and, when introduced by Stalin, was an innovation in the Communist movement. No one would dispute that Lenin's leadership of the Bolsheviks and the discipline that he enforced was what distinguished Bolshevism from the Russian Social Democratic movement as a whole. During the period between the two revolutions, 1906–17, or at any rate up to 1912, it was often very difficult to describe a Bolshevik in terms other than that of a Social Democrat prepared to accept Lenin's leadership without question or doubt. Nevertheless Bolshevism grew out of a democratic, not an authoritarian, tradition, which recognized the right of discussion and, until 1921, of dissent in the Party.

It is therefore legitimate and necessary to employ a term other than *führerism* to describe the nature of Communist rule during Lenin's active lifetime, and *Bolshevism* is a convenient, shorthand term. The problems which faced Lenin were quite different from

[1] See Leonard Schapiro, "The Political Thought of the First Provisional Government", in Richard Pipes, ed., *Revolutionary Russia* (Cambridge, Mass.: Harvard Univ. Press, 1968), pp. 105–12.

those which confronted Mussolini and Hitler, and again different from those which confronted Stalin. Neither Mussolini nor Hitler faced serious problems, or problems which they could not easily solve, of maintaining discipline in their respective parties. They were thus able to use Party members for their purpose of enforcing, or trying to enforce, their personal will on the existing institutions—though, of course, Hitler was much more successful in this respect than Mussolini. Lenin faced, especially towards the end of the civil war in 1920, an entirely different problem. His as yet relatively undisciplined Party was torn by internal dissent, and was facing increasing competition for the allegiance of both peasants and workers from Socialists, who had still not been completely suppressed. Moreover, Communist Party members were beginning to acquire institutional allegiances which were in conflict with the centralized policy which Lenin thought fit to impose—the trade union Communists demanded a kind of Communist-controlled trade union syndicalism, freed from the discipline of the Party centre; the Communists in the Soviets demanded independent power for the Soviets—under their own control, of course, but again free from the discipline dictated by the centre. There were many more instances of this type of almost anarchist libertarianism (libertarianism, of course, only for the Communists) during 1920 and 1921. By the spring of 1921 the position was rendered critical for the Communist Party by widespread strikes among workers, guerrilla war among the peasants, and by the Kronstadt revolt.

Lenin's methods of dealing with this situation, in which the survival of Communist rule, or at all events monopoly of rule, was under threat, must be seen in the light of these circumstances. The means which he adopted—the strengthening of the central machinery for control over the Party, the final forcible suppression of the Socialists and the elimination of dissent inside the Communist Party—are open to two main criticisms. First, that in putting the preservation of monopoly of Communist power before everything else he destroyed the democratic tradition within the Communist Party; and secondly, that in creating a "monolithic" party he laid the foundations on which Stalin was able to build his *führerist* party. There is truth in both these criticisms of Lenin's failure to see far enough into the future. But there are at least four reasons why the term *führerist* is not applicable to the Soviet Communist Party during Lenin's active lifetime. In the first place, the measures adopted in 1921 were supported by the great majority of Party members who realized that the alternative was at best sharing power with the Socialists, and at worst being swept away by popular dissatisfaction. Secondly, for all the rigid central discipline imposed by Lenin, the institutions of the Party were not destroyed and continued to function with some degree of vigour and genuine debate. Thirdly, Lenin never sought to set himself up as leader, to exact any personal adulation or to assert any kind of personal domination or ambition. And finally, since Lenin was out of action by early 1923, before the emergency which had produced the measures of the end of 1920 and of March, 1921 was over, the hope remained alive that the restrictions imposed were only temporary and would be lifted when better times returned.[1]

In sum: no one would deny that Lenin dominated his Party and used all means available to him to assert and to preserve his domination—at any rate until 1922. (It is possibly significant that during 1922, when Lenin was already being pushed aside by Stalin and Zinoviev, he made no really serious effort to reassert himself—though this could be explained by ill-health or disillusionment, or both). Nevertheless, the Party still retained under Lenin the recognizable contours of an institution—with its organs, its rules and its procedures. One has only to contrast 1921–2 with the position after 1936. By that date the Party ceases to have the contours of an institution at all: it is little more than an aggregate name for the individuals composing it, with the power of those individuals in turn depending almost entirely on their relations to Stalin.

The use made of their parties by Mussolini, Hitler and Stalin (after he had defeated his rivals and established his personal rule) was quite different. Mussolini's avowed aim was to use the Party,

---

[1] For a more detailed discussion of this problem see *The Origin of the Communist Autocracy* (cited above—p. 117, footnote 2), chaps. XIV–XVIII; and Leonard Schapiro, "Lenin after Fifty Years", in Leonard Schapiro and Peter Reddaway, eds., *Lenin: The Man, the Theorist, the Leader; A Reappraisal* (London: Pall Mall Press, 1967), pp. 3–22.

integrated into the state after 1926,[1] for the purpose of creating a "totalitarian" society in which all institutions were integrated in unity and harmonized in one will and purpose under his own leadership. He completely failed, and the Fascist regime remained a ramshackle conglomeration of discordant elements held together by some degree of terror. The monarchy retained its independence as an institution of which the legitimacy and continuity owed nothing to fascism.[2] The Church, if cautious and at times accommodating, never surrendered its spiritual supremacy. Fascism failed to dominate either the army or even the police.[3] For all his talk of "totalitarianism" as a doctrine, Mussolini failed much more than either Hitler or Stalin (who had no use for the term) to achieve it in practice.

Hitler's rule as leader, whose authority was "constitutionally" recognized as having the force of law, was in many ways much more independent of the Party than Mussolini's (or for that matter Stalin's until at any rate 1936–9). It was significant that, in Nazi doctrine, the glorification of the "totalitarian" state was a mere tactical device, and was abandoned after 1934 in favour of the glorification of the leader.[4] Hitler himself referred to the nature of National Socialist rule as "*autoritär*".[5] At any rate, until after the total mobilization brought about by the war, a considerable degree of independence remained in the Army, the bureaucracy and in industry. But the Party had supreme authority over the police, and the personal authority of Hitler made it possible for him to interfere arbitrarily at any point in society much more effectively than

[1] See the text of the Statute of the party of 1926, reprinted in Alberto Aquarone, *L'Organizzazione dello Stato Totalitario* (Turin: G. Einaudi, 1965), pp. 386–92.

[2] "Dramma della diarchia", as Mussolini described it after his fall. See "Storia di un anno", in *Opera Omnia* (cited on p. 117, footnote 3), XXXIV, 406–16. And cf. Mussolini writing to Himmler on October 11, 1942: "There are three of us in Rome: myself, the King and the Pope", quoted in F. W. Deakin, *The Brutal Friendship: Mussolini, Hitler and the Fall of Italian Fascism* (London: Weidenfeld & Nicolson, 1962), p. 55.

[3] See *The Brutal Friendship*, p. 329.

[4] See Franz Neumann, *Behemoth; the Structure and Practice of National Socialism 1933–1944* (New York: Harper Torchbooks, Harper & Row, 1966), pp. 62–5.

[5] There is no mention of the totalitarian state in *Mein Kampf*.

Mussolini. After the beginning of the war the direct authority of the Party was much more widely extended, and in particular its control was asserted over both the administration and over industry.[1] But this was a measure of the emergency conditions created by the increasing difficulties caused by the war, the new problems created by the occupied territories, the novel plans for the extermination of the Jews and for the mobilization of foreign slave labour and so forth, which the ordinary administration and the Army could not be expected to deal with. The fact that the Party was thus able to increase its control in an emergency was a measure of the Führer's authority and of the efficiency of the Party-controlled terror machine which had already existed before.

The case of Stalin at the height of his power was parallel in two respects. Like Hitler, the real source of all authority in practice if not in theory lay in himself. Secondly, the real strength of the Party as an instrument lay in the fact that Stalin had used the years between his accession to power and the end of the purges (1924–38) to transform the movement which Lenin had bequeathed to him, into something which approximated much more to the personal elite corps of adherents which the Fascist and Nationalist Socialist parties represented. Moreover, like Mussolini and Hitler, Stalin was concerned to assert his own supreme domination over a state which already had its institutions as created by Lenin after the Bolsheviks had come to power. Like Hitler he had faced and eliminated serious opposition in the Party, in the Army and elsewhere, though it had taken him many more years and much more bloodshed to do so. It is not therefore surprising that the Communist Party should have become, after 1938 and again after the end of the war, until Stalin's death in 1953, much more an instrument for effecting the personal domination of the leader than a revolutionary elite exercising a monopoly of rule.

STALIN'S RULE

It took Stalin thirteen years (from 1923 to 1936) to defeat the opposition with which he was faced within the Party leadership.

[1] See Neumann, *Behemoth*, pp. 468–9 and 530.

He then spent a further two years completing a mammoth purge of the entire Party membership in which some three-quarters of Central Committee members and certainly over a million of rank-and-file Party members either perished or were herded into concentration camps. It seems that after this operation he felt confident enough of Party loyalty to himself, at any rate until 1952, when a further Party purge was apparently in contemplation, and only cut short by his death.

It would not therefore have been surprising if Stalin, after the use of such methods (which far exceeded anything that Hitler and Mussolini had regarded as necessary to inflict on their parties), had found himself with a Party on which he felt he could rely to carry out his will. Yet nothing of the kind resulted. Stalin's form of Party rule, so far from being an enhanced form of Party rule as compared with that of Lenin, was in fact an emasculated and more limited form of Party authority than had been in existence before.

The most obvious symptom of this emasculation was the virtual atrophy of the functioning of regular Party organs. No Party congress met between 1939 and 1952. The Central Committee Plenum was not summoned for years on end. If Khrushchev's account is to be believed (and there is no reason to doubt it in this respect) even the Politburo seldom met as a full body, and was replaced by *ad hoc* meetings of two or three of the top leaders summoned at will by Stalin to take a decision. At the lower levels, meetings of Party organs were somewhat more regular. But since these had long become purely formalized instances for the endorsement of directives issued by the central Party apparatus, their existence did not add very much to the reality of the Party institutions. It is curious to note that the most regular persistence of the functioning of Party organs, in the later years of Stalin's life, took place in the Ukraine where Khrushchev was First Secretary of the Party. It is possible that this was due to the greater respect for the formalities of Party institutional life which Khrushchev was later to display after Stalin's death. It is also possible, as has been suggested, that this was a deliberate policy encouraged by Stalin in order to prevent so important an area as the Ukraine "from falling under the domination of a single pro-consul, who might have used it as the base for opposition" to him.[1]

There were other indications in the later years of Stalin's rule of this relative eclipse of the Party as the supreme institution of power at the central level. During the war, for example, by a decree of June 30, 1941, all power was concentrated in a newly created body—the State Committee for Defence (GOKO), with Stalin as Chairman. This Committee seems to have been designed to concentrate the best talent available in all the hierarchies—whether administrative or Party—and members of the Politburo (like Molotov) sat side by side with younger men who had acquired a reputation for their administrative talent, outside the Party hierarchy, like N. A. Voznesensky, the economist. GOKO acted in the provinces through plenipotentiaries who had the authority to override local Party and Soviet officials. There were also some local city GOKOs, whose chairman was invariably the local Party first secretary, but whose membership reflected the search for the best administrative talent, rather than the predominance of the Party as an institution.[2]

The rising prestige and influence of the economic directors were also reflected in a marked manner in the membership of the Central Committee elected at the Nineteenth Congress in 1952. However unimportant the Central Committee may by that date have become as an effective institution, membership of it was still a vital index of status in the hierarchy. The membership of the 1952 Party Praesidium (as the Politburo was renamed at the Nineteenth Congress) also reflected the growing importance of the technical leaders to an extent never reflected before in the membership of this body. Its numbers were considerably enlarged—a fact which gave rise to rumours (which were later given authority by Khrushchev in his speech in closed session to the Twentieth Party Congress in 1956) that Stalin's real intention in bringing in the new men had been to use them in order to get rid of and replace the older Politburo

[1] John A. Armstrong, *The Soviet Bureaucratic Elite; A Case Study of the Ukranian Apparatus* (New York: Praeger, 1959), p. 149.
[2] John A. Armstrong, *The Politics of Totalitarianism; The Communist Party of the Soviet Union from 1934 to the Present* (New York: Random House, 1961), pp. 134–5.

members. Certainly very few of them remained members of the Praesidium for any length of time after Stalin's death.[1]

Thus one of the effects of the rise of Stalin as a personal dictator was to diminish the role of the Party as an institution. Another was to blur the predominance in national leadership of the Party leaders in relation to the state or administrative leaders. The latter was much less true at the local levels, where the Party remained the predominant element in the administration. This was certainly true up to the period which is covered by the archive of the Smolensk Party organization—that is to say, up to 1938. At the regional and district levels in the later thirties it was invariably the local Party secretary who determined who was to be elected to the leading organs of the local Soviet administration, and laid down every step that was to be followed. It seems less certain that this situation persisted in quite such a marked degree in the period between the end of the war and Stalin's death in 1953. At any rate a study of the local Party conferences which preceded the All-Russian Party Congress in 1952 reveals an intense preoccupation by union-republican Party leaders to re-create or preserve some autonomy of action by the local Soviet administrative authorities.[2] There is no doubt at all that this uniformity in the union republics was the result of a directive from the centre. Such directives were not new, and indeed were quite consistent with Stalin's personal style of rule. Since all ultimate decision was concentrated in him it was a natural preoccupation for him to ensure the perpetuation of rival and dual instances of authority. Each could then watch the other, and moreover no decision of importance could be enforced at the local level without appeal to the centre, over which he maintained his ever-watchful control.

There were three other factors which made it possible for Stalin to ensure that no institution, whether the Party or any other, could build up any rival instance of authority to challenge his own. One was the dictator's tolerance of the most distinctive feature of

[1] Merle Fainsod, *How Russia is Ruled* (rev. ed.; Cambridge, Mass.: Harvard Univ. Press, 1963), pp. 323–7.

[2] Merle Fainsod, *Smolensk Under Soviet Rule* (Cambridge, Mass.: Harvard Univ. Press, 1958), p. 93. The reports of the union-republican party conferences can be studied in the Russian-language newspapers published in the capital of each union republic, beginning in the third week of September.

Soviet rule at all periods—the local clique. This took, and takes, the form of an alliance at the local levels of groups of leading officials in the various institutions—Party, police, procuracy, administration, etc.—who build up a kind of mutual aid and protection society, which cuts across the official institutions and their hierarchies, and enables all power to be concentrated, as it were, in a kind of Mafia, in a privileged group which can keep others out. These local cliques provide for a time a method of defence against the centre since they represent, as it were, a pooling of the personal influence which each member of the clique can exercise at the centre through his own personal connections. Their existence explains why the nature of the Soviet power structure must primarily be studied in terms of the kind of personal allegiances which powerful officials —whether of the Party or the administration—build up during their term of office. These personal allegiances are reflected in the subsequent promotions of members of the clique when one of their number succeeds in securing promotion to the centre of power in Moscow. But this aspect of Soviet politics would take us too far away from our subject. So far as the period of Stalin's later years of rule was concerned, the "clique" system had the advantage for him that it prevented any one institution, including the Party, from acquiring excessive power, or the kind of individual institutional allegiance which local parties had developed under Lenin. Of course, every now and again Stalin found it desirable to break up a group so as both to put an end to the corruption which they generated, and to ensure that they should not develop any sense of independence or security. But while they lasted they effectively prevented any predominance of Party institutions as entities with any kind of independence.

The second factor which prevented any kind of real Party supremacy during Stalin's period of ascendency was that neither at the local nor at the central level did the Party exercise control over the security organs—as happened in the early years of the Soviet regime, and as has happened again since 1953. Stalin retained personal control over his police at the centre. This was effected outside the machinery of the Central Secretariat, which is the general staff of the Party. Within this Secretariat Stalin maintained his own secret personal secretariat, probably identical with the Secret Department, which operated quite independently of the Central Committee Secretariat which he, Stalin, of course, also controlled. The heads of this personal secretariat were some of the most powerful men in the Soviet hierarchy—Tovstukha, Malenkov and Poskrebyshev among them. With their aid Stalin was able to use the security organs against the other institutions, including the Party, the Army and the administration. But, even more important, he was able, when he thought it necessary, to direct the edge of the purge against the secret police itself—as he did, for example, in 1938–9.

This leads to the third factor which characterized Stalin's rule—the clique or Mafia system at the very top. We have already drawn attention to the fact that Stalin avoided the risk of opposition forming to him in the Politburo by circumventing this body as a body, and taking decisions in *ad hoc* committees of two or three selected leaders. Parallel with this technique of government was his use of agents of personal rule in addition to his all-powerful personal secretaries, to operate outside the framework of the Party and state institutions. Notable among such were Vyshinsky, first Procurator General and then Chairman of the Legal Institute of the Communist Academy; and Shcherbatov, at one time Chairman of the Commission of Party Control. These men, and some others, played leading roles, under Stalin's personal direction, in the operation of the purges and the concomitant terror and achieved for him a degree of personal power which he could hardly have achieved through the medium of the Party as a fully institutionalized machine.

THE LEADER AND THE COMMISSAR IN CHINA

Turning to the Chinese case, an examination of the last thirty years of Communist history would show that at the outset of the Yenan period (1935–49) at least two different types of Communist parties existed.[1] This fact in the early revolutionary background of Chinese

[1] This section is based on Lewis, "Leader, Commissar and Bureaucrat", in Ping-ti Ho and Tang Tsou, eds., *China in Crisis; China's Heritage and the Communist Political System* (Chicago: Univ. of Chicago Press, 1968), 1, 449–81.

Communists by itself creates a sharp contrast with the totalitarian parties just described.

Operating in the relative safety of the Communist-controlled "red base areas", Mao Tse-tung laboured to build one type of leadership system in which his will was supreme. As Party Chairman, he stressed the creation of a direct relationship between his ideas and the general populace and denigrated the role of bureaucratic organization. On the other hand, in the Japanese- or KMT-occupied areas, powerful organization held the key to survival of the guerrilla movement. Here, the evidence suggests, Liu Shao-ch'i, among other top political commissars, emerged as a principal leader and within these more dangerous combat areas devised a more Leninist concept of Party structure and operation. Liu in particular commanded important elements of the Party apparatus and later insinuated them into the state structure with his key lieutenants assuming dual roles in both Party and state.[1] While Mao and Liu each in his own area built up a special type of Party organization, they seem to have worked harmoniously in joint operations, referring to each other's work with praise and approval.[2] During the *cheng-feng* campaign of 1942–4, moreover, the potentially complementary components of their two networks were explicitly emphasized and made to reinforce one another.

Doctrinally speaking, Mao's "mass-line" merged with Liu's principles of organization during this 1942–4 rectification campaign. As a tacit compromise, Liu adapted Party organization to "the thought of Mao Tse-tung" and gave Mao chief credit for Communist successes, while Mao placed increasing emphasis on the cadre apparatus and on the importance of explicit regulations and discipline for the guidance of the movement. By unifying operational structures throughout the Communist base areas the Yenan leadership attained centralization of authority while preserving substantial local autonomy, though each of the two networks within the Communist movement seems to have maintained a degree of its former

[1] For a discussion of the important December 9th Group associated with Liu, see the essay by Donald Klein, pp. 356–7.

[2] Mao, for example, mentions Liu in thirteen places in his *Selected Works*. The earliest reference is in November, 1938. See *Index to Selected Works of Mao Tse-tung* (Hong Kong: Union Research Institute, 1968), p. 93.

identity and apparently preserved the special characteristics of its own distinct power structure that had existed before 1942.

The now obvious fragility of the compromise should not lead us to the conclusion too quickly that the resultant amalgamation of the two networks after 1944 merely masked a factionalized Communist Party. Indeed, the compromise seems to have been quite real for the central leadership and worked well until the crisis following the failure of the Great Leap Forward after 1960. The scope of that failure upset the former balance and highlighted and intensified the latent, though long dormant, disagreement within the ageing leadership. The issue, naturally enough, was the definition of the pre-*cheng feng* revolutionary line or, at least the choice of which aspects of that line would be transmitted to the younger successor generation of leaders. In this context the distinctive qualities of the two types of parties became increasingly evident thereafter. Finally, under the impact of the Cultural Revolution in 1966, the long compromise was dramatically ruptured, and the Communist system in China once again had to contend with two types of parties, one close to the *führerist* type and the other approximating the Bolshevik type, in the sense described above. Drawing on the many statements released since that rupture, the following paragraphs will analyse the Party system that has been emerging, particularly in the early 1968 phase of the Cultural Revolution.

ATTACKS ON LIU AND THE COMMISSARS

Although it is probably unfair to give unqualified credence to the extreme accusations against Liu Shao-ch'i made by his foes in the Cultural Revolution, the range of accusations made does indicate the specific attributes of the old Party system that the Maoists have ascribed to Liu and now oppose. Their opposition has been expressed in terms of a movement to repudiate Liu's "Party-building line" and to replace it with the line of Mao Tse-tung.[1] Two of Liu's

[1] For major statements on the Maoist view of Liu Shao-ch'i's "Party-building line", see, for example, *Wen hui pao* [Cultural Exchange News], November 26 and December 28, 1967 and January 8 and 16, 1968; *Jen min jih pao* [People's Daily], November 18, 1967; *Chieh fang jih pao* [Liberation Daily], November 22 and December 6, 1967 and February 25, 1968; *Chieh fang chün pao* [Liberation Army Daily], article in *New China News Agency* [*NCNA*], October 25, 1967;

most prominent writings, "How to be a Good Communist" (1939)[1] and "On Inner-Party Struggle" (1941)[2] stand out in this denunciation movement. The outstanding characteristic of both these writings is Liu's preoccupation with organization, and it is alleged that for the sake of the organization Liu sacrificed Mao's political line and in general demeaned the "thought of Mao".

There seems to be no doubt that Liu did in fact attempt to build a professional, Leninist Party that could meet all threats to its survival and, to that end, adjusted the Party-building policies and tasks of the Party to meet all contingencies. It was Liu's type of Party that Mao referred to as a model for the white areas and cities in 1945,[3] and that prompted Chou En-lai's comment in 1967 that, in the ten years after the Tsunyi conference, "Liu was considered a model for his work in the white areas".[4] After the take-over in 1949, Liu approved the transformation of the Party into an instrument for China's modernization. Although the Maoist press has argued that Liu subverted the Party to his own purposes, what Mao seems to have abhorred most is the independence and degree of autonomy attained by those in the Party apparatus who adhered to Liu's "organizational concept". In January, 1968, for example, *New Anhwei Daily* described Liu's adherents in terms of "factionalism" because they had become divorced from Mao whose word is now equated to mean the "leadership of the masses".[5] Picking up a

NCNA, January 18, 21 and 30, 1968; and Shanghai Radio, November 17, 1967.

[1] Liu, *How to be a Good Communist* (Peking: Foreign Languages Press, n.d.). For the English translation of the 1962 revised edition, see Liu, *How to be a Good Communist* (Peking: Foreign Languages Press, 1964). For typical articles on this work, see *Current Background*, No. 827.

[2] Liu, *On Inner-Party Struggle* (Peking: Foreign Languages Press, n.d.). For typical recent criticism of this book, see *Kuang ming jih pao* [Bright Daily], April 7, 1967, in *Survey of China Mainland Press* [*SCMP*], No. 3923, pp. 4–8.

[3] See Mao's comments on Liu's "model" work in the white areas in "Appendix: Resolution on Certain Questions in the History of our Party", *Selected Works*, III, 198, 202, 203.

[4] *Hung chan pao* [Red Combat Bulletin], No. 15, November 29, 1967, pp. 1, 4 in *Joint Publications Research Service*, No. 44,574 (March 4, 1968), p. 28.

[5] Quoted on Hofei Radio, January 18, 1968. For text of *Jen min jih pao*, January 1, 1968 editorial see *Peking Review*, No. 1 (January 3, 1968), pp. 10–13. The campaign against factionalism may well have allowed supporters of Liu Shao-ch'i to return to power in Hopei province. Also on factionalism, see

theme of the New Year's Day editorial of *People's Daily*, this news-paper added, "When you are blinded by factionalism and have doubts about the decisions, instructions, and calls issued by the proletarian headquarters, headed by Chairman Mao, the sinister hand of the enemy stealthily reaches into your ranks to stir up trouble." The "most outstanding symptom of this factionalism", the editorial continued, was "exclusionism" whereby the Party apparatus becomes oriented to specific functions and tasks rather than to the supreme will of Mao.

Liu Shao-ch'i's "exclusionism" is traced in Red Guards' posters to personal corruption and, more fundamentally, to his impure class status. Such accusations have proved to be important because Mao technically headed the Party during the years that it fell under Liu's influence. The problem is to castigate the Party as an "evil instrument" without damning Chairman Mao at the same time. It is also necessary to preserve a minimum measure of Party authority in order to keep the bulk of its cadres loyal to Mao in the future.[1] Liu's influence is thus traced to a series of secret plots ranging from the formation of his personal power clique in 1936,[2] to his bureaucratic responses to all recent threats made to the Party's integrity and stability.[3] As examples of the latter, during the

Tientsin Radio, February 3 and 4, 1968; *Jen min jih pao*, January 25, 26 and February 5, 26, 1968; and *NCNA*, February 4, 1968. On factionalism in general, see as a sample of the many articles and broadcasts in this period *Wen hui pao*, January 12, 16, 1968 (as found in Shanghai Radio, January 11, 16, 28, 1968) and February 17, 1968 (Shanghai Radio, February 16, 1968); Hupeh Radio, January 31, 1968; *Hei lung chiang jih pao* [Heilungkiang Daily], January 23, 1968 in Harbin Radio, January 31, 1968; Hofei Radio, February 1, 1968; and Huhetot Radio, February 4, 1968.

[1] There has been a consistent emphasis on "trusting and relying on the majority of cadres". See, for example, *NCNA*, October 23, 1967, in *SCMP*, No. 4052, pp. 9–12; and next footnote.

[2] For a statement on Liu's building a personal machine in the Party, see the pamphlet "Down with Liu Shao-ch'i—Life of Counter-revolutionary Liu Shao-ch'i", by Ching-kang-shan Fighting Corps of the Fourth Hospital Peking, dated May, 1967 in *Current Background*, No. 834, p. 4; the pamphlet by the Peking Railway Institute of April, 1967, in *Selections from China Mainland Magazines* [hereafter *SCMM*], No. 591, p. 17; and *Hung ch'i*, No. 13 (1967), p. 25.

[3] For a rigorous review of these guidelines in parts of the Communist system,

"four clean-ups" movement in 1964 and the Cultural Revolution in schools during the "50 days" in 1966,[1] Liu allegedly dispatched Party work teams to smother the mass movement under the weight of Party bureaucrats and to prevent potential radicals from becoming too disruptive to the social order. In his first confession of October 26, 1966 Liu reportedly said:[2]

One wrong decision I made, for example, was the decision that a work team would be dispatched at the request of the various central ministerial committees and the Chinese Young Communist League headquarters... [W]hen the work teams were dispatched, they immediately adopted the method of suppressing the masses. For example, they banned the masses from going out in the streets to demonstrate and to put up wall newspapers; they also demanded a clear distinction between external and internal affairs.

In addition to insulating and protecting state and Party organizations from the activities of "Leftist" youth, Liu purportedly worked to divert the "revolution" to activities that would further consolidate state power and support programmes for production. The final gasp of the bureaucracy's response to the Cultural Revolution is described as a programme of "economism" through which the Party bureaucrats deliberately bribed workers to "lure them away" from the Maoist path.[3] By such methods Liu and his lieutenants are said to have given priority to national development and the programmes of professionalization of the elite, including the Army, at the expense of political indoctrination and struggle.[4]

see A. Doak Barnett, *Cadres, Bureaucracy, and Political Power in Communist China* (New York: Columbia Univ. Press, 1967).

[1] The "50 days" ran from early June to the third week in July, 1966. In his first attack on Liu, Mao said: "...in the last fifty days or so some leading comrades from the central down to the local levels have acted in a diametrically opposite way. Adopting the reactionary stand of the bourgeoisie, they have enforced a bourgeois dictatorship and struck down the surging movement of the great Cultural Revolution of the proletariat." Mao Tse-tung, "Bombard the Headquarters" (August 5, 1966), in *Peking Review*, No. 33 (August 11, 1967), p. 5.

[2] *Mainichi*, January 28, 1968.

[3] For a representative collection of articles on "economism", see *Current Background*, No. 818.

[4] On professionalism ("regularization and modernization") in the Army, see *Chieh fang chün pao*, August 30, 1967, in Peking Radio, August 30, 1967.

Liu is thus accused of paying little attention to the class purity of the Party, making it into a "hodgepodge" of class elements rather than into a proletarian "vanguard".[1] According to one Red Guards' leaflet Liu admitted that many had joined the Party to "find an outlet chiefly because they could find no [other] outlet in society— they have no job, no work and no schooling or they wanted to free themselves from family bondages or pre-arranged marriages".[2] By his approval of a broad-gauged recruitment policy Liu allegedly helped propagate the doctrine of the "Party of the whole people", a doctrine that had long been denounced as a central plank in Khrushchev's revisionist programme.[3]

This resulted in a downgrading of class criteria in the Party and a shift to bureaucratic control mechanisms to keep all new members in line. Coercion replaced rectification as the means to prevent them from reverting to habits learnt as members of hostile classes. Liu used the administrative and disciplinary machinery of the Party to mould the diverse recruits into a solid force and purportedly found it necessary to stress the absolute obedience or slavishness of all Party members. Even the principal internal publication of the Party on organizational behaviour, *Chih pu sheng huo (Branch Life)*, was used by Liu for shaping the rigid bureaucratic organization.[4] In sum Liu wanted "docile tools", robots religiously obeying the edicts of superiors and maintaining "peace"

[1] On the question of "impure" class elements in the Party see, for example, the pamphlet of the Peking Railway Institute, April, 1967, in *SCMM*, No. 591, p. 10; and the article on the proletarian dictatorship and China's Khrushchev in *Jen min jih pao*, August 26, 1967.

[2] Text of Red Guards' leaflet in *SCMM*, No. 591, p. 10. See also *Wen hua ko ming t'ung hsün* [Cultural Revolution Bulletin], No. 11 (1967) in *SCMM*, No. 599, p. 21. Teng Hsiao-p'ing made this statement at the Eighth Party Congress: "[N]owadays...it is easy to find people who have joined the Party for the sake of prestige and position" ("Report on the Revision of the Constitution", *Eighth National Congress of the Communist Party of China* (Peking: Foreign Languages Press, 1956), I, 209. Similar statements by Liu hardly suggest approval of such motives for joining the Party.

[3] For the standard Maoist treatment of this subject, see *The Polemic on the General Line of the International Communist Movement* (Peking: Foreign Languages Press, 1965), pp. 453–9.

[4] On *Branch Life*, see reference to it in *SCMM*, No. 603, p. 28, and No. 604, p. 25.

among themselves. These were the principal themes relevant to Liu's "Party line" in the denunciation of the deposed Party official during and following the Twelfth Plenum in October, 1968.[1]

At the core of the Party apparatus was the personal group Liu reportedly had gathered together in the years after 1936.[2] This elite group allegedly manipulated Party decisions through its control of communications and gave the Communist Party its bureaucratic, machine-like character. Because Mao found it difficult to attack the Party cadres as such he has emphasized the evils of this faction and traced the failings of the Party bureaucracy to the machinations of Liu and his group. Liu and the senior cadres are now depicted as men of incurable ambition whose corruption knew no bounds. Liu is even said to have wanted to replace Mao as the supreme leader and to have his works rank on the level of Marx himself.[3] Tainted by such ambition, Liu's past, once the subject of public praise, currently symbolizes total degradation.[4] Blame is heaped on Liu for every past defeat in the Party's history whether it was the victory of Chiang Kai-shek in the power struggle of 1927 or the near fatal hesitation of the Communists to take the initiative at the end of World War II. In this latter case Liu is charged with cowardice and "capitulationism" for his willingness to make a deal with Chiang and to change the Communist Party into a bourgeois-type parliamentary body.[5]

Men of power surrounding Liu Shao-ch'i could not have avoided being corrupted by him, according to the logic of the Red Guards. Thus it is not surprising to see the Maoists condemn those cadres associated with Liu for enjoying special privileges. Although Mao has accused only a "minority" of such failings,[6] the many stories of

[1] See, for example, *NCNA*, October 16, 1968; *Wen hui pao*, November 7, 1968; and *Jen min jih pao*, November 11, 1968.

[2] See above, p. 128, footnote 2 and p. 130, footnote 5. It is important to keep in mind that many of these accusations against Liu may be false or highly exaggerated.

[3] *Wen hua ko ming t'ung hsün*, No. 11 (1967), in *SCMM*, No. 599, p. 25.

[4] For a chronicle of Liu's history as seen by the Red Guards, see *Current Background*, No. 834.

[5] Peking Radio, November 17, 1967; and *Hung ch'i*, No. 13 (1967), pp. 49–50.

[6] Conversely Liu is said to have attacked the "majority" (or "suspected all") in his attempt to preserve his standing. See, for example, *P'i T'ao chan pao*

improper cadre behaviour during the first seventeen years of Communist rule deliberately give the impression that these failings were widespread. From the lowest levels, for example, come such stories as that of the West Peking Ch'eng-tzu Coal Mines in which the cadres insulated themselves from the senior leaders and ran the mines as a small kingdom or "Party outside the Party".[1] The cadres in this unit allegedly exploited and even executed workers, took liberties with the women workers and participated in all manner of "counter-revolutionary" activities with the help of local landlords. Meanwhile corrupt practices are also said to have been rampant among Liuist members of the central elite. Exclusive boarding schools were set up for the children of cadres,[2] and elite members of the cadre force reportedly were allowed to join a plush playboy-type club outside of Peking.[3] More widespread yet was a general attitude of "egoism" fostered, it is said, by the emphasis on self-cultivation in Liu Shao-ch'i's *How to be a Good Communist*. If the accusations against this book are valid,[4] Liu promoted careerism throughout the bureaucracy and promised the Party members huge rewards for small or temporary sacrifices.[5]

The lengths to which the Party under Liu went to preserve its privileged position and independence are also, of course, portrayed

[Criticize T'ao Combat Bulletin], No. 7 (April 10, 1967), in *SCMP*, No. 3962, pp. 1–5; and *Jen min jih pao*, April 2 and 4, 1967.

[1] *Huan ch'iu chih* [The Whole World is Red], No. 2 (June 27, 1967), pp. 1–3 (in *Joint Publications Research Service*, No. 41, 514, pp. 1–11). For another example, see *Hsüan chiao chan pao* [Combat Bulletin of the Communications System of Hsüan wu ch'ü Party Committee], May 26, 1967, in *SCMP*, No. 4051, pp. 8–11.

[2] *Ch'un lei* [Spring Thunder], No. 4 (April 13, 1967), in *SCMP*, No. 3940, pp. 6–15.

[3] *T'ien an men* [Gate of Heavenly Peace], No. 2 (March, 1967), in *SCMM*, No. 576, pp. 4–7.

[4] A collection of comments on this book can be found in *Current Background*, No. 827. For a typical discussion of egoism, see *Hung ch'i*, No. 15 (1967), p. 16.

[5] See above, p. 130, footnote 5. *Jen min jih pao*, November 18, 1967 stated that Liu "shamelessly advocated: 'the idea of gaining a little to lose a lot and of losing a little to gain a lot' conforms with the 'proletarian world outlook of Marxism–Leninism.' He also wantonly clamoured: 'It is not all public interest without self-interest; there should be room for self-interest in complete devotion to public interest; equal consideration should be given to both public and self-interest, placing public interest before self-interest'."

by tales of horror ranging from the imprisonment and torture of Maoists in Szechwan[1] to the setting up of mental hospitals for political suspects.[2] Confined to concentration camps or mental hospitals, persistent opponents of the bureaucracy are described as having been totally cut off from all outside communication, the extreme victims of the Party's insulation from the will of Mao.

This pervasive attitude of selfishness and isolation from Mao's leadership ideals is said to have influenced the writing of the Party constitution at the Eighth Party Congress in 1956. In preparing this document, Liu and others are accused of maliciously deleting all references to the "thought of Mao" from the final draft and giving undue emphasis to the role of the Party organization.[3] Indeed the part of Teng Hsiao-p'ing's 1956 report on the constitution dealing with the "cult of personality" is said to typify the Liuist attempt to turn the Party towards revisionism.[4] The suggestion for deleting the reference to Mao's thought apparently is traced to the discredited former head of the Army, P'eng Te-huai, and he and Liu Shao-ch'i are accused of having "prepared a secret report against Chairman Mao Tse-tung similar to the report prepared by Khrushchev against Stalin".[5] By camouflaging the attack on Mao in terms of de-Stalinization and the "cult of personality" and by having their views incorporated into the revised constitution, the Liuists thereafter could openly publicize their position as one dictated by the Party's regulations and rules.[6] In this third confession or self-criticism on August 1, 1967, Liu reportedly has acknowledged his errors in helping to draft the 1956 Party constitution in this way:[7]

[1] Kweiyang Radio, June 17 and 23, and July 7, 1967.

[2] See, for example, the story of the mental hospital in which various political attitudes were treated as mental disorders in the pamphlet " 'Maniacs' of the New Era", compiled by the Editorial Department of the Revolutionary Rebels of the Chinese Academy of Sciences, in *SCMM*, Nos. 602, 603 and 604.

[3] On the Party constitution, see *Pa erh wu chan pao* [August 25 Battle News], February 14, 1967, in *SCMM*, No. 574, p. 15; *Ching kang shan* [Chingkang Mountains], February 15, 1967, in *SCMP*, No. 3908, pp. 2–3.   [4] *Idem*.

[5] See *Ko ti t'ung hsün* [Correspondence from All Parts of the Country], No. 4 (September 13, 1967), in *SCMP*, No. 4081, p. 7; and *Pei ching jih pao* [Peking Daily], August 7, 1967, as given in *Tanyug* (Belgrade), August 6, 1967.

[6] *Jen min jih pao*, November 18, 1967.

[7] *Mainichi*, August 3, 1967. See also *Sankei*, August 2, 1967.

"Furthermore, my report speech to the Eighth Congress and its resolution were wrong and fell behind the Seventh Party Congress in that they did not mention that Mao's thought is the guiding thought of all the Party and is the guiding principle for all the Party and nation." This confession, of course, undermined the authority of the 1956 constitution, which has now been revised,[1] and doubts about its validity in turn helped sustain the broader attack on the entire Party structure associated with Liu Shao-ch'i on the eve of the Cultural Revolution.

MAO'S CULTURAL REVOLUTION

Mao's chief purpose in pressing the Cultural Revolution has been to destroy the autonomous character of the bureaucracy and to form it into a "docile tool" of his own. There can be no doubt that Mao wants such supreme authority over a Party wherein organizational requirements will be confined to a minor role. While hitting at the identity between "one's own matters" and "Party matters" in Liu Shao-ch'i's Party-building line, the purpose is not so much to destroy "selfishness" but to change the terms of identity to signify the complete subordination of "Party members" to the "thought of Mao".[2] Thus Mao's disciples argue that all ideology must be re-moulded in the course of political struggle so as to "achieve the complete ascendency of the thought of Mao".[3] This, it is said, is the only way to attain the "proletarian standpoint and remain a vanguard fighter of the proletariat, a genuine member of the Communist Party".

To bring down the bureaucracy and force it to adhere to the dictates of Mao's "revolutionary committees", the "revolutionary rebels" and Red Guards, until the line changed, did not hesitate to "doubt all and overthrow all" in carrying out Mao's order to

[1] For text of the revised constitution, passed at the Ninth Party Congress see *Peking Review*, No. 18 (April 30, 1969).

[2] *Jen min jih pao*, December 22, 1967.

[3] *Idem*. At the present time the "era of Mao's thought" is considered the third great "era" of communism, the first being associated with Marx and the second with Lenin. *Chieh feng chün pao*, article on China's Khrushchev in *NCNA*, September 23, 1967.

"bombard" his opponents.[1] For more than a year the Chinese press applauded the lawlessness of Mao's supporters when such lawbreaking was directed at his enemies. For example, *People's Daily* writing "in praise of 'lawlessness'" proclaimed that with the spirit of "lawlessness alone could the revolutionaries control their destiny". Speaking to an unspecified audience the newspaper declared: "Like the Monkey King who turns the heavenly palace upside down, we will destroy your 'law', smash your 'world', rebel against you and seize your power."[2] The label "anarchist", of course, has been loosely applied to "lawbreakers" acting against Mao, even when they included bureaucrats who were attempting to protect the order of the state from the destruction of the young rebels.[3]

By this kind of semantic juggling, the Maoists have supported their contention that only when it is subordinate to the Chairman is the Party a properly proletarian or Communist organization. *People's Daily* in November, 1967 described that subordination as the only valid definition of "democratic centralism" and ordered all cadres to oppose any other kind of subordination as a violation of Leninism.[4]

The approved model for all organizations continues to be the People's Liberation Army (PLA). Particularly since the launching of the movement to seize power in January, 1967—and at least until mid-1969—military leaders held the balance of power in the central political and economic institutions as well as in lower echelons.[5] All of the armed services played an important role in the Cultural Revolution, although by no means one that fully supported Mao. It is probable that the Army helped silence extremist voices in the Cultural Revolution in late 1967 and that even at present (late 1969) many Army leaders remain aloof or could be classified as sympathetic to positions ascribed to Mao's opposition. Neverthe-

[1] Harbin Radio, June 10, 1967.

[2] *Jen min jih pao*, January 31, 1967.

[3] For an article linking anarchism to factionalism, see *Wen hui pao*, February 17, 1968 in Shanghai Radio, February 16, 1968.

[4] *Jen min jih pao*, November 18, 1967. On democratic centralism as defined by Mao, see *Chieh fang chün pao*, February 16, 1968.

[5] For details on the movement to seize power, see *Peking Review*, Nos. 3–8 (1967).

less, until the present the Army has constituted the principal organized section of Mao's new system and has played the leading role in defining the proper place of the Communist Party in the future. Mao's present heir-apparent and "closest comrade in arms", Minister of Defence Lin Piao, has given what is perhaps the most authoritative definition of the relationship that must exist between the Party organization and the Maoists while at the same time re-iterating the position that the bulwark of the people's dictatorship remains its armed forces. Lin on August 9, 1967 said: "Since the start of the Cultural Revolution, some groups have fallen and a new state machine has to be built. The leadership group is very import-ant for it holds political power, and it itself is a state machine. The old leadership group of power-holders was incapable of becoming a state machine, fell, and has been taken over by the military."[1]

In the light of statements such as this it is not surprising that the cadres of China languish in a state of depression[2] and in the eyes of their constituents lack authority. According to *Liberation Army Daily* of October 25, 1967, Mao has proclaimed a new basis for the authority of officials and declared that "erroneous leadership harm-ful to the revolution should not be unconditionally accepted but should be resolutely resisted". Since it is not clear who has been exercising erroneous leadership, no more than a small percentage of the people would be likely to support any cadre wholeheartedly. The injunction that "in dealing with leading cadres we should employ class analysis to decide whether we should obey them or not"[3] does not help much, particularly since a good part of the definitive writing on class analysis was authored by deposed leader Liu Shao-ch'i. All cadres are suspect, and none can be sure that the cadre holding forth today may not be accused of being a "monster and freak" tomorrow. According to the Japanese press this situation has resulted in the petrification of major segments of the Party organiza-

[1] *Chu ying tung fang hung* [Pearl River East is Red], September 13, 1967, in *SCMP*, No. 4036, p. 6; and also citations on p. 140, footnote 4. The most obvious fact pointing up the importance of the Army is the position of Lin, who is referred to as Mao's "most ideal successor" (*tsui li hsiang ti chieh pan jen*), *NCNA*, February 25, 1968.

[2] *Chieh fang jih pao*, October 26, 1967.

[3] Harbin Radio, June 10, 1967.

tion. Duties formerly carried out by Party cadres are either no longer performed at all or the responsibility for them has been taken over by the Army.[1] According to the Japanese Communist newspaper *Akahata* of December 11, 1967 Party committees have been dropped from the list of addresses on certain Central Committee circulars with these orders now going directly to revolutionary committees and military commands. If *Akahata* is correct, Communist Party members in practice may temporarily be outside the functioning Communist system.

The problem for Mao, of course, has been to establish an alternative cadre apparatus where members loyal to him can be clearly identified as such and can organize themselves without falling into the errors of the purged Liu Shao-ch'i. As suggested above this has not proved to be an easy task because no one is quite clear which cadre merits the labels "revolutionary" and "new type".[2] The writings of one prominent member of the new leadership group in Peking have suggested, for example, that the Communists in effect have been caught up in circular reasoning. To be a Maoist one has to be a revolutionary but to be a revolutionary one has to support Mao.[3] Throughout the discussions on the "revolutionary committees" or "three-way alliances" that have seized power from the previous leading bureaucrats runs the recognition of the similar quandary concerning the criterion for choosing loyal cadres.[4] Endless articles deal with the desired ideal character for Mao's new cadre force by use of the negative example of the old bureaucracies,[5]

[1] See *Asahi*, October 19, 1967.

[2] See the definition of Mao's injunction in *Peking Review*, No. 1 (January 3, 1968), p. 11.

[3] He said: "At present we should consider whether or not they [the cadres] support Chairman Mao, his proletarian revolutionary line and the Great Proletarian Cultural Revolution and whether or not they stand on the side of Chairman Mao's proletarian revolutionaries" (*Jen min jih pao*, August 31, 1967). Later statements have described loyalty to Mao as the "first requirement of the times". See *Jen min jih pao*, March 4, 1968; and *Wen hui pao*, March 30, 1968.

[4] On the "revolutionary three-way alliance", see *Hung ch'i*, No. 5 (1967), pp. 5–8; and *Jen min jih pao*, February 17, March 10, 11, 15, 16, 19, 23, 25 and October 20, 1967.

[5] A convenient and fairly representative collection of articles on the question of cadres is in *Current Background*, No. 849.

and thus fail to clarify just what it is Mao hopes to accomplish with the new leaders. The continuing crisis in China would suggest that Mao has not made his point clear; no one knows who should be restored to power and who should be thoroughly and permanently repudiated. From all of the pages on the subject it is evident that Mao wants those who survive as cadres to toe his line and to step out smartly in support of his works. Yet the very act of stepping forward may bring forth accusations of ambition and spotlight a person as a convenient scapegoat from this or that faction in the power struggle. While heralding the new democracy of contention and struggle, the Communist official has never been so cowed by the cross-pressures introduced by the central leadership.

What we can conclude at this time is that Mao seeks to establish a new order that will displace the bureaucratic order built up in the past two decades. In Mao's new system the Party apparatus as such will not play a decisive role as it did in the past, and every cadre in it, as a directed propagator of Mao's dogma, will have to live with the fear that comes from responsibility for official acts when the very dogma he is proclaiming heaps suspicion on all officials.[1] Emphasis in Mao's new order falls on direct comradely relations between officials and the populace with a strong bias against the erection of any organizational barriers between the two.[2] In such a relationship the cadres, formerly the key element of the bureaucracy, are relegated to an ambiguous position without permanency. Thus Mao's longstanding opposition to routinization and specialization has evolved to the point that Party membership counts against the prospective leader. Mao has built his position by wrecking the institutional basis of the state. In this sense, his power has been directly correlated with the weakness of officialdom.

With every allowance made for the differences between Chinese and Soviet conditions, Mao's assault on the Party in his old age

---

[1] *Jen min jih pao*, November 18, 1967, quotes Mao as saying: "We Communists do not want to be officials; what we want is revolution." The whole tone of this article was to belittle officialdom with the statement that cadres should follow Mao whether or not his thought "is of a 'majority' and no matter at what 'superior level' it may be".

[2] See, for example, *NCNA*, December 15, 1967.

bears many striking resemblances to the all-out attack launched by Stalin on the Communist Party in 1936. The nature of the purges was quite different in the two countries, it is true; yet, in each case, extraneous forces (the NKVD, the Army and the Red Guards) were brought in by the leader in order to bring the Party to heel. Just as was Stalin, Mao is intent on bypassing the Party as the supreme, monopolistic instrument of power: as once did Stalin, Mao is seeking to break the institution so that it cannot thwart the will of the leader. In other words, both Stalin and Mao, as they become personal dictators, so they seek to circumscribe any independent role of the Party which might present any kind of challenge to their own personal, unlimited and arbitrary authority.

CONCLUSION

The foregoing analysis of four totalitarian systems appears to sustain Tucker's hypothesis concerning the Bolshevik and *führerist* types of party. When the leadership element in a totalitarian state is a Bolshevik party, at the beginning of that state's rule a powerful individual has usually emerged and led a struggle for personal dominance. This is exemplified in the cases of Stalin and Mao, both of whom asserted the absoluteness and infallibility of their leadership and in doing so deliberately undermined the Party organization. These two dictators, however, differed in their strategies for overcoming the Party bureaucrats. Well-placed within the apparatus, Stalin, for his part, chose to work within the Party as a way of enfeebling it. Through terror and selective purging the Russian leader virtually stripped the Party of its role as the central monopolistic organ of power in Soviet Russia. Unlike the *apparatchik* Stalin, Mao's strength lay outside the organization and rested on his charismatic appeal, his image of greatness among the general populace. Considering his major opponents to be the cadres controlling the Communist bureaucracy, Mao mobilized non-Party members to attack the central power organs. These included the youthful Red Guards and sympathetic officers within the Army. Compared to Stalin's approach, Mao's Cultural Revolution caused a far greater fragmentation of the leadership system possibly even laying the groundwork for a resurgence of regionalism and the forging of an unstable coalition of competing Party and non-Party groups to make up his power structure.

The trend initiated by Stalin and Mao can occur, of course, only when the original Party is Bolshevik rather than *führerist*. Hitler, by contrast, did not have to contend with the Nazi Party apparatus in his rise to personal power. Instead he could consider it one of several available instruments through which he could exercise his will from the beginning. Indeed, in order to counteract the increasing role of the officer corps in the Army at the time of the onset of World War II, Hitler deliberately augmented the importance and power of his Party officials, as suggested above, although even the enhanced role of the Nazi organization did not make it comparable in extensiveness to the Bolshevik organization under Lenin.

The unique totalitarian leader among those considered in this paper is certainly Lenin. Although he had begun to adjust his attitude on the relationship of leader and Party towards the end of his life, Lenin attempted to keep the Party organization strong and publicly played down his own role as leader. Nevertheless, in the cases of both the Bolshevik and Chinese revolutions, the Party that seized power proved to be transitory in character, giving way to a more bureaucratic type of organization.

To the extent that the Communist Party has retained its relevance its leaders have consciously adapted the Party organs to new conditions at the expense of ideological purity. Liu Shao-ch'i and Nikita Khrushchev are examples of leaders who gave the Party vitality in a changing society. Though it is beyond the scope of this paper, recent events in Eastern Europe suggest that "Liu-type" parties may be forced to make ever-wider adaptations to accommodate the demands of lower-level officials, intellectuals and others groups within the populace. Such demands may even develop in imitation of events outside the country and may reach the point where the leadership must give in or face the prospect of being replaced by popular movements. In a less dramatic fashion than the crises in Czechoslovakia or Poland, a fundamental choice of direction confronted the Chinese on the eve of the Cultural Revolution. But given the peculiar relationship between the "leader" (Mao) and the "commissar" (Liu),

Mao could not tolerate a shift that would have placed Liu in a more central position and would in Mao's opinion have set China on the road to "revisionism". Unlike Khrushchev, Liu could not act decisively. His disadvantage lay in the fact that he was not the only major leader in the system nor even the individual on top. Khrushchev for his part was in charge, but failed in his attempt to adapt the Party because he did not anticipate or respond to the reaction of senior leadership elements in the Party and in the government who felt he was going too far. The Russian leader in part antagonized senior Party officials by making them and their subordinates really responsible for their own decisions and actions; a burden that they had not previously borne.

We would conclude therefore that between the poles of Bolshevik and *führerist* parties there are many possible roles for a party under totalitarian dictatorships. In some cases a party is only one of several powerful instruments. The way a party relates to the system and retains any consistent position depends on the world view of the leader and his effectiveness in political combat. The importance of this can be seen by contrasting the rule of Hitler with that of Mussolini—the former being ruthlessly effective, the second often comically inept. But, as this study has attempted to demonstrate, considerations of personal outlook and leadership strength bring to bear only a fraction of the relevant variables. Problems of development and national power reduce and constrain a leader's alternatives even in a totalitarian system.[1] The impact of variables such as the increase in demand by minor cadres for greater local autonomy in an industrializing environment, the growth of opposition elements in regional organs of the party whose preservation is critical to attaining key national goals, and the conflicting pressure from party bureaucrats who support him may induce a leader to break the independent power of the party. Yet these same variables represent events in the life of the system that may be beyond his control. In most cases the resultant position of the party may be

[1] For a suggestive article on the pathology peculiar to totalitarian systems, see Karl W. Deutsch, "Cracks in the Monolith: Possibilities and Patterns of Disintegration in the Totalitarian Systems", in Friedrich, *Totalitarianism*, pp. 308–33.

characterized as falling somewhere along a continuum running from Bolshevism to *führerism* and as more or less stable in that position.

However, nothing in our analysis of the various countries concerned suggests to us that there is any kind of uniform pattern of evolution—from Bolshevik to *führerist* party, or the like. The case of Yugoslavia could indeed be cited to suggest the opposite path of development; and something of the kind was attempted in Czechoslovakia. What seems to us to emerge most strongly is the conclusion that the dominant factor in all the political systems we have discussed has been the personality of the leader—whether Mussolini, Stalin, Hitler or Mao: Lenin, as we have suggested, was not a leader in the same sense of the term, which may explain why Soviet Russia did not become totalitarian during his lifetime. But in the totalitarian system it is the leader who decides. He may, like Hitler, terrorize his party at the outset sufficiently drastically to be able to allow it some degree of institutional independence. But he may also, like Stalin or like Mao in his old age, decide to destroy the party as an institution for fear that it might rival his own personal power.

PART II

THE POWER ELITE IN
THEORY AND PRACTICE

4

THE REIGN OF VIRTUE: SOME BROAD PERSPECTIVES ON LEADER AND PARTY IN THE CULTURAL REVOLUTION

BENJAMIN I. SCHWARTZ

> 'When societies first come to birth', says Montesquieu, 'it is the leader who produces the institutions. Later it is the institutions which produce the leaders.'
>
> Whoever would undertake to give institutions to a people must work with full consciousness that he has set himself to change, as it were, the very stuff of human nature, to transform each individual who, in isolation, is a complete but solitary whole, into a part of something greater than himself, from which, in a sense, he derives his life and his being, to substitute a communal and moral existence for a purely physical and independent life with which we are all of us endowed by nature.
>
> J. J. Rousseau, *The Social Contract*, Book II, Chapter VII

One of the most arresting aspects of the Great Proletarian Cultural Revolution has been the confrontation between Mao Tse-tung (or the Maoist group) and the Chinese Communist Party. There is, to be sure, an area of vagueness and uncertainty concerning this whole matter. Have the Maoists attacked the Party as such? What indeed is the Party as such? The Party may be conceived of as the sum total of its actual members—of its human composition. It may be conceived of in terms of its organizational structure—its "constitution", rules and established mechanisms. To any genuine Marxist–Leninist, it is, of course, more than its cells and anatomy. It is a metaphysical organism which is more than the sum of its parts. The "soul" of this collective entity incarnates all those intellectual and moral capacities which Marx had attributed to the industrial proletariat.

Now there can be no doubt whatsoever that the Maoists have carried out a frontal assault on the human apparatus on the highest, middle and perhaps even on the basic levels of Party organization, at least in urban areas. There is also considerable evidence that Party structures and mechanisms are in a shambles and that even where they survive, as in the rump Central Committee and Army–Party branches, they have ceased to be an important vehicle of decision-making. The whole discussion of "Party building" which was a prominent theme at the end of 1967 and the early part of 1968 indicates the degree of Party wrecking which has been going on. The area of uncertainty is the third miasmic area of the Party as an ontological category—as a whole which may persist whatever the fate of its parts. In this area, it does not appear likely that the Maoist group is prepared to jettison the sacred label.

It is interesting to note that in another sector of what is still vaguely called the Communist world, the possibility of eliminating the role of the Party as such has emerged. In Regis Debray's book *Revolution in the Revolution?*, which is now regarded as a textbook of Castro ideology, we find the following striking assertions:

"Fidel says simply that there is no revolution without a vanguard but that this vanguard is not necessarily the Marxist–Leninist Party."[1] "The effective leadership of an armed revolutionary struggle requires a new style of leadership, a new method or organization."[2] "Parties are never anything but instruments of class struggle. Where the instrument no longer serves its purpose should the class struggle come to a halt or should new instruments be forged?"[3] Debray suggests that "an end be put to the plethora of commissions, secretariats, congresses, conferences, plenary sessions, meetings and assemblies at all levels—provincial, regional and local. Faced with a state of emergency and a militarily organized enemy such a mechanism is paralyzed at best, catastrophic at worst."[4] "There is no exclusive ownership of the revolution."[5] "Eventually the future People's Army will beget the party of which it is to be theoretically the instrument. Essentially the party is the army."[6]

Debray, to be sure, is discussing the period of revolutionary struggle and his doctrine is not incompatible with the view that after the victory a Party of the Communist type may be established.

[1] Regis Debray, *Revolution in the Revolution?* (New York: Grove Press, 1967), p. 78.
[2] *Ibid.* p. 101.   [3] *Ibid.* p. 104.   [4] *Ibid.* p. 102.
[5] *Ibid.* p. 125.   [6] *Ibid.* p. 105.

In some ways, however, M. Debray's assertions seem most applicable to China's Cultural Revolution. The Maoists insist that China is in a permanent state of revolutionary class struggle and that the Party, both in terms of its human composition and as a structure, has gone radically astray. Is it not possible that the Maoists are also ready to eliminate the Party's role in history as an instrument which "no longer serves its purpose"?

As against this possibility, however, one must note the fact that the concept of the Communist Party is now part of Chinese Communist sacred history, and that in pressing their own canonized revolutionary experience as the exclusive model for the Third World, the Chinese must inevitably stress the role of the Party in the revolutionary struggle. In Latin America, indeed, this brings them into direct collision with the Castro–Debray line which tends to express a studied contempt for the "pro-Chinese" groups in Latin America. The Maoists are constrained by their own history to reject Debray's elimination of the Party in the revolutionary struggle.

There is also the need to refute the current Soviet line on events in China. The Soviets have flatly asserted in their polemics that the "Maoist group" is bent on the destruction of the Chinese Communist Party.[1] The Chinese Party has, to be sure, always been defective, we are told, given its woefully weak proletarian base, but it was, after all, born under the inspiration of the October Revolution and for many years was guided by the directives of the Comintern. Even after 1949 it received much sound guidance from Moscow. Unfortunately the petty bourgeois Maoist group was able to establish its ascendency and is now bent on destroying it. One may still hope, however, that the bulk of Party leaders now in opposition will, ultimately be able to restore the Party to its legitimate role and also, hopefully, recognize Moscow's spiritual hegemony. In their discussion of the Cultural Revolution they have also dwelt at great length on the Maoist violation of Party constitutionality.

In the face of these Soviet efforts to identify themselves with the "legitimate" CCP heritage, the Maoists must deny Moscow's

[1] See for instance V. G. Gel'bras, "K voprosu o stanovlenii voenno-byuro-kraticheskoi diktatury v Kitae"("On the Establishment of a Military Bureaucratic Dictatorship in China"), *Narody Azii i Afriki*, No. 1 (1968).

claims. In a statement attributed to a "Stalin group"—a revolutionary organization in the Soviet Union[1]—we find a condemnation of "Soviet revisionist calumnies that China's Great Proletarian Cultural Revolution is 'directed against the Chinese Communist Party'... The fact that the broadest masses of the people are taking part in the Cultural Revolution together with the Party does not in the least impair the prestige of the CCP."

What is more, unlike Castro and Debray, the Maoist group (including such people as Ch'en Po-ta and K'ang Sheng) cannot but be profoundly conscious of the weight of the concept of the "Communist Party" in the history of Marxism–Leninism since 1917. Far from being a dispensable element, it lies at the very heart of Leninism. It was Lenin who insisted after 1917 that only Marxist–Leninist parties could act as the vanguard of the proletariat. It was Lenin who insisted that the Party structure be imposed on all "vanguards" abroad. It was Lenin who insisted that no revolution could be called socialist unless led by Communist parties and it was during Lenin's lifetime that the ultimate authority of the international Communist movement became lodged in one centre on the basis of a logic inherent in Communist Party organization. The Maoist group in China is still bent on capturing for itself this transnational Marxist–Leninist authority and it is most difficult to see how it can do so if it abandons the very concept of the Marxist–Leninist party.

And yet, the uncertainty of the Maoist attitude toward Party organization in China can be most graphically illustrated by the uncertainty of Peking's relations to its own Maoist followers in Belgium and France. In Belgium, the so-called "Rittenberg case" has thrown a glaring light on some of the issues involved. Sidney Rittenberg, an American Maoist of long standing residing in Peking, in the summer of 1967 wrote a pamphlet excoriating Jacques Grippa, the recognized leader of the Belgian Maoists, for his defence of Liu Shao-ch'i's "How to be a Good Communist". Grippa has, in turn, vehemently attacked Rittenberg and whoever may stand behind him, for attacking the Leninist principles of Party organization in the name of a "cult or idolatry with regard to a leader".[2] Grippa (a

---

[1] *New China News Agency* release, May 14, 1968.

[2] See *Joint Publications Research Service*, No. 44,204 (January 31, 1968), *passim*.

former Stalinist) is committed to the Party not only as a moral entity but as a Leninist structure. He is able to cull many telling citations from Lenin stressing the importance which Lenin attached to organizational principles and Party rules. The essence of those quotations is that the forms of Party organization are part of the very essence of what the Party is. One would gather that Grippa's standing in Peking is now very much under a cloud.

In France there are at least three "Maoist" groups, only one of which has constituted itself as a Marxist–Leninist party of the conventional type, while at least one of the other groups has refused to acknowledge that the older Party structure is any longer valid. It is apparently unclear whether any of these groups has as yet obtained Peking's official sanction. In all this, however, the issue is not necessarily whether the term "Party" is to remain in use but whether the old structure is to survive or indeed whether structure as such is to play a central role in a Maoist political universe.

When we turn our attention to recent developments in China itself as they are refracted through the murky media of the Cultural Revolution, one notes that at the end of 1967 and at the beginning of 1968 there were many references in the literature to "Party building". It is significant that even this literature hinted that the Party would somehow be restructured. During 1968, there was increasing discussion of the convening of the Ninth Party Congress, an act which, it was presumed, would once again affirm the Party's "legality". Chou En-lai is alleged to have asked a delegation of proletarian revolutionaries from Canton on November 11: "Haven't you discussed the subject of the Ninth Party Congress set for next year?"[1] This question would indicate, as one might suspect, that Chou at least was strongly committed to a return to as much organizational normalcy as possible under the prevailing conditions.

It is entirely possible that the Maoist group itself was interested in rebuilding the Party in some form or other[2] but by no means as interested as others in restoring power to the bulk of the former

[1] Cited in *Current Scene* (Hong Kong), VI, No. 4 (March 1, 1968), "The CCP—Orphan of Mao's Storm."

[2] One may speculate that some of the "ultra-leftists" actually may have conceived of the possibility of doing away with the Party entirely.

membership or in rebuilding the entire former machinery or even in restoring its position of centrality in the polity. The question would thus not be one of whether the Party should be rebuilt but how it should be rebuilt.

One may, of course, assume that the question of how the Party should be built was by no means entirely theoretical. Undoubtedly it was intertwined with the most ferocious power struggle. One would assume that former cadres would be most insistent on "Party legality" and the sacred character of Party structure and that the Maoists would be infinitely less committed to the "institutional charisma" of the Party. The very Red Flag editorial of July 9, 1967[1] which attempts to refute the charge that the Maoists do not "desire the leadership of the Party" makes it crystal clear that whatever charisma the Party may possess derives solely from the person and thought of Mao Tse-tung. It is made painfully clear that the Party derives its legitimacy from Mao Tse-tung and not vice versa. Any notion that Mao Tse-tung must legitimize his Cultural Revolution through established Party procedures is, in my view, not based on a correct reading of Cultural Revolutionary doctrine. Mao himself is the source of legitimacy and so long as his group remains more or less at the helm, he can legitimize any structure.

Since the Ninth Congress progress in Party building has again receded and one tends to feel that there has been no resolution of the conflicts surrounding the whole issue. Instead of discussions of Party building there has been a resurgence of attacks on the "Right" —on those nefariously attempting to "reverse verdicts". The "revolutionary committees" formerly treated as a provisional device seem to be emerging more and more (whatever they may be in actuality) as Mao's chosen vehicle of "proletarian dictatorship". If present trends continue they may themselves become the constituent units of any rebuilt Party. Concretely this would mean that the People's Liberation Army (PLA) and proven non-Party "proletarian revolutionaries" would play a dominant role at the heart of any reconstituted Party.

In discussing these matters we find ourselves *in medias res* and it

[1] *Hung ch'i* [Red Flag], No. 11 (1967), pp. 2–6.

would be futile to predict the future. The crux of the matter is not whether the Party survives in some form but whether it can ever recover its central sacred charter. The whole thrust of the Cultural Revolution has been to devalue and diminish its significance. The phrase "dictatorship of the proletariat" has never been used more obsessively and yet it is made crystal clear that the "dictatorship of the proletariat" and the Communist Party are by no means interchangeable terms. Just as the phrase "dictatorship of the proletariat" has long since been sundered from any actual reference to industrial workers, the Cultural Revolution has now demonstrated that the particular "general will" which it represents is quite detachable from the particular organization known as the Communist Party. For almost two years the Chinese were told that the dictatorship of the proletariat was being borne by the "Red Guards", by the PLA (the "main pillar of the dictatorship") and a whole assortment of non-Party "proletarian revolutionaries". They were even told that the battle between the "dictatorship of the proletariat" and the "dictatorship of the bourgeoisie" takes place within the arena of each individual soul. Far from possessing those self-purgative and self-regenerative powers which had always been attributed to it in the past, we find that the Party must be "reproletarianized" from without —by Mao Tse-tung standing above it and by the "revolutionary masses" standing below.

The fact that the PLA has become the "main pillar" of the "dictatorship of the proletariat" can, of course, be explained in quite mundane terms. In turning on the Party Mao and his supporters have been forced to fall back on the Army. However, as we are all aware, it is by no means clear that the Army as a whole is as solid a pillar as Mao would like it to be nor as thoroughly imbued with proletarian virtue. Assertions about the proletarian virtue of the Army, like many statements of this type, reflect not so much the complex actuality as the normative reality—the way things ought to be and will in good time become. Whatever its actual power role, however, the faith in the Army as the bearer of proletarian virtue certainly antedates the Cultural Revolution. We have the recent effort of the early sixties to turn the Army into a model of Maoist behaviour and behind that one has the central role of the army in the whole history of the Party since the early thirties. From the vantage point of the present, one is tempted to observe that Mao may have always implicitly seen in the PLA as much of a bearer of proletarian virtue as the Party itself. The isolated guerrilla fighter sacrificing his very life for the people has always been as much the epitome of higher virtue as the hard-working cadre.

It is, of course, entirely possible that with the demise of Mao or a reversal in the fortunes of the Maoist group, there will be an effort to restore the Party to its central position in Chinese life and to re-establish all its sanctified organizational forms. As already indicated, men such as Chou En-lai are probably deeply conscious of the role of the Party in Marxist–Leninist communism. The fact remains that the Cultural Revolution has unmasked many truths which will not be easily forgotten, particularly by the young who have participated in recent events. The Party may not have engaged in all the heinous bureaucratic crimes attributed to it in Red Guard newspapers but its profane nature as simply another bureaucratic organization devoid of any inbuilt proletarian grace or powers of self-redemption now stands revealed. The institutional charisma will not easily be restored.

Since the completion of this essay, there have been significant new developments in Party-building. Again, one is tempted to speculate that some of the major pressures for this "rebuilding" may come from those opposed to the inner Maoist group (particularly from former Party people). Yet as stated above, there is no reason to assume that the Maoist group is opposed to some sort of recrystallization of the "Party". The crux of the matter would still be not so much whether a "Party" should be rebuilt but what form such a Party should take. Current statements from the mainland would indicate that if the Maoists have their way, the cult of Mao and of his thought will reign supreme. The Party will derive whatever lustre it may have from the leader. The Party organization will be changed in significant ways and the mechanisms of election will play no great role. It is also implied that in some fashion the "revolutionary committees" will continue to function either inside or alongside the Party.

SOME HISTORIC PERSPECTIVES—WESTERN AND CHINESE

Instead of attempting to discern an unpredictable future, what I shall attempt in the balance of this article is an effort to see whether the notions which lie behind the Maoist attack on the CCP and behind the Cultural Revolution in general can be related to certain larger perspectives and contexts of ideas. If we are dealing with what many take to be a kind of madness, is this madness unique to Mao or does it relate in any way to a larger history of ideas—Western or Chinese? Is it indeed Western or Chinese or may it be said to feed on both cultural traditions?

In focusing on ideas and their genealogy there is no intention of implying that the Cultural Revolution or the conflict between the Party and the leader is solely a result of ideas in the head of Mao or to deny the role of power struggles, psychological motives or "objective factors". Mao's retreat to the "second line" of power during the years since 1959 may have been voluntary or involuntary or partially voluntary. Even if it was essentially voluntary (and I lean to the view that it was), the fact that the "first line" leaders of the Party were moving in a direction which the leader regarded as radically mistaken was, of course, not only an offence to his own vision of China's future but also to an enormous swollen sense of self-esteem which had become indissolubly tied up with this vision. The vision may be only one ingredient in the total complex. It is, however, an essential ingredient and it is on this ingredient that we shall concentrate our attention.

Mao Tse-tung has found that the CCP, both in its human composition and as an organizational structure, has failed at least for a time to embody the qualities of the "dictatorship of the proletariat". The latter phrase presumably designates the "social bearer" of certain social virtues and capacities but in current Maoist usage it often seems to refer to the assemblage of the virtues themselves— selflessness in the "service of the people", lack of self-interest, austerity, singularity of purpose, implacable hostility to the forces of evil, however defined, etc. The question of who the actual bearers of this "general will" are has indeed become a crucial problem of the Cultural Revolution.

In seeking out the provenance of these notions I shall concentrate attention in the first instance on the possible Western origins precisely because of the tendency among Western "pragmatic" academics to see something peculiarly Chinese in Mao's highly moralistic rhetoric. Furthermore, in dealing with Western sources, it will no longer suffice to confine our attention to the specificities of Marxist–Leninist ideology. As the Marxist–Leninist ideology moves into a period of advanced disintegration one becomes more and more conscious of some of the more general notions which lie behind Marxism–Leninism, notions which have become embodied in specific ways within the Marxist–Leninist complex (as well as in other ideologies) but whose origins go back at least as far as the enlightenment. These general notions have indeed proved more enduring than the specific ideologies within which they have found a lodging. Our particular quest here indeed leads us back as far as Jean-Jacques Rousseau and the Jacobin effort to apply the doctrine of that fruitful but ambiguous thinker.

It is not at all a question of whether Mao Tse-tung was ever a profound student of Rousseau or Jacobinism. There can be little doubt that in his youth he read about both but one need not argue any intimate contact. The significance of Rousseau here is that he gives a highly vivid expression to more general tendencies which can make their way without any intimate contact with the great thinker himself. In the case of Mao, one can indeed maintain that Marxism–Leninism itself has been a bearer of the strains of thinking with which we are concerned.

Turning back to Rousseau we find that, as Burke states, "Rousseau is nothing if not a moralist". As opposed to many of his contemporaries such as Turgot, Dalembert, Voltaire and Diderot who were overwhelmingly concerned with the progress of the "arts and sciences" and who regarded moral progress as a by-product of the accumulation of human knowledge, he was overwhelmingly concerned, in the first instance, with the question of how to make society virtuous and just. Amid the sophisticated and hedonistic libertines of the enlightened aristocracy and the new intelligentsia, he felt himself to represent the essential innocence of a man of the people and the sturdy virtues of a citizen of Geneva. The others were social

engineers concerned with how arts and sciences could be mobilized
to render society felicitous. He was overwhelmingly concerned with
society's moral progress: he had actually found in his "Discourses in
the Arts and Sciences" and "Discourses on the Origins of Human
Inequality" that the arts and sciences (technico-economic progress)
as they had developed until his time had actually run counter to
moral progress and contributed to all the corruptions of society.
His own "civic morality" was not a "new morality" but a morality
based on a kind of Plutarchian exaltation of ancient Roman and
Spartan virtues. His good society would be peopled by men who
would abnegate their private interests for the public good, men constantly inspired by a sense of duty to the fatherland, men who would
sacrifice themselves without stint, and men who would live simple
and austere lives. It is interesting to note that as the spiritual father
of modern nationalism (although again, the "antique" example is
here of overwhelming importance) Rousseau exalts the martial
virtues and even praises hatred of the national enemy as a unifying
cement of the sovereign people's will.

What makes Rousseau's ethic modern and revolutionary is, however, his lack of belief in the power of the individual to realize his
potentiality for virtue through his own individual efforts and his consequent tendency to link ethics indissolubly to politics. In his own
individual life he had discerned how impossible it is for a good man
to realize his moral potentialities within a bad society. "I saw", he
stated in his *Confessions*, "that everything depended basically on
political science, and that no matter how one views the problem every
people is just what its government makes it. What form of government is most suited to produce a nation which is virtuous, enlightened
and wise—in short, in the highest sense of the word, as perfect as
possible?"[1] The individual can realize his moral potential only by
submerging himself in that larger "moral entity", the people. The
people as a collectivity is not only the source of all sovereignty but
also of all virtue. It is only when the individual will somehow becomes
fused with the "general will" that the individual's own moral
potential can be realized. The question of how—in concrete political

[1] Cited in Cassirer's *Philosophy of the Enlightenment* (Boston, Mass.: Beacon
Press, 1966), p. 154.

terms—the "general will" comes to be internalized in the individual is, of course, one of the central enigmas of Rousseau's political thought and has been the subject of a vast literature. While related to the modern sociological view that the individual derives his "values" from "society" it is, of course, much more activist and political. What it asserts is that in some fashion the state is or should be the moralizing agency of human society. Its meaning is relatively clear when applied to an idealized ancient Rome and Sparta where citizens presumably expressed their "general will" in face-to-face primary assemblies and where the decisions of majorities were, in Rousseau's view, actually inspired by virtue. Even here he was forced to introduce a transcendent element in the form of that eighteenth-century device, the all-wise "legislator". It was Lycurgus who created an all-wise constitution and system of law which shaped the Spartans to virtue. "Of itself", we are told, "the people wishes the good; of itself it does not always see it."[1] Many enigmas emerge, of course, when this notion is applied to the modern nation-state. The question of how the virtue of the people is achieved in these vast societies is dealt with most cursorily by Rousseau and indeed he often expresses doubt whether social virtue is attainable in societies of this size.

In spite of its imprecision, the concept of a society in which the organized people would be able to crush all selfish individual group and factional interests and infuse its individual members with public virtue was to prove most powerful. The attempt to realize this ideal within the framework of the modern nation-state was, of course, to fall to Robespierre, St Just and Babeuf who found that the mere elimination of established vested interests and privileges as embodied in the old order did not automatically actualize the general will. Furthermore, as legislators of the general will they soon found that Rousseau's sharp distinction between the legislator who creates the general laws of the good state but who does not attempt to implement them and the "executive power" which applies them was to prove completely inapplicable in practice. Before one could even begin to create good laws, it was necessary to eliminate the manifestation of individual, group and factional egotism as well as

---

[1] "The Social Contract", Book II, chap. 3, in Sir Ernest Barker, *Social Contract: Locke, Hume and Rousseau* (New York: Oxford Univ. Press, 1962), p. 274.

the cynical sophistries of vain intellectuals which interfered with the establishment of good laws.

What happens here in essence is that Robespierre, not by any intent, himself becomes the embodiment of the general will not only as a "legislator" but also as a "magistrate". It is Robespierre himself who plays this role and not the Jacobin society which itself turns out to be susceptible to selfish factionalism. It is, after all, no accident that the transcendental factor in Rousseau's "Social Contract" is not an institution but an individual—the "legislator" who by dint of his god-like "great soul" is able to embody the indivisible public spirit. Institutions, made up as they are of many individuals, are hardly indivisible and may easily become the embodiment of "partial interests". Rousseau was not yet attuned to the notion of the dynamics of history which endow institutions with a kind of dynamic historic life of their own. He must accept Montesquieu's view that "leaders produce institutions". The Jacobin clubs were never to develop the distinctive personality later to be attributed to the Communist Party and Robespierre continually stressed that his Committee of Public Safety enjoyed its authority because of the purity and incorruptibility of its members rather than as an organizational entity.

The reign of virtue, as we know, was not established by the French Revolution and the question of why it was not established was to agitate a whole new generation of young thinkers including both the young Hegel and the young Marx. Both Hegel and Marx concluded that the "people" as a collective entity did not, in fact, embody the indivisible general virtue which Rousseau had attributed to it. It had turned out to be an agglomeration of all kinds of egoistic individual and group interests. Hegel was, of course, ultimately to find the realization of man's higher social virtue in the modern state while Marx was to find the social bearer of general virtue to be a particular segment of modern society, the industrial proletariat. It was, in the first instance, the economic origins of the proletariat which were to turn Marx's attention to the whole historic economic process which lay behind the rise of this redemptive class. However, Marx's growing interest in technico-economic progress during the forties was not wholly due to the necessity to explain the preconditions of the existence of the proletariat. His ideal of good society was no longer simply Rousseau's ideal of civic virtue. He had developed a genuine appreciation of the values of material progress which in his good society would be a precondition of cultural richness. His new man would be socially virtuous but would also live in material comfort and appreciate his Shakespeare and Homer. The proletariat was not only the heir of Rousseau's public virtue but as a stratum deeply immersed in technical life, it would also fulfil the role of Saint Simon's industrial–scientific elite. Thus Marx's concept of the mode of production fuses together, as it were, in an unstable complex the concepts of technico-economic and moral progress.

There is, of course, implicit in Marx's class conception something like the Rousseauist conception of a class "general will". He was not, however, inclined to go into the question of how the proletarian general will would find its realization. Unlike Rousseau, he was able to invoke a new dynamic principle, the impersonal forces of history. The unfolding mechanisms of the capitalist mode of production would themselves lead the proletariat to fulfil its historic role, to actualize both its moral and technico-economic tasks. It is in this way that the later Marx avoids the problem of class organization, the problem of politics itself.

With Lenin, however, who devoutly accepted Marx's conception of the historic mission of the proletariat, the problem of politics comes back to the very centre of the stage. The problem of how the general will of the proletariat is to be actualized becomes an immediate problem of political action. In Lenin's view, the virtues and capacities of the proletariat both in Russia and abroad had proven potential rather than actual and the impersonal forces of history had proven extraordinarily sluggish in carrying the proletariat along its destined path. The proletariat also required its "legislator" or its legislative vanguard to lead it on its destined path. Lenin probably never regarded himself as the living incarnation of the proletarian will. Indeed, he was quite sincere in his effort to create an organization which would play this role. Unlike the Jacobin clubs, the Bolshevik Party[1] was to be a highly articulated organization with a

---

[1] To Robespierre the word "party" was a bad word. There ought to be no "parties" within the sovereign people. The Marxist conception of class struggle,

distinct corporate life of its own. Grippa is quite right. To Lenin, the secret of his party lay not only in the virtues of its members but also in the efficacy of its organization. When one now scrutinizes the writings of Lenin on Party organization, one is struck by his vehement defence of the importance of organizational forms and well-formulated rules against all detractors of "formalism".[1] One is further struck by the fact that while Lenin's "professional revolutionaries" certainly should embody all the proletarian virtues, Lenin dwells not so much on their virtues as on their professionalism, their organizational expertise; first in the science of revolution, and then after the revolution as the technico-administrative elite of the post-revolutionary society. Lenin has shifted from "spontaneity" to "consciousness" but, as in the case of Marx, Rousseau and Saint-Simon are both present in his outlook.

Yet while Lenin was most intent on creating a Party institution with its own institutional charisma, the fact remains that during his lifetime it was Lenin rather than the Party who embodied the pro-letarian general will. Again and again he turned on his own Party and found it wanting. The institution had hardly replaced the leader.

When we turn to Stalin we find that he rises to power through a manipulation of the Party administrative apparatus. He thus seems to provide an instance of the "institution producing the leader". Yet the fact remains that the relationship between the leader and the Party remains as problematic as ever. In the case of Stalin with his jealous greed for power one is tempted to see here simply a particular instance of the universal struggle between the despot and his own bureaucracy. Yet within the Marxist–Leninist context, however, this also involved an extreme reluctance to share with any individual or any group the enormous, indivisible and total moral and intellectual claims attributed to the Party.

In retrospect, one is tempted to add that Stalin's *de facto* down-grading of the Party organization was due not only to his own power greed and mistrust, but also to the fact that the Party was unable to fulfil the tasks which Stalin felt that the times required. The

however, when added to the notion that parties represented classes, provided a much firmer foundation for the concept of a party.

[1] See particularly *One Step Forward, Two Steps Backward*.

"building of socialism" with its enormous emphasis on technocratic capacities naturally led Stalin to emphasize the "social engineering" aspect of the Party function rather than its moral virtues. In fact, the Party bureaucracy proved incompetent to perform in this capacity. If Mao was to find the Party insufficiently Red, Stalin found it insufficiently expert.

Nevertheless, while Stalin diminished the actual role of the Party, while he formed it into a personal machine, on the conceptual level he never veered in the slightest from the Leninist conception of the centrality of the Party. He claimed to the end to derive his legitimacy from the Party constitution however much he may have flouted it in practice. What is more, he left the formal lines of Party organization intact. Like Lenin, he insisted that it was the institution rather than the leader which embodied the proletarian general will. Unlike Rousseau's legislator who provides a static body of good laws for all eternity, Lenin's Party is required to act within the stream of history, to provide ever fresh yet infallible guidance through all the shoals and eddies of a changing world. To admit that the Party's transcendental capacities are totally dependent on the haphazard emergence of great leaders is to render its claims precarious indeed. This was appreciated by Stalin just as much as by Lenin.

Turning finally to the Mao Tse-tung of the Cultural Revolution period we find first that the problem of leader and institution assumes entirely new proportions, and second that the Rousseauist ethical emphasis again achieves a clear ascendancy.

The institution of the Marxist–Leninist party (as a world movement) has been in existence well over half a century. Yet in China it is now reiterated *ad nauseam* that the Chinese Communist Party is wholly dependent for whatever proletarian charisma it may have on the leader and his thought. What is more, the qualities of the proletarian dictatorship which find their fountainhead in Mao Tse-tung may be shared by groups, institutions and individuals which lie outside the Party. Indeed the Party as such, when considered apart from Mao Tse-tung and his thought, may wholly degenerate and become another "partial interest" in the Rousseauist sense. The future of communism is not guaranteed by the existence of the Party but by the "thought of Mao Tse-tung". It is the internalization of his thought which will realize general virtue and not the existence of the Party.

When we turn to Mao Tse-tung's thought itself (in its Cultural Revolutionary interpretation) we are struck, as stated above, by the overwhelming predominance of the social–ethical. When viewed in a Western perspective one must say that the Rousseauist element has pushed the Saint-Simonian technocratic element well into the background. The aged Mao is bent on achieving the reign of virtue as he understands virtue and remains unprepared to accept any progress of the "arts and sciences" which is not based on virtue. This does not mean, it must be stressed again, that Mao is against modernization. On the contrary, during the Great Leap Forward he fervently hoped that the energy of organized virtue would itself spur economic development. Maoist virtue, one might say, was to play the role of a kind of collectivistic Protestant Ethic. There is, however, no reason to believe that this ethic was regarded either then or now as nothing but a means to modernization any more than Weber's Calvinists regarded their own ethic as simply a means to economic ends.

Yet, however prominent the Rousseauist-Jacobin component in latter-day Maoism, key elements of the language remain Marxist-Leninist. "Proletariat," "bourgeoisie," "class struggle" and "dictatorship of the proletariat" are terms which occur in maddening iteration. The Maoist virtue remains "proletarian" and does not stem simply from the people or the masses. However capable the masses may be of proletarianisation, however necessary it is for "proletarian revolutionaries" to be in contact with the masses, the source of proletarian virtue lies somehow outside, above and beyond the masses just as the word "bourgeoisie" refers to forces of egotism on a world scale. The word "proletariat" still refers to some ill-defined transnational, transcendental historic force and it is as the embodiment of this force that Mao confronts both his own people and the world. The Maoist dream of reconstituting a new world Communist movement centred in Peking remains indissolubly tied to this vocabulary.

We have spoken of Maoism within a Western perspective. It may well be suggested at this point that many of the dominant notions of the Cultural Revolution seem to suggest the greater cogency of a

Chinese cultural perspective (in spite of the explicitly anti-traditional stance of the Maoist group). If we choose to personify ideas, may not Mencius be more relevant than Rousseau?

It is interesting to note that in early Meiji Japan as well as in early twentieth-century China affinities were often noted between Mencius and Rousseau. Is it possible, in fact, to make meaningful comparisons between the eighteenth-century political philosopher and the ancient Chinese sage? Much of the prevailing historicist and social scientific dogma would reject this possibility. Yet it seems to me that comparison (which involves both difference and similarity) is, in fact, possible. To inquire why such comparison may be possible would carry us very far afield. It might simply be noted, in passing, that for some reason the ancient Chou thinkers and the eighteenth-century philosopher do, oddly enough, confront the human situation from a similar perspective, the perspective of vicarious statesmen who have prescriptions for "society" as a whole.

One is immediately struck by certain similarities in the relationship of ethics to the political realm. As in the case of Rousseau, the majority of men in Mencius are potentially good (they possess the roots [*tuan*] of goodness) but seem incapable of realizing their goodness through their own efforts. In both cases the unfavourable social environment negates the possibility of such realization. In both cases the people's ethical potentialities can be realized only through political mediation. Yet Mencius manages to avoid many of the enigmas surrounding Rousseau's abstract conception of the general will of the people. The moralizing agency of his society is clearly an ethical elite and the superiority of this elite resides in the moral superiority of its individual members who are somehow able to actualize through individual self-effort their own potential virtue and wisdom.[1] Unlike the mass of mankind, these *chün tzu* are able to realize their own potentialities by "following that part of themselves which is great".[2] They are able to transcend their environment and are thus also able to transform the people below

[1] In the ideal society of the past, the ethical initiative had been taken by single individuals, the sage-rulers Yao, Shun and Yü.

[2] *The Book of Mencius*, Pt. I, chap. XVII, II, 419 in James Legge, *Chinese Classics* (Hong Kong: Hong Kong Univ. Press, 1960).

them through the power of example, education and proper policy. Thus Mencius accepts the principle of hierarchy gladly and without hesitation.

Rousseau, on the other hand, sets out from a rejection of hierarchy. His ideal society is one in which all citizens fully participate as "free" and equal citizens on the idealized ancient Roman model. The attainment of the ideal is immediately cast into doubt, however, by all sorts of tragic dilemmas. There is not only the dilemma raised in the question, "How can the multitude which often does not know what it wants because only rarely does it know what is for its own good undertake an enterprise so extensive and so difficult as the formulation of a system of laws?"[1] Mencius himself might have recognized this dilemma. There is also, however, Rousseau's clear realization that princes, magistrates and all those who govern (the "executive power") are made of the same clay as the people. Rousseau can solve his dilemmas only by introducing the *deus ex machina* of the transcendent legislator, that rare genius of unaccountable "greatness of soul" who is able to create a system of general laws which educates the people to virtue.[2] Rousseau is, after all, an heir to Western legalism and ultimately seems to believe in the rule of law. It is the law itself which plays a determining role in forming the general will.[3]

With the Jacobins, however, this sharp distinction between the legislative and executive breaks down and Robespierre must represent the general will as both legislator and magistrate. In Leninism it survives in the feeble guise of Party constitutionality and legality. Here, however, we perceive the enormous contradiction between Rousseau's intentions and the unintended uses to which his doctrines have lent themselves.

When we turn to Mencius' account of the famous sage–rulers Yao, Shun and Yü, we find that the distinction between legislator and prince does not exist. These mythic figures are in a sense

[1] *The Social Contract*, Book II, chap. VI, in Barker, *Social Contract*, p. 289.
[2] And even he should not rule. "When Lycurgus gave laws to his country he began by abdicating his royal power." *Ibid*. p. 293.
[3] Although here too we find ambiguities. Ernest Barker points out that in spite of his emphasis on law, Rousseau "felt in his bones that the nation made the law and not the law the nation". *Ibid*. p. xxxix.

"legislators" in that they create or make manifest the sacred institutional framework of society but they are also the active rulers of society who stand high above the institutions which they have formed. The institutions are simply the channels through which they spread their spiritual–ethical influence. The Confucian tradition even in its Mencian interpretation is hardly anti-formalistic. Even to Mencius, the virtues of rulers and of the *chün tzu* must be channelled through an institutional setting and find their objective expression in the rules of propriety. Yet in Mencius (as opposed to Hsün-tze) it is not the institutions which mould the sage–rulers and the men of virtue; it is the sage–rulers and *chün tzu* who irradiate their ethical power through the institutions.

When one examines the idiom of the Cultural Revolution one somehow feels that the untroubled image of Mao as the fountainhead of all morality, standing high above all laws and institutions, may owe more to certain Chinese cultural perspectives than to any Western source of inspiration. One feels this also in the tremendous emphasis on the power of example attributed to such paragons as Lei Feng and Men Ho, who may, to be sure, be men of the people but who are nevertheless capable of heroic acts of ethical self-transcendence. Again, they are capable of these acts only because they draw inspiration from the sage–ruler himself.

One is further tempted to speculate that even the aged Mao's anti-formalism and anti-institutionalism may have their indigenous roots in the heterodox strains of the Chinese heroic (*yu hsia*) tradition so vividly expressed in the epic novels which were his favourite childhood reading. Here we find the heroic bands of blood-brothers fighting for the right under leaders recognized by all for their natural qualities of leadership. The ties which bind here are not the institutional forms of the corrupt traditional establishment but the moral cement of shared sentiments. These literary images must blend easily in the leader's mind with the actual experience of the Hunan-Kiangsi and Yenan days.

In all of this the Chinese perspective may explain much which cannot be explained in terms of a purely Western perspective. There are, however, areas in which the particular Chinese perspectives and the particular Western perspectives, far from being mutually exclusive, prove to be mutually reinforcing. There are also areas where only the Western perspective can adequately account for a new reality. The concept of the masses as active and total participants in the whole political process (whatever may be the actual situation) has, of course, become an essential part of the "thought of Mao Tse-tung". As in the case of Rousseau, Mao Tse-tung's masses are the masses not necessarily as they are but as they "ought to be" and there can be no doubt of the leader's aspiration to make them what they ought to be. They are to be made public spirited and their virtue is no longer to be passive and negative, but active and dynamic. It is to be a moral energy consolidated in the service of the nation. What is more, this moral energy is to be unified in a positive aggressive struggle against all the forces of evil. Here both the nationalist motif of Rousseau and transnational image of Marxism–Leninism are united into one.

One could go on in this scrutiny of Western and Chinese perspectives. Perhaps of more significance than the question of cultural origin is the fact that we are here dealing with issues that have now assumed a transcultural significance. The fact that groups of the young in heart of the modern West profess to find in the Mao of the Cultural Revolution (by a painfully selective interpretation) answers to their own discontents points to this transcultural aspect. On the one hand they respond to the Maoist anti-institutionalism and anti-formalism. On the other, they respond to the Rousseauist emphasis on morality in reaction to the preponderantly technocratic version of the theory of progress. In responding to their version of Mao, they are thus responding to an element of their own cultural past.

5

THE PARTY IN
CHINESE COMMUNIST IDEOLOGY

STUART R. SCHRAM

As the title indicates, this article deals with the image of the Party in Chinese Communist ideology. Obviously the conception of the Party and its role put forward in theoretical writings cannot be isolated from the reality of the Party, if only because ideology is shaped by practice and serves as a rationalization of practice. But the emphasis here will be on the analysis of statements about the Party, and their evolution over the past three decades.

Even on the level of ideology, it is not possible to treat the problem exhaustively in a brief article. In a word, I shall endeavour to concentrate on those aspects of Chinese views of the Party which best serve to define their originality as compared to the Leninist tradition. Thus, the emphasis will be less on the principles and methods of organization, which are basically similar to those of all other Communist parties (and indeed have been imitated by other non-Communist or even anti-Communist parties and movements), than on such decisive concepts as the nature of the Party, the locus of authority within the Party, and the Party's relation to other organizations and social groups.

On these and other points, the dominant conceptions within the Chinese Communist movement have varied over the years. But there have also been, at any given time, divergent views on the subject. In the first portion of my article, surveying the history of the question from Yenan days to the aftermath of the Great Leap Forward, I shall limit myself to a considerable extent to a comparison of the views of Mao Tse-tung and of Liu Shao-ch'i. Apart from saving space, such an approach has the advantage that at least we are dealing with identifiable tendencies, whereas a wider selection of authors would have involved us in a great deal of speculation about factions, or at least about ideological sympathies, within the top leadership group.

It is certainly not my intention to read back into the past the present sharp conflict between Mao Tse-tung and Liu Shao-ch'i, and to assume that they have for many decades been as violently at odds as Mao would now have us believe. But although one obviously cannot take at face value the historiography of the Cultural Revolution, neither should one discount it altogether. It is clear that there have, in fact, long been serious tensions and disagreements among the Chinese leaders, which most observers—including myself—have tended to minimize because of their faith in the myth of the monolithic unity of the Chinese Communist Party. In particular, such divergences are visible in writings of Mao Tse-tung and Liu Shao-ch'i dating from well before the establishment of the Chinese People's Republic in 1949.

These divergences reflect, to be sure, the differing personalities and early training of Mao and Liu, but they reflect perhaps even more the differing experience which shaped, during the years 1921–41, their conception of the Party and its role. Fundamental in this respect is the fact that only rarely in the course of these two decades had Mao Tse-tung found himself in the presence of a Communist Party like those in other countries, namely a powerful organization operating largely on its own, and employing essentially political methods. To a large extent, the "Party" was for Mao merely a name for the leading nucleus in another organization—the Kuomintang from 1922 to 1927, the Red Army thereafter. The only time when the Party as such had confronted Mao as a real entity was in the days of the Kiangsi Soviet Republic, and then it had been a foreign and hostile body which effectively excluded him from the exercise of power and insisted on applying policies which he believed to be erroneous.

The most important and most typical experience of the Party for Mao was, however, as a soul or parasite inhabiting the body of the Red Army. Although the two were theoretically distinct, the *de facto* symbiosis between them, persisting as it did over a long period of time, could not fail to affect the manner in which the Chinese Communists perceived the Party—and this was especially true of those such as Mao who were not particularly well grounded in Leninism. This situation led, on the one hand, to a conception of armed struggle as the only form of class struggle, and to the subordination of the existence and development of the Party to armed struggle. Thus, in his editorial for the first issue of the inner-Party journal *The Communist* in October, 1939, Mao wrote:

Apart from armed struggle, apart from guerrilla warfare, it is impossible to understand our political line and, consequently, to understand our Party-building...We know that in China there would be no place for the proletariat, no place for the people, no place for the Communist Party, and no victory for the revolution without armed struggle. For eighteen years the development, consolidation, and Bolshevization of our Party have been undertaken in the midst of revolutionary wars *and have been inseparable from guerrilla warfare*. Without armed struggle, *without guerrilla warfare*, there would not have been such a Communist Party as exists today. Comrades throughout the Party must never forget this experience gained at the cost of blood.[1]

But this situation—and no doubt Mao's own turn of mind— led not only to the subordination of political to military struggle, but also to a personalized idea of the Party in general, and of Party leadership in particular. The fact that the Party did not emerge in its own right as a palpable reality, although it was theoretically supposed to be in control of the whole struggle (witness Mao's famous statement, reprinted in the *Quotations from Chairman Mao*, "The Party commands the gun, and the gun must never be allowed to command the Party"), naturally gave rise to the identification of "Party" leadership with obedience to the correct line. And since there was thus a Party line, but no visible Party, the ultimate consequence was to define fidelity to the Party as obedience to the author of the correct ideology—in other words, to the leader.

This aspect of Mao's thinking is strikingly expressed in his speech of December 21, 1939 on the occasion of Stalin's sixtieth birthday, when he said:[2]

[1] S. Schram, *The Political Thought of Mao Tse-tung* (rev. ed.; Harmondsworth: Penguin Books, 1969), p. 374. The words in italics have been eliminated in the present official edition.

[2] *Jen min jih pao* [People's Daily], December 20, 1949. Emphasis supplied. For a full translation see *The Political Thought of Mao Tse-tung*, Text X, G, pp. 425–8.

Both the revolutionary and the counter-revolutionary fronts must have someone to act as their leader, someone to serve as their commander. Who is the commander of the counter-revolutionary front? It is imperialism, it is Chamberlain. Who is the commander of the revolutionary front? It is socialism, it is Stalin. Comrade Stalin is the leader of the world revolution. Because he is there, it is easier to get things done. As you know, Marx is dead, and Engels and Lenin too are dead. *If we did not have a Stalin, who would give the orders?* This is indeed a fortunate circumstance. Because there is in the world today a Soviet Union, a Communist Party, and a Stalin, the affairs of the world can be more easily dealt with. What does a revolutionary commander do? He sees to it that everyone has food to eat, clothes to wear, a place to live, and books to read. And in order to attain these objectives, he must lead a thousand-odd million men in struggle against the oppressors, and bring them to final victory. This is precisely what Stalin will do. Since this is the case, should not all those who suffer oppression congratulate Stalin? I think they should, I think they must. We should congratulate him, support him, and study him.

The sentence in italics is extremely suggestive. It is hard not to see in it a prefiguration of Mao's attitude towards his own role in recent years. In any case, it is in sharp contrast with the viewpoint expressed at the same period by Liu Shao-ch'i.

Liu also shared, of course, to a certain extent, the experience of political struggle as guerrilla warfare. But he also spent considerable periods in clandestine work in the enemy-occupied "white areas", in conditions corresponding far more closely to the premises of orthodox Leninism. And his Russian experience and knowledge of Soviet ideological writings predisposed him, more than Mao, to consider the struggle in the countryside as a concession to reality, rather than as the source of new theoretical norms.

A number of Liu Shao-ch'i's most important and best-known writings belong, like the Mao texts just quoted, to the years 1939–43. In July, 1939 at the Marx–Lenin School in Yenan he delivered the lectures which were later published as Parts I and II of the book which used to be called in English *How to be a Good Communist*, and is now entitled, translating more literally, *On the Self-Cultivation of Communists*. After his transfer to Central China, where he assumed responsibility for political work in the New Fourth Army following the incident of January, 1941, he gave other lectures at the Central China Party School, of which the best known are perhaps those composing *On Inner-Party Struggle*, dating from July, 1941. But none of these texts deal at such length with the central issues at stake here, namely the role of the Party as an organization, as distinguished from the men who compose it and the personalities of their leaders, as does Part III of *On the Self-Cultivation of Communists*, entitled "On Organizational and Disciplinary Self-Cultivation". Moreover, as this text was printed only for study within the Party, it also has the advantage of being somewhat more outspoken than materials for open circulation.[1]

Central to Liu's whole analysis is the vital importance of organization and discipline in giving to the Party its distinctive character. He goes even farther than Mao Tse-tung had yet done at the time[2] in recognizing that the Communist Party, like every organization (and, more broadly, like "all other things") is "a contradictory entity". This contradiction creates problems in the shape of the

[1] When I mentioned this work in the first edition of *The Political Thought of Mao Tse-tung* (New York: Praeger, 1963), pp. 49–50 and note 70, p. 88, I had not yet identified it as part of *How to be a Good Communist*. Franz Schurmann, who originally called this document to my attention, and who has discussed it in his book *Ideology and Organization in Communist China*, (Berkeley & Los Angeles: Univ. of California Press, 1966), pp. 54–5, was also unaware of this. The first edition of Part III known to me was published by the Hsin Hua Shu tien (Chi chung chih tien) as a companion volume to the edition of Parts I and II issued by the same publisher in November, 1939. This edition is undated, but the lectures must have been delivered during the latter part of 1941. They cannot have been given before June of that year, since they mention the German-Soviet war as having already begun. A hostile reference to them by Yao Wen-yüan (note 27 to "Comments on T'ao Chu's Two Books", *Peking Review*, No. 38 (September 15, 1967), p. 17), which is probably accurate in this respect, gives the date as 1941. I therefore conclude that they were delivered during the second half of that year. I am citing here from the text of the three parts which appears in Liu Shao-ch'i, *Lun tang* (Dairen: Ta-chung Shu-tien, 1947), pp. 29–190. Incidentally, this volume is not, and does not even contain, Liu's report on the Party Constitution delivered at the Seventh Congress, which usually goes under the same title of *On the Party*.

[2] In Mao's known writings explicit reference to contradictions between the leaders and the led occurs only in 1957, in the speech on the correct handling of contradictions among the people. For a lengthier discussion of Liu Shao-ch'i's views on this theme in 1941, see *The Political Thought of Mao Tse-tung* (revised edition), pp. 94–5.

complementary but nonetheless opposite exigencies of democracy and centralism, but these contradictions must be endured, for without a hierarchical structure the Party cannot function effectively:[1]

The structure of our Party is not that of a mixture. It is not simply the grouping together of several hundred thousand Party members, and it is not without a definite structure; on the contrary, it is the union of several hundred thousand Party members in accordance with a definite organizational form and definite rules. It is a union of contradictory elements, comprising the leaders and the led, the Party leaders and Party members, the upper-level and lower-level organizations of the Party. It is this type of organizational structure which gives to the Party its great fighting strength; otherwise, it would be *nothing but an undisciplined mob*.

This is, of course, an entirely orthodox position. From it flows a strong emphasis on the duty of the individual Party member—*every* Party member—to obey the organization. To be sure, Mao Tse-tung had also asserted on many occasions the need for obedience—for example, in a passage from his report of October, 1938 which appears in the *Quotations from Chairman Mao*:[2]

We must affirm anew the discipline of the Party, namely:
 (1) the individual is subordinate to the organization;
 (2) the minority is subordinate to the majority;
 (3) the lower level is subordinate to the higher level;
 (4) the entire membership is subordinate to the Central Committee
Whoever violates these articles of discipline disrupts Party unity.

But there is some doubt whether, for Mao, even in 1938, these principles really applied to the man at the top. Liu, on the other hand, declared bluntly:[3]

Every Party member, whatever his capacities, his activities and his influence, is merely one of several hundred thousand Party members, he is merely one element of the contradictory structure which constitutes the

---

[1] Liu Shao-ch'i, *Lun tang*, p. 135. Emphasis added.

[2] *Quotations from Chairman Mao Tse-tung* (Peking: Foreign Languages Press, 1966), p. 255.

[3] Liu Shao-ch'i, *Lun tang*, pp. 138–9. Liu also declares that, although the influence of a leader of the Party is great, and that of a simple member very small, it is the Party which decides what the post of each shall be, and promotes people from the ranks if they are capable of playing an important role. *Ibid.* pp. 141–2.

Leninist Party. He must place himself within the Party in order to lead and urge forward the Party as a whole, and not outside the Party or above the Party in order to lead it. Lenin and Stalin both placed themselves within the Party in order to lead the Party and urge it forward, they both played their role as a single Party member within the Party.

Moreover, he did not scruple to apply these general principles to Mao, declaring:[1]

In our Party, there are no special privileges for individuals; any leadership which is not exercised in the name of the organization cannot be tolerated. Comrade Mao Tse-tung is the leader of the whole Party, but he, too, obeys the Party...

We obey the Party, we obey the Central Committee, we obey the truth; we do not obey individuals. No individual merits our obedience. Marx, Lenin and Mao Tse-tung have done their work well; they represent the truth, and it is only for this reason that we obey them.

It will be seen that a contradiction has here crept into Liu Shao-ch'i's reasoning by virtue of the fact that the purely organizational criterion for the right to obedience has been enlarged to include also the notion that the leader deserves to be followed because he stands for the truth. Liu could hardly avoid this problem, given the history of the Russian Social Democratic Workers' Party itself. He deals with the matter as tactfully as possible:[2]

The content and essence of the Party's unity is the ideological unity *created by Marxism*. This ideological unity is the most fundamental unity of all, and without it the Party's cohesion cannot be assured, and the Party's unity will be split. Hence, if there are ideological differences, differences of principle, within the Party, struggle must be unleashed in order that unity may once more be achieved. If there is a minority of Party members which persists in its errors of ideology and principle, and refuses to abandon them, in the end this minority must be expelled (for example, the Trotskyites and Rightists). If it is the majority within the Party which persists in holding to such an erroneous ideology and erroneous principles, then in the end it will be inevitable to split with them and set up another organization (for example, Lenin left the Social-Democratic Party and set up a separate Communist Party).

[1] *Ibid*. pp. 154–5.   [2] *Ibid*. p. 136.

The trouble with this explanation is that, as Liu himself points out, all the "renegades" of the past—Ch'en Tu-hsiu, Li Li-san, Lo Chang-lung, Chang Kuo-t'ao and others—had used this argument to justify their opposition to the Central Committee, which they said was following an erroneous line, and to set up their own rival organization. Liu's answer is that one should be extremely prudent in following such historical precedents as the creation of the Bolshevik faction because "Firstly, you are not Lenin, and secondly, Lenin was opposing the Second International, whereas you are opposing the Chinese Communist Party, led by the Third International."[1]

It may be of some interest to note, in the light of subsequent events, that Liu cites three examples of Communist leaders who have shown great merit and forbearance in obeying the majority even when they knew the majority was wrong: Marx, at the time of the Paris Commune; Lenin, at the time of Brest Litovsk; and himself, in the early years of the Chinese Communist Party, when the workers insisted on launching a strike which he knew would fail.[2] Mao is not included in this select list.

In concrete political terms, Liu very soon changed his attitude and came to terms with the reality of Mao's leadership. Thus, whereas he had previously shown little respect for Mao's achievements as a theoretician,[3] in his article of 1943, "Liquidate Menshevik Thought in the Party", he paid his tribute to the Mao cult which had begun to develop the previous year during the Rectification

---

[1] *Ibid.* pp. 147–8. [2] *Ibid.* pp. 174–6.

[3] In a letter dated simply July 13, and apparently written in 1941, to Comrade Sung Liang, Liu Shao-ch'i deplored the fact that although the Chinese Communist Party was extremely strong in its organizational work, it was exceedingly weak on the theoretical side. In particular, he complained that little headway had been made in the Sinification of Marxism. Liu Shao-ch'i, *Lun tang*, pp. 339–44. Mao, too, at about the same time, noted the lack of progress in this domain, despite his appeal of 1938 (see his speech of May 5, 1941. "The Reconstruction of Our Studies", in Boyd Compton, ed., *Mao's China*. Party Reform Documents, 1942–4 (Seattle: Univ. of Washington Press, 1952), pp. 59–68. But he did not, like Liu Shao-ch'i, attribute this unhappy situation to the fact that "the number of members of the Chinese Communist Party who can read the works of Marx and Lenin in the original is very limited" (*Lun tang*, p. 344), since this did not leave much place for his own contribution.

Campaign,[1] and in 1945 at the Seventh Party Congress he delivered the most fulsome eulogy yet of Mao's colossal theoretical achievements.[2] But despite this political *rapprochement*, which may well have been based on some bargain or agreement between the two men, there remained a great gulf between Liu's veneration for the Organization with a capital "O", to which he attributed a kind of metaphysical significance and an existence apart from the concrete individuals who composed it, and Mao's nostalgia for a Stalin who would "give the orders".

It is extremely suggestive that, although one of the aims of the *cheng-feng* movement of 1942 was to instil Leninist concepts of organization into the very large number of new recruits who had been taken into the Chinese Communist Party during the Anti-Japanese War, Mao himself had almost nothing to say on this theme in his two long speeches launching the movement. He left these problems to Liu Shao-ch'i, and to the authors of the various translated Soviet and Comintern materials such as Stalin and Dimitrov.[3] To be sure, one could say that this means little, since it simply proceeds from a functional specialization on the part of Mao and other comrades in the Chinese Communist Party. But surely it likewise reflects Mao's conviction that neither his own originality nor that of the Chinese Revolution lies in this domain. For him, the essential attributes of the Party he was bent on creating were to be found rather in its intellectual outlook, characterized by the integration of theory with the realities of Chinese society, and in the moral temper of its members.

In the few brief references he did make to problems of organization in his rectification speeches, Mao came down even more heavily than Liu Shao-ch'i on the side of order and discipline. Whereas Liu had declared, in his 1941 lectures, that democracy and centralism were equally important, since neither could exist without the other,

---

[1] Translated in Boyd Compton, *Mao's China*, pp. 255–68.

[2] Extracts of the most eloquent passages are to be found in H. Carrère d'Encausse and S. Schram, *Marxism and Asia* (London: Allen Lane The Penguin Press, 1969), Text IX, 1, pp. 259–61.

[3] As Boyd Compton points out in his introduction to the *cheng-feng* documents (*Mao's China*, p. xlv), these translated materials are similar to those which were used in other Communist Parties at the time.

Mao said: "The Communist Party not only needs democracy, but it needs centralization even more." And he added:[1] "We must definitely build a centralized, unified Party and make a clean sweep of all unprincipled factional struggles. We must combat individualism and sectarianism so as to enable our whole Party to march in step and fight for one common goal."

The classic statement of the "mass line" itself, Mao's directive of June 1, 1943, while it emphasizes the importance of closely linking the activity of "the leading group" with that of "the broad masses", makes it very clear that this leading group must be "strong" and "united", and that it must be characterized not only by "contact with the masses", and "capacity for independent work", but by "observance of discipline". Moreover, in a sentence eliminated from the current edition, Mao states that, in general, the two extremes among the masses—the "relatively active" and the "relatively backward"—are small, the great majority belonging to the middle group. In other words, people as a whole are not regarded here as a great reservoir of spontaneous creative energy; Mao views them rather, in altogether Leninist terms, as an inchoate mass to be taken in hand by a revolutionary elite. There is, however, a hint of the old Mao of the Chingkangshan—and of the Mao of recent years—in the statement that, in the course of any great struggle "the composition of the leading group should not and cannot remain entirely unchanged throughout the initial, middle and final stages; the activists who come forward in the course of the struggle must constantly be promoted to replace those original members of the leading group who are inferior by comparison or who have degenerated". For in the original text of this directive, the word "heroes" (*ying hsiung*) appears in parentheses after "activists", as an appositive explaining its meaning.[2]

Mao employed the same language in 1940, when he wrote in *On New Democracy* that the heroes and brave fellows (*ying hsiung hao han*) in the colonies and semi-colonies must take their stand either on the side of imperialism or on the side of world

---

[1] *Selected Works* (Peking: Foreign Languages Press, 1961–5), III, 43–5.

[2] For the original text, see *Chieh fang jih pao* [Liberation Daily], June 4, 1943; compare *Selected Works*, III, 117–22.

revolution.[1] It reflects his persistent tendency to evaluate the political merit of individuals by their own greatness of soul, and not by their status in an organization.

The conquest of power marked, as Mao himself pointed out at the time, the transition to a new stage in the history of the Chinese Communist Party. As he put it in March, 1949, in a report recently re-issued in the course of the Cultural Revolution:[2]

From 1927 to the present the centre of gravity of our work has been in the villages—gathering strength in the villages, using the villages in order to surround the cities and then taking the cities. The period for this method of work has now ended. The period of "from the city to the village" and of the city leading the village has now begun.

In other words, a Communist Party which had hitherto been in many ways unorthodox in its composition and methods was to become more orthodox. The efforts to achieve this during the early years of the Chinese People's Republic, in particular by drawing more workers into what had been largely a peasant party, are well known. What interests us here is the influence of these circumstances on Mao's conception of the Party, and that of his comrades. An interesting indication of the spirit in which Mao Tse-tung envisaged the problem at this time is provided by his statements, in "On People's Democratic Dictatorship", regarding the withering away of the Party:[3]

Like a man, a political party has its childhood, youth, manhood and old age. The Chinese Communist Party is no longer a child or a lad in his teens but has become an adult. When a man reaches old age, he will die; the same is true of a party. When classes disappear, all instruments of class struggle—parties and state machinery—will lose their function, cease to be necessary, therefore gradually wither away and end their historical mission; and human society will move to a higher stage... For the working class, the labouring people and the Communist Party, the question is...one...of working hard to create the conditions in which classes, state power and political parties will die out very naturally and mankind will enter the realm of Great Harmony.

[1] *The Political Thought of Mao Tse-tung*, p. 376.
[2] Report of March 5, 1949 to the Second Plenary Session of the Seventh Central Committee of the Chinese Communist Party, *Selected Works*, IV, 363.
[3] *Selected Works*, IV, 411–12.

It is true that this idea is to some extent implicit in the original Marxist view of the transformations which would ensue once the proletarian power had been established. Thus, in the *Manifesto*, Marx and Engels wrote: "When, in the course of development, class distinctions have disappeared, and all production has been concentrated in the hands of a vast association of the whole nation, the public power will lose its political character."[1] If the organization of society is to lose all political character, one might conclude, as Mao does, that political parties, including the Communist Party, will then have no further role to play.

But Mao was writing not in 1849 but in 1949, and not merely as a disciple of Marx, but as a disciple of Lenin. To.be sure, Lenin himself, in one of his rare forays into Utopia—that most un-Leninist work *The State and Revolution*—had likewise written of "the transformation of public functions from political into simple functions of administration".[2] But by his whole doctrine of the Party, which did not exist in any such form in the thought of Marx himself, Lenin had in fact introduced a new element into the problem. "By educating the workers' party", he wrote, discussing the situation after the victory of the revolution, "Marxism educates the vanguard of the proletariat, capable of assuming power and leading the whole people to socialism, of directing and organizing the new system, of being the teacher, the guide, the leader of all the working and exploited people in organizing their social life without the bourgeoisie and against the bourgeoisie."[3] This passage refers explicitly only to the first phase of communism, that of proletarian dictatorship, and not to the higher phase which will reputedly see the withering away of the state; hence it does not directly contradict Mao's ideas as set forth in "On People's Democratic Dictatorship". But if the ultimate withering away of the Party, as well as of the state, is compatible with Lenin's thinking, it is not a point on which he, or most other Communist writers, have chosen to dwell.

For the average Communist in all countries—including, probably, Liu Shao-ch'i and many other leaders and cadres in China—the Party

---

[1] See the last paragraph of chapter II of the *Communist Manifesto*.
[2] V. I. Lenin, *Selected Works* (Moscow: Progress Publishers, 1967), II, 314.
[3] *Ibid*. p. 285.

as an organization has become such an important reality that its disappearance can scarcely be imagined. Even when it has ceased to have a "political" character, they no doubt think of it as living on in the role of "teacher and guide...in organizing...social life" attributed to it by Lenin. Mao's sensibility in these matters is clearly different, as is underscored by his further discussion of the same theme of the withering away of the Party in 1956, in his speech on "The Ten Great Relations". Here he makes explicit what could only be guessed from his 1949 essay, namely that the Communist Party will wither away *simultaneously* with the various other democratic parties which still survive in China:[1] "In the last analysis, is it better to have one party or several parties? As we see it at present, it is better to have several parties. Not only was this the case in the past, but it may also be the case in the future, right down to the time when all parties naturally wither away."

By declaring not merely, as he did in 1949, that the Communist Party, like all other parties, would one day wither away, but that it would not necessarily enjoy even a brief period during which it was the only party in existence, Mao gave one more proof that he sees the Communist Party as merely one instrument among others, and not as something unique and sacred which is in itself the embodiment of legitimacy.

Taking as he does a fundamentally utilitarian view of the Party, Mao has repeatedly revised his ideas in the course of the past twenty years, in the light of the contribution which, in his judgement, this particular form of organization was actually making to the revolutionary transformation of China. The development of his thinking in this domain is thus inextricably linked to the mutations in his conception of revolution since 1949.

In the broadest terms, the evolution of Mao's thinking about "building socialism" since he achieved victory displays a striking parallel with the development of his ideas about the road to power prior to 1949. In both cases, he first accepted on faith an orthodox Leninist approach inspired by Moscow, based on the cities and the urban working class, and shifted to a different model, relying above

[1] See paragraph 7 of Mao's "Lun shih ta kuan hsi", on "Relations between the Party and Non-Party People and Organizations." Translated in Jerome Ch'ên, *Mao* (Englewood Cliffs, N. J.: Prentice-Hall, 1969), pp. 65–85.

all on the peasants in the countryside, only when more orthodox methods failed to work. After the disasters of Shanghai and Canton, he took the road to the Chingkangshan and to Yenan; after he became convinced that Soviet methods of planned economic development would leave basic values and patterns of thought largely unchanged, he embarked on the path of the communes, the Great Leap Forward, and ultimately of the Cultural Revolution.

This shift involved the re-evaluation of a whole series of factors which are linked among themselves and at the same time directly related to Mao's attitude towards the Party: organization and leadership as opposed to spontaneous action by the masses, the working class as opposed to the peasantry, the technical and managerial elite as opposed to rank-and-file ingenuity, material factors as opposed to moral factors. On all of these issues, Mao has, as everyone now knows, moved away from Leninist orthodoxy and from the majority position of the Party leadership.

Just as he had stressed the "consciousness" of the intellectuals as the decisive element in building the revolutionary Party prior to the conquest of power, so Lenin displayed what might be called a "technocratic bias" in his approach to socialist transformation after the conquest of power. In his view, only a profound change in the material conditions in which men lived would ultimately make it possible to modify their patterns of behaviour, and such a change could only be achieved by planned economic development based on organization, discipline and technical competence. Above all, what was required was industrialization, which would shake the peasants out of their torpor and force them to assimilate the values of the city.

This technocratic bias was continued and intensified under Stalin. It meant attributing to the workers a role in "building socialism" not unlike that which Lenin had granted to them in establishing the Party, and which could be likened to that of non-commissioned officers. Just as they had required the bourgeois intellectuals to become truly conscious of the interests and mission of their own class, they needed the managers and engineers to guide them in the work of economic development. But they were possessed, both before and after the conquest of power, of organizational talents and technical skills denied to the peasants, and hence could provide the disciplined backbone which the amorphous rural masses were incapable of generating themselves.

In this whole broad domain of attitudes towards organization and attitudes towards technical factors in social change, Mao began to move in 1955 from a Leninist reliance on the elite to a populist reliance on the masses. Thus, in the years ahead, he put forward the view that in China, because of the special conditions prevailing in the country, collectivization must precede mechanization.[1] This was in direct contradiction not only with the view which Liu Shao-ch'i had expounded in 1950—now denounced as "China's Khrushchev's reactionary theory of 'mechanization before collectivization'"[2]—but with the ideas of Lenin and Stalin. At the same time, Mao began to reassess the role of the Party.

Mao's views on the Party at this time are set forth most clearly in the commentaries he contributed to the collection of documents entitled *Socialist Upsurge in China's Countryside*, of which the first Chinese edition was sent to the press in December, 1955. In these, he did not hide his own conflict with the cadres of the Party. Thus, he declared: "In many localities there is a practice prevalent almost to the point of being universal: right opportunists within the Party, working hand in glove with the forces of capitalism in society, are preventing the broad masses of poor and lower middle peasants from taking the road to the formation of co-operatives."[3] In other words, many cadres at the grass-roots level were not applying Mao's policies. But at the same time, he continued to attribute to the Party the decisive role in the economic, social and political transformation of China.[4] Similarly, in his speech of January 25, 1956, before the

[1] See his speech of July 31, 1955 on the agricultural cooperative movement' conveniently available in *Selected Readings from the Works of Mao Tse-tung* (Peking: Foreign Languages Press, 1967), p. 335. For a more extended discussion, see the forthcoming revised edition of my biography of Mao Tse-tung.

[2] Liu made his statement of 1950 in his report on land reform, found in *The Agrarian Reform Law of the People's Republic of China* (third edition; Peking: Foreign Languages Press, 1952) p. 88. For the denunciation of his "reactionary theory", see *Peking Review*, No. 12 (March 22, 1968), p. 27.

[3] *Chung kuo nung ts'un ti she hui chu i kao ch'ao*, p. 729; p. 159 of the English translation.

[4] He said, for example: "Whether or not the socialist transformation of our agriculture can keep pace with the rate of advance of industrialization in our

Supreme State Council, presenting his twelve-year programme for agricultural development, Mao displayed an emphasis on the economic aspect of revolution, and a respect for the role of technical competence in furthering modernization, which has since largely disappeared from his thinking. In carrying out the "vast design" of "transforming the backward economic, scientific, and cultural conditions in our country so as to attain rapidly an advanced level by world standards", the "factor which decides everything" he declared to be "the need for cadres, the need for a sufficient number of scientific and technical specialists".[1]

In a word, Mao's view of the Party at this stage appears to have been that it was an organization with bureaucratic and rightist tendencies but an organization which, despite these defects, was still the only available instrument, and indeed the only conceivable instrument, for leading the revolution. Moreover, he was still prepared to recognize the importance and utility not only of politically dedicated Party cadres, but of "scientific and technical specialists". Although it is obviously too early for any definitive analysis of relations between Mao and the Party during the past two decades, it appears likely that the Eighth Party Congress in September, 1956 marked a decisive stage in the deterioration of these relations.

Attention has been focused on the deletion of the reference to "Mao Tse-tung's thought" as the guide for all the Party's work in the new version of the Party constitution adopted at this Congress, which is now said to have been a plot by Liu Shao-ch'i and Teng Hsiao-p'ing, abetted by "traitor P'eng Te-huai".[2] But on re-reading the record of the Congress one discovers many statements which can scarcely have been in accord with Mao's views, and quite a few which must have been intensely repugnant to him.

country, whether or not the co-operative movement can develop in a healthy fashion..., depends on whether or not the local Party Committees at all levels can quickly and correctly shift the emphasis to this task...A change of this kind depends first and foremost on the secretaries of the Party committees at various levels..." *Ibid.* pp. 1125-6 of the Chinese edition and pp. 206-7 of the English edition.

[1] *Jen min jih pao*, January 26, 1956.

[2] See the anti-P'eng materials translated in *Current Background*, No. 851, and now available in *The Case of Peng Teh-huai* (Hong Kong: Union Research Institute, 1968), pp. 119-20, 201.

Once more, as in 1941, Liu Shao-ch'i emphasized the primacy of the collective, and attributed Mao's success as a leader to his modesty and self-effacement:

As everyone knows, the reason why the leader of our Party, Comrade Mao Tse-tung, has played the great role of helmsman[1] in our revolution and enjoys a high prestige in the whole Party and among the people of the country is not only that he knows how to integrate the universal truth of Marxism-Leninism with the actual practice of the Chinese revolution, but also that he firmly believes in the strength and wisdom of the masses, initiates and advocates the mass line in Party work, and steadfastly upholds the Party's principles of democracy and collective leadership.[2]

For his part, Teng Hsiao-p'ing, while recognizing the importance of leaders, stressed, like Liu Shao-ch'i in 1941, that they must stand "not above the masses, but in their midst, not above the Party, but in it". They must, he said, set an example in obeying the Party organizations and observing Party discipline. "Love for the leader", he declared, "is essentially an expression of love for the interests of the Party, the class and the people, and not the deification of an individual. An important achievement of the 20th Congress of the Communist Party of the Soviet Union lies in the fact that it showed us what serious consequences can follow from the deification of the individual."[3]

Such a rejection of the "cult of the individual" naturally goes hand in hand with the valorization of the Party as a collective entity. But since the will of the Party can be expressed only by the human beings who compose it, the authority of the leader can be circumscribed only by stressing the role of some other component in the organization. It is typical of Liu Shao-ch'i's thinking—and also entirely in harmony with the spirit of Leninism—that he should attach special significance to the cadres. Thus he declared: "The amount of experience gained by the Party and the choice of leaders do have an important bearing on whether the Party makes mistakes,

[1] Liu had in fact hailed Mao as "the helmsman of the Chinese nation and of the Chinese people's revolutionary struggle" in the peroration of his report of May 14, 1945 on the revision of the Party constitution.

[2] *Eighth National Congress of the Communist Party of China* (Peking: Foreign Languages Press, 1956), I, 104–5.

[3] *Ibid.* p. 200.

but what is more important is whether the rank-and-file Party members, *and primarily the high-ranking cadres*, can, in the various periods, apply the Marxist–Leninist stand, viewpoint and method to sum up experience in the struggle, hold fast to the truth and correct mistakes."[1]

As I have already suggested, these questions of the structure of authority in the Party cannot be separated from the broader issues of the role of the Party in the revolutionary process. In particular, they are linked to the problem of the Party's class basis. It is, of course, agreed by everyone that the Chinese Communist Party is the party of the proletariat. Thus, the very first sentence of the Party Constitution adopted in 1956 read: "The Chinese Communist Party is the vanguard of the Chinese working class, the highest form of its class organization." On the other hand, article 1 of chapter 1 declared that membership was open to "any Chinese citizen who works and does not exploit the labour of others". To what extent did Mao, Liu, Teng and the others regard all non-exploiters as equally good potential members of the workers' party, and to what extent did they consider it vital that the party should contain a higher percentage of genuine urban workers? Although one would have expected all the "orthodox" Party leaders to take a similar line on this question, in fact Liu Shao-ch'i has appeared throughout to attach more importance to the real workers, and to be more sceptical regarding the revolutionary capacities of other classes, and especially of the peasantry, than Teng Hsiao-p'ing—not to mention Mao Tse-tung.

Teng Hsiao-p'ing, on the the other hand, went very far in 1956 in minimizing the importance of objective class origins altogether. Thus he declared, in discussing the abandonment in the 1956 constitution of the more rigorous selection procedures previously in force for non-workers applying for Party membership:

The distinction that was hitherto made in the procedure of admitting new members has been removed because the former classification of social status has lost or is losing its original meaning... The difference between workers and office employees is now only a matter of division of labour within the same class. [!]...Poor and middle peasants have all become

[1] *Ibid.* p. 98. Emphasis added.

members of agricultural producers' cooperatives, and before long the distinction between them will become merely a thing of historical interest ...The vast majority of our intellectuals have now come over politically to the side of the working class, and a rapid change is taking place in their family background. The conditions in which the city poor and the professional people used to exist as independent social strata have been virtually eliminated. Every year, large numbers of peasants and students become workers, large numbers of workers, peasants and their sons and daughters join the ranks of the intellectuals and office-workers, large numbers of peasants, students, workers and office-workers join the army and become revolutionary soldiers, while large numbers of revolutionary soldiers return to civilian life as peasants, students, workers or office-workers. What is the point then, of classifying these social strata into two different categories?[1]

Although some details of the above passage, such as the statement that the distinction between former poor and middle peasants will soon be of merely historical interest, are not in harmony with subsequent developments, Teng here adopts an approach basically similar to that of Mao in recent years, namely that the "class nature" of Party members depends rather on subjective attitudes than on objective family origins. At the same time, it is worth noting that Mao himself, as late as February, 1957 in his speech on contradictions among the people, stated that although there would still be class struggle in China, "the turbulent, large-scale, mass class struggles characteristic of the revolutionary periods have in the main come to an end".[2]

If Mao proceeded to move, in the course of the ensuing year, to

[1] *Ibid.* pp. 213–14.

[2] Mao Tse-tung, *On the Correct Handling of Contradictions Among the People* (Peking: Foreign Languages Press, 1957), p. 50. Mao was, in fact, honest enough to recognize, even in October 1966, during the high tide of the Cultural Revolution, that the ideas put forward by Teng Hsiao-p'ing in 1956 had not represented merely an individual deviation, but had reflected the climate in the whole Party at the time. When K'ang Sheng denounced Liu and Teng for this past heresy in the course of a meeting, Mao promptly interrupted him to say: "We all read the report, and it was adopted by the Congress. One cannot hold only the two of them responsible." See the collection of statements and directives by Mao entitled *Mao Tse-tung ssu hsiang wan sui!* (n.p., n.d.), p. 46; translation in *Current Background*, No. 891, p. 72.

revive not only "class struggle" as the conflict between bourgeois and proletarian ideological tendencies, but the atmosphere of "turbulent and large-scale mass movements" which he declared in February, 1957 to be largely a thing of the past, it was no doubt in considerable part because of his disillusionment at the outcome of the Hundred Flowers episode. Mao's statements during the years 1955–6 regarding the pre-eminent importance of cadres and technical knowledge were rooted in the conviction that by now the vast majority of the population had been persuaded of the superiority of the socialist system and was basically loyal to the principles of the new regime. The political foundations having thus been laid, one could concentrate on techniques. But the reaction when the floodgates were opened to criticism early in 1957 soon convinced Mao that the political and ideological revolution was far from accomplished, and must be given first priority.

Mao's new approach finds graphic expression in his contribution to the first issue of *Hung ch'i* in 1958, in which he first put forward publicly the thesis that the Chinese people were possessed of superior revolutionary capacities because they were "poor and blank".[1] The idea that "poor people want revolution" bears some resemblance to Marxism, though Marx saw in the proletariat the class capable of redeeming society not only because its members were economically exploited and deprived of the fruits of their labour, but also because of the decisive role they played in the productive process. Mao's praise of "blankness", on the other hand, is in profound contradiction with the logic of Marxism. Marx, who had the greatest respect for the technical and economic achievements of the bourgeoisie, attributed to the proletariat the capacity for becoming the leading class in society not only because it incarnated the moral values of protest against injustice, but also because it was the heir to the technical knowledge of the bourgeoisie. Because the peasant societies of Asia did not possess these technical skills and economic drive, Marx proclaimed explicitly that the only solution for them lay in "Europeanization".

---

[1] He had first expounded this idea, in a somewhat attenuated form, in his unpublished speech of April, 1956 on the Ten Great Relations. Ch'ên, *op. cit.*, pp. 83–4.

For Mao Tse-tung, the implications regarding the inferiority of the Asian nations and their need to learn from the West "how it is done" implicit in the logic of Marxism are clearly intolerable. Hence his attempt to make of "blankness" a virtue, a symbol of the moral purity of the Chinese people, who are not afflicted with the maladies of materialism and individualism that have perverted not only the West but the Soviet Union.

It may appear that the contrast between Mao's vision of revolution by the poor and blank and the logic of Marxism has little to do with the Party. In fact, it seems to me that it has everything to do with it. For the Party is by definition the bearer of organizational expertise, and also to a certain extent of technical knowledge. This is the case not only of orthodox Leninism, but of the thinking of Liu Shao-ch'i and of Mao himself during the early years of the Chinese People's Republic. Thus Mao declared in March, 1949: "We [i.e. the Party] can learn what we did not know [i.e. the new skills necessary for developing the economy]."[1] And Liu Shao-ch'i said more explicitly in 1956:[2]

In all work the Party should and can play a leading role ideologically, politically, and in matters of principle, and policy. Of course, that does not mean that the Party should take everything into its own hands, or interfere in everything. Neither does it mean that it should be content with being a layman in things it does not understand. The Party calls on its cadres and members to study painstakingly in order to master the things they do not understand in their work. For the more we study, the better will we be able to lead.

As already suggested, it is in part because Marx attributed these two qualities of organizing ability and technical knowledge to the proletariat that he saw in it the class capable of achieving not merely the moral redemption but the continuing material progress of society. Lenin, and still more Stalin, further emphasized these attributes as inherent in the working class. It was, for example, in the name of this postulate that groups of workers were sent out from Moscow and Petrograd in 1929–30 to help (or coerce) the peasants into forming the collective farms which they were presumably incapable

[1] *Selected Works*, IV, 375.   [2] *Eighth National Congress*, p. 96.

of organizing themselves.[1] Obviously, Mao could never have accepted an orthodox Social-Democratic interpretation of Marxism, under which the social development of a given country must progress to a point where there were large numbers of real workers endowed with the peculiar virtues of the proletariat before revolution could take place. But why could he not model himself on the Soviet example, in which a so-called proletarian party had taken power in the name of an embryonic working class, and had then so transformed society in the course of half a century as actually to create its own supposed class basis?

The essential reason, I would submit, is that if China were to follow the Soviet example, and gradually transform a predominantly rural society under the guidance of a Party which was "proletarian" in the sense of genuinely embodying the values of the real working class, the members of this Party would remain for a very long time far more foreign, in their mentality and way of life, to Chinese society as a whole than were the Bolsheviks in Russia. They would thus be more prone to become a privileged and bureaucratic stratum detached from the masses of a still largely agrarian China. Moreover, as the bearers of knowledge actually acquired in many cases outside the country, and in any case ultimately transmitted from the West (including the Soviet Union), they would appear in a sense as the instruments of the kind of foreign domination regarded as intolerable by Mao Tse-tung.

In 1958, despite the radicalism of the Great Leap Forward, it still appeared that Mao *was* prepared to work through a Party of the traditional type. For example, in the resolution of the Sixth Plenum of the Central Committee dated December 10, 1958, it was laid down:

In running a people's commune well, the fundamental question is to strengthen the leading role of the Party. It is only by strengthening the Party's leading role that the principle of politics in command can be realized, that socialist and communist ideological education among the cadres and commune members and the struggle against all kinds of

[1] See Thomas P. Bernstein's article "Leadership and Mass Mobilisation in the Soviet and Chinese Collectivisation Campaigns of 1929–30 and 1955–56: a Comparison", *The China Quarterly*, No. 31 (July–September, 1967), pp. 1–47.

erroneous tendencies can be conducted in a thoroughgoing way, and that the Party's line and policy can be implemented correctly.[1]

But this passage is immediately followed by this curiously prophetic sentence: "There are some people who think that with the emergence of the commune the Party can be dispensed with, and that they can practice what they call 'merging the Party and the commune in one'." The resolution adds that "This kind of thinking is wrong", and there is no proof that such was Mao's own view at the time. Indeed, Kuan Feng, who later emerged as one of the principal members of the extreme leftist faction in the Cultural Revolution, declared in an article on the "great historical significance of the people's communes" published in the autumn of 1958 that one of the advantages of the communes was "the strengthening of Party leadership in the basic organizations". And he further stated that the "high level of centralization" practised in the communes would contribute to this desirable end.[2] But in the long run, Mao's utopian vision was to prove incompatible with the orthodox Leninist conception of the Party and its role.

During the crucial years 1962–5, when in many respects the groundwork for the Cultural Revolution was being laid, the statements regarding the Party issued by Mao or his spokesmen became increasingly ambiguous. One very important document of this period is the ninth Chinese reply to the Soviets, entitled "On Khrushchev's Phoney Communism and its Lessons for the World", which contained extensive quotations and paraphrases of Mao's views on the form of the dictatorship of the proletariat, and in particular on the role of the Party. In the summary of the "main contents of the theories and policies advanced by Comrade Mao Tse-tung in this connection", the fifteenth and last point begins:[3] "As the vanguard of the proletariat, the Communist Party must exist as long as the dictatorship of the proletariat exists. The Communist Party is the highest form of organization of the proletariat. The

[1] See paragraph VII of the resolution.

[2] *Che hsüeh yen chiu* [Philosophical Research], No. 5 (1958), pp. 1–8. Translation in my monograph *La "revolution permanente" en Chine* (Paris: Mouton, 1963).

[3] *Peking Review*, No. 29 (July 17, 1964), p. 26.

leading role of the proletariat is realized through the leadership of the Communist Party...".

There is here implied, of course, the notion of the withering away of the Party put forward by Mao in 1949, and re-stated in 1956. Apart from this, Party leadership at the present stage is duly mentioned—but if it would not be quite fair to say that it is added as an afterthought, it is certainly not very heavily stressed in the context of the statement of Mao's views as a whole. This same editorial note also made public for the first time the now familiar quotation from Mao's note of May 9, 1963 warning that if proper vigilance was not exercised, "the Marxist–Leninist Party would undoubtedly become a revisionist party or a fascist party, and the whole of China would change its colour".[1] Even more striking in a sense than this remark—which certainly did not indicate a very high level of confidence in the Party—was another argument used against the Soviet conception of the "party of the entire people":[2]

If Marxism–Leninism has really become the world outlook of the entire people, as you allege, does it not then follow that there is no difference in your society between Party and non-Party and no need whatsoever for the Party to exist? What difference does it make if there is a "party of the entire people" or not?

This passage clearly expresses a point of view which is implicit elsewhere in this long editorial, and which has obviously come to underlie more and more Mao's thinking in recent years, namely that the Communist Party is simply an assemblage of like-minded people, and not an entity with a definite structure, still less an organization having an existence and a significance of its own. The "proletarian party", from the tightly organized and disciplined instrument conceived by Lenin and used (and misused) by Stalin, has become simply the totality of all the "proletarians" in a given society. It only remained to define "proletarian" as not merely right-thinking, but faithful to the leader, in order to reach today's paradoxical situation in which a pro-Mao "revolutionary rebel" outside the Party represents the Party, whereas the Party's regularly appointed leadership does not.

[1] *Loc. cit.*　　　　　[2] *Ibid.* p. 19.

In January, 1965, in the 23-point directive on the "socialist education movement" in the countryside (which is now, like virtually every other important directive issued in the past few years, attributed to Chairman Mao in person), it was stated for the first time that the principal enemy was to be found within the Party. "The important point in this campaign", the directive stated, "is rectifying those people within the Party who are in authority and are taking the capitalist road." Some of these, it was said, were to be found even in the departments of the Central Committee. At the same time the de-emphasizing of the Party which had been in evidence since the Great Leap Forward was carried a step further. Thus, in the six criteria which were said to have been put forward in June, 1964 by Mao Tse-tung for carrying out the socialist education movement well, the Party as such was not even mentioned, although the fourth item read: "Has a good leadership core been established or not?"[1]

The ambiguity persisted, however, even in the celebrated May 16th directive of 1966, which is supposed to have marked Mao Tse-tung's reassertion of control over the Cultural Revolution. For, after denouncing "those representatives of the bourgeoisie who have sneaked into the Party, the government, the army and various cultural circles" as "a bunch of counter-revolutionary revisionists", the document went on to warn: "Once conditions are ripe, they will seize political power and turn the dictatorship of the proletariat into the dictatorship of the bourgeoisie."[2] By this it is suggested that the Party still occupies a unique and decisive position in the political system, since the "revisionists" within the Party could use their positions to seize the levers of power. Such a situation, in which status and power depended on a given individual's place in the hierarchy of an organization, and not on his good pleasure alone, was clearly intolerable to Mao. Hence the statement, attributed to Mao in the same directive: "Put destruction first, and in the process you have construction." In other words, smash the Party, and then the true "proletarian" revolutionaries (i.e. those loyal to Chairman Mao) can build a new order.

[1] See the extracts translated in *The Political Thought of Mao Tse-tung*, Text VI, C, 10, pp. 323–5.　　[2] *Peking Review*, No. 21 (May 19, 1967), p. 9.

Mao's dictum about putting destruction first was spelled out in picturesque and highly un-Marxist language, which throws an instructive light on the meaning to be attached to the word "proletarian", in the *tatzupao* said to have been put up by the Red Guards of the Middle School attached to Tsinghua University on June 24, 1966. (This document was first published only in August, 1966, following the first Red Guard rally in Peking, at the same time as Mao's slogan "To rebel is justified!") "Revolution is rebellion, and rebellion is the soul of Mao Tse-tung's thought", began the poster. "Daring...to rebel is the most fundamental and most precious quality of proletarian revolutionaries. *This is the fundamental principle of the proletarian Party spirit!*"[1] The definition of "party spirit" or "*partiinost*" as rebellion against the Party (or in any case against the majority of its leadership) is obviously the logical culmination and *reductio ad absurdum* of the tendency to define fidelity to the Party exclusively in terms of loyalty to "Mao Tse-tung's thought" which had been developing for several years.

The singular mixture of revolutionary and traditional imagery which characterizes the whole of the Cultural Revolution is extraordinarily well illustrated by the last paragraph of this poster:[2]

Revolutionaries are Monkey Kings, their golden rods are terrible [*li hai te hen*], their supernatural powers far-reaching and their magic [*fa li*] omnipotent, for they possess Mao Tse-tung's great invincible thought. We wield our golden rods, display our supernatural powers, and use our magic to turn the old world upside down, smash it to pieces, pulverize it, and create chaos—the greater the confusion the better [*yüeh luan yüeh hao*]! ...We are bent on creating a tremendous proletarian uproar, and hewing out a proletarian new world!

It would be hard to find a more striking epitome of Mao's view according to which membership in the proletariat is defined above all by a state of mind, which anyone can acquire through study, or simply in a flash of illumination, and thus change his objective class essence.

[1] *Jen min jih pao*, August 24, 1966; translation in *Peking Review*, No. 37 (September 9, 1966), pp. 2–21.
[2] *Loc. cit.*

As regards the political tactics of the Maoist faction, Mao himself had declared that construction must follow destruction, and he had long shown too clear a grasp of the importance of organization as a political weapon to imagine that his aims could be achieved merely by adolescent "Monkey Kings". Indeed, in a letter of August 1966 to the authors of the *tatzupao* just quoted, who had sent him a copy of their manifesto, Mao subtly transformed the slogan justifying "rebellion", which he himself had coined in 1939, to read "It is right to rebel against reactionaries." In other words, rebellion was not an end in itself, to be indulged in merely for the sake of letting off steam, but a means to get rid of "reactionaries", i.e., those of whom Chairman Mao disapproved.[1]

The phase of destruction was therefore followed by the phase of the seizure of power. This period, which began in January, 1967 and came to a close only in the autumn of 1968, raises, of course, the most complex questions as to what actually happened, and in particular as to the role of the Army. Here our concern is rather with the ideological justifications put forward by Mao and his spokesmen, especially as they affect the Party. In this respect, while the ideological rationalizations of the "triple union" put forward in early 1967 are couched in more Marxist language than the Red Guard eloquence cited above, they go in some respects even farther than these earlier texts in overturning established Leninist principles regarding the role of the Party.

One of the most significant documents in this respect is the *Hung ch'i* editorial entitled "On the Proletarian Revolutionaries' Struggle to Seize Power". First, this text goes to the extreme of applying to the "handful of persons within the Party who are in authority and taking the capitalist road" several of Mao's statements directed against the "imperialists" in general or the United States in particular. Thus, as in the case of the Soviet leaders, the "revisionists" within the Chinese Communist Party have ceased to be regarded as misguided comrades to be re-educated, and are completely assimilated to the enemy. Secondly, it is stated that "the revolutionary masses have become clear as to who are the chief figures among those in the Party who are in authority and taking the capitalist road".

[1] See the translation in *Current Background*, No. 891, p. 63.

In other words, the "revolutionary masses" are better judges of "proletarian" virtue than the "proletarian party" itself. Thirdly, and most important, it is asserted:[1]

A number of units, where a handful of persons within the Party who are in authority and taking the capitalist road have entrenched themselves over a long period, have become rotten. There these persons have been exercising bourgeois dictatorship, not proletarian dictatorship. The Marxist principle of smashing the existing state machine must be put into practice in the struggle for the seizure of power in these units.

In other words, the best way to preserve the Party as a symbol is to smash the concrete organization of the Party whenever it fails to obey Mao's will. This is not merely an inference on my part; it is clearly laid down in the editorial just quoted, when it is declared: "The current seizure of power from the handful of persons within the Party who are in authority and taking the capitalist road is not effected by dismissal and reorganization from above [i.e. by the organization itself] but from below by the mass movement called for and supported by Chairman Mao himself." Thus, while the Party still subsisted as an organization, it had become a group of rather suspect individuals, like the national bourgeoisie, only tolerated on good behaviour. The "soul of the Party" lay henceforth in the mysterious communion between the "great leader", Chairman Mao, and the masses.

One reason for Mao's onslaught on the Party was of course the fact that it was no longer an obedient instrument for carrying out his will. But while resentment at Liu Shao-ch'i, Teng Hsiao-p'ing and the other Party leaders who had thwarted him in the application of his radical policies undoubtedly influenced his attitude, his recent course corresponds too closely to tendencies long present in his thought and behaviour to be explained merely by pique and vanity. Stalin decimated the Party bureaucracy in order to maintain his own power, but he had nothing against bureaucracy as such; on the contrary, he could conceive of no other way of governing and of running the economy. Mao, on the other hand, although he exhibited very early a grasp of the importance of organization as a political

[1] *Hung ch'i* [Red Flag], No. 3 (1967), translation in *Peking Review*, No. 6 (February 3, 1967), pp. 10–15.

weapon which I have called "natural Leninism," has constantly sought to prevent all organizations, including the Party, from becoming ends in themselves. In the past, he combated the bureaucratization of the Party both from within, by the repeated rectification campaigns in which the cadres were obliged to participate, and from without, by constantly exposing the Party organization to popular scrutiny in accordance with the formula of the "mass line". This time, he chose to treat the Party cadres not, as in 1942 or 1957, as patients to be cured, but as enemies to be terrorized by the Red Guards and publicly humiliated.

In March, 1967, impressed by the slogans about "smashing the bourgeois state machine," I went so far as to suggest that there might be no place at all for the Party in the new scheme of things Mao was striving to create, except perhaps as a label for right-minded people. Recent developments, during and after the Ninth Party Congress, have shown that this was going too far. But they also show how singular is Mao's conception of the Party today.

The most astonishing and spectacular expression of the totally unorthodox character of current Chinese thinking about the Party is to be found in the paragraph of the new Party constitution designating Lin Piao as Mao's successor.[1] This passage has received abundant attention as a clue to the balance of power within the Chinese elite, but its ideological implications have perhaps not been sufficiently spelled out. In this sense it comes as the culmination of Mao's attempt to set himself openly above the Party as the incarnation of the will of the "proletariat". This is something which Stalin himself never ventured to do. Even as he established his own arbitrary dictatorship and purged the Party bureaucracy with the aid of the secret police, Stalin claimed to be merely the servant of the Party, exercising its collective authority in his capacity as Secretary General. This conception of the leader as, in theory at least, simply the person who happens to be occupying a given office in the Party at a given time, should logically rule out any idea of a personal successor. It is true, of course, that a great effort was made in the Soviet Union to build up Stalin as Lenin's

[1] For a translation of the new Party constitution, see *Peking Review*, No. 18 (April 30, 1969), pp. 36–9.

"closest comrade in arms" and therefore to establish a kind of personal succession. But by formally laying it down in the Party constitution that Lin Piao will be *his* successor, Mao not only carries this process of the laying on of hands a step farther, but effectively denies to the Party as a collective entity a right which unquestionably belongs to it, namely that of choosing a new Chairman when the post becomes vacant. Thus the individual authority of the leader is seen to exceed the collective authority of the organization not only during his lifetime, but beyond. This is the utter negation of the Leninist conception of the Party as an order made up of individuals who collectively incarnate the will of the proletariat. Mao's conception of "open-door Party consolidation", as expressed in a directive quoted in an editorial published on 1 July 1969, in commemoration of the 48th anniversary of the founding of the Chinese Communist Party,[1] is in fact a deliberate attempt to break down the privileged status of the Party members by inviting the non-Party masses to "attend the meetings and give comments". Mao's aim—to prevent Party cadres from taking on the airs of the former imperial bureaucracy—is a laudable one, but these policies are nevertheless in flagrant contradiction with the whole logic of Leninism.

Another expression of Mao's leader-centred conception of the Party is, of course, the provision in the new constitution that individual members may bypass their immediate superiors and appeal directly to the Central Committee and to its Chairman. This tendency to establish direct links between the leader and the grassroots is carried a step farther in the provision that "leading organs of the Party at every level must ... constantly listen to the opinions of the masses both inside and outside the Party and be subject to their supervision".[2]

It is no accident that the two points just mentioned occur in the same paragraph of the new Party constitution. For if Mao has placed himself above the Party, he has done so, in his own eyes, only in order that the Party may not place itself above the masses—

[1] "Long Live the Communist Party of China", translated in *Peking Review*, No. 27 (July 4, 1969), pp. 7–9.
[2] See Article V.

in order that the spontaneity of the masses should not be inhibited by the dead hand of a bureaucratic organization. Spontaneity was, of course, a dirty word for Lenin. In fact, Mao's spontaneity is, of course, a spontaneity tempered or limited by military control, but he probably does not see in this a contradiction, since by definition a guerrilla-minded army cannot be bureaucratic.

CONCLUSION

As already suggested, the tendency towards the generalization of the spirit of Yenan which characterizes Mao's thought and policies since 1955 implies an emphasis on struggle rather than rationality, and on mass action rather than the technical and managerial elite, which in fact goes against the grain not only of "Khrushchevite revisionism" (with or without Khrushchev), but of Leninism itself. A parallel has been suggested, and does in fact exist, between certain aspects of Stalin's assault on the Party during the purges of the thirties, and Mao's assault on the Party today. But the similarities should not blind us to the profound differences between these two series of events, still less lead us to accept some theory of the identical wave of violence which grips all Communist regimes two decades, more or less, after they are established. Stalin leaned on the government bureaucracy as a counterweight to the Party; Mao leans on the Army, and this in itself is significant. Even more important, Stalin used mass hysteria backed by terror to exclusively political ends, to break resistance to his own rule. He did not regard mass mobilization as a useful instrument of economic progress. On the contrary, he stressed, like Lenin, both technological factors and organization as basic to the transformation of society. Worse still, for one praised today in Peking as a genuine revolutionary, he regarded not unselfish devotion to the common good, but material incentives, as the principal source of inspiration for "building socialism". Egalitarianism, he declared in 1934, was "a reactionary petty-bourgeois absurdity worthy of some primitive sect of ascetics".[1]

The accent on organization, rationality and technical competence

[1] See his report to the Seventeenth Congress of the CPSU.

can, as already pointed out, be traced back to Marx himself, who saw in the European proletariat the class which would not only put an end to the injustice of capitalism, but at the same time inherit and carry on the promethean mission of the bourgeoisie. Lenin made of the need for consciousness and organization the key to his whole revolutionary system, as it related to tactics both before and after the conquest of power. Mao, on the other hand, came to power not as a result of a skilfully engineered coup by a minority, but after two decades of guerrilla warfare during which he had survived only by involving the whole of the Chinese people, or a large part of it, in the struggle to transform its own fate.

Out of this very different revolutionary experience have come the contrasting visions of revolution which we encounter today in China and in the Soviet Union. Once again, the writings of Stalin himself show how far removed was the spirit of the Soviet Union under his leadership from that which reigns in China today. Contradictions in socialist society, he declared in 1950, were resolved not by revolutions, but by gradual change, without qualitative leaps. Even such a profound transformation as agricultural collectivization in the Soviet Union had taken the form of a gradual transition, without ruptures, because it constituted "a revolution from above".[1] In fact, the conception of "revolution from above", by those who know best, is very much a part of the Leninist tradition. Mao, on the other hand, though he proposes to re-shape the "poor and blank" Chinese people, attempts to do so from within, rather than from above.

At the basis of all Mao's policies today lies (apart from the obvious concern with maintaining his own power) a profound anxiety lest the process of industrialization and modernization under way in China lead to the emergence of the same tendencies which have been engendered by economic development in other countries: increasing functional differentiation and the birth of new forms of social stratification, the subordination of moral values to technical rationality, the primacy of economic incentives. The fact that the domination of a bureaucratic and technocratic elite in the Soviet Union appears to him to be linked to the development of such

[1] See his *Marxism and Questions of Linguistics.*

"capitalist" tendencies in the homeland of the October Revolution is the ultimate root of his distrust of the Party. It remains to be seen whether a society can function effectively without an elite enjoying an assured status, or whether the new elite thrown up by the Cultural Revolution will be less bureaucratic than the old.

6

FACTIONALISM IN THE
CENTRAL COMMITTEE

PHILIP BRIDGHAM

In the 16 years since the founding of our people's republic, the Marxist-Leninist leadership of the Chinese Communist Party Central Committee headed by Comrade Mao Tse-tung has waged three big struggles against anti-Party revisionist cliques.

—*Jen min jih pao* [People's Daily] editorial, "Long Live Mao Tse-tung's Thought", July 1, 1966.[1]

A fascinating by-product of the "Great Proletarian Cultural Revolution" has been the disclosure of new information on factionalism within the Chinese Communist Party since its rise to power in 1949. One purpose of these disclosures has been to demonstrate the validity of Mao Tse-tung's most recent "creative development" of Marxism–Leninism—"that classes and class struggle exist in society throughout the historical period of the dictatorship of the proletariat".[2] A second purpose has been to discredit and incriminate Mao's high-ranking opponents within the Party by charging them with varying degrees of complicity in these earlier "anti-Party" struggles.

Because of the questionable nature of this new evidence, it must of course be used with great care. It is necessary, for example, to be extremely wary of allegations of misconduct unless supported by statements of the accused uttered at the time and reproduced in verbatim form. It is also necessary to attempt to place these statements in the proper context, both of the speech or report from which they are drawn and of the policy guidelines prevailing at the time. With these caveats in mind, it is believed that these disclosures do

[1] *New China News Agency* [*NCNA*], June 30, 1966, in *Survey of China Mainland Press* [*SCMP*], No. 3773, p. 4.

[2] Joint *Hung ch'i* [Red Flag] and *Jen min jih pao* [People's Daily] article, "A Great Historic Document", *NCNA*, May 18, 1967, in *SCMP*, No. 3943, p. 3.

provide new and valuable insights into the process of policy formation and the structure of power in the Chinese Communist Party over the course of the past nineteen years.

Reduced to the broadest common denominator, the "three big struggles" that have taken place within the Chinese Communist Party since 1949 have been, as Mao's propagandists assert, "struggles for and against Mao Tse-tung's thought". At the same time, they have necessarily involved considerations of power and in all cases have been regarded by Mao as challenges to his leadership of the Party. The recurring nature of these challenges—the "anti-Party alliance of Kao Kang and Jao Shu-shih" in 1953, the "Right opportunist, or revisionist, anti-Party clique headed by P'eng Te-huai" in 1959, and the open-ended "counterrevolutionary clique" (headed initially by P'eng Chen and Lo Jui-ch'ing and later by Liu Shao-ch'i and Teng Hsiao-p'ing) in 1965–7—suggests, more over, that factionalism, carried on beneath a façade of unity, has been a continuing feature of Party life in Communist China since 1949.

As an aid to the reader in understanding what is at best an imprecise and difficult concept, the term "factionalism" is used in this paper to mean the activities of "an opinion group with organized force behind it".[1] This definition reflects a basic prerequisite for engaging in factional struggle—the need for an independent power base or, in Chinese Communist terminology, "an independent kingdom". A second feature of this definition is that it does not necessarily imply conscious opposition to the Party leadership or an attempt to expand the existing power base.[2] This is of particular importance, it is believed, in understanding the phenomenon of factionalism in Communist China in recent years. The basic factor determining what constitutes factional activity, after all, is the view of this activity by the dominant group within the Party leadership.

[1] This definition appears in Franz Schurmann, *Ideology and Organization in Communist China* (Berkeley and Los Angeles: Univ. of California Press, 1966), pp. 55–6.

[2] In discussing the Great Proletarian Cultural Revolution, the Chinese Communists themselves admit that many Party cadres have "practiced factionalism ...unconsciously...." See, for example, the *Jen min jih pao* editorial "Arm the 700 Million People With Mao Tse-tung's Thought", *NCNA*, October 1, 1966.

In the final analysis, factionalism, like beauty, is in the eye of the beholder.

The purpose of this chapter is to reappraise the nature and extent of this phenomenon of factionalism within the Central Committee on the basis of new evidence brought to light during the course of the past two years. Although each of these struggles is unique and possesses an intrinsic interest of its own, an attempt will be made to identify features common to all. The ultimate purpose of this chapter, then, is to seek to illuminate the origin and nature of the latest and most momentous of these factional struggles—Mao Tse-tung's Great Proletarian Cultural Revolution.

THE KAO KANG–JAO SHU-SHIH ANTI-PARTY ALLIANCE

The criminal aim of the Kao Kang–Jao Shu-shih anti-Party alliance was to split our Party and to overthrow the leading core—the long tested Central Committee of the Party headed by Comrade Mao Tse-tung—with the aim of seizing the supreme power of the Party and the State. Their means to achieve this aim was conspiracy. This was the principal hallmark and program of this anti-Party alliance.

—*People's Daily* editorial, "Tremendous Victory of the Party in History", April 10, 1955.[1]

Red Guard disclosures have added a new dimension to our understanding of the first big struggle against factionalism in the Chinese Communist Party since it came to power—that waged against the Kao–Jao "anti-Party alliance" in the years 1953–5. The principals in this affair were, of course, Kao Kang and Jao Shu-shih who, in running the regional Party organizations in the industrial areas of Northeast and East China, had constructed, it was charged, "independent kingdoms". Although relatively few and fragmentary in character, these new disclosures suggest that this first challenge to Mao Tse-tung's leadership was more broadly based and formidable than indicated at the time.

One aspect of the Kao–Jao affair, it has now been revealed, was an effort to persuade Mao Tse-tung to give up one of his leadership positions, to resign either as Chairman of the Party or the state

[1] *NCNA*, April 10, 1955, in *SCMP*, No. 1026, p. 3.

(almost certainly the latter). A leading figure in this effort apparently was the revolutionary war hero Chu Te, charged subsequently by Lin Piao (in the autumn of 1959) with having "tried to become the leader himself...advocating the idea at the time of the Kao Kang incident of becoming Chairman in turn".[1] Another prominent figure in this effort was T'an Chen-lin (at the time *de facto* head of the East China Regional Bureau) who (it is now disclosed) "in 1953... took the lead in sending a joint letter asking our great leader Chairman Mao to 'take a rest'".[2] Although presumably a number of other Party officials signed this letter, only one other signatory has been identified—the recently deposed First Secretary of the Shanghai Muncipal Party Committee, Ch'en P'ei-hsien.[3]

Differentiating this effort from the activities of Kao and Jao at this time was the fact that it was carried on openly, utilizing normal channels of communication within the Party. It could be justified, moreover (as Ch'en P'ei-hsien has asserted in his defence), as a move designed to protect "Chairman Mao's health" by removing part of the burden which active leadership of both Party and state entailed.[4] By contrast, the "principal hallmark" of the Kao–Jao "anti-Party alliance" was, as noted above, "conspiracy".

As indicated in the March 31, 1955 Party "Resolution on the Kao Kang–Jao Shu-shih Anti-Party Alliance" (still the best single source of information on the activities of this group), Kao had claimed "that the Central Committee of the Party and the Government should... be reorganized...and that he himself should for the time being be General Secretary or Vice-Chairman of the Central Committee of the Party and the Premier of the State Council".[5] A recent account of the role of T'ao Chu (then a Secretary in the South-China Sub-Bureau) illustrates the manner in which Kao sought through "secret talks" in 1953 to recruit support for this endeavour. Holding forth

[1] *Mainichi*, February 9, 1967.

[2] Brief excerpts from this letter appear in "Letter to the People of the Whole Country", in *P'i T'an chan pao* [Combat Bulletin for Criticising T'an Chen-lin], June 1, 1967, p. 1. Also see Shanghai Radio, March 20, 1968

[3] Shanghai Radio, March 20, 1968. Also see "Criticism of Ch'en P'ei-hsien's Five Sham Self-Examinations", *Kung jen tsao fan pao* [Workers' Rebellion Journal], in *SCMP*, No. 4131, pp. 3–4.

[4] *Ibid.*   [5] *NCNA*, April 4, 1955, in *Current Background*, No. 324, p. 4.

the prospect of "a high position in the Government", Kao allegedly said to T'ao: "They (meaning members of the anti-Party clique) all agree that I should be Vice Chairman of the Party. What do you think?" Although T'ao gave an equivocal answer, he did not report this incident and, only after "exposure" of this scheme in Peking, did he then "hurriedly make a false confession".[1]

A more basic and serious charge in this Party resolution was that Kao had attempted to secure support in the army for his conspiracy against the Central Committee by advancing the "utterly absurd 'theory' that our Party consisted of two parties—one, the so-called 'party of the revolutionary bases and the army', the other, the so-called 'party of white areas'—that the Party was created by the army".[2] In terms of this theory, Kao could claim that the first "party" (which he represented) deserved to "hold the major authority" in the new structure of power in Peking since it had acquired greater "revolutionary merit" in defeating the Japanese and winning final victory over the Kuomintang. As leaders who had spent much of this time in the "white areas" (i.e. those areas under the rule of the Nationalist Government), Liu Shao-ch'i and Chou En-lai would have to settle, under this theory, for a secondary role in the new Party and government structure.[3]

It is of considerable interest to note, in the recent revelations of the Cultural Revolution, that this proposal apparently elicited varying degrees of support from high-level military leaders at the time. As noted above, one of these was the founder of the Red Army, Chu Te. Another was P'eng Te-huai who in 1953 had just returned to Peking in triumph after commanding the Chinese forces in the Korean War. Although some of the accusations against P'eng (e.g. that he actually "headed" the Kao–Jao "anti-Party alliance") are obviously untrue, the central charge that he had been involved and that, as a consequence, he had made a "self-criticism" at the

---

[1] "How T'ao Chu Got Off After the Exposure of the Kao–Jao Affair", in *P'i T'ao chan pao* [Combat Bulletin for Criticising T'ao Chu], April 10, 1967, in *SCMP*, No. 3962, p. 9. The reference in parentheses to an "anti-Party clique" appears in this source.

[2] *Current Background*, No. 324, p. 4.

[3] For a discussion of this point, see Peter S. H. Tang, *Communist China Today: Domestic and Foreign Policies* (New York: Praeger, 1957), p. 87.

time appears credible.[1] Indeed, there is support for this view in the communiqué which described the March, 1955 Party conference as "carried out in a full spirit of criticism and self-criticism" and the speeches delivered there (by P'eng Te-huai and many others) as having "brought out the various crimes of Kao Kang and Jao Shu-shih against the Party and the people".[2]

In retrospect, it appears that Kao Kang's claim to a dominant role in the Chinese Communist leadership in the early 1950's was based primarily on his achievements as head of the Party, government and military organizations in the strategic and advanced industrial area of Northeast China. The following passage (in an earlier "Resolution on Strengthening Party Unity" adopted by a Central Committee plenum in February, 1954) appears clearly to have been directed at this challenge by Kao Kang:

Since the victory of China's New Democratic Revolution, there has grown up among some of the cadres within the Party a most dangerous kind of conceit. They lose their heads over certain achievements they have made in their work... They exaggerate the role of the individual... They think there is no one equal to them in the wide world. They listen only to others' flattery and praise but cannot accept others' criticism and supervision... They even regard the region or department under their leadership as their individual inheritance or independent kingdom.[1]

Developing this theme, a later *People's Daily* editorial charged that "they regard the area and department under their leadership as their individual inheritance and vainly attempt to use it as their capital and instrument for fulfilling their individual ambition of undermining and splitting the Party".[4]

The specifics of this charge were spelled out a year later, at which time the campaign against Kao and Jao was in full flood. Now they

---

[1] This charge appears in the "Resolution of the Chinese Communist Party Central Committee Concerning The Anti-Party Clique Headed by P'eng Te-huai", August 16, 1959, in *SCMP*, No. 4004, p. 2.

[2] *Current Background*, No. 324, p. 2.

[3] "Fourth Plenary Session of Seventh Central Committee of Chinese Communist Party Issues Communique", *NCNA*, February 18, 1954, in *SCMP*, No. 751, p. 4.

[4] Editorial entitled "Heighten Revolutionary Vigilance", *Jen min jih pao*, April 4, 1954, in *SCMP*, No. 787, p. 3.

were attacked by name for having "regarded all work achievements in the Northeast and East China regions as their own 'merits', created the myth that they are 'always correct', 'men of great ability' and 'well-trained in theory' and with the aid of such fantastic lies, aroused others to blindly worship them".[1] It was also suggested at this time that policy issues had played a part in this first "big struggle" within the Central Committee, as in the allegation that Kao Kang had "preached absurd ideas of the 'special character of the Northeast', and 'the Northeast has always been more advanced', set various 'leftist' or rightist policies against the correct policies of the Party center, and even refused to carry out the directives and resolutions of the center".[2]

Since Kao Kang was in close contact with large numbers of Russian economic advisers and military officials throughout this period, these charges suggest that one of the unstated but nevertheless real policy errors committed by Kao was that he had been too zealous in promoting the Soviet model of economic development which featured concentration on heavy industry and relative autonomy for professional management. The latter concept Kao advocated quite openly, as, for example, in his statement in mid-1950 describing the role of a factory manager in China's emerging industrial economy: "If the manager is made answerable not to state authorities or industrial control organs of a higher level but to the Party committee or the Party branch...then there will no longer be any unified leadership."[3] This presumably was but one instance of a tendency on Kao's part (in the words of the March, 1955 Party resolution) "to belittle the role of the Party..." That Kao may have been encouraged by the Russians in this and other programmes which challenged the Party centre in Peking is indicated

[1] Hsiung Fu, "Learn Lessons From the Incident of the Kao Kang–Jao Shu-shih Anti-Party Alliance", *Chung kuo ch'ing nien*, [China Youth], April 16, 1955, in *SCMP*, No. 1036, p. 15.

[2] Chou Ming, "Smashing the Kao Kang–Jao Shu-shih Anti-Party Alliance Is a Great Victory", *Shih shih shou ts'e*, April 25, 1955, in *SCMP*, No. 1052, p. 9.

[3] *Jen min jih pao*, June 5, 1950, as quoted in John Wilson Lewis, "Revolutionary Struggle and the Second Generation in Communist China", *The China Quarterly*, No. 21 (January–March, 1965), p. 130. For a more extensive discussion of this point, see Schurmann, *Ideology and Organization*, pp. 267 ff.

by the recent charge (without supporting evidence, it is true) that he and his colleagues "maintained illicit relations with foreign countries..."[1] In any case, two of the main ingredients of the more recent phenomenon of "revisionism"—the stress on expertise and professionalism at the expense of political control, and reliance on the Soviet model and Soviet support to promote China's economic development—appear to have been present in the Kao–Jao affair.

It is ironic that the net effect of this first struggle against incipient "revisionism" was to strengthen the position of Liu Shao-ch'i and Teng Hsiao-p'ing who are now denounced as the two leading "revisionist" villains within the Central Committee. Teng, who led the attack on the Kao–Jao "anti-Party alliance" at the Party conference in March, 1955, was immediately elevated to the Politburo at a Central Committee Plenum the following month.[2] It is interesting to note that Lin Piao was also promoted to membership in the Politburo on the same occasion, possibly reflecting Mao's dissatisfaction with his other two top military leaders Chu Te and P'eng Te-huai for having become involved in the Kao–Jao affair.[3]

It was not until the reorganization of the Party structure at the Eighth Party Congress in September, 1956, however, that the full extent of the increased power of Liu Shao-ch'i and Teng Hsiao-p'ing would be revealed. By this time, the concept of "collective leadership" (which had emerged in the Soviet Union following the death of Stalin and in China following the Kao–Jao affair) had been further strengthened by the striking disclosures of Stalin's paranoia in Khrushchev's "de-Stalinization" speech. Moreover, as Teng Hsiao-p'ing stated in his "Report on the Revision of the Constitution of the Communist Party of China" at this Congress, it was considered necessary "to set up additional central organs" in the Central Committee "owing to the pressure of Party and government work".[4]

[1] This charge appears in the *Hung ch'i* [Red Flag] editorial, "From the Defeat of P'eng Te-huai to the Bankruptcy of China's Khrushchev", *NCNA*, August 15, 1967.

[2] *Current Background*, No. 324, p. 2.

[3] Another explanation for Lin Piao's relative inactivity in the early 1950's, it should be pointed out, is that he was in poor health, possibly suffering from tuberculosis.

[4] *Eighth National Congress of the Communist Party of China: Documents* (Peking: Foreign Languages Press, 1956), I, 222.

The combined result of these developments and pressures was a substantial delegation of political power by Mao Tse-tung at the Eighth Party Congress to Liu Shao-ch'i (as the senior Vice-Chairman of the newly established Standing Committee of the Politburo) and to Teng Hsiao-p'ing (as head of the Secretariat charged with "attending to the daily work of the Central Committee").

A decade hence, at an important Central Committee work conference in October, 1966, Mao Tse-tung would refer to this delegation of power as a "mistake", the consequences of which had necessitated the Great Proletarian Cultural Revolution. As Mao would explain on this occasion, it had been his idea to "divide the Standing Committee of the Politburo into first and second line fronts", to "place Liu Shao-ch'i and Teng Hsiao-p'ing in the first line" where they would respectively "preside over...important conferences" and "take charge of the daily operations" of the Party. This had been done to provide for a smooth succession in the leadership (and thus avoid the errors committed in the Soviet Union)— "to foster these people's authority so that no great changes would arise in the country when the time came for me to meet my Heavenly King (God)". Mao's confidence in his principal Party lieutenants, however, had been misplaced. They had abused his confidence ("we overtrusted others"), had committed a number of "mistakes", and (like Kao and Jao before them) had constructed "independent kingdoms".[1]

The end result of the first factional struggle within the Central Committee in the post-1949 period, then, was to augment the power of Liu Shao-ch'i and Teng Hsiao-p'ing who would one day be charged with the same crimes of disaffection and disloyalty for which Kao Kang and Jao Shu-shih had been purged. Before that, however, Mao Tse-tung would have to face a challenge more formidable than that which Kao and Jao had posed, when Minister of National Defence P'eng Te-huai would lead a spirited attack on Mao's radical Great Leap Forward and commune programmes at Lushan in the summer of 1959.

[1] *Yomiuri*, January 7, 1967. For a discussion of this important speech, see Gene T. Hsiao, "The Background and Development of 'The Proletarian Cultural Revolution'", *Asian Survey*, VII, No. 6 (June, 1967), 392 ff.

THE P'ENG TE-HUAI AFFAIR

> At the Lushan meeting of the Party in 1959, a handful of
> ambitious bourgeois careerists and schemers . . . who had
> the support of the Khrushchev revisionist clique launched a
> ferocious attack on the Party's Central Committee headed
> by Comrade Mao Tse-tung.
>
> —*People's Daily* editorial, "Long Live Mao Tse-tung's
> Thought" July 1, 1966.[1]

If differences over policy played a part in the first factional struggle after 1949, policy issues were at the heart of the second big struggle —that waged at Lushan in July and August, 1959 against a "Right opportunist, or revisionist, anti-Party clique" headed by the then Minister of National Defence P'eng Te-huai. For the first time since 1935, Mao Tse-tung's personal leadership and programmes were openly subjected to attack by a long-time "comrade in arms" who, moreover, had managed to muster considerable support within the Central Committee. Although Mao would triumph at Lushan, the opposition to his radical domestic and foreign policies would persist and finally precipitate the Great Proletarian Cultural Revolution.

In contrast with the fragmentary nature of new disclosures about the Kao–Jao affair, important documentary evidence has come to light in the past year concerning the intra-Party struggle at Lushan. Thanks to a Red Guard publication, we now have the text of the "Letter of Opinion" (dated July 14, 1959) which P'eng Te-huai sent to Mao at an early stage of the Lushan conference.[2] We also have the text (in excerpt form) of the Central Committee resolution condemning the "anti-Party clique headed by P'eng Te-huai" which was passed on August 16 at the conclusion of this conference.[3] Using these documents and other Red Guard revelations, it is now

---

[1] *SCMP*, No. 3733, p. 5.

[2] "P'eng Te-huai's So-Called 'Letter of Opinion' to Chairman Mao, at the 1959 Lushan Conference", in *Ko ming ch'uan lien* [Exchange of Revolutionary Experience], August 24, 1967, in *SCMP*, No. 4032, pp. 1–5.

[3] "Resolution of Chinese Communist Party Central Committee Concerning Anti-Party Clique Headed by P'eng Te-huai", August 16, 1959, in *SCMP*, No. 4004, pp. 1–4.

possible to reconstruct with some confidence the main outlines of the great debate on policy staged at Lushan.

P'eng's "Letter" to Mao Tse-tung makes fascinating reading, containing, as it does, one of the most cogent and damning indictments of Mao's radical Great Leap Forward and commune programmes produced in or outside China. That he received help in the preparation of the "Letter" (probably from another alleged member of the "clique", the then Deputy Foreign Minister Chang Wen-t'ien) seems clear, lending colour to the charge in the Party resolution that activities of the "anti-Party clique" at Lushan were "purposive, prepared, planned and organised".[1] That it was an act of courage, motivated at least in part by a sincere conviction that the policies he criticized had brought hardship and suffering to the Chinese people, is equally clear. For despite its "outward pretensions of support for the general line and for Comrade Mao Tse-tung" (in the words of the Party resolution), P'eng's "Letter" did amount (as the resolution further asserted) to "a fierce onslaught on the Party's general line and the leadership of the Central Committee and Comrade Mao Tse-tung . . ."[2]

The first charge in P'eng's indictment was that capital construction under the Great Leap Forward had been "hasty" and "excessive", tying up capital, creating "imbalances" in the economy and, by reducing the supply of commodities on the market, creating a "political" problem in the relationship between "the workers and peasants". This had resulted from lack of familiarity with "the work of socialist construction", in particular with "the socialist law of planned and proportionate development" of the economy.[3]

Next, P'eng discussed somewhat gingerly the "shortcomings and errors" which had attended the formation of rural communes. There had been "a period of confusion regarding the question of the system of ownership" and this, in conjunction with unrealistic estimates of grain production, had led to "free supply of food" in violation of the socialist law of "distribution according to work". P'eng concluded his brief discussion of the communes by admitting that most of these defects and errors had been recognized and were in the process of correction.[4]

[1] *Ibid.* p. 2.   [2] *Ibid.* p. i.   [3] "Letter of Opinion", pp. 2–3.   [4] *Ibid.* p. 2.

P'eng Te-huai reserved his most withering fire, however, for that most distinctive characteristic of Mao Tse-tung's Great Leap Forward approach to economic development—reliance on mass movements in economic construction, especially the mass movement to make iron and steel. He, "like many comrades", had been "bewildered by the achievements of the great leap forward and the passion of the mass movements", by the "habit of exaggeration" which had spread throughout the country and the "unbelievable miracles" which had been reported in the press. P'eng's explanation for all of this—which had "done tremendous harm to the prestige of the Party"—was that it had resulted from "petty-bourgeois fanaticism". This was a state of mind which rendered one liable to commit such "'Left' mistakes" as "wanting to enter into communism at one step" and "demanding that targets which could be accomplished in several years or more than a decade be fulfilled in one year or even several months".[1]

P'eng then attributed these "Leftist" mistakes and tendencies to a misunderstanding and misapplication of the principle of "putting politics in command" over economic construction. Since this was an issue which would figure prominently in the early stages of the Cultural Revolution, P'eng's formulation of this charge deserves to be quoted at length: "Putting politics in command is no substitute for economic principles, still less for concrete measures in economic work. Equal importance must be attached to putting politics in command and to effective measures in economic work; neither can be overestimated or neglected."[2]

P'eng concluded his "Letter" by calling for "a systematic summing up of the achievements and lessons gained in our work" with the objective of "distinguishing right from wrong and raising our understanding" and thus "uniting the whole Party". In keeping with the constructive nature of his proposal and the urgency of the task, P'eng then expressed the hope that "on the whole, there should be no investigation of personal responsibility".[3]

Mao Tse-tung's response, as revealed in the August 16 Party resolution, was to launch a bitter attack on P'eng Te-huai and his other critics at Lushan, branding them as members of a "Right

[1] *Ibid.* p. 4.   [2] *Ibid.*   [3] *Ibid.* p. 5.

opportunist anti-Party clique" engaged in an unprincipled and un-scrupulous struggle "to sabotage the dictatorship of the proletariat and undermine the socialist revolution..." Instead of discussing the merits of the charges raised in P'eng's "Letter" (they were dismissed as "exaggerated...out of all proportion"), the Party resolution concentrated on denigrating P'eng's character and im-pugning his motives, characterizing him as "essentially a representa-tive of the bourgeoisie" who had been conducting "anti-Party activities" for 30 years.[1] Instead of heeding P'eng's recommendation that in the interests of Party unity there should be no "investigation of personal responsibility", Mao called for waging a new "inner-Party struggle against Right opportunism headed by P'eng Te-huai" in order to "further strengthen the ranks of the Party and the people and heighten their militancy".[2]

The resolution also provides new evidence for assessing the amount of support P'eng was able to muster at Lushan. There were, of course, the other members of the "clique" identified by name—Huang K'o-ch'eng (Chief of Staff of the People's Liberation Army), Chang Wen-t'ien (alternate Politburo member and Vice-Minister of Foreign Affairs) and Chou Hsiao-chou (First Secretary of the Hunan Provincial Party Committee). That there were a number of others who provided varying degrees of support was revealed in the resolu-tion statement that "because of his tactics of feigning candor and frugality, P'eng Te-huai's activities could and did mislead a number of people" and consequently were "fraught with danger for the future of the Party and the People's Liberation Army".[3]

Other sources indicate that P'eng received substantial support from other senior military figures, including the Director of the General Logistics Department Hung Hsüeh-chih (who was purged); Director of the General Training Department Hsiao K'o (attacked as a "military dogmatist"); Director of the General Political Department T'an Cheng (criticized in the *Kung tso t'ung hsün*); and a half dozen lesser military leaders who have been out of the news since 1959.[4] What is more, recent Red Guard publications

---

[1] "Resolution Concerning P'eng Te-huai", pp. 1–2
[2] *Ibid*. pp. 3–4.   [3] *Ibid*. p. 2.
[4] See, for example, David A. Charles, "The Dismissal of Marshal P'eng Te-huai", *The China Quarterly*, No. 8 (October–December, 1961), p. 73. This

have disclosed that Chu Te also came to P'eng Te-huai's defence at Lushan,[1] an act for which he was roundly condemned by Lin Piao (P'eng's successor as Minister of National Defence) at an expanded plenum of the Military Affairs Committee shortly thereafter.

Lin Piao's speech at this plenum suggests an important truth about the Lushan conference. According to Lin, the struggle at Lushan was not unexpected, since it represented the culmination of a process under way for some time. As Lin pointed out, "Chairman Mao stated a number of times that there was a possibility of a split arising in the Party. As a matter of fact, he was referring to P'eng Te-huai and Chu Te."[2] It is in this sense that the charge contained in the Party resolution denouncing P'eng's "clique"—that their "activities represent a continuation and development of the anti-Party alliance of Kao Kang and Jao Shu-shih"—appears to have been true. Kao Kang's earlier challenge, which had called for a larger role for military leaders in the determination of Party affairs (under the theory that "the Party was created by the army"), had been repeated by P'eng Te-huai at Lushan.

As recent Red Guard publications have charged, P'eng Te-huai personified the threat of "military professionalism" (what the Chinese Communists call the "bourgeois revisionist military line"). Specifically, P'eng is charged with having attempted (1) to put "the army before the Party"; (2) to counterpose "regularization and modernization" against "proletarian revolutionization of the army"; (3) to substitute "the system of one-man leadership" for the "collective leadership of the Party committee" in the Army; and (4) to "place military technique in the first place" in Army building.[3]

article, based on refugee reports, is a good early account of the P'eng Te-huai affair. A number of the findings in this article which appeared controversial at the time of publication have been confirmed by the revelations of the Cultural Revolution.

[1] *Asahi*, January 16, 1967.

[2] *Mainichi*, February 9, 1967. Also see "Vice Chairman Lin Piao Criticises and Repudiates P'eng Te-huai", *Ko ti t'ung hsün* [Correspondence From All Parts of the Country], September 13, 1967, in *SCMP*, No. 4081, p. 2.

[3] "Principal Crimes of P'eng Te-huai, Big Ambitionist and Schemer", *Ching kang shan* [Chingkang Mountains] and *Kuang tung wen i chan pao* [Kwangtung Literature and Art Combat Bulletin], September 5, 1967, in *SCMP*, No. 4047, p. 4. Also see *Jen min jih pao* article "Settle Accounts with P'eng Te-huai...", *NCNA*, August 20, 1967.

Finally, and perhaps most important, P'eng is charged with having "opposed the policy advanced by Chairman Mao of creating an independent and complete network of modern national defence industries by relying on our own efforts", advocating instead "depending...on the Khrushchev revisionist clique for improvement of our army's equipment and the development of up-to-date military science and technology..."[1] As evidence for the latter, P'eng is quoted as having argued for a division of labour between China and the Soviet Union in the event of war, with "China... contributing troops and the Soviet Union, atom bombs".[2]

It was at this point that P'eng's interest in opposing Mao's leadership and policies coincided with that of Khrushchev. The revelations of the Cultural Revolution (appearing in both official and Red Guard publications) confirm what had already been credibly reported in the West—that when P'eng Te-huai launched his attack at Lushan he "had the support of the Khrushchev revisionist clique..." For his part, P'eng is alleged to have "made secret deals with Khrushchev", to have "provided Khrushchev with anti-China 'ammunition'", and to have "openly expressed his opposition to the Party's general line, the great leap forward and the people's communes and to Chairman Mao and the Party Central Committee...in the presence of the Khrushchev revisionists". In return, Khrushchev is said to have shown his support by "launching an open attack against our people's communes" four days after P'eng delivered his July 14 "Letter" and by openly praising P'eng after the event as "correct and brave" and as his "best friend".[3]

In fact, it is reasonable to assume that Khrushchev's offer of support was more substantial and tangible than this, including perhaps a pledge of increased (or at least undiminished) Soviet military, technological and economic assistance in return for certain Chinese concessions. Following so soon after the sudden Soviet cancellation on June 20, 1959 of its October, 1957 agreement to assist the Chinese in the development of advanced weapons, it is possible that P'eng

[1] *NCNA*, August 20, 1967.   [2] *SCMP*, No. 4047, p. 5.
[3] *Ibid*. p. 8.

recruited support at Lushan on the basis of a pledge to reinstate this agreement once Soviet conditions were met.[1] Whatever P'eng may have hoped to gain by approaching (or listening to) Khrushchev, it is clear that this scheme backfired. To the standard epithets used to denounce P'eng could now be added the charges of "conspiracy" and "treason".

Another motive prompting P'eng to challenge Mao is suggested by the charge in the Lushan Party resolution that his "anti-Party clique" contained elements who "bear a grudge against the Party" (for which read Mao Tse-tung). Personal animus fuelled by the conviction that he had been badly used in the past is revealed in the statement P'eng addressed to Mao (as subsequently reported by Mao) at Lushan: "In Yenan, you cussed me for 40 days. Now you will not allow me to cuss you for 20 days."[2] As a member of the "Returned Student Clique" who had been a leading target of the "rectification" (cheng-feng) campaign in Yenan, Chang Wen-t'ien also had ample cause to "bear a grudge against the Party". The venerable Chu Te would also fit into this category if, as Red Guard publications have frequently asserted, he felt that his earlier services in the revolutionary war had not been properly rewarded in the postwar structure of power. At minimum, these disclosures cast serious doubt on the efficacy of Mao's famous "unity–criticism–unity" policy for dealing with erring comrades, the policy of "learning from past mistakes to avoid future ones and curing the illness to save the patient". In these cases, the "illness" of disaffection and opposition to Mao had clearly lingered on.

Despite this evidence of the unreliability of the "rectification" process, Mao decided once again to treat the challenge of P'eng Te-huai and his supporters as a "contradiction among the people". Although they were dismissed from positions of authority within the government and Party structure, they were permitted, as the Party resolution pointed out, to "keep their membership or alternate

[1] See Ellis Joffe, "The Conflict Between Old and New in the Chinese Army", *The China Quarterly*, No. 18 (April–June, 1964), pp. 132–3.

[2] *Wu ch'an chieh chi wen hua ta ko ming ta shih chi* [The Great Proletarian Cultural Revolution—A Record of Major Events] February, 1967, in *Joint Publications Research Service* [*JPRS*], No. 42,349, p. 4.

membership in the Central Committee or the Politburo..."[1] In return, they were to "admit and disclose all their mistakes before the Party and rectify them in action".[2] The contents of P'eng Te-huai's confession, reported as taking the form of a short letter to Mao, have not been revealed, but it was apparently contrite enough to enable him to return to his home province of Hunan (he was reported as being there in 1961) where (according to a later report by his wife) he "passed his time breeding fish and growing vegetables".[3] What is more, it is now known that P'eng was assigned in late 1965 (on the eve of the Great Proletarian Cultural Revolution) to the Southwest Bureau of the Central Committee where he served as "third deputy director of the Construction Committee".[4]

In the communiqué of the Tenth Plenum of the Eighth Central Committee issued on September 28, 1962, the Lushan conference would be praised for having "victoriously smashed attacks by Right opportunism, i.e. revisionism..."[5] In retrospect, it appears that P'eng Te-huai in many respects was the prototype of those who would be attacked during the "Cultural Revolution" as "Khrushchev-type revisionists" within the Chinese Communist Party. In criticizing Mao's radical Great Leap Forward and commune programmes, P'eng represented a large group of the more pragmatic and technically minded administrators and professionals within the Party, government and Army who had come to see the folly of these

[1] The fact that Mao, in the face of considerable provocation, decided to adopt a policy of leniency in itself suggests that P'eng Te-huai received substantial support on the policy issues raised at Lushan. Mao would apply this same policy of "ideological strictness" and "organizational leniency" in dealing with Liu Shao-ch'i and Teng Hsiao-p'ing in the early stages of the "great proletarian cultural revolution". For an interesting discussion of this point by Madame Liu Shao-ch'i, see the article by Liu T'ao (Liu's daughter) entitled "Rebel Against Liu Shao-ch'i, Follow Chairman Mao to Make Revolution for Life", in *Ching kang shan* [Chingkang Mountains], December 31, 1966, in *Current Background*, No. 821, p. 12.

[2] *SCMP*, No. 4004, p. 3.

[3] "Trial of P'u An-hsiu (P'eng Te-huai's Wife)", in *Ta p'i t'ung hsün* [Mass Criticism and Repudiation Bulletin], in *SCMP*, No. 4124, p. 8.

[4] Chengtu Radio, September 23, 1967.

[5] "Communiqué of the Tenth Plenary Session of the Eighth Central Committee of the Chinese Communist Party", *NCNA*, September 28, 1962, in *Current Background*, No. 691, p. 4.

programmes. In their stead, P'eng may be said to have advanced an alternative model of economic and military development, one patterned more closely on Soviet experience and featuring Soviet military economic and technical assistance. As the symbol both of Soviet "revisionist" influence and of opposition to Mao, the P'eng Te-huai affair would cast a long shadow over the years that followed. As is now well documented, it was Mao's conviction that Wu Han's play "Hai Jui's Dismissal" constituted a defence of P'eng Te-huai and therefore an attack on him personally which would precipitate the launching of the Great Proletarian Cultural Revolution in the autumn of 1965.

THE GREAT PROLETARIAN CULTURAL REVOLUTION

Bombard the Headquarters

> In the last 50 days or more some leading comrades from the central down to the local levels . . . have enforced a bourgeois dictatorship and struck down the surging movement of the great proletarian cultural revolution . . . How vicious they are. Viewed in connection with the right deviation in 1962 and the apparently 'left' but actually right deviation in 1964, shouldn't this prompt one to deep thought?
>
> —Mao Tse-tung's First Wall Poster, August 5, 1966.[1]

Mao Tse-tung's first wall poster, produced at the Eleventh Plenum of the Eighth Central Committee in early August, 1966, would (in the words of a subsequent *Red Flag* editorial) "blast the lid off" a struggle "between the proletarian headquarters" headed by Mao Tse-tung and "the bourgeois headquarters" headed by "China's Khrushchev" (i.e. Liu Shao-ch'i) which "had existed in the Party over a long period of time".[2] Although it is necessary to make allowance for polemical language and *ex post facto* exaggeration, the record does suggest (as the wall poster indicates) that Mao had begun to question Liu's leadership of the Party apparatus as early as 1962; that these suspicions were strengthened by what Mao considered to

[1] Quoted in *Hung ch'i* editorial, "Completely Smash the Bourgeois Headquarters", *NCNA*, August 6, 1967.
[2] *Ibid.*

be further resistance by his top Party lieutenants in 1964; and that Mao had been preparing for nearly 18 months for the struggle with his high-level opponents within the Party which surfaced at the Eleventh Plenum. In terms of the subject matter of this paper, it might be said that Mao first perceived in 1962 that Liu Shao-ch'i, Teng Hsiao-p'ing and others in control of the Party machine might constitute a faction in opposition to his leadership; that Mao's suspicions of disloyalty had hardened by the end of 1964; and that by early 1965 Mao was already engaged in planning the third and by far the most momentous factional struggle within the Chinese Communist Party since 1949—the Great Proletarian Cultural Revolution.

Developments in the three-year period following the Lushan Plenum (1959–62) demonstrated that in important respects, in the great debate over domestic and foreign policy staged at this historic meeting, P'eng Te-huai had been right and Mao Tse-tung had been wrong. The combined effect of irrational economic policy, successive bad harvests and the Soviet withdrawal of technicians in the summer of 1960 dealt Mao's Great Leap Forward programme of economic development a shattering blow. Confronted with the threat of economic and political collapse, the Chinese Communist regime responded with a series of urgent corrective measures in the winter of 1960–1 and then, reluctantly and painfully, with even more drastic remedies in a period of further retreat from mid-1961 to mid-1962.

The result, as Merle Goldman makes clear in her essay later in this volume, was the worst outbreak of intellectual dissidence since the founding of the Chinese People's Republic. Disaffected by the widespread suffering caused by the disastrous Great Leap Forward programme, a number of China's leading intellectuals resorted to the use of historical allegory, of pseudonyms, and of Aesopian language to criticize Party policies and even Mao Tse-tung himself. Wu Han's play "Hai Jui's Dismissal" (published in early 1961) exemplified this criticism of Mao Tse-tung by likening the case of P'eng Te-huai to that of a Ming Dynasty official who had been unjustly dismissed by the Emperor.

By the winter of 1961–2, disillusionment with Mao's policies and programmes apparently extended into the ranks of the Politburo, to include a number of those standing in the "first line" of leadership who were charged with the responsibility for coping with this domestic crisis. As Mao Tse-tung would subsequently point out (in an October 24, 1966 speech to a Party work conference), the resistance he encountered beginning at this time was of two kinds— that carried on "secretly" by "the P'eng Chen group" and that carried on "openly" by "the Liu Shao-ch'i–Teng Hsiao-p'ing group".[1] The progressive awareness by Mao (and a small coterie of trusted advisers) of the extent of this opposition would culminate, in the autumn of 1965, in the decision to initiate one of the most extensive and violent Party purges in the history of the world Communist movement.

A good example of the first type of opposition was a secret conference convened by the powerful Mayor and First Secretary of Peking, P'eng Chen, in December, 1961. The purpose of this conference, it is now charged, was to make a critical review of all documents issued by the Central Committee since 1958, to find "problems" and "mistakes" and thus, by "attacking the general line, the great leap forward, and the people's commune", discredit and "oppose" Chairman Mao.[2] Once these data were collected, the problem remained how to make use of them. One participant allegedly expressed the hope that the conference would lead to "correcting the Central Committee's mistakes and allowing Chairman Mao to calm down and examine himself". A more realistic view was expressed by another participant, however, who first characterized China's predicament as resulting from "mistakes of line" made by "Chairman Mao and the Party Central Committee" and then pointed out: "In the history of the Party, no mistakes of line have been corrected by those who made them."[3] For this reason, the findings of this conference—the first act in the "conspiracy" of the "P'eng Chen group"—were kept secret.

Of far greater importance for understanding the Great Proletarian

[1] *Yomiuri*, January 8, 1967.

[2] Cheng Hsüan, "Big Exposure of a Conspiracy to Usurp the Party and State Leadership", *Kuang ming jih pao* [Bright Daily], August 9, 1967, in *SCMP*, No. 4014, pp. 3–5.

[3] *Ibid*. p. 6.

Cultural Revolution, it is believed, was an enlarged Central Committee work conference held a month later in January, 1962. For it was at this conference, attended by some 7,000 Party cadres, that Liu Shao-ch'i, in a lengthy report summing up political and economic work in the preceding year, made such a gloomy assessment of the results of the Great Leap Forward and commune programme as to cast doubt on the validity of these Maoist programmes.

The evidence for concluding that Liu at this conference criticized, obliquely but unmistakably, several of Mao's policies is impressive. Although the recent claim that on this occasion "a vigorous struggle was waged between the proletarian headquarters headed by Chairman Mao and the bourgeois headquarters headed by China's Khrushchev"[1] is exaggerated, it seems clear that Mao and Liu revealed divergent views in their speeches to this conference concerning the gravity of China's domestic problems and the methods that should be employed to cope with these problems. In a sense, their speeches and those of their supporters represented a continuation of the great debate which had taken place earlier at Lushan. What is more, the policy issues in this debate would figure prominently in the ensuing Cultural Revolution.

As portrayed in various Red Guard and official publications, Mao Tse-tung and Lin Piao stood on one side in this debate breathing "revolutionary optimism", as expressed in Mao's assertion that "the situation is very favourable".[2] From other excerpts of this speech, it is known that Mao warned of the danger posed by China's intellectuals and by "bourgeois representatives" in the Party, and of the consequent need to recognize and carry on a "protracted, complex and at times... very violent class struggle" in China's socialist society.[3] Expounding his view that the main danger was one posed by "class enemies", Mao called on the cadres present at this conference to "think carefully" about "the possibility of a [capitalist] restoration" in China, and stressed the necessity for

[1] *NCNA*, November 12, 1967.

[2] *Down with Liu Shao-ch'i—Life of Counterrevolutionary Liu Shao-ch'i*, Peking pamphlet, May, 1967, in *Current Background*, No. 834, p. 20.

[3] "Chairman Mao's Important Instructions on Literary and Art Work...", *Wen i hung ch'i* [Red Flag of Literature and Art], May 30, 1967, in *SCMP*, No. 4000, p. 22.

"arousing the masses and...supervision by the masses" (a salient feature of the Cultural Revolution) to prevent this from happening.[1]

The solution to China's problems advanced by Lin Piao at this conference was to improve political and ideological work—to study "Mao Tse-tung's thought...the soul and the very life of all work. When one masters it, one becomes proficient in everything".[2] Reflecting this viewpoint, key *People's Daily* and *Red Flag* editorials earlier in December and January had suddenly revived long-dormant concepts of the "revolutionary enthusiasm" and the "subjective initiative and creativity" of the masses and called upon Party cadres to "fully mobilize" this enthusiasm for production by carrying out intensive "ideological and political work".[3]

Aligned on the other side of this debate were Liu Shao-ch'i, Teng Hsiao-p'ing and other top leaders who stood in the "first line" and thus were charged with devising practical measures for coping with this domestic crisis. Responding to Mao's optimistic assessment, Liu in his speech pointed out: "The very favourable situation the Chairman has discussed refers to the political situation. But the economic situation cannot be said to be very favourable; it is very unfavourable." In discussing the causes of this economic crisis, Liu repeated what he had been told by peasants in Hunan that it had resulted primarily ("70 per cent") from "man-made disasters"; observed that the view of "some comrades" that "the people's communes were premature" might be "true"; and criticized "the loss of balance" and other mistakes in implementing the Great Leap Forward as rendering the results of this programme "not worthwhile".[4]

Liu Shao'ch'i is also charged with having depicted (probably at

[1] Joint *Hung ch'i, Jen min jih pao* and *Chieh fang chün pao* [Liberation Army Daily] editorial, "An Epoch-Making Document", *NCNA*, May 16, 1968.

[2] "Expose the Great Conspiracy Behind the Three Editions of the Book 'On Self-Cultivation by Communists'", *Jen min jih pao*, April 12, 1967, *NCNA*, April 13, 1967. Also Kweiyang Radio, June 17, 1967.

[3] See, for example, the editorial entitled "Summon Up Full Vigor, Strive for New Victory in Socialist Construction", in *Hung ch'i*, No. 1 (January 1, 1962), in *Selections From China Mainland Magazines* [*SCMM*], No. 298, pp. 9–13.

[4] "Chronicle of Liu Shao-ch'i's Crimes Against the Party, Socialism and Mao Tse-tung's Thought", in *Ching kang shan* [Chingkang Mountains], April 18, 1967, in *SCMP*, No. 3946, pp. 3–4. For a similar account, see *Current Background*, No. 834, pp. 20–1.

later Party meetings in the spring) China's economy generally as being "on the brink of collapse"; China's financial difficulties as "grave"; and the losses in China's agriculture of such magnitude as to require "seven or eight years" to repair.[1] To help cope with the crisis in agriculture, Liu is reported to have advocated "any method which is useful to arousing the activism of the peasants in production..." Among the methods specified by Liu at this time were "fixing output quotas according to the household and individual farming",[2] practices later attacked as "the three freedoms and one contract" or, more simply, as "going it alone" in agriculture.

Of even greater interest, for the purposes of this paper, was Liu's advocacy at this January Party work conference of greater democracy and of the right of dissent in inner-Party discussion. Liu's justification was the need to rehabilitate a large number of those Party cadres and technical specialists who had spoken up in opposition to Mao's Great Leap Forward and commune programmes in 1959 and, like P'eng Te-huai, had been labelled "Right opportunists". In this undertaking to "reverse the verdicts" at Lushan and elsewhere in 1959, Liu made a distinction between P'eng Te-huai who had been "guilty of treason" (i.e. "maintained illicit relations with foreign countries") and of "organizing an anti-Party clique" and those who had merely "shared P'eng Te-huai's viewpoint". The latter, Liu argued, had been unjustly treated since 1959 (subjected to "ruthless struggle and merciless attack") and deserved to be "vindicated".[3]

Liu Shao-ch'i's reference to "the mistake of 'ruthless struggle and merciless attack'" was significant, for in Party history this mistake had only occurred when a "Leftist" leadership had been in control. As described, for example, in Teng Hsiao-p'ing's report on the revised Party constitution at the Eighth Party Congress in September, 1956, this mistake resulted from "pushing inner-Party struggle to the extreme" and resulted in "severe damage" to

[1] Ibid.
[2] Ibid. Also see the joint Hung ch'i–Jen min jih pao article "Along the Socialist or the Capitalist Road?", NCNA, August 14, 1967.
[3] "Chronology of Events in the Struggle Between the Two Lines on the Cultural Front..." in Wen hua ko ming t'ung hsün [Cultural Revolution Bulletin], May, 1967, in Current Background, No. 842, p. 4.

"Party unity, inner-Party democracy and the initiative of the rank and file Party membership..."[1] It was in keeping with the provisions and spirit of the Party constitution, then, that Liu went on to advocate that "those who speak at Party meetings shall not be punished" and to call for "an open opposition...within the Party".[2]

Liu could, and probably did, rationalize his admission of "error" by the Party leadership at this time as essential to regain the confidence and support of the rank and file of Party cadres assembled at this extraordinary conference. In calling for "an open opposition", Liu could cite as justification the well-established Party concepts of "democratic centralism" and "collective leadership". It is unlikely, moreover, that Liu identified himself with the "opposition" at this time, for he himself had been closely associated with the radical Great Leap Forward and commune programmes which he now felt compelled to criticize. Liu's subsequent defence (in his "self-criticism" at an October, 1966 Central Committee work conference) of his performance at this time is credible—that for the most part Mao not only was kept informed about but also approved the decisions of these Party meetings and that it was only later (at the Tenth Plenum in September, 1962) that "he expressed his basic disagreement with our evaluation and our way of doing things" and "corrected our mistakes for the first time".[3]

Whatever the case, it now seems clear that Mao Tse-tung (who only a year earlier had informed Marshal Montgomery that Liu Shao-ch'i would be his successor)[4] had by the autumn of 1962 become suspicious of the loyalty and reliability of his top Party lieutenants. As Mao would put it in his wall poster of August 5, 1966, the activities of Liu Shao-ch'i and other top leaders at this time (described as "the Right deviation in 1962") constituted the first of several grave political errors by "leading comrades" which would lead to the Great Proletarian Cultural Revolution. To correct this "Right deviation", Mao apparently decided in the summer of 1962 to reclaim at least some of the powers which he had delegated

[1] *Eighth National Congress of the Communist Party of China*, I, 207.
[2] *Current Background*, No. 842, p. 4. Also *NCNA*, August 14, 1967.
[3] *Mainichi*, January 28, 1967.
[4] Richard Hughes, "Most Likely to Succeed in Red China", *New York Times Magazine*, October 21, 1962, p. 90.

at the Eighth Party Congress to Liu Shao-ch'i and Teng Hsiao-p'ing in the interests of efficient administration and an orderly succession. The occasion for reversing his earlier decision to establish a "first line front" and a "second line front" of command in the top leadership of the Party was the Tenth Plenum of the Eighth Central Committee held in September, 1962, at which time (as Mao would put it in an October 25, 1966 speech to a Party work conference) "the second-line front was abolished".[1]

The immediate problem confronting Mao was to devise a rationale which would justify his reassertion of more direct control over the Party and at the same time explain the opposition within the Party to his policies and programmes. This rationale, which Mao revealed in an important speech to the Tenth Plenum, was to revive and develop to a new and higher stage the concept of "class struggle" in socialist society. By means of this concept, Mao was able to explain past failures and criticism of his policies as largely the handiwork of "foreign and domestic class enemies", against whose poisonous influence ("revisionism") it was now necessary to inoculate all segments of Chinese society by means of a massive "socialist education" campaign.[2] Of particular interest is the fact that Mao singled out China's "leaders...even old leaders" as a special target for this campaign[3]—in effect, serving notice on his old "comrades in arms" of the Long March that they were no longer exempt from the painful process of "rectification" and "thought reform" which previously they had inflicted on their subordinates.

In April, 1966, in a *Liberation Army Daily* editorial publicly launching the Great Proletarian Cultural Revolution, it was disclosed that the "socialist education" campaign initiated at the Tenth Plenum comprised an integral, if formative, phase of the Cultural Revolution.[4] It is in the sense, then, of a final test by Mao of the loyalty and trustworthiness of his old "comrades in arms" that the unfolding and ultimate surfacing of the Cultural Revolution in the years following the Tenth Plenum can best be understood. His earlier suspicions of disloyalty strengthened by the display of

---

[1] *Yomiuri*, January 7, 1967.   [2] *Mainichi*, March 9, 1967.   [3] *Ibid.*
[4] *Chieh fang chün pao* editorial, "Hold High the Great Banner of Mao Tse-tung's Thinking", *NCNA*, April 19, 1966.

further resistance by top leaders throughout this period, Mao then decided to undertake a rectification–purge campaign of a new type, directed at Party cadres in positions of authority and designed to make the Chinese Communist Party and ultimately the Chinese people once more responsive to his will.

Two developments in the winter of 1964–5 suggest that Mao was already blaming Liu Shao-ch'i, Teng Hsiao-p'ing and other leaders of the Party apparatus for the growth of "revisionism" in China. First, in a major work report to the Third National People's Congress in December, 1964, Chou En-lai denounced publicly a number of the emergency policies and programmes instituted in the period of recovery following the Great Leap Forward as the handiwork of "class enemies".[1] Although not revealed at the time, it is now known from Red Guard and official publications that most of the policies which Chou criticized in his report had been either advocated or approved by Liu and Teng in this earlier period.

The fact that Chou En-lai initiated this new attack (indirect, of course) against Liu Shao-ch'i and Teng Hsiao-p'ing is in itself significant and deserves further explanation. On record in October, 1960 with a glowing tribute to Mao's thought[2] (an act of obeisance which Liu Shao-ch'i did not see fit to perform throughout this period), Chou is also credited in a Red Guard publication with having joined Lin Piao at the fateful January, 1962 work conference (discussed at length above) in "defending the thought of Mao Tse-tung and the proletarian revolutionary line represented by Mao Tse-tung".[3] There is good evidence, moreover, that the Premier supported Mao's new tough line on literature and art at various Party meetings in the period following the Tenth Plenum.[4] Thus, whatever his real views on policy (Chou has been generally regarded as the symbol of relatively moderate forces within the Chinese Communist Party), the record suggests that Chou En-lai defended Mao

[1] Chou En-lai, "Report on the Work of the Government", December 21–22, 1964, *NCNA*, December 30, 1964.

[2] This tribute appears in the February 6, 1961 issue of *Kung tso t'ung hsün* [Bulletin of Activities].

[3] "Events Surrounding the 'Chang kuan lou' Counterrevolutionary Incident", in *Tung fang hung* [The East Is Red], April 20, 1967, p. 7.

[4] *Current Background*, No. 842, pp. 10 ff.

against his critics during this crucial period and by this act of loyalty demonstrated his fitness to serve as one of the principal leaders in the ensuing Great Proletarian Cultural Revolution.

More important than this attack, however, was one which Mao launched at a Central Committee work conference held in January, 1965. One purpose of this conference, as recent Red Guard and official publications have disclosed, was to criticize and rectify mistakes committed by Liu Shao-ch'i in directing the rural "socialist education" or "four clearance" campaign in 1964. These mistakes are said to have included (1) making too gloomy an assessment of the results of the campaign; (2) advocating stringent measures against basic-level cadres as a whole; (3) denigrating one of Mao's work methods—that of holding "investigation meetings"; and (4) substituting his own views in place of Mao's theoretical formulations concerning the nature of the "four clearance" movement.[1] As Liu would admit subsequently in his October, 1966 "self-criticism", these constituted "mistakes which appeared 'Leftist' but were actually rightist"[2]—the second grave political error for which Mao would attack Liu Shao-ch'i in his August 5, 1966 wall poster.

It must have been clear to those present, moreover, that Mao was levelling a serious political attack on Liu at this work conference. Views which Liu had advocated the preceding September at another Party meeting were denounced in the document drawn up under Mao's supervision ("Some Current Problems Raised in the Socialist Education Movement in the Rural Areas" or, more simply, "The 23 Points") as "not Marxist–Leninist"[3]—a serious charge in a Communist state. In addition, this document revealed that a new target had been selected for the "socialist education" campaign in urban and rural areas, the same target as that which would be selected for the Great Proletarian Cultural Revolution—"those within the Party

[1] For one account of these mistakes, see *SCMP*, No. 3946, pp. 7–8.
[2] *Mainichi*, January 28, 1967.
[3] For a discussion of this important document secured in Taipei, see Charles Neuhauser, "The Chinese Communist Party in the 1960's: Prelude to the Cultural Revolution", *The China Quarterly*, No. 32 (October–December, 1967), pp. 13 ff. The passage quoted above appears in the second section of this document.

who are in authority and are taking the capitalist road". And when the document further asserted that these "class enemies" within the Party were being supported and protected by Party officials "at higher levels...even provincial and central levels",[1] it must have been evident to those present that Mao was intent upon extending the scope of his latest rectification–purge campaign into the highest echelons of the Party leadership.

Together with the Lushan plenum in August, 1959, the January, 1962 conference of 7,000 Party cadres, and the Tenth Plenum in September, 1962, this Party work conference in January, 1965 was an important milestone on the road to the Great Proletarian Cultural Revolution. Recounting the events leading up to this Cultural Revolution, Chou En-lai would subsequently underline the importance of this conference as follows: "At that time, Chairman Mao expressed his...disappointment in Liu Shao-ch'i. Despite his help for 20 years, Liu had not lived up to expectations, and at this time, our deputy supreme commander Comrade Lin Piao had become the choice of the masses."[2]

If Chou's recapitulation of events is taken as correct, it was at or shortly after this conference that Mao finally decided that Liu Shao-ch'i, Teng Hsiao-p'ing and other top Party leaders were, by virtue of their past and continued opposition, guilty of "revisionism" —that they constituted an "anti-Party revisionist clique" which would have to be removed in order to protect the integrity and ensure the continuity of Mao's revolutionary doctrines. This would prove to be a long and difficult process, however, which would in time necessitate launching the Great Proletarian Cultural Revolution. One reason it would take so long is that Mao had to move cautiously and circumspectly against his old "comrades in arms" because of their entrenched position in control of the Party apparatus.

Since, as subsequent developments would strongly suggest, Mao's "revisionist" opposition encompassed the great majority of Party leaders at the central, regional and provincial levels, it would appear that it was Mao and his supporters who comprised the real

[1] *Ibid.*
[2] "Premier Chou's Criticism of Liu Shao-ch'i", in *Wen ko t'ung hsün* [Cultural Revolution Bulletin], October 9, 1967, in *SCMP*, No. 4060, p. 10.

"anti-Party clique" or faction at this time. Forced to plan and run this campaign outside normal Party channels, Mao apparently created his own organization and channels of communication at an early stage of the Cultural Revolution, with those performing leading roles destined to replace the purge victims. Among those to whom Mao now turned for advice and support were Lin Piao (his long-trusted military leader), Ch'en Po-ta (his former political secretary), Chou En-lai, K'ang Sheng (a long-time intelligence specialist) and last but not least, his wife, Chiang Ch'ing. Since it was directed principally at powerful leaders who controlled much of the Party apparatus, Mao would also find it necessary to look outside the Party for support and assistance in carrying out this campaign, turning first to the People's Liberation Army and then to such extra-Party mass organizations as the Red Guards.

Eighteen months would elapse before Mao Tse-tung would convene the Eleventh Plenum of the Eighth Central Committee to depose Liu Shao-ch'i and name Lin Piao as his "revolutionary successor". Before he could do this, it was first necessary to solve "the problem of Peking" where, as Mao would put it in his October, 1966 work conference speech, Mayor and First Secretary P'eng Chen had constructed an "independent kingdom" so tight that "there was not even room to drive in a needle".[1] The story of Mao's entrapment of P'eng Chen (i.e. using one of P'eng's subordinates, Wu Han, as a stalking horse) is well known and will not be repeated here.[2]

It was also necessary to get rid of the other members of "P'eng Chen's group", principally Communist China's second-ranking military leader Lo Jui-ch'ing, who had attempted, it was later charged, "to establish...an independent kingdom in the army". As Chief of Staff, Lo personified continuing resistance within the People's Liberation Army to Mao's views on Army-building (featuring political indoctrination and productive labour at the expense of military training). For these and other reasons, as the record of charges suggests, both Mao and Lin Piao had by February, 1965

[1] *Yomiuri*, January 7, 1967.
[2] See Philip L. Bridgham, "Mao's 'Cultural Revolution': Origin and Development", *The China Quarterly*, No. 29 (January–March, 1967), pp. 18 ff.

come to distrust Lo Jui-ch'ing.[1] Occupying a powerful position in the Chinese Communist hierarchy, it is not surprising that Lo was the first casualty of the Great Proletarian Cultural Revolution, disappearing in late November, 1965.

Finally, it was necessary to construct a trap with which to ensnare Liu Shao-ch'i and all others in the Party apparatus who had continued "openly" to oppose Mao Tse-tung. The strategy in this case was to incite "revolutionary teachers and students" (the precursors of the Red Guards) in June and July of 1966 to rise up against the "work teams" sent by Liu Shao-ch'i, Teng Hsiao-p'ing and other leaders to reassert the authority of the Party over Mao's Cultural Revolution in China's cultural and educational institutions. Once the Party apparatus had been challenged and had counterattacked, its leaders could then be indicted for the same crime charged against P'eng Chen—that of attempting to suppress "the proletarian Left".[2]

This was the third and by far the most serious charge levelled by Mao Tse-tung in his August 5, 1966 wall poster—that Liu Shao-ch'i and his supporters at "the central right down to the local levels" had "enforced a bourgeois dictatorship and struck down the surging movement of the great proletarian cultural revolution..." The time had come to spring the trap on Liu Shao-ch'i, Teng Hsiao-p'ing and a large number of other high-ranking Party leaders, a trap which in retrospect it appears Mao Tse-tung may well have been preparing since early 1965.

CONCLUSIONS

As portrayed in the disclosures of the Great Proletarian Cultural Revolution, factionalism in the Chinese Communist Party Central Committee since 1949 has been motivated by considerations of power, policy and personal rivalry. That these factors have been present in each of the "three big struggles" of the past nineteen years suggests that they will continue to produce tension and conflict within the Chinese Communist political system.

[1] "Lo Jui-ch'ing Deserves To Die Ten Thousand Times for His Crimes" in *Ching kang shan* and *Kuang tung wen i chan pao* September 5, 1967, in, *SCMP*, No. 4046, pp. 9 ff.

[2] Bridgham, "Mao's 'Cultural Revolution'", pp. 23–4.

The first of these, the power factor, reflects the first prerequisite for engaging in factional struggle—the need for an independent power base (or "independent kingdom"). These have been both geographical (e.g. the regional power bases of Kao Kang and Jao Shu-shih in Northeast and East China and of P'eng Chen in Peking) and institutional (e.g. the People's Liberation Army in all three struggles and the Party apparatus in the Great Proletarian Cultural Revolution) in nature. The pivotal role of the Army, the most powerful institution outside the Party, in all three struggles demonstrates the continuing validity of Mao Tse-tung's famous warning in the late 1930's that the Party must "direct the gun, and never allow the gun to direct the Party". It is pertinent to ask, however, how Mao intends to enforce this principle now that his Party apparatus has been largely destroyed and replaced by new "revolutionary" organs of power largely dominated by the military.

The second factor—the policy factor—has been especially prominent in the last two factional struggles within the Central Committee. Although involving foreign policy, the dispute has centred on domestic policy, in particular the proper strategy for promoting China's economic, social, political and military development. The central issue in this debate has been Mao's contention that the same techniques of ideological and political mobilization which worked so well in the early years of revolutionary struggle can be applied to the construction of a modern society. The ultimate expression of this political indoctrination, "mass line" approach to economic and social development was, of course, the Great Leap Forward. It was this reliance on mass movements in economic construction on which P'eng Te-huai focused his attack at the Lushan Plenum.

By defending those who had earlier criticized Mao's radical Great Leap Forward and commune programmes at the January, 1962 Party work conference, Liu Shao-ch'i set in motion a series of developments which would lead in time to the Great Proletarian Cultural Revolution. Although he could cite the Party constitution as justifying an "open opposition", Liu must have suspected that Mao would resent his call to "reverse the verdicts" on those who had shared P'eng Te-huai's viewpoint. Liu may have felt that the strength of his argument combined with the strength of his position in control of the Party apparatus rendered him immune to attack.[1]

The third factor—the factor of personal rivalry—is also indispensable for understanding the "three big struggles" within the Central Committee since 1949. A prominent feature in both the Kao-Jao and P'eng Te-huai affairs, this element of personal antagonism and conflict has played an equally important role, it is believed, in the Great Proletarian Cultural Revolution. For it appears in retrospect that Mao Tse-tung did interpret Liu Shao-ch'i's statements at the January, 1962 Party work conference as being critical both of his policies and himself, and began to have serious doubts concerning Liu's loyalty and fitness to serve as his "revolutionary successor". When these suspicions of disloyalty were strengthened by developments in the ensuing three-year period, Mao then decided to make new arrangements for a "revolutionary successor".

The consequences of this decision would be momentous. It would mean, instead of the smooth succession which Mao had hoped to achieve by conferring power and prestige on Liu Shao-ch'i as head of the Party apparatus, the start of a succession struggle. It would necessitate a thorough purging of all those in the Party apparatus who had staked their careers on the eventual succession to power of Liu Shao-ch'i and Teng Hsiao-p'ing and, as a result, had espoused the views and policies of these Party machine leaders. It would require enlisting the support of other leaders whose bases of power lay outside the Party apparatus, principally Lin Piao (who controlled the People's Liberation Army) and Chou En-lai (also important as an able administrator and representative of the government bureaucracy). It would require the construction of an elaborate trap with which to ensnare Liu Shao-ch'i and Teng Hsiao-p'ing and their supporters in the Party apparatus, and the creation of

[1] The Chinese Communists have advanced this view themselves to explain Liu's conduct in the years preceding the Cultural Revolution. See, for example, the charge that "Liu Shao-ch'i always overestimated his strength" in the joint *Hung ch'i*, *Jen min jih pao* and *Chieh fang chün pao* editorial "Study the History of the Struggle Between the Two Lines Conscientiously", *NCNA*, November 24, 1968.

such extra-Party mass organizations as the Red Guards to supply the element of force needed to spring this trap. In short, this decision to select a new "revolutionary successor" would lead, after the necessary preparations had been made, to the launching of Mao Tse-tung's Great Proletarian Cultural Revolution.

PART III

THE COMMUNIST PARTY AND CHINESE SOCIETY AFTER THE TAKE-OVER

7

KEEPING THE REVOLUTION GOING: PROBLEMS OF VILLAGE LEADERSHIP AFTER LAND REFORM

THOMAS P. BERNSTEIN[1]

Two threats arose in China after land reform[2] that imperilled the transition from the anti-feudal, new democratic revolution of land reform to the socialist revolution of collectivization. One threat came from "below", from the village environment; the other from "above", from the hierarchy of Party and government. Both threats centred on the basic-level leadership and activists who had been recruited into political roles during the guerrilla years and especially during land reform. One threat arose as the interests of the peasants in the maintenance of the small-producer economy affected the attitudes and behaviour of village leaders, leading them to such responses as wanting to withdraw from political involvement. The other threat arose as the rural administrative system became increasingly burdened by numerous tasks and assignments. As pressure to produce results increased, rural leaders, oriented towards getting each task done quickly, tended more and more to mobilize peasants by issuing commands and using coercion. This approach caused a variety of problems; for example, it jeopardized a central goal of the socialist transformation of agriculture of securing peasant support and cooperation with this change.

The purpose of this article is to see how serious the two threats

[1] The author would like to acknowledge with thanks the support of the East Asian Research Center, Harvard University.

[2] In the old liberated areas, land reform was implemented in the years 1946–9; in the new liberated areas occupied by the PLA in 1948 and 1949, land reform was carried out in the years 1950–3. Many, but by no means all, of the examples used in this essay come from old liberated villages in Shansi. Despite variations in local and regional conditions, the problems here described appear to have occurred everywhere at least in some measure.

were and what the Chinese Communist Party (CCP) did about them. The focus will be on the immediate post-land-reform period. Two developments will be examined. One is the "rightist" trend in 1950–1. The other is the campaign against "bureaucracy, commandism, and violations of laws and discipline" in 1953, a campaign carried out against the background of widespread abuses in policy implementation in 1952 and early 1953.

THE THREAT FROM "BELOW"

Two cases

As illustrations, let us take two cases of village cadre behaviour after land reform. Wang Yung-sheng was head of a *hsiang* (administrative village) in Kiangsi province. Wang had been a poor peasant who had suffered from landlord exploitation. When the communists came to his village in about 1949 he was politically "awakened". During land reform he displayed great political activeness and zeal. In rapid succession he became a *hsiang* cadre, then *hsiang* chief. He was chosen a *hsien* (county) labour model, joined the Youth League, and became Youth League secretary. Shortly after land reform he "gloriously" became a candidate Party member. As a result of land distribution, he received 20 *mow* and a draught animal. His acquisitions enabled him to get married. His wife, of middle-peasant origin, also brought in property, and Wang was now a well-off middle peasant. As the prospect of prosperity took hold, Wang began to look upon his political obligations as costly and undesirable chores. Wanting to farm, he neglected his political work and became more and more passive. Repeated education by *ch'ü* Party committee members had little effect on him.[1] He was dismissed from his post of *hsiang* chief, but this didn't bother him, since he could, as he said, earn his *hsiang*-chief supply compensation by working for a few days on his own. Soon after he was dismissed from the Youth League, and his candidacy for Party membership was terminated. Wang commented, "I know it is not right not to do

[1] The *ch'ü* was an administrative unit between *hsiang* and *hsien* of considerable importance in the early 1950's.

[political] work. After I make a little money I'll become active again."[1]

The second case is that of Chang Shui-ts'e, a *ts'un* chief (then an administrative village equivalent to *hsiang*) in Shansi province. Like Wang, Chang had a long history of exploitation as a farm hand. The Communists came to his area in 1940, and Chang joined the cause. The account does not tell us whether he became a part-time guerrilla or joined the Army, but only that he participated in the struggles during World War II for reduction of rent and interest, and against Han-traitors and despots. His life improved, but did not take a dramatic turn for the better until land reform in 1947, when he received land, and, like Wang, got married.[2] During land reform he distinguished himself, became secretary of the Peasant Association and joined the CCP. For three years after land reform he actively led the peasants in movements to increase production and also in organizing labour exchange teams—the most rudimentary form of mutual-aid. Chang was honoured as a *hsien* labour model and elected *ts'un* chief.

Then, just about the time when the civil war ended, Chang began to feel that the revolution was a success and that the road to personal prosperity was open. He bought a draught animal and engaged in sideline production, for the development of which he hired a long-term labourer. Chang thus became an "exploiter".[3] Simultaneously, he lost interest in politics. When he received instructions from the higher level (*ch'ü*), he would simply pass them on instead of exerting himself to implement them. When a peasant group elected him head of a mutual-aid team, he felt himself to be in an unhappy predicament. If he refused to run the team, he would be criticized by his Party superiors; if he accepted, he would not be able to devote as much time to his own property. So, he accepted the post but compromised by doing an indifferent job (*ma ma hu hu*), and as a

[1] *Ch'ang chiang jih pao* [Yangtze Daily], November 2, 1951.

[2] Opportunity to get married seems to have been a rather widespread by-product of land reform in the case of formerly impoverished peasants. Land reform thus had the immediate consequence of re-enforcing the institution of the family as well as attachment to property.

[3] The distinction between long-term hiring of labour and the temporary engaging of harvest help was a criterion defining exploitation.

result of this lack of dedication, the team disintegrated shortly thereafter. After the autumn harvest in 1951, the *hsien* committee ordered him to attend a Party training class at the *hsien* to study Party reform (*cheng tang*). He went, but was preoccupied with his farm affairs, feigned a good attitude, but in fact retained his hired man. His example and influence led three other Party members also to employ long-term hired hands. Because the Party members could no longer lead by setting a personal example (*tai t'ou*), all work in the *ts'un* now became backward. Newspapers went unread, guards did not challenge strangers, a people's school (*min hsiao*) was closed, mutual-aid teams existed only on paper. By all these indices Chang's village had turned from a model one into a backward one in the course of less than three years.

In June, 1952, a three-man team came down from the *hsien* committee of the Party. The three led the local cadres in making a class analysis of the village, which consisted of finding out who had had to sell land and who didn't have enough to eat as a result of all this capitalist activity. The article provided no information on class differentiation, but as a result of the work team's efforts, Chang now became aware of his class origin, and he was sick at heart about the "damage" he had done to people and Party. Chang apologized to the Party, to Chairman Mao, and to the people (in that order). He swore eternal fealty to the Party, promising that he would resolutely overcome his capitalist ideology, and would henceforth lead in mutual aid and cooperation by his personal example. This is how the story ends; the patient was cured and was apparently not dismissed from his posts or expelled from the Party.[1]

As these two illustrative accounts suggest, there were two interrelated threats to the regime's goal of maintaining the village political base built up before and during the years of land reform. One was simply the trend towards withdrawal from political involvement, as basic-level leaders sought to enrich themselves and their families (*fa chia chih fu*). This trend towards political passivity threatened to erode the regime's organizational linkages with the village. The other trend was expressed by cadre Wang's remark,

[1] *Shan hsi jih pao* [Shansi Daily], June 25, 1952. Another such case was reported in the same paper on July 3, 1952.

"After I make a little money, I'll become active again." The threatened consequence of this trend from the CCP's point of view was that the rural leadership would become so well off and even rich (in the technical Marxist–Leninist sense) that it would become not only useless for socialist transformation, but even worse, a resisting obstacle.

Disinvolvement from Communist politics

The desire to withdraw from political involvement was undoubtedly very widespread after land reform. Basic-level cadres failed to see why they should continue to be active. For them the revolution was a success (*ko ming ch'eng kung*), and the real business of life was no longer politics but farming. Speaking of cadres in North China, Po I-po said in mid-1951:

[They] wanted a rest and laid down, holding that the driving away of the Japanese imperialists and Chiang Kai-shek and the carrying out of agrarian reform were to them a revolutionary success. Hence they become politically vulgar, could not visualize what things to do, and felt contented with a "basket of bread, a pot of sour vegetables and sitting on a *k'ang*". They don't bother with such great movements as the suppression of counter-revolutionaries and the Resist-U.S. and Aid-Korea campaign.[1]

A study of 87 Party branches in P'ing-ting *hsien*, Shansi, showed that only half of 1,013 members, or 538, were working actively, while 101 were doing no political work at all. Passive members were most heavily concentrated in 16 backward branches.[2] If cadres in the old liberated areas wanted to withdraw from politics, even though they had been participating in Communist-sponsored political work for many years, it stands to reason that indifference to politics was even greater in the new liberated areas, where cadres had been politically involved for only one or two years.[3] The case

[1] Po I-po, "Strengthen the Party's Political Work in the Countryside", *Jen min jih pao* [People's Daily], June 29, 1951, in *Current Background*, No. 161.

[2] *Shan hsi jih pao*, January 8, 1953.

[3] See also *Shan hsi jih pao* editorial and article, January 20, 1951, on Party reform in the old areas. Chalmers Johnson's point on peasant nationalism as a central ingredient in the Communist victory may well be valid, but judging by the press accounts in the early 1950's, not even peasant cadres seem to have

of Wang Yung-sheng, in fact, was a model discussed all over Kiangsi in an effort to counteract the tendency. Each province in the Central-South Administrative Region had its own model "Wang Yung-sheng", which is suggestive of the seriousness of the problem.[1] According to a survey of one *ch'ü* in Chekiang, 8 out of 10 *hsiang* cadres wanted to devote their time to production rather than to politics.[2]

As for Party members and cadres becoming economically well-off, this was a problem that disturbed the Chinese leaders throughout the period between land reform and collectivization. Let us look at the extent to which Party members and cadres became "exploiters", i.e., behaved like rich peasants. In early 1952, Kao Kang castigated the "increasing practice of rural members of employing farm labour under the fantastic pretext that to 'hire labour is mutual help'" and he warned:

If no active steps are taken to lead the peasants towards the path of co-operative economy rather than to the rich peasant economy, then the rural village government is sure to deteriorate into a rich peasant regime. If the Communist Party members all hire labour and give loans at usurious rates, then the Party will become a rich peasant party. This would mean the complete collapse of the people's regime and the Party organ in the face of attacks launched by the rural bourgeoisie. This, of course, would be intolerable to us.[3]

Data on exploitation by Party members comes mainly from old liberated areas, where more time elapsed between the completion of land reform and the onset of vigorous promotion of policies of

retained a lasting and powerful commitment to the system outside the village. See his *Peasant Nationalism and Communist Power* (Stanford: Stanford Univ. Press, 1962).

[1] Honan had its "Lei Yü ssu hsiang" campaign: see *Ho nan jih pao*, [Honan Daily], December 27, 1951; Hunan had Li Ssu-hsi: see *Jen min jih pao*, September 26, 1951, and also Wang Shou-tao, "P'i p'an Li Ssu-hsi ssu hsiang, chia ch'iang kan pu ssu hsiang chiao yü" [Criticise Li Ssu-hsi's Thought, Strengthen Cadres' Ideological Education], *Hsüeh hsi* [Study], No. 12, October 1, 1951; and Hupeh had its "Wang Jen-ying ssu hsiang" campaign, see *Ch'ang chiang jih pao*, December 2, 1951.

[2] *Che chiang jih pao* [Chekiang Daily], January 27, 1952.

[3] Kao Kang, "Overcome the Corrosion of Bourgeois Ideology; Oppose the Rightist Trend in the Party", *Jen min jih pao*, January 24, 1952, in *Current Background*, No. 163.

socialist transformation. A study of 6 Party branches in Ch'ang-chih Special District, Shansi, showed that 39 of 141 Party members engaged in exploitation.[1] An analysis of the more than 5,000 Party members in 185 Party branches of Wu-hsiang *hsien*, Shansi, published in July 1952 yielded the following three-grade breakdown in quality:

Grade I: 49 Branches. Indicators: very strong mutual-aid and co-operation: over 90% of households "organized". Party members' thought is pure, branches are actively leading in policy implementation; work results quite good.

Grade II: 132 Branches, of which 88 were adjudged to be closer to Grade I in quality, and 44 closer to Grade III.

Grade III: 4 Branches. Indicators: very serious capitalist thought; members have "basically changed colour". Except for a few who are leading mutual-aid and cooperation, most farm on their own (*tan kan*), and they engage in all varieties of exploitation.

Thus, while only four branches had lost their political effectiveness as implementers of Party policy, 44 others had deteriorated in the same direction, for a combined total of 21% of the branches. The report added that 5% of the members were not in mutual-aid teams, and were also persisting in acts of exploitation, while another 15% of the members were passive, failed to set a personal example, and were thus backward.[2]

These scattered data suggest that a minority of Party members—and as Party members their obligations to maintain model standards were of course greater than for non-Party cadres—was not only not responsive to regime policies but was also succumbing to the temptations of the "capitalist road". This impression is reinforced by national data on Party reform (*cheng tang*) in rural basic-level organizations carried out intensively in 1952-3. According to data on 75,000 branches (out of a total of 180,000 then in existence), 90% of the members met the conditions for continued membership.[3]

[1] *Shan hsi jih pao*, November 30, 1952.   [2] *Shan hsi jih pao*, July 26, 1952.
[3] "Nung ts'un cheng tang kung tso ti chi tien ching yen" [Model Experience of Village Party Reform Work], *Jen min jih pao*, April 2, 1953, in *Hsin Hua yüeh pao* [New China Monthly], No. 5 (May, 1953).

An Tzu-wen, reporting on *cheng tang* in 40,000 branches, said that 3–5% of the members were expelled as bad elements, while 5–7% resigned voluntarily after having come to understand their unsuitability.[1] In Shantung province, the first wave of *cheng tang* involved 60,360 Party members, of whom 2,363 were expelled and 5,892 were persuaded to resign from the Party, yielding a total reduction of 13·5%. In addition, 1,856 received disciplinary punishment (*ch'u fen*).[2] Although complete information on the purge of rural Party members does not seem to be available either for individual provinces or for the nation, the partial data indicate a rather high purge rate that ranged between 8% and 13·5% of rural members. As far as I know, this was the severest purge of rural Party members between 1950 and 1957.[3] It compares in severity with the purge of rural Party members undertaken in the Soviet Union on the very eve of all-out collectivization, in 1929, when 14% of the cell members were expelled.[4]

These purge data require two qualifications. One is that Party members were expelled or persuaded to resign not merely for passiveness, and for class offences such as rich-peasant behaviour, sheltering counter revolutionaries, being disguised landlords, etc. The other important causes for purge were corruption and abuse of power in implementing policy. *Cheng tang* was undertaken together with a campaign against violations of laws and discipline, directed against cadres who were coercing and oppressing the peasants in various ways (see below). Hence, only an unspecified fraction of the over-all loss rate of 10% is attributable to the failings we have been discussing. The other qualification goes in the opposite direction; that is, the purge rates understate the prevalence of Party-members'

[1] An Tzu-wen, "Nationwide Struggle Against Bureaucratism, Commandism and Violations of Law and Discipline", *New China News Agency* [*NCNA*], February 9, 1953, in *Current Background*, No. 251.

[2] *Ibid.*

[3] For example, in the Party reform movement in 1950–1 in old liberated areas, there apparently were very few expulsions; see *Shan hsi jih pao*, January 20, 1951.

[4] For comparative data, see my article, "Leadership and Mass Mobilisation in the Soviet and Chinese Collectivisation Campaigns of 1929–30 and 1955–56: A Comparison", *The China Quarterly*, No. 31 (July–September, 1967), pp. 1–47.

offences of all kinds. Leniency, as expressed in the principle of "magnanimous treatment for past deeds, but rigorous treatment for new deeds", was the order of the day. In February, 1953, the North China Bureau of the Central Committee published "Provisions for dealing with employment of labour, issue of loans, operation of commercial enterprises and renting of land by members of the Party. . ."[1] which stressed that those persisting in these proscribed acts were to be expelled. According to the report on six Shansi branches cited above, 39 of 141 members had engaged in exploitation; only 15 were dismissed as incorrigible.[2] Thus the Party leaders were more interested in salvaging the rural cadre base than in destroying it. While the precise dimensions of the problem are unclear, it can be reasonably concluded that there was a significant tendency of rural Party members and cadres generally to disengage themselves from politics and to take the road to personal enrichment.

Reasons for disinvolvement

From the cadres' point of view, the desire to withdraw to private life was a rational response. They could contrast the attractions of farming with the burdens of being a cadre. The latter offered the prospect of arduous work and the uncomfortable position of being at the boundary of the political system and the society, exposed to the pressures of both. As some basic-level cadres complained: "If we don't do a good job, we get criticized by the higher level. If our attitude isn't good, the masses complain [yu i chien]. If we neglect our farms, the wives grumble. So, the best thing is not to be a cadre."[3]

Moreover, the material rewards of an official post in the administrative village were not great, even for those two or three full- or half-time officials who received compensation from the state. The rest had to combine farming with political work and had some-

[1] "Provisions for Dealing with Employment of Labour, Issue of Loans, Operation of Commercial Enterprises and Renting of Land by Members of the Party during the Period of the Readjustment of the Party Organizations", *Jen min jih pao*, February 26, 1953, in *Survey of the China Mainland Press* [*SCMP*], No. 532.

[2] *Shan hsi jih pao*, November 30, 1952.

[3] *Che chiang jih pao*, January 27, 1952.

how to reconcile the competing demands on their time. Moreover, many basic-level cadres harboured feelings of frustration and resentment at having to remain in the village at a time when many others were being promoted. In the years of national take-over, many jobs had to be filled in the cities and in the administrative levels above the village. Those who were picked for these posts could take satisfaction, as did a successful Kwangtung peasant cadre, who said, "This truly is Chairman Mao's good leadership, we peasants can also become *ch'ü* chiefs."[1] But many of those who stayed behind felt keenly the injustice of their lowly state.[2] These grievances were apparently quite widespread in the old liberated areas, since many cadres had been transferred from them to the new liberated areas. As priority was being given to industry and the cities, the old bases once again became remote backwaters (which presumably had been the reason why they had become guerrilla bases in the first place). Cadres remaining there felt neglected and undervalued, resulting in a morale crisis of considerable proportions and accentuating tendencies towards passivity and withdrawal.[3] Again Po I-po provides a generalized appraisal:

What is worse, they not only carry on no revolutionary work, but ask "repayment of debt" from the Party, ask for position, for enjoyment. If they can't have their way, they complain, "The donkey is killed after turning the mill", "peasants are forgotten after the entry into the cities." They consider that the Party is unfair to them, not that they have separated themselves from the revolution.[4]

In contrast, individual farming offered tempting vistas of prosperity. When a cadre said "all my life I have suffered hardship. Now that I have been given land, I am completely satisfied, so why

[1] *Nan fang jih pao* [Southern Daily], October 4, 1952.

[2] As one unpromoted cadre said, when his thinking had been rectified: "I have been brooding about the injustice of the Party's not recommending me, but this is nothing but subordinating the Party's general interest to the individual interest and it is not compatible with the criteria for being a Party member. Henceforth I will be able to work free from worry." *Jen min jih pao*, August 8, 1953.

[3] For a report on a conference dealing with the problem in Ch'ang-chih Special District, an old area in Shansi, see *Shan hsi jih pao*, July 17, 1952.

[4] Po I-po (*Current Background*, No. 161). Translation slightly modified.

continue to make revolution",[1] he was speaking as a participant in the small-producer economy. In Lenin's celebrated phrase, such an economy generates capitalism continuously, hourly, and on a massive scale. What this actually means is that as long as peasants have a chance, they will strive to become "capitalists". Rich peasants, in other words, are the model of what other peasants would like to become; they serve as their reference group. Given a chance, peasants will try to enlarge their holdings, hire labourers, loan money at the highest obtainable interest; that is, do what rich peasants do. Land reform intensified these normal peasant attitudes. Now, not only was there the desire to become rich but also the reality of opportunity, as reflected in the mass appearance of new middle peasants as well as of some new rich peasants.[2] As upwardly mobile property owners, many cadres also took the rich peasants as their reference group. As Party members, or prospective Party members, they were supposed to be aware of the political definition of rich peasants as evil and threatening exploiters. They were supposed to take the lead in repudiating the rich peasant model, and persuade everyone of the inevitable futility in store for most of those attempting to follow it. They were to hold out the road to common prosperity of the "get organized" movement, that is, take the lead in organizing mutual-aid teams, in due course Lower Producers' Cooperatives (LPC), and ultimately collective farms.

From this vantage point, the CCP had failed in a timely and vigorous way to counterbalance and overcome the attractions of individual enrichment for the cadres. For some time, longer in the old than in the new liberated areas, the regime allowed basic-level cadres to become disoriented with respect to the direction which rural development would take (towards socialism). This disorientation was in part the product of a policy of explicit encouragement of individual enrichment. The reason for this was simply the

[1] *Jen min jih pao*, September 26, 1951; the cadre was the Hunan model for withdrawal, Li Ssu-hsi.

[2] Marxist–Leninist theory predicts, of course, that class differentiation will lead to the separation of the village into two sharply polarized groups of exploiters and exploited majority. In fact, as a result of land reform, the opposite happened, as middle peasants of various types came to constitute the majority in the village, a state of affairs that did not significantly change before all-out collectivization.

immediate, short-run need of the country for maximum food output. As long as there were few mutual-aid teams and virtually no producers' cooperatives, encouraging individual peasants to believe that the "four freedoms" (freedom to rent, buy and sell land, to hire labour, to lend money, and to engage in trade) were legitimate and long-term rights was the only way to attain this goal. The need to reassure the peasants—to "stabilize their production enthusiasm"—arose also because of land reform itself. During land reform peasants had understandably been reluctant to maximize production by using all possible inputs such as hired labour for fear of promotion to class-enemy status.[1] On the other hand, land reform, with its expropriations and redistributions of property, also gave rise to ideas of "Utopian" peasant socialism, including egalitarian notions of "everyone eating out of the same pot". To allay these fears and sentiments, the slogan of family enrichment (*fa chia chih fu*) was raised.[2] In mid-1950, a writer in *Hsüeh hsi* noted that some peasants would indeed become rich, while others, not as hardworking or not as well-equipped, would again become poor and labourers. He added approvingly:

This kind of differentiation is advantageous for the development of production...Many peasants...will work hard, striving to enrich their families. The rich peasant economy will have better productive forces at its disposal than the small peasant economy. Its productivity will be higher because it has better conditions for improving implements, raising technology, using fertilizer, etc. Therefore, class differentiation is today definitely not to be feared.[3]

The indulgent policy towards rich peasants did not of course last, and when the general line of the transition to socialism was announced in 1953, the one-sided encouragement of small-peasant production had already been subjected to criticism.[4]

[1] *Nan fang jih pao*, February 19, 1953, in *SCMP*, No. 527.

[2] Po I-po (*Current Background*, No. 161); Kao Kang, in a speech given in March, 1950, "Stand at the Forefront of Economic Reconstruction in the Northeast", *Jen min jih pao*, June 5, 1950, in *Current Background*, No. 163.

[3] Shang Ko-tung, "T'u kai hou hsiao nung ching chi ti fen hua wen t'i" [The Differentiation of the Small Peasant Economy after Land Reform], *Hsüeh hsi*, July 16, 1950.

[4] *Jen min jih pao*, November 17, 1953. In view of the current attacks on Liu Shao-ch'i's "black line", it is worth pointing out that Mao Tse-tung too was

Nonetheless, for a time cadres did find themselves in a situation in which their personal preferences received official encouragement. As one Party branch secretary in Shansi ingenuously explained, "Hiring a long-term labourer is not exploitation, but taking the lead in developing production."[1] The Party never officially tolerated exploitation by Party members, of course, but for a time the official response was quite lenient. Contrast the uncompromising tone of Kao Kang in the 1952 speech quoted above (see p. 000) with the tone of a speech of his in March 1950:

Some families of Party members may have become rich by productive labour after agricultural reform. If they intend to withdraw from the Party, their application should be granted. Those who are lukewarm towards Party work should have their Party membership suspended... As to those who do not wish to withdraw from the Party though their attitudes have become somewhat unenthusiastic, we shall reserve their membership so long...as they exercise no bad influence upon the masses. But any Party member who has changed his faith and political outlook and lost the minimum qualification for Party membership is to be expelled from the Party in order to ensure its integrity.[2]

The disorientation of rural cadres resulting from the shifting relations between short- and long-term policies was strongly reinforced by their widespread ignorance about what socialism and communism meant. Again, short-term considerations had intruded:

very sensitive to the issue of production. For example, in 1948, he suggested that new rich peasants who had appeared in the years of Communist rule in the old areas should be treated as well-off middle peasants, "for the sake of agricultural production". Mao, "On Some Important Problems of the Party's Present Policy", *Selected Works* (Peking: Foreign Languages Press, 1961), IV, 185. This does not of course prove that the leaders were unanimous on this issue. Most likely, what was in dispute was not the policy of encouraging rich peasants as such, but its timing and duration. Speaking of socialist transformation generally, one could probably say that all leaders were in agreement on the desirability and necessity of this goal, but that there was disagreement over the timing, nature and content of the change. Thus, the speed of collectivization was a matter of dispute at least until the second half of 1955. Disagreement on such issues is the stuff of politics and its existence should not occasion surprise, and it does not by itself prove the existence of unified factions with an established policy position.

[1] *Shan hsi jih pao*, July 36, 1952.

[2] Kao Kang, "Stand at the Forefront of Economic Reconstruction in the Northeast" (*Current Background*, No. 163).

in order to mobilize the participation of peasant activists in land reform, one of the main incentives held out to them had been the promise of land and of subsequent personal prosperity.[1] However, ignorance of the Party's objectives after the anti-feudal revolution extended not only to the most recent recruits in the new liberated areas, but also to Party members of long standing. In 1951, a survey of the attitudes and opinions of the 109 members of four Shansi village branches was made. The branches had been set up between 1937 and 1939; one-third of the current membership had joined during the anti-Japanese war; two-thirds joined during the third revolutionary war (1946–9). All knew that the ultimate goal of the party was "Communism". But none had any but the foggiest notions of the nature of the intervening steps; while some professed willingness to go along with the Party, others felt that the *status quo* was pretty satisfactory. The author of the report attributed their ignorance to the fact that the Party members had never been exposed to systematic study of "Marxism–Leninism and the thought of Mao Tse-tung".[2]

Ignorance of the official ideology did not mean that many village Party members did not have some ideas of their own. Thus the press voiced considerable concern over manifestations of "peasant ideology" (*nung min ssu hsiang*). Peasant Party members not only harboured ideas about the attractiveness of the small-producer economy, but even explicitly rejected such key tenets—strongly emphasized in the early 1950's—of working-class leadership. "The world was won by the peasants, peasants should rule the world",[3] and, "The CCP should be a peasant party since many Communist Party members are of peasant origin."[4] Peasant Party members did not think it right for the urban working class (*kung*

[1] *Fu chien jih pao* [Fukien Daily], February 1, 1952; see also the materials on Li Ssu-hsi, *Jen min jih pao*, September 26, 1951.

[2] *Shan hsi jih pao*, August 22, 1951. A related problem was that many of the rural cadres were illiterate or semi-literate. The survey showed that of the 109 members, 37 were illiterate and 35 had had up to two years of schooling. Aside from teaching them how to read, the CCP coped with this by relying heavily on oral communication, and especially group study as techniques for spreading knowledge of ideology and policies.

[3] Po I-po, (*Current Background*, No. 161).

[4] *Shan hsi jih pao*, August 10, 1951.

jen chieh chi) to be elevated to the leading position, to the position of the "elder brother" of the peasants, to whom the peasants should defer and from whom they should learn. Rural Party members argued that the peasants had fought in the PLA, had borne the brunt of the struggle, and had liberated the workers in the cities. Moreover, they argued, there are many peasants and few workers, and the peasants feed the cities, so why should peasants now have to play second fiddle to the workers?[1]

What is important in the notions of peasant supremacy and resentment of the superior position now being accorded to the cities is that these ideas were the closest approximation that one can find to a positive, programmatic articulation of peasant interests. For the most part, rural cadres simply withdrew from political activity to devote themselves to family prosperity, and by doing so they articulated an interest in the maintenance of the *status quo* in only a passive and defensive way. As far as one can tell, no well-off Party member tried to formulate his interests in programmatic form or tried actively to mobilize peasants in support of these interests. Instead, the threat they posed was a defensive one. When a village became politically "backward", regime programmes either were not being implemented or they were distorted in some way to accommodate particular local interests or preferences. This defensive or passive interest-articulation manifested itself in reluctance of Party members to join mutual-aid teams. Cases such as that of a village in T'un-liu *hsien*, Shansi, where only one out of 34 Party members was in the teams, were not isolated in 1951 or 1952.[2] Or, where mutual-aid teams did function, Party members and other cadres might use them in their own interests, e.g., by taking advantage of poorer peasants in the exchange relations of labour and draught animals on which the teams were based.[3] The erosion of linkage

[1] *Shan hsi jih pao*, September 23, 1951. The same attitudes were also found in the South, as reported in the case of one training class for prospective Party members in the villages of Kwangtung. See *Nan fang jih pao*, August 2, 1952. In their case, a visit to factories, where they could admire the superior skills of the workers, reportedly dispelled these confused notions.

[2] *Jen min jih pao*, May 8, 1952; also *Chieh fang jih pao* [Liberation Daily], July 15, 1952.

[3] *Fu chien jih pao*, January 8, 1953; August 27, 1952. See also Kao Kang, "Overcome the Corrosion of Bourgeois Ideology; Oppose the Rightist Trend in the Party", *op. cit.*

between regime and peasant cadres thus did not threaten the existence of the Communist system as such. It did threaten the goals of the CCP of introducing fundamental change through non-compliance or outward compliance while actually the content and purpose of the policies were being distorted.

Making cadres responsive to socialist transformation

The CCP did not permit rural cadres to succumb to their spontaneous preferences. In a series of increasingly vigorous efforts that began in about the summer of 1951 and gained momentum in 1952, the regime sought to make cadres responsive to the goals of socialist transformation. As is already clear, a variety of approaches and techniques were utilized, such as the selective purge in 1952–3, with its accompanying pressure on cadres to rectify their ways and to undertake "penetrating self-examination".[1] Outstanding among the techniques for revitalizing cadres' political involvement was the cultivation of a sense of threat and danger from enemies.[2] Propaganda strongly emphasized the theme that withdrawal from politics would provide opportunities for landlords to reseize their property and to recapture power and influence in the villages, especially in new liberated areas where land reform had only just been completed. Possibly the threat was a real one. When cadre commitment to political activity declined, vigilance also declined. Complacent attitudes of "universal peace" took hold. Consequently, militia units and village security committees disintegrated and the system of formal control imposed on landlords and registered counter-revolutionaries became less effective. In response, the press played up instances of the old elite making a comeback, plotting and infiltrating local organizations. Instances of arson and poisoning of livestock were attributed to class enemies as part of the effort to raise cadre vigilance.[3]

[1] *Shan hsi jih pao*, February 20, 1953.

[2] As R. H. Solomon has suggested, the use of enemies has not just been a technique in the arsenal of political approaches but is really an internalized part of the Maoist world view. See Richard H. Solomon, "America's Revolutionary Alliance with Communist China: Parochialism and Paradox in Sino-American Relations", *Asian Survey*, VII, No. 12 (December, 1967), 831–50.

[3] *Ch'ang chiang jih pao*; the issues of November 2, November 8, and December 26, 1951 carried stories on these issues.

The cultivation of a sense of threat was also used in order to widen the mental horizons of cadres beyond the confines of their village. The "Resist-U.S., Aid-Korea" campaign was particularly important in this regard. It afforded an opportunity to activate cadres in a cause more readily comprehensible than socialist transformation—national defence—and to ask them to lead peasants in patriotic production movements and bond drives. The CCP skilfully tied the U.S. threat to past dangers and struggles with which rural cadres had had direct experience. In areas that had been under Japanese occupation, for example, the anti-U.S. campaign was linked with U.S. intentions to rearm Japan.[1] Elsewhere, the U.S. threat was tied to the Kuomintang and to the landlords. As one cadre reportedly exclaimed, "We must definitely not let the Chiang bandits, the landlord class, and U.S. imperialism harm us again; I'll certainly make revolution through to the end."[2] Once cadres were active again, it was not difficult to channel their efforts into the desired socialist direction. The step from leading a patriotic production drive to leading a mutual-aid team was not a large one.

In its educational work the CCP sought to teach cadres some clear and simple propositions about the direction of future change, about the elements of the doctrine and about the meaning of Party membership. Thus the reason why the CCP stressed the concept of working-class leadership was not only that it wanted to come as close as possible to orthodox Soviet conceptions of what a Communist party should be. More fundamentally, inculcating acceptance of this concept was a major way of teaching peasant Party members to understand and be responsive to new socialist goals that by definition went beyond the cognitive horizon of peasants. Acceptance of the notion of the CCP as the vanguard of the working class rather than of the peasants—one of the eight criteria for Party membership—signified the conscious shedding of one's petty-bourgeois peasant standpoint, and the acceptance of the two goals of collectivization of agriculture and of industrialization, in which agriculture would play a supporting role.

To prod cadres into renewed activity, the CCP combined

---

[1] For one account, see *Jen min jih pao*, April 14, 1953.
[2] *Ch'ang chiang jih pao*, August 24, 1951.

education with more or less unspoken pressures. It laid stress on the inevitable failure of the capitalist road and on the inevitability of change in the direction of socialism. The unspoken warning behind this message was that cadres had better rejoin the cause since the alternative would be an existence that threatened to become less and less viable and that might ultimately expose them to unpleasant sanctions. Probably this was an effective way of revitalizing cadre activeness. The CCP had already once demonstrated its capacity effectively to carry out a major rural revolution: land reform. When it made clear its determination to make another change, cadres had no reason to question its capacity to do so.

Factors of personal interest also entered into the cadres' calculus of reasons in favour of activeness. Cadres could compensate for the frustrations and difficulties of organizing and managing village producers' collectives by the hope and even the expectation that loyal service would ultimately be rewarded by a more comfortable job in the higher levels of Party or government as socialist transformation generated demands for more full-time officials on the state's payroll.[1] For the time being, on the other hand, the choice in favour of commitment was made easier in that in 1952 and 1953, cadres and activists were expected mainly to lead mutual-aid teams and lower-stage cooperatives, in which they did not have to abandon the ties to private property all at once. Whatever the exact mix of cadre perceptions, it is clear that in the case of most cadres, the CCP did overcome the tendency towards withdrawal from politics that manifested itself after land reform. Thus by late 1953 and 1954, except for full-time administrative cadres, virtually all cadres and activists were leading producers' collectives.[2]

In looking at the revitalization of cadres' activeness, we have emphasized various techniques used by the regime to attain this goal.

[1] When higher-stage cooperatives were organized on a national scale in 1956, many new positions for full-time cadres did in fact open up. It is interesting that during the Cultural Revolution Liu Shao-ch'i's "cadre line" was severely criticized for allegedly holding out to lower-level cadres the prospect of advancement to higher and more prestigious positions. See, for example, "Thoroughly Repudiate Liu Shao-chi's Counter-Revolutionary Revisionist Line on Party Building", *Peking Review*, No. 51 (December 20, 1968).

[2] For some data on the percentages of village cadres in the producers' cooperatives, see for example *Kuang ming jih pao* [Bright Daily], July 1, 1954.

This implies that the regime secured cadre responsiveness primarily through its own efforts, and that internalized commitments played a much smaller role or none at all. It implies that few cadres had any genuine commitment to the cause or to ideas, goals, or entities going much beyond the normal horizon of the village, such as nationalism, socialism–communism, the CCP, or Chairman Mao. Very possibly this is an overstatement. For instance, we have been speaking only of a minority of Party members, and judging by some of the data there was another minority on the other side who were responsive and about whom the CCP had no cause to worry. Also, it seems implausible that such major changes as collectivization in the mid-50's could have been accomplished without some genuine commitment. But the main point seems to be that even if many cadres did have a predisposing commitment to the Communist system, the commitment had to be reinforced constantly; it was not a self-sustaining one. It had to be reinforced by unremitting efforts from above, by pressure to participate, by education campaigns and study, and it had to be reinforced horizontally by other village cadres. As a newspaper article put it a year or so after these particular campaigns, "if the *ch'ü* committee and the branch relax leadership and education over them [the village Party members], spontaneous forces will grow and they will waver in their thinking".[1] The "threat from below" was a continuing one, and there is much evidence that problems similar to the ones that have been discussed here arose in later years as well, as after the Great Leap, and that the regime responded in roughly the same ways as it did in 1951–3.[2]

THE THREAT FROM "ABOVE":
BUREAUCRATISM AND COMMANDISM

The main purpose of revitalizing the links between system and village leadership was to make it possible to introduce more change to the village. In 1952 and 1953, an increasing number of programmes

---

[1] *Hsin Hu nan pao* [New Hunan Newspaper], August 31, 1954.

[2] For example, after the Great Leap, cadres no longer wanted to carry the burden of wanting to be cadres, and they were affected by spontaneous forces. For discussion, see Richard Baum and Frederick C. Teiwes, "Liu Shao-ch'i and the Cadre Problem", *Asian Survey*, VIII, No. 4 (April, 1968), 323–45.

and policies were being implemented in the rural areas. These included not just the normal administrative work, such as tax collection, but programmes related to cultural modernization, as for example sanitation measures, literacy movements, and the enforcement of the marriage law. Most important, agricultural production was increasingly politicized; that is, increasingly becoming the responsibility of political leadership. Not only were there movements to increase production, anti-drought campaigns, and drives to make peasants use new tools, but in 1952-3 the first major campaign to establish mutual-aid teams and cooperatives on a wide scale was pressed forward. The burden of implementation fell on the basic-level leadership, although, being inexperienced, they were supposed to be guided and supervised by cadres from the *ch'ü* and the *hsien*.[1] As is normal in China, programme implementation took place under pressure. In much of 1952 an anti-rightist campaign had been in progress to rectify the very shortcomings that we discussed in the preceding section. The problems that arose in policy implementation arose at least in part because many cadres corrected for "Rightist" mistakes by making "Leftist" ones.[2]

The results of the efforts were not good. Instead of a deviation from the official norm, coercion or commandism (*ch'iang p'o ming ling*) was the norm. As An Tzu-wen reported:

In the basic level organizations of the Party and the government... commandism and alienation from the masses prevail... In the agricultural production and patriotic health movements directly serving the interests of the masses, the commandist style of work is quite serious. Under such a bad style of work, the masses suffer tremendously in the anti-drought work, the promotion of improved seeds, the issuing of agricultural loans, and the anti-epidemic work. In some places the situation is even more serious where the *ch'ü*, *hsiang*, and part of the *hsien* cadres violate laws and discipline, suppress criticism, shield counterrevolutionaries, and harm good people... The existence of these phenomena has seriously menaced

[1] Indeed, the *ch'ü* often had direct operational responsibility in the early years, because of the weakness of the *hsiang ts'un* leaders.

[2] For an article describing the consequences of struggle against Right deviation, see *Shan hsi jih pao*, February 20, 1953; the article is characteristically entitled "Forcing the Masses to Merge Mutual-aid Teams Turned a Good Thing into a Bad One".

the interests of the people, twisted the Party policy, and undermined the relations between the Party and the masses.[1]

For example, to combat drought, a campaign was launched in some northern provinces to mobilize peasants to dig wells. Cadres implemented the programme by forcing peasants to contribute funds and coercing them to dig the wells to such a point that, according to Hopeh's Party secretary, Lin T'ieh, some people were driven to suicide. Or, cadres forced peasants to buy water wheels even though they had no use for them. In some cases, they mobilized the militia to force peasants to work on the public projects. In another case, a Party branch secretary physically beat the peasants, and this was not an isolated instance.[2]

The mutual-aid and cooperative campaign of 1952–3 was characterized by "blind advance", "hastiness", "crude methods", all of which adds up to coercion. Cadres forced peasants to join teams and to agree to their amalgamation into larger units (in some cases into a very large cooperative farm of over 100 households). Force consisted of threatening to treat people as class enemies ("not to join mutual-aid teams is a sign of capitalist thought"), of imposing fines, withdrawing irrigation rights, etc.[3] In one case, cadres made dozens of non-farmers join mutual-aid teams in order to increase the enrolment percentages.[4]

The result of these widespread deviations from the model[5] was

[1] An Tzu-wen, "To Struggle for Eradication of the Passive Attitude and Unhealthy Conditions in Party Organizations", *Jen min jih pao*, February 12, 1953, in *Current Background*, No. 231.

[2] Lin T'ieh, "Chien chüeh fan tui kuan liao chu i, jen chen cheng tun tang ti chi ts'eng tsu chih" [Resolutely Oppose Bureaucratism, Seriously Reorganize the Party's Basic-level Organisations], *Jen min jih pao*, February 3, 1953. See also *Jen min jih pao*, editorial, February 11, 1953.

[3] For some sources on the movement, see *Jen min jih pao*, March 24, 1953, March 29, 1953; *Fu chien jih pao*, February 20, 1953; *Shan hsi jih pao*, February 20, 1953. An enormous number of other sources is available.

[4] *Shan hsi jih pao*, February 20, 1953.

[5] The model approach, it should be noted, is not what is normally understood as the mass line, i.e., an approach based on persuasion, mass participation, and voluntariness. The approach legitimate from the CCP's point of view is more complex, and always includes a measure of coercion, however disguised and indirect. This includes, for example, coercion directed against particular class enemies, which, naturally enough, has an impact on the response of those who

first and foremost peasant dissatisfaction and alienation, which jeopardized the regime's goal of securing peasant cooperation in such central matters as raising agricultural output. More specifically, blindly coercive policy implementation caused economic damage, as in the case of Tientsin Special District, Hopeh, where 40,000 of 70,000 wells dug ("decorative wells") turned out to be useless.[1] In another case, cadres, under pressure to have peasants make use of a new type of seed, forced them to uproot already growing plants.[2] In the mutual-aid team and cooperative campaign, some property losses occurred as peasants killed livestock rather than have it socialized. In addition, the movement was severely set back as the regime found it necessary to dissolve a proportion of the newly set up producers' collectives.[3] In other cases, once the pressure for compliance was off, the newly formed institutions, lacking any staying power of their own, simply disintegrated. For all these reasons, a purely coercive approach to programme inplementation was undesirable from the regime's point of view.

In the official analysis of what had gone wrong, "bureaucratism" (*kuan liao chu i*) at the levels of responsible leadership (province, special district, and *hsien*) was held accountable for commandism at the basic level. Bureaucratism consisted of these failings: higher-level officials had made no effort to understand conditions in the villages. They did not understand the backwardness and lack of skill of the basic-level cadres, nor did they grasp the limitations of what could immediately be done to change the ways of the peasants. Hence higher-level departments attempted to do too much too quickly without regard for objective limitations. This tendency was

are not classified as such, at least for the time being. Also, it includes public criticism, and "helpful advice" to deviants, which has coercive overtones. Official definitions have specifically excluded "criticism" and "education" from the definition of what constitutes commandism, as in North China Central Committee Bureau regulations. What matters are the proportions of the various approaches, and what is at issue is the more or less exclusive reliance on coercion.

[1] Lin T'ieh, in *Jen min jih pao*, February 3, 1953, and July 26, 1953, in *Current Background*, No. 259, Appendix, September 15, 1953.

[2] *Kuang ming jih pao*, January 14, 1953.

[3] In North China, 2,600 LPCs of 9,000 in existence at the time the movement was broken off in March, 1953 were turned back into mutual-aid teams; 400 apparently dissolved. See *Shan hsi jih pao*, July 21, 1953.

fostered by competition among various departments and by apparently quite inadequate coordination of projects by the Party committees. Each department assigned priority to its particular project and demanded immediate fulfilment from the basic-level cadres. They put blind pressure on the village cadres in failing to define the scope and limits of what it was they wanted done, hence the excesses. In fact some higher-level officials felt that pressing down with assignments (*ya jen wu*) was the best way to combat the tendency of village cadres of withdrawing from political and administrative work. Higher levels assigned tasks without regard to the contribution that the particular programme would make to the over-all goal of socialist transformation; they adopted the "pure business viewpoint" (*tan ch'un jen wu kuan tien*). They were precocupied with quantitative indices of performance which they could use to demonstrate their merit: number of wells dug, percentage of households organized in mutual-aid teams, number of people taught how to read, etc. They were satisfied with the reported results, and they failed to go and see what was actually happening in the villages. Instead they were contemptuous of the village cadres, treated them like errand boys, and kept them busy collecting non-essential information.[1]

Bureaucratism at the higher levels caused commandism at the level of implementation, in the villages. Indeed, it can hardly be considered surprising that basic-level cadres, under heavy pressure to carry out a bewildering array of complex tasks with inadequate

[1] Some of the sources for these points:

(i) An Tzu-wen, "To struggle for eradication of the passive attitude and unhealthy conditions in Party organisations", *op. cit.*

(ii) Lin T'ieh's article in *Jen min jih pao*, February 11, 1953, *op. cit.*

(iii) A decision by the North China Bureau of the Central Committee, "Ta li kai chin tui yü nung ts'un ti ling tao kung tso" [Greatly Improve the Work of Leading the Village], *Shan hsi jih pao*, June 23, 1953.

(iv) For a report on "ya jen-wu", see Lung Shou, "Chieh shao Hsin Hu nan pao kuan yü Li Ssu-hsi ssu hsiang ti t'ao lun" [Introducing the Discussion in *New Hunan Newspaper* on Li Ssu-hsi's Thought], *Hsüeh hsi*, No. 11 (September 16, 1951).

(v) For a report on how higher levels treat *hsiang* leaders as messenger boys (*p'ao t'ui*), *Chieh fang jih pao*, August 27, 1953.

(vi) On keeping village leaders busy collecting non-essential information, *Shan hsi jih pao*, February 8, 1953.

knowledge, guidance and experience should have used the simplest method—coercion—to get them done. As may be seen from this list of failings, bureaucratism not only caused commandism, but had the additional consequence of freeing villages from higher-level control. "Independent kingdoms" appeared in the villages. Just as some basic-level cadres preferred to withdraw from political activity when higher-level pressure was off, others preferred to exploit their positions of power and to lord it over the peasants for their own ends. As a statement by the North China Bureau of the Central Committee put it:

In the cases of small numbers of *ts'un* cadres who exploit their authority and adopt such illegal methods as detention and physical force in interrogations, thereby...encroaching on human rights and putting innocent people to trouble to the extent of forcing them into death, or who are corrupt, traffic in narcotics, and have incurred the hatred of the broad masses, they shall be treated as bad elements who have violated law and Party discipline.[1]

Hapless peasants exposed to the tyranny of such cadres found that it didn't pay to try to complain to higher levels of authority. For one thing, the village cadres were frequently in a position to retaliate against the complainers.[2] For their part, higher-level bureaucrats tended to pigeonhole letters from the public. In the first half of 1952, 100,000 such letters, some of which contained information exposing village "despots", accumulated in Shantung Party and government offices.[3]

Bureaucratism also made it possible for basic-level cadres to cope with the multitudinous demands by deceiving their superiors. Quite a few reports of false reporting (*hsü pao*) appeared in the press. During Party reform in a Shansi *hsien*, it was found that 93 of 414 Party members had at various times submitted false per-

[1] North China Bureau of the Central Committee, "Provisions for Dealing with Problems Relating to Corruption, Waste, and Commandism on the Part of Members and Cadres of the Party during the Period of the Readjustment of Party Organization", *Jen min jih pao*, February 26, 1953, in *SCMP*, No. 532. Translation slightly modified.

[2] An Tzu-wen, "To Struggle for Eradication...," *Jen min jih pao*, February 12, 1953.

[3] Case reported in *Jen min jih pao*, April 9, 1953, in *SCMP*, No. 557.

formance reports that inflated results.[1] In Kao-yang *hsien*, Hopeh, 2,400 year-round mutual-aid teams were reported; 400 actually existed.[2] In Shansi, a *ch'ü* committee told *ts'un* cadres to organize such teams; within a few days, one village sent a report that 90% of the households had been organized. The *ch'ü* committee did not quite believe this, so it sent a report up to the *hsien* saying that half the village's manpower had been enrolled.[3] Sometimes higher-level ignorance concerning the actual state of affairs in the villages was a product of long neglect, especially in mountainous areas with poor communications. Some *hsien* and *ch'ü* committees in Shansi, for example, didn't know how many Party branches and Party members they had under their jurisdiction.[4] In another case, reported from Chekiang, leadership at all levels above the villages remained ignorant of the true proportions of a famine affecting 309 *hsiang* in the spring of 1952, and it was only an apparently fortuitous letter to the Chekiang provincial committee that initiated investigation and a vigorous response.[5] It goes without saying that such breakdowns in upward and downward communication were deeply disturbing to a regime bent on introducing fundamental change, for which it required a maximum of information and control.

Corrective measures

It also goes without saying that it was easier to diagnose these deficiencies than to remedy them. At least some were deficiencies of the system itself and hence have been recurring problems. The CCP tackled them both by means of campaigns designed to shake things up and also by more long-range organizational adjustments and training programmes. The major campaign was the one against "bureaucratism, commandism, and violations of laws and discipline" in 1953. At the higher levels, especially the *hsien*, fire was concentrated on officials' ignoring mass criticism and public opinion, on failing to guide the local cadres and failing to maintain

[1] *Shan hsi jih pao*, February 8, 1953.
[2] Lin T'ieh in *Jen min jih pao*, February 11, 1953.
[3] *Shan hsi jih pao*, July 30, 1952.
[4] *Shan hsi jih pao*, March 21, 1953.
[5] *Chieh fang jih pao*, December 28, 1952, in *SCMP*, No. 491.

an upward flow of accurate information.[1] In opposing commandism at the basic level, the emphasis, as already noted in the earlier discussion on exploitation, was on leniency. In view of the conditions in which they had had to function, village cadres were not held fully responsible for force and commandism. Instead, such violations of the model approach were handled primarily as an educational problem. Disciplinary and legal sanctions were applied in only the most flagrant criminal abuses.[2] As can be surmised, it is difficult to appraise the impact of such a corrective campaign. While it probably did rectify a number of particularly nasty situations, there is little evidence, for example, that, after this campaign, fear of the masses reporting cadre misdeeds was an effective constraint on cadre behaviour.

In addition to correcting the most immediate abuses by means of a campaign, an effort was made in 1953 to streamline the relationship between different levels of the hierarchy of Party and government. Several practices emerged into wider use during this time. One was that Party secretaries and Party committees, especially the *hsien* committee, would take much more decisive charge of the coordination of projects in line with current priorities. "Unified arrangement" (*t'ung i an p'ai*) would prevent unrestricted access by higher-level departments and officials to the village cadres. The

[1] See *Jen min jih pao*, editorial, July 26, 1953, in *Current Background*, No. 259, Appendix, September 15, 1953. It is worth noting that this anti-bureaucracy campaign followed closely on the heels of the *san-fan* movement (three antis: against waste, corruption, bureaucracy). This campaign seems to have been relatively ineffective in the rural areas. An Tzu-wen reported that it reached the *hsien* organs in 1952 and was generally completed by October, but apparently the focus of attention was mainly corruption. An Tzu-wen added that the *ch'ü* level organs were too weak to sustain a vigorous *san-fan* campaign, while *san-fan* methods were "even less applicable" in the villages. "In February and March 1952, the 3-anti movement was spontaneously launched in certain rural areas, and this led to great confusion...causing unrest among the masses, and nearly bringing all work to a state of stoppage. Accordingly, we had to resolutely stop the 3-anti movement in the rural areas." An Tzu-wen, "Nationwide Struggle Against Bureaucratism, Commandism, and Violations of Law and Discipline", *NCNA*, February 9, 1953, in *Current Background*, No. 251. Evidently the lower-level cadres required a more lenient and educational approach than was characteristic of the struggles of the *san fan*.

[2] "Provisions for Dealing with Problems Relating to Corruption...", *Jen min jih pao*, February 26, 1953.

hsien committee would order all tasks around the central task (*chung hsin kung tso*), that is, the most important programme of the moment. In this way the system sought to cope with "dispersionism" (*fen san chu i*), and prevent the village cadres from getting caught up in an unmanageable maze of tasks.[1] Also, following the troubles in policy implementation in 1952–3, the use of key or strongpoint villages was emphasized. Higher-level cadres would first personally try out a new project in a particular village, enabling them to gain the necessary practical experience which could then be more widely applied.[2]

More intensive efforts were undertaken to train the basic-level cadres and improve their leadership skills and work methods.[3] Higher-level work teams were instructed not merely to press for implementation but above all to teach local cadres appropriate skills, and to stop treating them as errand boys. Village cadre training programmes were stepped up. Emphasis was placed on mastery by the village party branch of skills of the division of labour (*fen kung*), which would enable the branch secretary to allocate tasks to the growing substructure of cadres and activists, thus broadening the base of political participation and involvement in policy imples mentation.[4] From 1953 on, the "Party life" columns of the provincial press were full of materials on model organization of rural branches, which reflected a training effort designed to help these branches acquire an "independent work capability".[1] These organizational

<hr />

[1] *Shan hsi jih pao*, June 23, 1953; and Teng Yün, "Chien ch'uan tang wei chih" [Strengthen the Party Committee System], *Hsüeh hsi*, No. 9 (September 2, 1953).

[2] *Jen min jih pao*, editorial, July 26, 1953.

[3] In the summer of 1953, a campaign was begun against the "five too many": too many meetings, tasks, organizations, concurrent posts, official documents, and forms. Ma T'ieh-ting, "Fan tui 'wu to', pu shih fang ch'i ling tao" [Opposing the Five Too Many Doesn't Mean Abdication of Leadership], *Hsüeh hsi*, No. 9, (September 2, 1953).

[4] As more villages acquired Party organizations, and as the pace of post-land-reform recruitment was stepped up, especially in 1955, the branch replaced the village government as the "leading core" of the main decision-making unit.

[5] E.g., *Fu chien jih pao*, April 21, 1953; and some long reprints from *Shan hsi jih pao*, in *Jen min jih pao*, April 14, 1953, and August 14, 1953. See also my article, "Leadership and Mass Mobilisation in the Soviet and Chinese Collectivisation Campaigns of 1929–30 and 1955–56: A Comparison", *The China Quarterly*, No. 31 (July–September, 1967), pp. 1–47.

improvements took effect in the following few years, and they are of central importance in accounting for the ability of the villages to absorb a vastly stepped-up pace of change, especially of course in collectivization. At the same time, these improvements only mitigated but did not eliminate tendencies inherent in a campaign-oriented and highly pressurized administrative and political system; namely, the tendency to excess, to over-response, and to consequently irrational results. These tendencies continued to manifest themselves in the years following 1953, and they were compounded when programmes with which the local cadres were not familiar were being introduced.

Together with these efforts at improving the organizational effectiveness of rural leaders came growing emphasis on politics in command and on the mass line. The notion of the "pure business viewpoint" and of "concrete" task implementation without reference to politics was repudiated. Instead, the regime sought to relate each task to the broader goal of the CCP in the villages, i.e., socialist transformation. Given the goal of introducing fundamental change, it is worth pointing out that this was not an irrational approach. What the regime wanted was to get the peasants to abandon one way of life and adopt a new one, that is, exchange the small-producer life for that of the collectivized farmer. This required changing the peasants' outlook and value system. A functionally specific approach to task implementation could contribute very little to this goal. Instead, it easily led, in the Chinese context, to methods that alienated people rather than maximizing their willingness to accept change.[1] In contrast, the mass line and an integrated approach to policy implementation made it possible for the system to work on the problem of changing peasants' outlook by involving them in the process of change through the mechanisms of participation,

[1] An American sociologist studying the relations between welfare bureaucracies and lower-class groups in the U.S. has suggested that bureaucracies generally are ineffective in getting lower-class people to change their ways, because a functionally specific approach fails to treat with the whole person, "...helps to keep the lower-class person in his place and inhibits change. In fact, modern bureaucracies have proved to be singular failures in resocializing their clients." Gideon Sjoberg, "Ideology and Social Organization in Rapidly Developing Societies", *Comparative Administrative Group—Occasional Papers* (Bloomington: Indiana Univ., December, 1966).

persuasion, and the mobilization of group pressures. In this process of change the village leaders were expected to play a major role; hence their importance for the continuity of the revolution.

CONCLUSION

In this essay we have looked at obstacles that arose in the early 1950's when the CCP sought to make use of village-level leaders to implement the new goals and tasks of socialist transformation. A "threat from below" arose as village cadres responded not to Communist demands, but to attitudes, interests, and preferences that were widely found in the small-producer village and that had in fact been re-enforced by the property changes of land reform. A "threat from above" arose as the bureaucratic hierarchy, anxious to transform the village overnight, pressed the cadres so hard that programmes backfired.

The CCP did succeed in coping with these problems. In the autumn of 1953, after more than half a year of retrenchment and consolidation, it announced its general line on the transition to socialism. This policy triggered a massive effort to organize producers' collectives, to enforce a state monopoly over the marketing of grain, and to teach the peasants the virtues of the socialist road. An accelerated pace of change led to completion of the collectivization of agriculture within three years. At the same time, however, both types of problems recurred, both during the collectivization years and later on as well. Village cadres continued to be influenced by their peasant environment; there was an ever-present possibility of their taking action at variance with regime policy. Village cadres also continued to be subordinate to an administrative hierarchy bent on introducing changes at a pace too rapid for the village to absorb; hence the recurrence of "commandism".

8

PARTY POLICIES TOWARD THE INTEL-
LECTUALS: THE UNIQUE BLOOMING
AND CONTENDING OF 1961–2

MERLE GOLDMAN

From its inception until at least the Cultural Revolution, the Communist regime in China has had a twofold aim for its intellectuals: it has sought to indoctrinate them with the exclusive ideologies of Marxism–Leninism–Maoism, and it has tried to utilize their skills to develop an industrialized and modernized society. The Chinese Communist Party has attempted to implement these two policies by an insistence on the strict orthodoxy of the intellectuals, on the one hand, and by the encouragement of intellectuals to work creatively at their jobs on the other. This contradictory approach has resulted in a policy towards the intellectuals that has been alternately severe and relaxed. Though the main trend is usually in one direction or the other, there have always been countercurrents present which can be revived when necessary.

SIMILARITIES OF 1961–2 WITH OTHER RELAXATIONS

An episode in this cycle of alternating policies that has not been sufficiently studied is the period of relative relaxation that began in 1961 and went through the autumn of 1962. It was in this time that several ingredients that eventually produced the combustion of the Cultural Revolution appeared. The 1961–2 interlude was both unique and similar to two earlier periods of relaxation under the Chinese Communist regime. Before discussing its uniqueness, let us first discuss its similarities to the relaxation in 1953 and the first half of 1954 and the famous Hundred Flowers movement of 1956 and the first half of 1957.[1] The shift to relaxation at these times was in large part governed by internal economic factors. In 1953 the Party announced the start of its First Five-Year Plan, but immediate problems occurred because of insufficient or over-ambitious planning. As a result, the Plan was temporarily halted so that its defects could be studied and remedied. In the latter half of 1955, the Party once again moved ahead with its Plan by escalating the conversion of peasant land holdings into cooperatives and speeding the pace of industrialization. But because of shortages and wasting of resources, the rapid rate of growth of the early 1950's began to falter. Likewise the big push of the Great Leap Forward produced acute food shortages and hampered industrial development. In each of these economic thrusts, the Party whipped the intellectuals into line in order to achieve its economic goals. However, as it encountered difficulties in implementing its programme, the Party slackened its drive to harness the economy. It reduced the size of collective farm units, allowed private plots and trade fairs, sanctioned the practice of service trades and permitted material incentives. Similarly it relaxed its grip on the intellectuals in an effort to secure their help in solving the problems it faced.

The relaxation of 1961–2 shared another factor with the preceding periods of moderation. It followed a period of intellectual repression. The respite of 1953–4 came after the three-anti and five-anti campaigns and the ideological remoulding of professors; the Hundred Flowers episode followed the campaign against the Left Wing writer Hu Feng and the counter-revolutionary movement; and the 1961–2 relaxation occurred after the anti-rightist campaign and the Great Leap Forward. Each one of these thought-reform drives demoralized substantial numbers of Party and non-Party intellectuals who became increasingly passive in the face of intense criticism

[1] The relaxations in 1953–4 and the Hundred Flowers are discussed in the author's book *Literary Dissent in Communist China*, (Cambridge, Mass.: Harvard Univ. Press, 1967). There have been numerous books on the Hundred Flowers movement, among them Roderick MacFarquhar, *The Hundred Flowers* (New York: Praeger, 1960) and Theodore Chen, *Thought Reform of the Chinese Intellectuals* (Hong Kong: Hong Kong Univ. Press, 1960). Dennis Doolin wrote an article on the 1961–2 relaxation in *Current Scene*, II, No. 19 (September 1, 1963).

and enforced labour reform. [1] Scholars in the social sciences, humanities, arts and even in the more-favoured sciences hesitated to make innovations. Desperately in need of the services of the intellectual community, the Party eased its pressure in the hope that intellectuals would be reactivated. The shifts from repression to relaxation were governed by this dialectical process, as well as by political and economic factors. These interludes of a more moderate, more flexible approach towards the intellectuals were in part a by-product of the earlier period of repression. When the drive towards intellectual conformity appeared to be destroying the initiative of the intellectuals, Party leaders would relent until they perceived that their political control was threatened.

There is reason to believe that the moving force behind the relaxation of 1961–2 was Liu Shao-ch'i rather than Mao who had been instrumental in initiating the previous relaxations, particularly the free-ranging Hundred Flowers period. Mao is said to have charged during the Cultural Revolution that after the Great Leap Forward he had been forced out of his leadership position by Liu and his associates. The tone set during the relaxation of the early sixties substantiates this charge. Nevertheless, though the director may have been different, the methods used in 1961–2 were similar to those of previous relaxations. The Party functionaries, the cadres, for example, were ordered to relax their administrative grip on the academic realm. Party leaders acknowledged that during the previous ideological remoulding campaign tensions had arisen between the cadres and intellectuals. They did not blame these tensions on their own policies but on their underlings, the lower and middle level cadres who, they claimed, distorted the policies in practice. The Party thus remained infallible. The cadres were charged with bureaucratic attitudes, ignorance of the specialized work under their command, and disrespect for scholars. More attention was focused on the suppressive and authoritarian practices of the cadres than on the unorthodox thinking and undisciplined habits of the intellectuals.

Simultaneously, in 1961–2 the Party sought to enhance the

[1] The decisions as to when a campaign would be launched, what form it would take and who would be the major scapegoat were usually made by the Politburo. The apparatus which carried out the campaign was the Party's Propaganda Department.

prestige of the intellectuals at the expense of the cadres. It reversed its previous policy of downgrading intellectual achievement and stressed the crucial role of the intellectuals and the professionals in the development of China. The cadres and masses were told that ideological orthodoxy, administrative abilities, and labour could not alone. build a modernized society; the techniques and professional skills of the intellectuals must also be used. In contrast to the preceding period of repression, the leadership decreed that intellectual endeavour and professional proficiency, rather than ideological orthodoxy, should be the standard of achievement. In fact, the cadres were informed that in certain technical areas the intellectuals, rather than they, should take the lead.

Also, as in the Hundred Flowers movement, scholars were surrounded with all the tokens of esteem. No longer were they called reactionary and backward as they had been for the last three years. The intellectuals were ranked right behind the workers and peasants in their devotion to the Communist cause. The Party now conceded that the mystical forces of the masses could not replace the scientific learning and technical know-how of the intellectuals. In contrast to the Great Leap Forward, the work and prestige of the scholars were elevated; peasant and worker illiteracy was correspondingly downgraded. The Party also tempered its policy of integrating the intellectuals with workers and peasants. There were to be fewer interruptions of school and research for work in the fields and factories. *Hung ch'i*, the official ideological organ of the Party, declared that "Scientific conclusions cannot be obtained through casual experiences or inspirations...Often some ordinary workers and peasants can make good suggestions...but this does not indicate that without knowledge as background one can express any expert opinion."[1] The cadres were likewise criticized by the leadership for lacking scientific and technical knowledge. Liu Shao-ch'i admitted that the masses of cadres did not have much time to read books and consider the problems under their command with objectivity.

[1] Li Shu-chih, "Concerning the Question of Letting All Schools of Thought Contend", *Hung ch'i* [Red Flag], No. 11 (1961), pp. 23–6, in *Selections from China Mainland Magazines* [*SCMM*], No. 266, p. 32.

As in the past, the Party demonstrated its benevolence towards the intellectuals by convening academic forums throughout the country. It hoped to entice intellectuals into debate by assuring them that they need not discuss the class struggle and Marxism–Leninism. Also, as in the Hundred Flowers, anyone taking a minority view in these forums was allowed to retain his opinions, offer adverse criticism, and defend his position. This approach was forthrightly stated in *Hung ch'i*'s editorial "Let 100 Flowers Bloom in Academic Research". "The atmosphere becomes lively in any field so long as there are controversies, mutual exchanges of opinion and mutual criticism. Such an atmosphere is beneficial and necessary to science for raising the level of scientific workers. Questions of right and wrong in artistic and scientific circles should be settled through free discussion."[1]

The Party made another effort to win the cooperation of intellectuals by giving them freer range within their own specialties. The leadership went so far as to admit that Marxism–Leninism had little relevance in certain academic areas, especially in the natural sciences. Less leeway was given to the social sciences and humanities, but even in these fields a greater variety of viewpoints and more tolerance of differences were permitted. Intellectuals were even urged to use the academic forums to criticize the cadres in charge of their respective fields. The Party assumed that this relaxation and enhancement of prestige would prompt intellectuals to work more effectively. Even more important, the Party hoped that these concessions would make intellectuals more willing to support the current ideological and political line. In this way thought reform and ideological indoctrination continued during the periods of relaxation but they were carried out in a more subtle manner than the direct pressure used in the preceding periods of tightening up. The methods changed, but the Party goal remained the same: the development of a corps of productive intellectuals obedient to the Party's will.

The intellectuals, at first, were hesitant to take advantage of these overtures from the leadership. Their recent experiences with the pressures of thought reform and the cadres' reluctance to

[1] Reprinted in *Peking Review*, No. 12 (March 24, 1961), p. 6.

release their grip at this time made them distrustful of their new freedom. Initially, the leadership was far more active in criticizing the cadres and demanding greater freedom for the intellectual than were the intellectuals themselves. The Party blamed this silence on the dictatorial practices of the cadres. After repeated and energetic encouragement from the leadership, some intellectuals eventually stepped forth to debate. Among them a few brave souls ventured beyond the broader limits prescribed by the Party. They not only voiced dissident opinions within their own fields, but went even further and showed how the intellectuals' value system conflicted with the regime's.

CHRONOLOGY OF THE 1961–2 INTERLUDE

The 1961–2 relaxation was a delayed movement that had its beginnings in the late 1950's. In fact, several conflicting movements were initiated at the end of the fifties that presaged later stages. At this time, the Party apparently was in a state of indecision. When the Great Leap Forward began to fail towards the end of 1958, the punitive campaign against the rightists quickly came to an end. In the first half of 1959, discreet but clear signs of relaxation began to appear. Several groups of rightists were pardoned. Economists were allowed to criticize the irrationality of the Great Leap Forward and the communes publicly. The scientific and technical knowledge of scholars in the universities and institutes was given preference over the practical experiments of workers in factories and peasants in the countryside. Professional writers were permitted to criticize the do-it-yourself poetry of the peasants. T'ao Chu, then first secretary to the Kwangtung Party Committee, was active in promoting this relaxation in the first half of 1959. In an article in *Jen min jih pao* on June 3, 1959, he wrote: "It is my opinion that to face squarely the defects and errors in our work will not harm in the least the achievements of our great enterprise. Like the black spots on the sun, we do not have to be afraid of mentioning defects and errors in our Party."

But these concessions were withdrawn in the second half of 1959, as suddenly as they were given, with the attack at the Lushan conference on P'eng Te-huai and his associates for their criticism of the Great Leap Forward. There was a return to the downgrading of intellectual endeavour, reminiscent of earlier periods of repression. Economists who had freely criticized Party programmes a few months before were condemned. One of these, Ma Yin-ch'u, was removed from his position as President of Peking University. Scientists were rebuked if they failed to take seriously the scientific achievements of the masses. Amateurs were again encouraged to lead professionals. A drive was launched to combat revisionist thinking inside China. This was exemplified by the attacks on the old Left Wing writers, Pa Jen and Hsü Mou-yung. They were labelled representatives of revisionist thinking because they sought similarities rather than differences among people and thereby obscured the class struggle. They were accused of fostering literary works which depicted the universal in human feeling. Most significant, intimations of themes later to be used in the Cultural Revolution appeared in September, 1960. An effort was made to teach the youth about the revolutionary traditions and the revolutionary ways of the Yenan period. The future heirs of the Chinese Communist Party were directed to become imbued with the ascetic life their hard-working leaders had led in Yenan. Even so, because of economic difficulties, this tightening-up process was less oppressive in 1960 than it had been at the outset of the Great Leap Forward.

In 1961, there was another sudden switch in the Party's policy towards the intellectuals. The drive to revolutionize China's youth was postponed. It was eclipsed by a period of relaxation that had its timid beginnings in 1959. In large part, this shift was due to the complete withdrawal of Soviet scientific and technical experts occurring at the same time as the disruptions of the Great Leap Forward hit the population most severely. Faced with serious food shortages and the disruption of its industrial programme, the Party made concessions in the economic sphere. It modified the commune system, reduced the size of collective farms, and allowed the cultivation of private plots. The Party, as in earlier periods of retrenchment, did not blame itself for the three years of economic downturn, but blamed its lower echelons. A major rectification drive to discipline erring cadres was begun at the lowest levels of the Party in the countryside and factories.

Similar concessions were made in the intellectual sphere. Because of the removal of Soviet experts, the Party needed the assistance of the senior intellectuals more than in the earlier periods of economic difficulty. Even the army cadres, considered more disciplined than the Party cadres, were criticized for under-estimating the role of the intellectual in China's development and for setting ideological standards that were too strict. Army cadres were accused of treating intellectuals like parasites rather than giving them special consideration for their professional achievement. In fact, they were advised that on professional and technical matters "We should...let [the intellectuals] have...responsibility and authority, a free hand to go ahead in their work and courage to assume responsibility. Party members should obey administrative and professional leadership and cannot make themselves privileged persons."[1]

Superficially, the relaxation of 1961–2 had many of the same trappings and slogans as the Hundred Flowers movement. This interlude was heralded by a high official, Vice-Premier Ch'en I, in a speech given August, 1961, reminiscent of the one Chou En-lai gave in January, 1956, to usher in the Hundred Flowers movement. Ch'en I, like Chou En-lai earlier, sought to invigorate the intellectual community by urging that greater respect be shown the scholar and higher regard be given his contribution to the nation. As had the leadership during the Hundred Flowers period, Ch'en explained that several years of Party indoctrination had rendered the intellectuals politically trustworthy. In fact, Ch'en had so much confidence in the transformation of the intellectuals that he believed they need no longer spend time in political sessions and manual labour to the neglect of their own work. Ch'en declared, "As long as experts show results in their profession and contribute to the construction of socialism, there should be no objection to their taking only a small part in political activity."[2] Furthermore, he announced that the intellectual need not be thoroughly versed in Marxism–Leninism and completely committed to the Party ideology.

[1] Chester Cheng, trans., *Politics of the Chinese Red Army* (Stanford: The Hoover Institution, 1963), p. 755.

[2] *Kuang ming jih pao* [Bright Daily], September 3, 1961, p. 2. This is the text of Ch'en I's speech given at the Peking Institute of Higher Studies in August, 1961.

Using himself as an example, he confessed that he too was still influenced by Confucius, Mencius, and bourgeois ideas. He also minimized class origin as a factor in evaluating one's work. He admitted that the majority of the Party's Central Committee did not come from worker and peasant families, but from landlord and middle-class backgrounds.

Ch'en even went further than had Chou En-lai in de-emphasizing ideological conformity and class origins. He redefined Communism in terms closer to Khrushchev's pragmatic interpretation than to the Chinese Communist Party's more ideological approach. The intellectual demonstrated his political spirit, Ch'en declared, not by constantly professing his devotion to the regime or to its political system, but by contributing to the development of modern industry, agriculture, science, and culture. In Ch'en's view, such activity was "a manifestation of the politics of socialism". He feared that unless there were changes in attitude towards the intellectuals, "Our country's science and culture will lag behind forever."

Mao's concept of the contradictions among people was also emphasized at this time with an interpretation similar to the one presented by him in his famous speech "On Correct Handling of Contradictions Among the People" of February 27, 1957. In 1961–2, as in 1957, the population was informed that contradictions can exist among people and between the leaders and the led. Thus the Party sought to close the widening gap which it acknowledged had grown even wider during the Great Leap Forward, particularly between the cadres and the intellectuals.

It made a special effort to win the cooperation of the scientists. At the 1961 Ninth Plenum of the Eighth Central Committee, the Party attempted to resuscitate the scientific community and rectify the lowering of scientific standards during the Great Leap Forward. The Ninth Plenum called for improvement in the quality of scientific work. Scientists were assured sufficient time for personal research and given added material incentives. They were also allowed more responsibility in directing their own work. Administrators at all levels were directed to heed the advice of scientific personnel on technical matters. Even individual research as opposed to group research was promoted in an editorial of *Jen min jih pao* on December

28, 1961 which declared that "In science, personal research will forever remain important." Most important, as Ch'en I had declared earlier and as *Kuang ming jih pao* stated on November 5, 1961, "We should not judge a scientist's achievement in natural science by the standard that he is a materialist or an idealist in his philosophical thinking. A scientist who is philosophically an idealist may attain great achievement in natural science..." As during the Hundred Flowers, courses were given in Morgan genetics and such depreciated scientists as Newton, Copernicus, and Einstein were spoken of favourably. Similarly, more attention was paid to providing students with a broader, theoretical scientific education than to giving them merely specialized, technical training. With scientists and technicians given wider discretion in meeting their obligations to the state, the Party, in reality, had created the conditions for the emergence of a new class of specialists whose decisions would be based on apolitical standards and whose activities represented a potential threat to Mao's political hegemony.

Even in the social sciences, intellectuals were given more latitude. It was frankly stated that the knowledge and the legacy of the Western academic community could be as valuable to the social scientists as to the scientists and technicians. Social scientists were encouraged to explore different methods of research, conduct various experiments, and raise different assumptions. The most provocative article to appear on this subject was by Feng Ting, a well-known ideological authority who had held high posts in the Propaganda Department and Cultural Ministry and was Chairman of the Peking Philosophical Society. This article "Concerning Redness and Vocational Proficiency" appeared in the June 12, 13 and 14, 1962 issues of *Kuang ming jih pao*. Even though admitting that the social sciences, unlike the natural sciences, had class character and were even directly related to politics, he declared that they had independent features. With this view of the social sciences as related and yet distinct from the political struggle, Feng Ting asserted that it was permissible and even beneficial to learn some of the techniques used by the social scientists in the west. He wrote "Even if (knowledge) was accumulated in a capitalist society and disseminated by bourgeois scholars earlier than capitalism, it should be learned and mastered...Many of the problems brought forward by bourgeois social scientists in academic fields are precisely what we want to explore and solve."[1]

In opposition to the "proletarianization" of knowledge during the Great Leap Forward, Feng Ting demanded that the social sciences like the natural and physical sciences be treated as a professional, individual endeavour. He described this approach with the analogy that "In a row boat, it is important that there be someone there who can handle the rudder, but there is no need for the rudder to be handled by everyone in the boat."[2] In his view, the scientists and social scientists could not solve China's problems by engaging in mass campaigns. Instead of devoting themselves to political and social action, he urged students and scholars to devote the greater part of their time to study and acquiring technical skills. Feng advocated that the social scientist be allowed to use a wide range of methods in order to test his hypotheses. "As long as the social scientist...displays the spirit of persisting in the truth... anybody may insist on his own view and gather more data."[3]

This kind of encouragement to the social scientists was not only given by scholar–officials like Feng Ting. Several articles in the authoritative journal *Hung ch'i* followed a similar though less forthright line—on August 10, 1961 in "On Free Discussion of Academic Problems", *Hung ch'i* likewise acknowledged that the social sciences need not concentrate on subjects directly related to the political and class struggle. With such urging, some unprecedented discussions occurred, particularly in the field of economics. Several economists offered suggestions that paralleled the ones being made by reforming economists in the Soviet Union. They, like their Soviet counterparts, called for a pragmatic, rather than an ideological, approach to economic problems. They advised that profitability and efficiency, instead of political expediency, be made the basis of investments and that the market-place, instead of administrative decisions, determine prices. In addition to the profit and price mechanism, the economists also recommended the use of mathematical methods, differentiated rent, economic accounting, and

---

[1] *Survey of China Mainland Press* [*SCMP*], No. 2776, p. 8.
[2] *Ibid*. p. 5.　　　　　　　　　　　[3] *Ibid*. p. 15.

interest on capital as means for promoting China's modernization.

This period of relative relaxation also produced a form of cultural renaissance. Although intellectuals were allowed to turn away from Marxism–Leninism, they could not look outward as they did during the Hundred Flowers because of the dispute with the Soviet Union and with the West. The only place they could turn was inward, into China's past. The retreat to traditional Chinese thought and culture has been a characteristic of intellectual movements in Chinese history. It occurred during the relaxation of 1953–4, when there was renewed interest in Chinese history and in traditional Chinese literature, particularly old popular novels like *The Dream of the Red Chamber*. Also at that time, there were discussions on Confucius, a subject that had been avoided until then.

Similarly, in 1961–2 there was a revival of interest in Confucius and Chinese history even though just a year before, in July, 1960, the philosopher Feng Yu-lan was severely reprimanded for an article in which he affirmed some aspects of Confucianism. Now there was animated discussion of Confucianism in which various schools of thought debated with one another. One group called Confucius a representative of the slave-owning nobility and, therefore, reactionary; another called him a representative of the new emerging class and, therefore, progressive; and another called him an advocate of gradual change and, therefore, a reformer. In the field of historiography, the use of the dialectic and the applicability of the class struggle to Chinese history were questioned. There was more concentration on historical data and less on the application of Marxism–Leninism to Chinese history. More attention was given to re-evaluating the contribution of the dynastic reigns of Han Wu-ti, K'ang Hsi, and the Empress Wu of the T'ang dynasty than to the role of peasant rebellions.

The latitude granted to writers in 1961–2 was similar in scope to that granted them in previous periods of relaxation. Writers, as in earlier interludes, were urged to use a variety of literary styles and methods of expression. Socialist realism and revolutionary romanticism were no longer prescribed as the only literary forms. In addition, there was emphasis on more professional literary standards and on the intrinsic value of art. This more creative approach was not merely tolerated, but was actively promoted by Party leaders. As in the Hundred Flowers, writers were not only allowed diversification of style, but also diversification of subject matter and theme. An editorial in *Wen i pao* declared that "Definite regulations on subject matter have not only limited the development of many kinds of literary style and spirit, they have had an unfavourable influence on the brilliance and development of literary work."[1] Therefore *Wen i pao* demanded that "A writer, according to his different circumstances, freely select and arrange the material with which he is most familiar and which he enjoys."[2] No longer did writers have to depict construction projects or even the class struggle, they were allowed to describe family life, love affairs, and the small details of everyday living.

Yet, unlike the Hundred Flowers, the few intellectuals who did speak out in 1961–2 limited their statements to a parroting of the official line. Though the debate by the economists certainly had political implications, the regime refrained from counterattack at this time. The anxiety of Party leaders during this period of economic crisis was evident from their willingness to explore or at least permit the publication of comparatively revolutionary economic suggestions that might lead to more efficient use of scarce resources. Similarly the discussion on Confucianism was not subversive to the Party's interest because it drew intellectuals inward and away from the West. Also, it was in line with the Party's appeal to nationalistic spirit, cultural pride, and self-reliance. The reinterpretation of Confucius fitted into the regime's effort to inherit facets of the traditional culture that enforced the Party's authoritarian rule.

Even an apparently bold article by the novelist Pa Chin, "The Writer's Courage and Responsibility", written in commemoration of the Twentieth Anniversary of Mao's Yenan "Talks on Art and Literature", conformed to the Party line. Though his arguments were strongly stated, they coincided with the regime's effort to cast off its image as a bureaucratic establishment and loosen the cadres' stranglehold on China's cultural life. Pa Chin directed his offensive specifically at the literary bureaucratics. His essay began on a

---

[1] *Wen i pao* [Literary Gazette], No. 3 (1961), p. 2.   [2] *Ibid.* p. 3.

note of sadness as he expressed anxiety over growing old without having created anything he considered worthwhile. Instead of fulfilling his responsibility as a writer, he lamented: "I have spent myself on all kinds of things. I have advanced much politically, but I have written little and moreover have written it badly."[1] Therefore, he resolved "to use this limited time well, to write better and write more".[2] What hindered him in this desire and what prevented him from carrying out his duty as a writer, Pa Chin asserted, were the literary bureaucrats, who dictated what he could write. He described these bureaucrats as "people with a hoop in one hand and a club in the other who go everywhere looking for persons who have gone astray...They enjoy making simple hoops ...and wish to make everyone jump through them...If there are people who do not wish to go through their hoops and if there are some who have several kinds of flowers blooming in their gardens... these people become angry, raise up their clubs and strike out."[3]

In Pa Chin's view, these bureaucrats with hoops and clubs did not understand literature, nor did they represent public opinion. They were merely interested in maintaining themselves in power and elevating themselves to a superior position above others. Consequently, many writers, himself included, had become frightened and cowardly. They only did what they were ordered so that they could be left alone and not be battered with one of the clubs. However, now was the time, Pa Chin asserted, for writers to become literary warriors and to battle the people with hoops and clubs. He defined literary warriors as writers who upheld the truth, that is, their own vision of reality. He claimed that "I only know that the more the truth is discussed, the clearer it will become. I have not heard that the more the truth is slandered the clearer it is."[4] What the times needed, Pa Chin declared, was "brilliant creative work... through the diligent, unceasing effort of writers not men with hoops and clubs".[5] In this way, writers will fulfil the responsibility of their profession and will demonstrate the bravery of their calling. He did not draw the obvious conclusion that the existence of bureaucrats with hoops and clubs was due to the policies of the leadership.

---

[1] *Shang hai wen hsüeh* [Shanghai Literature], No. 5 (1962), p. 3.
[2] *Ibid.*   [3] *Ibid.*   [4] *Ibid.* p. 4.   [5] *Ibid.*

Speaking in more general terms, he stressed the need, as did the regime at this time, for greater unity between those who lead and those who are led. He proposed that this be done by the democratic method of expressing diverse viewpoints rather than by the authoritarian method of frightening people with different opinions into submission. In conclusion, he stated that "in order to unite we should...with sincerity allow the free exchange of feelings".[1]

Outwardly, therefore, this period of relaxation appeared to be in the spirit of the original Hundred Flowers, but in actual fact, it was not. It was more like the limited relaxation of 1953–4—the regime wanted academic debate without political ferment. Like 1953–4, the relaxation of 1961–2 extended to every sphere of cultural endeavour and permitted a wider range of discussion and of study, but from the very start its scope was restricted to scientific and academic subjects. As soon as the relaxation began, the Party called for a clear-cut distinction between contention in the academic sphere and contention in the political arena. Rebellious intellectuals had previously demanded this separation so they could express themselves more freely in their own fields without the imposition of political criteria. The regime now demanded it so that the intellectuals would not interpret the Party's tolerance of freer discussion in academic subjects as a sanction to examine political issues as happened in 1957.

As in 1953–4, the Party continued its thought-reform sessions while it called for a limited degree of academic freedom. The contradictory nature of this relaxation is seen in the same speech of Ch'en I that urged intellectuals to contend. Along with his emphasis on intellectual merit and de-emphasis on political reliability, he still insisted on the need for continued ideological indoctrination. However, as in 1953–4, thought-reform was carried out in a different manner than in the more intense periods of regimentation. The Party sought to indoctrinate the intellectual by making his acceptance of Marxism–Leninism a voluntary rather than an enforced act. This aim was clearly stated by Ch'en I when he declared that "Since thought-reform relies chiefly on the indi-

[1] *Ibid.* p. 6.

vidual's consciousness, the individual must come to conclusions himself. Therefore, it is not feasible to use forceful measures and exert popular pressure."[1]

Again, as in 1953–4, the Party sought to induce the intellectual's voluntary acceptance by conducting thought-reform sessions in an atmosphere which was psychologically and politically less oppressive. The Party called these sessions of the early sixties "meetings of the immortals" to distinguish their more easy-going approach from the intense pressure applied during the criticism and self-criticism sessions of the preceding campaigns. The meetings were to leave one with an ethereal feeling as if he were immortal; instead of reforming the intellectual by coercion, they were to wash him with "gentle breezes and mild drizzle". This phrase was also used in the Hundred Flowers, but then it was used to encourage intellectuals to criticize the cadre with gentleness rather than have the cadres censure the intellectuals with discretion.

Ch'en I informed the cadres that in reforming another individual one must "not hurt his feelings or deal blows to his soul. One must be patient and understanding."[2] As before, the intellectuals were divided into small study groups but the discussions in these groups were to be conducted as informal chats rather than as confessions extorted by the cadres. If ideological "mistakes" were made in the course of a chat, the individual was not ostracized but was to remain part of the group and treated in a comradely fashion. The Party's aim as stated in *Jen min jih pao* was that "By exchanging thoughts and helping one another, all people will naturally... acquire an identical, definite understanding of right and wrong."[3]

The Party's call for a clear division between debate in academic and political spheres was meant to confine the intellectuals' discussions to the academic realm, but it was not meant to confine the Party to the political realm. The Party, as in the past, sought to exert its controls over scholarship, particularly the non-scientific fields. The restrictions that were belatedly imposed two weeks after the termination of the Hundred Flowers movement were invoked

[1] *Kuang ming jih pao*, September 3, 1961, p. 2. [2] *Ibid*.
[3] Liu Kuo-chün, "Meetings of Immortals Drive the Intellectuals Forward in Self-Remolding", *Jen min jih pao*, May 16, 1961, in *SCMP*, No. 2512, p. 11.

from the very beginning of the 1961–2 movement. The one most pertinent to the intellectuals prescribed that there be only academic discussion useful to the Party. Therefore, the same kind of contradictory goals that characterized the whole movement also characterized the Party's policy in the academic realm. The Party sought to foster intellectual and scientific endeavour while at the same time it strengthened its ideological control over academic thinking. Scholars were urged to look for the truth, but the truth could not be contrary to Mao's teaching or to the Party's current programme. Consequently, the emergence of independent groups and journals engaging in a spontaneous exchange of ideas was not permitted at this time as it was in the Hundred Flowers period.

THE UNIQUENESS OF THE RELAXATION OF 1961–2

Though 1961–2 resembled the Hundred Flowers period in some respects and the less extensive relaxation of 1953 and early 1954 in others, it differed in several crucial respects from both these interludes. It was a unique period in the history of the Chinese Communist regime. Unlike 1953–4 and the Hundred Flowers when criticism came principally from the intellectual community and from students, the criticism that was heard in 1961–2 came from officials high in the Party hierarchy, specifically in the Propaganda Department and the Peking Party Committee, the very organizations instrumental in implementing the relaxation. With a few exceptions, most intellectuals were reluctant to participate because of the undefined nature of the new freedom and because of their past experience. They feared that the movement was designed to investigate their minds rather than to enrich culture and science. Pointing to the ambiguity between the line dividing debate in the political and academic spheres, several refused to express their own opinions. They claimed that their views on academic questions would be construed as opinions on political issues. Still others excused themselves from debate with the plea of insufficient knowledge.

What made this relaxation even more unique was the target of the criticism. Though criticisms were couched in literary and academic discussions, they went beyond the limits of the Hundred Flowers. Whereas in 1956 and the first half of 1957 the more radical critics dared to challenge the one-party rule of the Chinese Communist Party, in 1961–2 these officials did not hit at the Party of which they were a part, but at Mao himself.[1] Though their attacks took diversified forms, officials both in the Propaganda Department and the Peking Party Committee focused on three main issues. One was resistance to the glorification of Mao; they were willing to accept Mao as their leader but not as an omnipotent god. Secondly, they were disturbed by the failure of the Great Leap Forward which they believed was due to Mao's unwillingness to face up to the economic realities of Chinese life. Finally, they supported the opposition of individuals such as P'eng Te-huai who had dared to criticize the wrongs they saw before them despite the consequences. What had started out as a campaign to activate the intellectuals turned into an indirect attack on Mao and his policies by a small group of cultural officials.

The relaxed atmosphere of the early sixties, the increasing disillusionment with the Great Leap Forward and the concern over the capabilities of China's ageing leader, still do not fully explain why these high officials, who were well aware of the consequences of dissent, chose to speak out publicly. They may have felt that they were somewhat immune from reprisal. As yet we do not have substantive information to prove the charges made during the Cultural Revolution that Liu Shao-ch'i and Teng Hsiao-p'ing were the patrons of this group and the behind-the-scenes manipulators of the onslaught on Mao. Nevertheless, these allegations may have some validity because it is unlikely that such officials as Chou Yang and maybe even P'eng Chen would have allowed their underlings to initiate or sustain their attack on Mao's policies unless they had the tacit support of some member of the Standing Committee of the Politburo.

[1] The sources for this criticism of Mao are of uneven quality. The full texts of some of the criticism have been published, as for example Teng T'o's "Evening Talks at Yenshan". For other criticisms such as those voiced at the Dairen conference, it was necessary to rely on the lengthy excerpts reprinted in newspapers and journals. These speeches made at the conference were never published in full.

DAIREN CONFERENCE

Paradoxically, among the most vigorous challengers to Mao's policies were the top officials in the Propaganda Department's literary establishment, the very ones who directed the imposition of controls on the intellectuals in the earlier periods of repression. This group was headed by Chou Yang and his principal lieutenants who had been the scourge of the intellectual and literary community since the early 1940's. Yet these same literary bureaucrats unleashed a devastating blast against Mao's Great Leap Forward at a two-week meeting held in Dairen in August, 1962, presided over by Chou Yang. Several of them had come from peasant stock and had returned to the countryside to observe what had happened in the aftermath of the Great Leap Forward. Ostensibly, the conference was called to discuss short novels about the countryside, but in actuality, the forum became a platform from which these bureaucrats called for the depiction of the misery and poverty that had befallen the peasantry. They denounced the use of mass campaigns, crash programmes, and rash actions. They urged writers to show the Great Leap Forward not as the Utopia it was decreed to be, but as an illusion, a great tragedy that had befallen China. They called it a mere theory which had not shown results, but had produced disaster.

These themes were stressed over and over again at the conference. One of the most outspoken was K'ang Cho, a protégé of Chou Yang, who became one of the editors of *Wen i pao* after Chou had forced his old rivals, Ting Ling and Feng Hsüeh-feng from the editorship of this most important cultural journal. In 1962, K'ang Cho was vice-president of the Hunan branch of the Chinese Writers Union. Even before the conference was convened, K'ang had already expressed some of these themes, though somewhat obliquely, in an article "On Short Stories in Recent Years". In this essay, he insisted that the contradictions in society had shifted. They were no longer between the old and new society. Instead, new contradictions had arisen which split the present social system. He insisted that because current literary works are in "excessive pursuit of romanticism", they have covered over these new contradictions in society. He complained "There still do not appear to be many pieces of writing which profoundly reveal the backward phenomena and short-comings in life."[1] To remedy this he called on writers to use more realism and less romanticism.

At the Dairen conference, K'ang spelled out these themes in concrete terms. He plainly stated that the old contradiction between capitalism and socialism had temporarily been relegated to a secondary position. For the present "The main contradiction is between the socialist ideological leadership and the actual needs of the peasants."[2] He accused the "leaders of socialism" of failing to live up to their ideals. This was the same complaint voiced by the literary idealists from the Yenan period on, except this time it was K'ang who had formerly attacked these idealists who now took up their cause. As he saw it the ideals of socialism had been destroyed by the Great Leap Forward of which he said "It is too destructive... I feel the important thing is to write down its painful lessons...even if it must be in tragic terms."[3]

K'ang urged writers in their short stories to show that this policy had produced privation and despair in the rural population. At the same time he called on the regime to change its policy towards the peasants and provide them with a better life. He warned "We have not yet taken the initiative in removing the burden placed on the heads of the peasants by the state, cities and cadres..."[4] Though he did not spell out any exact economic measures such as a return to private enterprise in agriculture, he went so far as to suggest that perhaps a socialist planned economy and the peasant mode of life and production were incompatible. He implied that the peasant was opposed to Mao's brand of socialism because the peasant would rather become rich than be revolutionary. He urged the regime to retreat from its present course by approaching its rural

[1] K'ang Cho, "Shih lun chin nien chien ti tuan p'ien hsiao shuo" [On Short Stories in Recent Years], Wen hsüeh p'ing lun [Literary Criticism], No. 5 (1962), p. 26.
[2] SCMP, No. 3750, p. 3. K'ang Cho's speeches at the Dairen Conference have not been reprinted, but large excerpts from them were published in Canton, Yang ch'eng wan pao, July 7, 1966.
[3] Ibid.   [4] Ibid.

problems like a runner "turning back to try again after failing to clear the pole in a high jump".[1]

Another confidant of Chou Yang conspicuous at this Dairen Conference for his denunciation of the regime's treatment of the peasantry was Shao Ch'üan-lin. Though originally a short-story writer, he was known primarily as a powerful literary bureaucrat. After the Party take-over of the mainland, he rapidly made a name for himself as a leader of the thought-reform campaigns. Starting as one of several vice-chairmen of the Chinese Writers Union in 1953, by the outset of the anti-rightist campaign, he held the important position of secretary of the Party Committee of the Chinese Writers Union. By 1960, he appeared to stand right behind Chou Yang as a major spokesman in the literary and art realm.

Yet, at this conference Shao presented views diametrically opposed to the ones he had been preaching as a Party bureaucrat. This switch in Shao's thinking and his sudden concern with the peasantry do not seem so unusual when one views some of his ideas expressed in the early 1940's prior to his joining the Party. Then he wrote a most revealing book of short stories, entitled *Ying hsiung* (Heroes). These stories were published a little over a year before Mao in his "Talks on Art and Literature" had established the dogma that the peasants and proletariat must be depicted as flawless heroes. In his introduction, Shao wrote that the task of the writer is to portray the struggle, difficulties, and tribulations that go on in the ordinary peasant or worker as he goes through the long, complicated process of transformation. Writers should not pursue epic subjects of glory and grandeur, but instead portray the actual people within their own familiar circle. He urged writers "to understand the real face of social change and feel its love, hatred, anger, and joy".[2] Similarly, works that extol "brightness" and expose "darkness", Shao asserted, were not honest nor artistic because "in reality, both brightness and darkness are intertwined".[3]

After Mao's "Talks", Shao's views remained dormant for twenty years. They finally came to life again with less eloquence but with

[1] *Ibid.* p. 5.
[2] Shao Ch'üan-lin, *Ying hsiung* [Heroes] (Shanghai: n.p., 1948), p. 2.
[3] *Ibid.* p. 3.

the same meaning, in the relaxation of the early 1960's. Why did Shao revive them at this time and not in the more far-reaching relaxation of the Hundred Flowers period? Perhaps, the deification of peasant and worker heroes in the preceding Great Leap Forward had reawakened the core of Shao's thinking which, even after several decades of ideological remoulding, had not changed. Moreover, Shao probably thought he had finally reached a position high enough to be able to state unorthodox views with relative impunity. Whatever the reasons, in 1961 and into the summer of 1962, he repeated his unorthodox views over and over again at meetings of the editorial staff of *Wen i pao*. He amplified these views further at the Dairen conference where he denounced the literary strictures established by the Party, strictures which he himself had had a large part in imposing. He denounced the depiction of fictional characters as simplified, one-dimensional figures who "all have red faces". Though he had indicted Hu Feng for the very same criticism seven years earlier, he now implored writers to "smash oversimplification, doctrinairism, and mechanical theories".[1] Echoing dissident writers whom he had earlier attacked, he demanded the destruction of dogmatism in literature so that writers could present a more realistic picture of the world in which they lived.

Like K'ang Cho, Shao claimed that the main contradiction in society was no longer between different classes, but, unlike K'ang, he saw the contradiction as concentrated in the individual himself. In Shao's view, most workers, particularly peasants, were not the perfect heroes the Party ordered writers to describe but people in an intermediate stage between "backward" and "advanced" thinking. Most people had both positive and negative elements within themselves. Instead of depicting heroic and villainous extremes, Shao urged writers to portray the vast majority of the population whom he termed "the people in the middle", as yet uncommitted to the revolution.

Shao insisted on the delineation of the anguish of the revolutionary struggle going on within the individual consciousness, not the

[1] *Wen i pao*, Nos. 8–9 (1964), p. 15. Shao Ch'üan-lin's remarks, like K'ang Cho's, were not published at the time he gave them. However, excerpts were reprinted after he was attacked in 1964 in *Wen i pao*, Nos. 8–9 (1964), pp. 15–20.

end result. To him this anguish was especially acute in the intellectuals and peasants. He gave a vivid picture of what he meant by describing the intellectual as his thought was being remoulded. "For the intellectual, the change from the old to the new is a painful process. He has to be immersed in clear water three times, bathed in bloody water three times, and cooked in salt water three times."[1] A similar process, Shao claimed, went on within the peasant as he moved from a system of individual land-ownership to a collective economy.

Like the leadership, Shao believed that literature was a form of propaganda, but, in his view, literary works would be far more effective propaganda if they presented characters with whom the reader could identify, rather than standard heroes and villains whom no one could believe. Furthermore, he maintained that literature would affect the reader more profoundly if reality were depicted with art and accuracy instead of with idealized images and ideological exhortations. He further suggested that the writer would have a greater impact on his readers if he merely raised problems without solving them. "Let the reader draw his own conclusions...Let people see the cause and effect themselves."[2] Not only should the work speak for itself, but Shao also demanded that the author speak for himself. "Let each develop his own style. Let him see the greatness in common events. Let him look at life with a smile or knotted brows. We need not be angry with him or try to interfere."[3]

Besides clashing with the Party's dictum that literature focus on the ideal, Shao's approach struck directly at the Party's basic political and ideological teachings. Couched in his discussion of literary characters, Shao exposed the differences between the Party's official view of reality and what actually existed. He maintained that at present the millions of Chinese workers and peasants, who supposedly were the bulwark of the revolution, were not the exemplary revolutionaries the Party had pictured. In reality, those who wavered between the "progressive" and the "backward" path were not only a small number of bourgeoisie and intellectuals as the Party claimed but the vast majority of the population. He forthrightly asserted that the Party's prime allies also vacillated towards

[1] *Ibid.* p. 18.　　　　[2] *Ibid.* pp. 17–18.　　　　[3] *Ibid.* p. 18.

the revolution and were also riddled with mental conflicts and contradictions. Finally, Shao disclosed that after years of protracted struggle and learning from Mao, the regime was still confronted with an unstable, uncommitted multitude, its rural population.

THE THEATRE

It was in the theatre that the most subversive moves against the cult of Mao and the Great Leap Forward occurred. In line with the cultural renaissance of the time, the majority of the plays performed in the early sixties were based on historical characters. Among the myriad of plays produced, the most controversial were "The Dismissal of Hai Jui" by the prominent historian and Vice-Mayor of Peking, Wu Han, and "Hsieh Yao-huan" by the chairman of the Union of Chinese Stage Artists, the playwright T'ien Han. Both plays were produced in the summer of 1961 and possessed remarkable similarities. Both eulogized historical figures who had fought against the exploitation of the peasantry and who had demanded the return of land confiscated from the peasants. The plays' heroes raised their voices against misguided, arbitrary government and urged immediate reforms. Both plays criticized the severe punishment of those who had risen in protest against these injustices. Finally, both plays warned that unless something was done to alleviate the peasant's plight the regime would not last long.

Wu Han and T'ien Han had specifically written that their historical plays were comments on contemporary events. Wu Han in his introduction to "The Dismissal of Hai Jui" had said "The position of Hai Jui in history should be confirmed as some of his good qualities are worthy of emulation today."[1] Likewise, T'ien Han in an article in *Wen i pao* wrote "The educational significance of good historical plays on people today is no less effective than of modern plays...We see the present through the past...The task of the playwright is not just to transmit some historical knowledge to the people...the main task is in creating vivid images of historical figures on the basis of historical fact which

[1] Wu Han, *Hai Jui pa kuan* [The Dismissal of Hai Jui] (Peking: Pei ching ch'u pan she, 1961), pp. 7-8.

may educate the people of today."[1] In other words, the purpose of both men in their plays was to use historical events and characters to criticize present-day conditions. This is a traditional Chinese technique of historical analogy with double meaning. It is quite obvious then from the contexts of their plays that these authors were expressing the peasants' discontent with the Great Leap Forward and the communes, their admiration for officials like P'eng Te-huai who had dared to criticize such policies, and their opposition to Mao's policies.

Before Wu Han produced his play, he had written several essays on Hai Jui, a high official in the Ming dynasty stationed in the Soochow area from 1569 to 1570. One of the first to appear was "Hai Jui Scolds the Emperor", in *Jen min jih pao* on June 16, 1959 under the pseudonym Liu Mien-chih.[2] Wu Han quotes Hai Jui as protesting to the Emperor that "Present taxes and labour levies are abnormally high... These ten years or more have been chaotic." Hai Jui implies that the ruler has increasingly lost touch with reality and might be approaching a state of senility. He states that "In earlier years, you did quite a few good things, but... all officials in and out of the capital know that your mind is not right, that you are too arbitrary, too perverse. You think you alone are right, you refuse to accept criticism and your mistakes are many... This is the most serious problem in the country." This description of an historical ruler as tyrannical and irrational, most likely meant as criticism of Mao, was reiterated by others in the early 1960's.

Wu Han's play, "The Dismissal of Hai Jui", which was produced two years later, focused on the plight of the Soochow peasants whose land had been confiscated from them by local officials. The villagers come before Hai Jui complaining "Our properties have been occupied by officials... yet we continue to pay taxes and live in poverty."[3] Despite threats and bribes from the local officials, Hai Jui demands that all the land that was illegally confiscated be returned. He also orders the death of a landlord's son because

[1] *Union Research Service*, XXV, No. 2, p. 23. Reprint of an article by T'ien Han, "The Problem of Choosing a Theme", *Wen i pao*, No. 7 (1961).

[2] James Pusey called my attention to this article. His monograph on "The Wu Han Campaign" will be published in the Harvard East Asian Monograph series.

[3] Wu Han, *Hai Jui pa kuan*, p. 24.

he had killed an elderly peasant. The local landlords and officials appeal to the Emperor who spares the landlord's son and dismisses Hai Jui. Though presented in an historical context, this play seemingly symbolizes the experience of the peasants with the communes and P'eng Te-huai's dismissal.

T'ien Han, a skilled playwright, presented similar themes in "Hsieh Yao-huan", a play of vivid dramatic quality. T'ien Han intimated that he was working on a play of social criticism in an essay that appeared shortly before the play was produced. In it he wrote "There is a lack of courage to write about internal contradictions among the people." He insisted that "If souls of characters cannot be more deeply revealed in contradictions and conflicts based on laws of dramatic art...then why do it?"[1] "Hsieh Yao-huan" was T'ien Han's advice put into practice. Unlike most of China's modern playwrights who first appeared on the literary scene in the 1930's, T'ien Han was of peasant stock. In 1960 and 1961 he had visited several rural areas where he had taken extensive notes and convened numerous meetings in an effort to understand the happenings in the countryside. Most likely "Hsieh Yao-huan" was the result of this experience.

Like Wu Han, T'ien Han used an historical figure to criticize the contemporary scene. His character, Hsieh Yao-huan, was a lady of the court of the Empress Wu in the T'ang dynasty. She, like Hai Jui, was concerned with the suffering of the peasants. The play takes place in the last years of Empress Wu's reign, analogous to the twilight of Mao's rule. Some of her ministers and closest advisers have seized peasant land, oppressed the peasants, and rocked the state's foundations. In words very similar to those used by Wu Han in his essay "Hai Jui Scolds the Emperor", Hsieh Yao-huan informs the Empress that although once her regime had been close to the people and she had been considered a defender of their interests, her administration recently had become so estranged from the people's needs that it had become antagonistic to the masses. She warns the Empress that she is unaware of the miseries in the countryside because flatterers of the court persecute those who try to bring these problems to her attention. "In recent years", Hsieh

---

[1] *Union Research Service*, XXV, No. 2, p. 20.

declared, "most of the good laws based on the even distribution of land...have been abandoned. The powerful families and elite annex land and force people to lead a hard life."[1]

When the peasants subsequently mass to rebel against these conditions, one faction of the court demands they be suppressed militarily. Another faction, led by Hsieh, pleads with the Empress to check the expropriation and to resettle the insurgents so that "There is land for the tillers and food for the hungry. By the time of the return of spring, the people will sing praise of your wise rule."[2] Note the use of the term "the return of spring", a phrase repeated by several critics at this time and similar to the term "thaw" used by Soviet writers in their demands for liberlization. Hsieh implores that unless such action is taken "The water which carries the boat now waits to overthrow it."[3] The implication is that the peasants who once supported the regime now wish to overthrow it.

The Empress, misled by rumours, hesitates to act, and consequently Hsieh is killed by opposing officials at the court. The play then ends with a warning to the Empress by Hsieh's husband, "Please open your eyes and ears to loyal counsel so that the people will lead a happy life and suffer no more. If you favour and trust the crafty and trample under those loyal to you, I fear there will be considerable trouble in the country."[4] A similar prophecy was voiced by Hai Jui in Wu Han's play, "With...ruthless bureaucrats preying on district commissioners, the common people have to flee to other places. The people are impoverished and the national economy is in jeopardy...Unless the seized land is returned, [your rule] will not last long."[5]

TENG T'O

This feeling of pessimism and fear for the future was repeated by others at this time, most notably by Teng T'o, former editor of *Jen min jih pao* and director of the ideological and cultural activities

---

[1] T'ien Han, "Hsieh Yao-huan", *Chü pen* [Theatre Book], July–August, 1961, p. 9.
[2] *Ibid.*   [3] *Ibid.* p. 19.   [4] *Ibid.* p. 28.
[5] Wu Han, *Hai Jui pa kuan*, p. 27.

of the Peking Party Committee since 1959. The concern with the well-being of the peasantry, the anxiety over Mao's mental capacities and his unwillingness to face up to economic realities, and the defence of those who dared to criticize, climaxed in a series of essays written by Teng T'o under the heading "Evening Talks at Yenshan". For almost a year and a half, this column and several other articles by him were published in the three main newspapers of Peking, *Pei ching wan pao* (Peking Evening News), *Pei ching jih pao* (Peking Daily), and *Ch'ien hsien* (Frontline), the theoretical organ of the Peking Party Committee.

Like Wu Han and T'ien Han, Teng T'o obliquely criticized contemporary people and events by using ancient characters and historical incidents. On the surface, his essays appeared to be mild social and historical commentaries, but in reality they were devastating, though subtle, criticism of Mao's leadership and policies Like Lü Hsun, his essays were written in Aesopian language intended to be understood by a limited circle of like-minded intellectuals and leaders.

Teng T'o more than the other dissidents at this time was forthright in his denunciation of the cult of Mao. Several of his essays emphasized the need for the ruler to listen to others' views and then act accordingly. He saw himself and his colleagues as playing a dissident role similar to that of the Tung-lin faction during the Ming dynasty. In an essay "A Concern for All Things" first published in *Pei ching wan pao* on October 8, 1961 he quoted the following verse associated with the Tung-lin group: "Matters of household, the rain and the book—all are of concern [to us]."[1] He interpreted this verse to mean that "Learning must always be accompanied by a keen interest in politics."[2] He suggested that the intellectuals in present-day China follow the example of the Tung-lin movement. Despite the fact that its members came from a feudal society, he insisted that "they were better than scholars who showed no concern at all or studied as a means to attain fame, position or other benefits".[3] Though he said it was not necessary for intellectuals to

[1] Teng T'o, "A Concern for All Things", *Yen shan yeh hua* [Evening Talks at Yenshan], (Peking: Pei ching ch'u pan she, 1962), II, 60.
[2] *Ibid.*   [3] *Ibid.* p. 61.

become an opposition party, he believed "it is important [for them] to realize the close association between scholarship and a concern for politics".[1] Then in an indirect attack on the cadres, he said "to be learned without being interested in politics is just as bad as being politically inclined without being learned".[2] He concluded that "Even our ancestors understood and saw clearly the relationship between scholarship and politics. Let us live up to and strive for a deeper understanding of this principle."[3]

With the Tung-lin faction as his example, Teng T'o proceeded to attack Mao and his policies through a discussion of historical events. In an essay "Is Shrewdness Dependable", published in *Pei ching wan pao* on February 22, 1962, he told of an official during the Sung dynasty who exhorts the prominent statesman Ssu-ma Kuang: "I hope that you will invite other persons to make suggestions because it is not necessary for you to be the author of every scheme."[4] When this happens "flattery will find its way to meet your every wish".[5] Then with an obvious analogy to Mao, Teng T'o quotes the official as stating there are "some persons...who always want to assert their own ideas, attempt to win by surprise and refuse to accept the good ideas of the masses under them. If persons with such shortcomings do not wake up and rectify their shortcomings themselves, they will pay dearly one day."[6] Here again, Teng expressed the same kind of premonition that was voiced by Wu Han and T'ien Han in their plays. This essay and several others of a similar nature warned that it is impossible for one man or even a small group to understand everything and command everything. The true shrewdness in Teng's view came only from consulting widely and heeding the sentiments of the masses.

Teng T'o developed this theme further in an essay, "A New School of Thought", in which he wrote about a seventeenth-century scholar Liu Hsien-t'ing who because he came in personal touch with the people was able to help them. Teng said of him: "In later years, he travelled widely in the country in order to come in direct contact

[1] *Ibid*. p. 62.   [2] *Ibid*.   [3] *Ibid*.

[4] Teng T'o, "Is Shrewdness Dependable", *Yen shan yeh hua*, IV, 17–19, in *Current Background*, No. 742.

[5] *Ibid*.   [6] *Ibid*.

with the people and widen his own horizon. Because of this he was able to understand the peasant rebelliousness and upheavals."[1] This was an obvious appeal to Mao to follow a similar example.

Besides his plea that the leadership go out into the countryside and learn personally of the peasants' plight. Teng also urged that all policies be carefully studied and their implications be fully understood before they were enacted. In another essay, "Understanding", he wrote, "We will find that the more we study...gradually we will be able to understand what the books are saying. It is completely impossible to understand everything at once."[2] He quoted a great Chinese scholar to the effect that though we think we understand what we are reading, we "actually are vague about the subject until we have met with some practical application of that knowledge".[3] Developing this theme further in the essay, "A Small Key", he wrote that if one wants to concentrate on a special field, one must study everything on the subject from whatever source it may come including foreign ones, because "It is only after much logical reasoning, practical proofs and detailed analysis that success in that field will be achieved."[4]

He urged further that China's young scientists and scholars be consulted before any actions were carried out. In the essay, "Talking Nonsense", he criticized those who dismissed the work of these scholars as "nonsense". He said such people considered their work "nonsense" because they themselves had limited knowledge. In his view, "Scientific theories on the one hand should not be considered constant or unchangeable; on the other hand, new conclusions or new agreements as long as they are backed with reasonable proofs should be accepted."[5] He then concluded that "It is our duty to encourage young people to liberate their thoughts, to be more outspoken and to do more outstanding and daring research."[6] Besides scientific inquiry, Teng also talked in "New Lyrical Poems" about the need for literature "to express the joy, anger, sorrows and frustration of the present age".[7]

---

[1] Teng T'o, "A New School of Thought", *Yen shan yeh hua*, II, 13.
[2] Teng T'o, "Understanding", *Yen shan yeh hua*, II, 90.   [3] *Ibid*. p. 91.
[4] Teng T'o, "A Small Key", *Yen shan yeh hua*, II, 97.
[5] Teng T'o, "Talking Nonsense", *Yen shan yeh hua*, II, 23.   [6] *Ibid*.
[7] Teng T'o, "New Lyrical Poems", *Yen shan yeh hua*, II, p. 68.

Teng T'o's concern with the need of the leadership to have direct contact with the peasantry, the need for more considered and scholarly judgments, and the need to heed the anguish of the times led virtually to a direct appeal to Mao in an essay entitled "Study More, Criticize Less". This time Teng T'o used the Sung official Wang An-shih as his symbol for Mao. To Teng, Wang represented an official who initiated untested, unrealistic programmes. He said of Wang An-shih: "He certainly had new ideas, but lacked practical experience and concrete knowledge. He considered everyone else inferior to himself and used to criticize them vehemently on no grounds at all. His major shortcoming was his lack of humility."[1] Teng insisted that if one does not understand a certain situation or lacks substantial knowledge about it, he should "have a sense of humility and willingness to learn. We should not be rash. This is the most valuable advice that has been handed down to us by past experience."[2]

Stronger than even Wu Han in "Hai Jui Scolds the Emperor", Teng, along with Wu Han and Liao Mo-sha, another official of the Peking Party Committee, under a column "Notes From a Three Family Village", implied that Mao suffered from a form of insanity that led him to irrational behaviour and decisions. In an article "A Special Treatment of Amnesia" published in issue number 14 of Ch'ien hsien, they wrote that "People suffering from this disease... often go back on their word and do not keep their promises...This disease will not only bring forgetfulness, but will gradually lead to abnormal pleasure or anger...easiness in losing ones temper and finally insanity..." Their advice, obviously directed to Mao, was that under such conditions "A person must promptly take a complete rest, must not talk or do anything." And again they warned as in earlier essays that "If he insists on talking or on doing anything, he will make a lot of trouble."[3]

As sharply as Teng questioned Mao's ability to rule, he lashed into his policies, specifically the Great Leap Forward. One of his earliest criticisms of the Great Leap Forward appeared in an

[1] Teng T'o, "Study More, Criticize Less", *Yen shan yeh hua*, II, 84.   [2] *Ibid.*
[3] *Current Background*, No. 792, p. 4. "A Special Treatment of Amnesia", *Ch'ien hsien*, No. 14 (1962) under the column *Notes from a Three Family Village*.

article "The Theory of Treasury Labour Power" written April 30, 1961. This essay protested against the forced use of peasant labour to work on large-scale construction projects. Once again he used the example of ancient rulers to criticize the present ones. He wrote that "Even as early as the Spring and Autumn period and the Warring States, our great politicians already understood the meaning of caring for human labour."[1] He quoted the *Book of Rites* which said that the labour power of the people can be requisitioned no more than three days a year. "From this we can see", he said, "that we must take into account the strength of the people and must not do the impossible."[2] He concluded that "We should draw new enlightenment from the experience of the ancients and take care to do more in every way to treasure our labour power."[3]

In another essay "An Egg as an Asset", Teng indirectly denounced the Great Leap Forward as merely a dream unrelated to reality which had no basis in practical experience or economic principles. He did this by telling the story of a merchant who gets an egg from a hen and then quickly dreams he will make a fortune. Excitedly he tells his wife that because the hen can lay fifteen eggs each month after three years he will become a very rich man. Teng said this story teaches us several lessons; the most important was that wealth could not be produced by whipping up great enthusiasm. In his view, the merchant's plan to build up great riches in a few years, starting with just a single egg, could only end up with his losing the egg itself. Of the man, Teng said "obviously he...did not like to follow the proper and usual way of production in order to increase his wealth. He was just speculating."[4] Teng observed that "Only an honest labourer...who works industriously can create and accumulate wealth for his society, country and self."[5] His story ridiculed the Great Leap Forward as having substituted an illusion for reality.

In another essay in "This Year's Spring Festival" published in 1962, but omitted from the published collection of "Evening

[1] Teng T'o, "The Theory of Treasuring Labour Power", *Yen shan yeh hua* (Peking: Pei ching ch'u pan she, 1961), 1, 56.

[2] *Ibid.* p. 57.   [3] *Ibid.* p. 58.

[4] Teng T'o, "An Egg as an Asset", *Yen shan yeh hua*, 1, 77.   [5] *Ibid.*

Talks at Yenshan", Teng directly referred to the food shortages caused by the Great Leap Forward and showed that previous governments had guarded against these shortages, but the present one had not fulfilled its responsibility to the people. He wrote "Our people have always attached importance to storing food...It was a very important practice of past dynastic days; they appealed to peasants to save up to one-half or one-third of their yields. This approach and its underlying motives are not without merit and should not be completely negated."[1]

But then, in contrast to his earlier pessimism, a note of hope appeared in this essay perhaps in response to the modifications in the commune system and the granting of small plots to individual farmers then underway. He wrote "The chilly season brought on by the north wind will soon come to an end. In its stead the mild east wind will quickly bring about a thaw on the frozen ground and then all things will show vitality and growth."[2] Here is another reference to a "thaw".

In one respect, Teng went beyond his fellow critics in his criticism of Maoist policies. Not only did he attack Mao's economic and agricultural programmes, his estrangement from the masses, his arbitrary, irrational behaviour, and his intolerance of criticism, but he openly demanded closer relations with the Soviet Union. In several essays, Teng urged the leadership to follow Soviet methods in modernizing China.

In one of these articles "From Three to Ten Thousand", Teng wrote that because the process of education is gradual and the teacher's guidance is necessary, the student must not dismiss the teacher. In an apparent reference to China's rejection of Soviet assistance, Teng warned that "If a man with a swelled head thinks he can learn a subject easily and then kicks out his teacher, he will never learn anything."[3] In another essay, "How to Make Friends", he advocated allying with more advanced countries. Again to prove his point, he quoted a statesman of the Ming who

[1] Ch'en Chao-chi, "Black Goods That Can in no Way be Tucked Away", Canton, *Yang ch'eng wan pao*, May 16, 1966, in *SCMP*, No. 3706, p. 12.
[2] *Ibid*. p. 11.
[3] Teng T'o, "From Three to Ten Thousand", *Yen shan yeh hua*, I, 33-34.

said "Some like to ally with those who are as good as they are, but do not like to unite with those who are better than they are, because they lack a humble attitude."[1] The statesman advised that it is most "important to make friends with others, especially with those in a competitive position"[2] in order to learn from them.

Teng even called for closer contact with the United States in an essay "Who Were the Earliest Discoverers of America". In line with the nationalist spirit of the times, Teng insisted that it was actually the Chinese who, by way of the Aleutian Islands and Alaska, discovered the United States. The Chinese did this in the fifth century, a thousand years before Columbus. Some even believe, Teng claimed, that the culture of the Aztecs of Mexico came from ancient China. Thus Teng concluded that "We can be sure that there has been a close association between the Chinese and Americans as early as the fifth century. This long tradition of Chinese–American friendship is an important historical fact."[3]

He ridiculed Mao's rejection of both the Soviet Union and the West in his essay "Great Empty Talk" published in *Ch'ien hsien*, on November 10, 1961 under the column "Notes from a Three Family Village" again written with Wu Han and Liao Mo-sha. In this essay he mocked Mao's statement that "The East wind will prevail over the West wind" by quoting a child's poem: "The East wind is our benefactor and the West wind is our enemy". Though the child's poem has such eye-catching words as "East wind", "West wind", "benefactor" and "enemy", Teng said these words "are just hackneyed phrases without much meaning. They only cause more confusion." He asserted "I want to offer my friends who are fond of big talk, this piece of advice: read more, think more and talk less."[4]

The last article Teng published in his series "Evening Talks at Yenshan", was entitled "Thirty-six strategies", written September 2, 1962 just prior to the convening of the Tenth Plenum. It was obvious that he sensed the end of the relaxation of the early

---

[1] Teng T'o, "How to Make Friends", *Yen shan yeh hua*, I, 51.   [2] *Ibid.*

[3] Teng T'o, "Who Were the Earliest Discoverers of America", *Yen shan yeh hua*, II, 3.

[4] *Current Background*, No. 792, p. 2. "Great Empty Talk", *Ch'ien hsien*, No. 21 (1961), published under the column *Notes from a Three Family Village*.

sixties. He wrote that he would discontinue "Evening Talks" because he had recently turned his attention to other things. He then described the thirty-six strategies used by a general in the Six Dynasties when caught in a difficult situation. Of these, Teng said, the best one was to retreat safely. That is what Teng attempted to do by ending his "Evening Talks at Yenshan".

As Teng had anticipated, the September, 1962 Tenth Plenum of the Eighth Central Committee revived the class struggle and informed the intellectuals once again that they were infected with "bourgeois" germs. It was no longer possible to be "expert" without being "red". Though more leeway was given in the sciences, the toleration of different viewpoints in the social sciences, humanities and arts was halted. There were several reasons for the termination of this period of relaxation. By the autumn of 1962, the economy had begun to improve and confidence was somewhat renewed. Most likely the regime believed there was less need to loosen its control over the economic structure than over the intellectual community.

Even more important, Mao probably ended the respite of 1961–2 to stop the subtle though clear criticism of himself, his treatment of P'eng Te-huai, the Great Leap Forward, and the plight of the peasantry by officials of the Propaganda Department and the Peking Party Committee. They were the pace-makers. As Propaganda officials called for the depiction of "people in the middle", stories began to appear with imperfect, non-revolutionary heroes as the main protagonists. Newspapers adapted the form of "Evening Talks at Yenshan" and published special columns of essays. These works were gaining a widening circle of readers. Hence, Mao declared a halt to this unique period of relative relaxation in the autumn of 1962 though dim echoes of it were to be heard for a long time after. The criticisms by the leaders of the Peking Party Committee and the Propaganda Department in the early sixties set in motion forces that ultimately produced the Cultural Revolution, "the trouble in the land" which Wu Han, T'ien Han and Teng T'o had prophesied so accurately several years before.

This 1961–2 relaxation repudiates the theory that a Communist regime invariably is in opposition to the intellectuals. In this episode and the earlier relaxations, there was an informal joining together of the Party and the intellectuals. Yet here again there are sharp differences in these alliances. As stated previously the moving force in the Hundred Flowers was Mao, but in the 1961–2 relaxation most likely it was Liu Shao-ch'i and the Party apparatus. Another difference was in the purposes of these alliances. During the Hundred Flowers, Mao sought the support of the intellectuals in his drive to curb the bureaucratism and dogmatism of the cadres. In 1961–2 the Party apparatus wanted the help of the intellectuals in their effort to repair the damage caused by Mao's Great Leap Forward. A similar kind of an alliance occurred in the Soviet Union when Khrushchev sought the assistance of the intellectuals in his attack on Stalinism. These have been instances, admittedly of short duration, when the regime and the intellectuals have joined together to counteract or control a common enemy. It could very well be that at some time in the future the Party in its reconstructed form will again ally itself with the intellectuals in an endeavour to check the forces unleashed by the Cultural Revolution.

9

GETTING AHEAD AND ALONG IN COMMUNIST CHINA: THE LADDER OF SUCCESS ON THE EVE OF THE CULTURAL REVOLUTION

MICHEL OKSENBERG

By the mid-1960's, the leaders of the Chinese Communist Party (CCP) had given structure to the opportunities and career choices available to the Chinese people. In their individual decisions, the Chinese people had to confront the questions Mao wanted them to face, such as whether to join the Party, to serve the people, and to become heavily involved in political life. Mao and his associates had helped to shape the determinants of social mobility and delineate the skills needed to get ahead and along in China. The violence, uncertainty and turmoil which characterized lives during the revolutionary era had given way to a period of more stable, predictable and structured career patterns.

What did the institutionalization of the revolution mean for the opportunities enjoyed by individual Chinese? What was the impact of the Communist revolution upon career opportunities established by the CCP? And what were the consequences for the CCP of the emergence of a well-defined ladder of success? These are the questions pursued in the subsequent pages.

It should be stressed that the observations in this paper are presented in the form of hypotheses derived primarily from my own lengthy interviews undertaken during 1964–5 of seven former residents of the mainland,[1] shorter interviews of several others,

---

[1] The seven included two former employees of ministries in Peking, three former college students (from Peking, Fukien and Shansi) who were also briefly employed on the mainland before joining relatives outside China, a youthful ex-accountant of a production brigade in Fukien, and a university professor at a leading normal school. For discussion and references to other analyses of this

and an interview project of peasant migrants which I sponsored. In addition, my thoughts have been influenced considerably by my reading of the interview protocols recorded by Ezra Vogel, John Pelzel, and Stanley Lubman, coupled with my reading of the Chinese press, the writings of former mainland residents,[1] and secondary sources.[2] Further, my interpretations have been improved by comments of others on an earlier draft.[3] But the firm data required

source, see my "Sources and Methodological Problems in the Study of Communist China", in A. Doak Barnett, ed., *Chinese Communist Politics in Action* (Seattle: Univ. of Washington Press, 1969).

[1] See in particular, Chow Ching-wen, *Ten Years of Storm* (New York: Holt, Rinehart & Winston, 1960); Eric Chou, *A Man Must Choose* (New York: Knopf, 1962); Robert Loh, *Escape from Red China* (New York: Coward McCann, 1962); Mu Fu-sheng, *The Wilting of 100 Flowers* (New York: Preager, 1962); Teng Chi-ping, *The Thought Revolution* (New York: Coward McCann, 1966); and Morris Wills, as told to Robert Moskin, *Turncoat* (Englewood Cliffs, N.J.: Prentice-Hall, 1968).

[2] For secondary sources, see in particular: A. Doak Barnett with Ezra Vogel *Cadres, Bureaucracy, and Political Power in Communist China* (New York: Columbia Univ. Press, 1967); James Townsend, *Political Participation in Communist China* (Berkeley: Univ. of California Press, 1967); Jerome Alan Cohen, *The Criminal Process in the People's Republic of China, 1949–1963* (Cambridge, Mass.: Harvard Univ. Press, 1968); Stanley Lubman, "Mao and Mediation: Politics and Dispute Resolution in Communist China", *California Law Review*, LV, (November, 1967), 1284–1359; and the series of extremely perceptive articles by Ezra Vogel, "From Friendship to Comradeship: The Change in Personal Relations in Communist China", *The China Quarterly*, No. 21 (January–March, 1965), pp. 46–60; "From Revolutionary to Semi-Bureaucrat: The 'Regularization' of Cadres", *The China Quarterly*, No. 29 (January–March, 1967), pp. 36–60; "Voluntarism and Social Control", in Donald Treadgold, ed., *Soviet and Chinese Communism: Similarities and Differences*, (Seattle: Univ. of Washington Press, 1966), pp. 168–84; and "A Preliminary View of Family and Mental Health in Urban Communist China", an unpublished paper prepared for the September, 1966, conference at Greyston House on "Kinship in Chinese Society", sponsored by the Sub-committee on Research on Chinese Society of the Joint Committee on Contemporary China. Also, I have drawn freely upon conclusions reached in my "Local Leaders in Rural China, 1962–5: Individual Attributes, Bureaucratic Position, and Political Recruitment", in A. Doak Barnett, ed., *Chinese Communist Politics in Action*.

[3] This paper hopefully reflects the helpful discussion by the participants of the Conference on the Chinese Communist Party, particularly A. Doak Barnett, Thomas Bernstein, and John Lewis, as well as the insightful comments made by others who read the earlier draft: Steven Goldstein, Kenneth Lieberthal, Kenneth Prewitt, Maurice Simon, G. William Skinner, Frederick Teiwes, James Townsend, and Ezra Vogel.

to document a paper on career patterns in Communist China have not yet been gathered. As a result, the paper is suggestive and exploratory, rather than definitive.

PARTY AND SOCIETY

But why, it might be asked, in a book on the CCP would an article appear on career opportunities and strategies throughout Chinese society? In such a volume, why not limit analysis to career opportunities and strategies, recruitment and mobility within the CCP? Several interrelated answers to these questions provide the rationale for this paper, and they deserve to be elucidated.

To begin with, the boundary between Party and society was difficult to draw. An institution such as the CCP can be defined as a set of interrelated roles; that is, the CCP was the sum of millions of Party roles, such as the roles of branch secretaries, branch members, and the Chairman of the Party. The problem in defining the boundary of the Party, then, rests in differentiating among Party and non-Party roles. And here, disagreement easily arises—not only among Western students of the CCP but among CCP members themselves. For example when P'eng Te-huai was Minister of Defence, he probably conceived of his position as a Party responsibility, while Mao perceived that by 1959, P'eng had used his position to play an anti-Party role. In another vivid example, Chiang Ch'ing to the chagrin of many succeeded in extending the definition of Party roles to include her position as Mao's wife. It was not easy, in short, to determine when someone was performing a Party role.

Delineating the boundary between Party and society became particularly difficult in the study of Party recruitment. Actually, recruitment occurred gradually, with the formal inscription of a new member on the Party rolls culminating a long process. In behavioural terms, a person was recruited into the Party not when he formally joined the Party, but when he started acting like a Party member, and that occurred even before his admission into the Party. An undeterminable number of Chinese, the so-called "activists", in fact had adopted the code governing the behaviour of Party members and were behaving much as if they were Party members. Meanwhile, many Party members who faced conflicts between the role they were expected to play as Party members and the other role obligations they had (such as commitments to family, profession, or local community) de-emphasized their Party roles. Thus, what might be called the "effective Party membership"—that is the people who gave primacy to Party roles—included many who were not formally Party members and did not include all Party members.

Nor did the rulers assist in marking a boundary between Party and non-Party behaviour by providing different models to guide the conduct of Party and non-Party members. The same ideal pattern of behaviour applied to both, although it was expected that non-Party members were less interested in attaining the ideal.

In spite of these conceptual difficulties, however, the CCP was an institution in society, not coterminous with it. An analogy to concentric rings is appropriate here, with the distance from the centre ideally representing a person's responsiveness to Party Chairman Mao and his associates: at the core, the top leaders; the next ring composed of people in the Party apparatus; the next ring, the "effective Party members"; the next ring, the more loyal supporters of the Party, and the outer ring, the more passive elements of society. The boundaries between each ring, at any moment, were not clear, and through time people moved from one ring to another.

The analogy reveals another reason why a volume on the CCP should contain an article on career opportunities and strategies throughout society. The Party must be studied in relation to its social milieu, and the concepts of Party membership and political careers become meaningful only when they are compared with non-Party careers. Although its leaders structured the CCP to be an instrument of political control and social change, to a certain extent the leaders became captives of their environment. At least, a frequent complaint of Mao and his supporters during the Cultural Revolution was that many Chinese were quite aware of the determinants of career and attempted to manipulate these determinants to their advantage. Increasingly, Chinese used the system for the limited advantages it could bestow upon them and made their plans on this basis. On the eve of the Cultural Revolution, unwritten "rules of the game" had developed which guided people as they planned their lives. Hence, the study of career opportunities and strategies throughout society illuminates why, as barnacles encumber a streamlined hull, many who grouped themselves around the Party core hindered the leader's ability to initiate social change.

IMPORTANT ASPECTS OF CAREER MOBILITY

By the 1960's, the major features of career mobility in China were rather clear. Among the more important aspects was the extremely limited range of choice available to most Chinese. If a distinction is made between the extent to which individuals were able to affect their careers, and the extent to which the system imposed constraints and shaped alternatives, then the greatest weight must be placed upon the latter. Even for the young, the ability of parents to pay school tuition, family connections, and the status of one's family influenced a child's desire and ability to attend a good middle school.

A second striking aspect of careers in China was the intense competition, the risks, and the dangers involved. No matter what hierarchy or how far up someone had moved, he still felt the threat of being demoted far down the hierarchy. Though the threat had become routinized and people had learned to anticipate and minimize it, the threat still existed.

Another salient feature of careers was that the realistic options usually involved either seeking promotion in one's organizational hierarchy or building a secure position within it. Some career options available in more affluent, free societies were less available in China. Chinese in general did not have many opportunities for voluntary, mid-career lateral mobility, involving a transfer, with no loss of rank, into other hierarchies. Examples of such lateral mobility would be academicians freely moving into government, or government employees accepting executive positions in industry, or agricultural workers seeking employment as unskilled workers on the urban labour market.

To be sure, people constantly had the opportunity to volunteer for hardship posts in the more remote areas of the country, such as

Sinkiang. But Chinese tended to consider such transfers to involve downward rather than lateral mobility. Further, there was considerable lateral mobility within the Chinese bureaucracy, as cadres were shunted from one position to another, but such lateral transfers were more the result of unanticipated, hard-to-influence orders. The very terminology usually used to describe such transfers (*tiao tung* or *tiao p'ei*) did not suggest volition. Interviews further suggest the difficulty someone faced in changing jobs. To quit and seek new employment required personal recommendations and the approval of the Personnel Department and, in some instances, the CCP's Organization Department. The transfer had to fit into the annual personnel plan and the table of organization (*pien chih*). And the transfer had to be justified in terms of the interests of the state.

As an exception, personnel with rare skills did have some opportunity for lateral transfer. Although it was against administrative regulations for one agency to raid another, this sometimes occurred. For example, an agency with a shortage of competent book-keepers sometimes recruited a book-keeper from another agency and assisted in cutting the red tape involved in the lateral transfer. In spite of such instances, however, it apppears that the principal career option involved the choice of whether to seek promotions within an organization or to build oneself into a specific position.

Another important feature of careers in Communist China was that once someone had opted for goals found outside the political system, he could not decide at a later date to pursue the goals offered by the political system. The principal exception was in the countryside, where apparently it was possible for a rather passive person to become politically active in his forties, winning a cadre position on the team and brigade level. In general, however, once a person had been labelled passive, the label stuck. To a lesser extent, the opposite was also true. The more someone opted for and secured the goals offered by the political system, the more difficult it became to opt out of an active involvement in political life and to pursue successfully those goals found outside its realm. That is, once someone became an "activist", and particularly if he had joined the Party, he found it hard to opt out. He could become less active, but to resign from the Party was politically suspect. As a result of drifting into the "activist" role as a teenager, and then securing membership in the Communist Youth League, it was possible for Chinese to find themselves deeply enmeshed in politics, with little recourse but to sustain the level of activism necessary to retain the position they had attained.

Most importantly, the political system continually impinged upon career choices. Underlying the specific concerns of each career stage was the common concern of how the individual dealt with the world of politics. Did he choose to pursue goals offered within the system or outside the system? Here was the consequence for the individual of the CCP's slogan, "politics takes command," or more literally, "politics controls all affairs."

A narrowly proscribed range of choice, high risks, little opportunity for voluntary lateral mobility, few "second chances" to retrieve an option once surrendered, and the constant impingement of governmental power upon careers—these were the major factors which anyone planning a career in Communist China had to face.

CAREER STAGES

In addition to these general considerations, Chinese faced particular problems and decisions, depending upon their age and career stage. In broad terms, Chinese passed through four career stages. The first stage involved the problems of initially responding to the incessant demands of the political system. The second stage involved problems of organizational affiliation, education and acquisition of skills, and selection of an occupation. The third stage involved the pursuit of ambitions, while the fourth involved the tempering of ambition and the pursuit of security. The stages in an individual's life cycle in China on the eve of the Cultural Revolution were not unique; men everywhere seem to pass through similar ones. But Chinese tended to face somewhat distinctive problems and pressures at each stage in their lives.

While young teenagers, Chinese, either consciously or unconsciously, responded to the whole problem of "volunteering". The question was not whether a typical Chinese teenager participated in political activities—everyone participated—but rather, to what extent did he participate? That is, how enthusiastically did he join in the various movements involving youth? If by 18 he consistently had displayed reluctance to participate in political life, in effect he already had significantly reduced his chances of obtaining an advanced education, joining the army, or entering the Communist Youth League (CYL). But if he had displayed considerable enthusiasm, he may have initiated a process that began to have a momentum of its own, entailing ever-increasing political involvement.

This led to the second group of career questions, typically confronted by youths between 15 and 25. Essentially, the questions clustered around a teenager's response to the political system. Did he wish to pursue goals found within the political system such as political power, the respect of peer groups imbued with the Maoist ethic, and the satisfaction of building the society envisioned by Mao? Did he try to join the two important organizations open to youth, the CYL and the People's Liberation Army (PLA)? Did he cultivate the relations necessary for joining these organizations and undertake the activities required to enter them? If by 25 a youth had responded negatively to these questions, for the rest of his life he was likely to be able to pursue only goals found outside the political system, such as emotional security and quietude, the respect of peer groups whose values were more traditionally or more technically oriented, and the equitable and just society envisioned by non-Maoists.

Between the ages of 15 and 25, a Chinese youth, particularly in urban areas, also confronted a set of questions centring on problems of education and occupation. What skills did he wish to acquire, and in what institutions could these skills be acquired? Although Chinese youths were assigned to particular jobs, schools, and departmental majors, they were able to affect the complex bureaucratic process through which such assignments were made. Not all middle schools were of equal prestige or calibre, for example, and students and their parents often tried to pull strings in order to be placed in the middle schools which increased their chances for entry into college. In some localities, moreover, middle-school graduates were asked to rank a specified number of universities they wished to attend. If they passed the standardized entrance examinations, their preferences were taken into account. If no slots were open at their preferred universities, however, they then were assigned to another university. Further, an applicant often could rank his preferred departmental majors.

Given these limited choices, youths had to decide to what university and department they should apply. Since they could indicate a preference for only a limited number of universities, listing the more competitive and prestigious universities (such as Peking University) automatically eliminated the possibility of mentioning a university more easily entered, and increased the chances that one would be arbitrarily assigned to a university one did not wish to enter. Similarly, competition for some departmental majors varied, and some students adopted a strategy of applying for departmental majors they knew they could secure.

If a student failed the college entrance examination and had independent financial support (because his family had sufficient income or he received remittances from overseas Chinese), did he refuse his job assignment, remain unemployed, and study independently, in preparation for the next year's examinations? Apparently, some urban youth selected this option, even though it made them vulnerable to charges of idleness and failing to serve the people.

Further, what kind of employment did a school graduate seek? Middle-school and college graduates were able to indicate where they preferred to work, and sometimes were able to encourage prospective employers to hire them, as a result of job interviews and letters of recommendation from senior Party members. Did a graduate seek a job which made him vulnerable to the incessant, harsh demands of the political system, or did he seek employment in occupations less involved in politics? Did he wish to work in urban areas, or was he willing to work in the rural or remote areas of China? And, if he did not like his job assignment, was he willing to appeal against the decision—recognizing that appeal might mean he then would be assigned to an even less desirable position?

Already in the second stage of a career, though even more so in the third stage of his career, a person confronted the problems associated with the pursuit of ambition. No matter what his goals, did he pursue them diligently and purposefully? Actions during this period were a measure of drive to climb the ladder of success. Did someone seek promotions and do the things that earned them? Did he base his marriage upon career considerations? (An aspiring Party member risked his career by marrying a girl of questionable class background.) And if he had a high need for power, wealth, or public achievement, he often confronted the question: How many people was he willing to harm in order to achieve his objective? The Chinese system in many ways was a brutal one; to rise, it was often necessary to join in the bitter denunciations of innocent men.

While the second stage of the life cycle in China involved defining ambitions and being funnelled into specific careers, in the third stage Chinese between the ages of 25 and 40 typically confronted the problems associated with specified ambitions. Essentially, this stage posed the problem of achieving promotion and success within an organization. To a considerable extent a career depended both upon individual performance and the record of the entire unit as well; if a unit failed to meet its targets or was judged ideologically impure, everyone in the unit would bear the consequences. Thus, Chinese seeking advancement not only had to do things which insured their personal success but also had to make sure their unit was successful.

At some point, though the moment may have come either early or late in life, most Chinese became aware of the high personal costs of ambition. They choose to seek no further promotion, but rather to build themselves securely into a particular position. In a sense, their prime value had become security. After the age of 30, increasing numbers of Chinese entered the final career stage of their lives. This phase was dominated by attempts to build secure positions, somewhat immune from the demands of the political system. At this stage, paramount concerns were to develop a network of protective mutual obligations and to become quietly indispensable at work. People in this stage tended to prefer positions in factories and enterprises, organizations which provided relatively more job security, and to shun employment in state administration and the Party apparatus, where employees were more susceptible to transfers and the turmoil of campaigns.

Since in 1965, the People's Republic was only 16 years old, no

Chinese actually had experienced all four career stages under Communist rule. People in their late thirties and forties, in fact, had selected their profession by 1949. But certainly by 1965, the bulk of the population perceived a defined pattern to life under communism. Indeed the more perceptive Chinese had identified the broad outlines of these patterns by the mid and late 1950's. As people embarked upon their careers, they adjusted their behaviour in anticipation of predictable pressures.

But, in any society, the way individuals respond to the pressures depends upon two interrelated considerations: their personal preferences and the objective opportunities available to them. That is, who climbs the ladder of success and how they climb it depends upon the interrelated combination of "systemic selection" and "self-selection". "Systemic selection" refers to the way the social structure facilitates the advance of some while blocking or eliminating others, depending upon their sex, family background, native place, occupation, personality, and so on. "Self-selection" means that some people attempt to advance, while others decide to remain in their existing station, and others voluntarily give up the fight. The variation in individual decisions, in turn, is explained through a combination of the different perceptions of opportunities, the different values and needs of individuals with distinctive childhood experiences and formal education, and perhaps the differences in genetically acquired characteristics.

The study of social mobility involves the attempt to identify and attach weights to these variables, an analysis presently impossible for Communist China because of data problems. The next two sections, however, deal with subjects related to career mobility for which the information is sufficient to form general impressions: the risks, rewards, and interrelationship of various goals which people might select, and the factors affecting the chances of achieving these goals.

CAREER GOALS

Among the goals which men pursue, either for their intrinsic or instrumental worth, are political power, high income, equity and justice, respect, and security. Not all men pursue the same goals, however, nor do men enjoy equal opportunities in their pursuit. In addition, the interrelationships among these goals differ among societies. For example, although in most societies, high income leads to political power, in some, high income yields little power. What qualities were attached to these goals on the eve of the Cultural Revolution? How were these goals interrelated? Who in society was in the best position to pursue particular goals?

Political power

Power yielded privileges unavailable to the general populace. For example, top provincial officials apparently had access to luxury swimming pools, vacation retreats, and air-conditioned offices. Power-holders also were able to command superior health services as well as superior educational opportunities for their children. Moreover, many people in power apparently were able to enjoy somewhat more relaxed relations with friends.

While power had its rewards, its pursuit was arduous. Members of the CCP, even those at the pinnacle of power, led hectic lives. To a certain extent, they had to savour power for its own sake, for its possession entailed many burdens and dangers. They were expected to volunteer for the most difficult tasks; they had to "take the lead", as the Chinese put it, in instilling enthusiasm in society. They were subject to the intense pressures of campaigns, and risked the dangers of purge. In short, power generally did not produce stable or tranquil lives.

The locus of political power in China was the CCP, particularly its Organization Department, the political–legal apparatus, and the Party secretariats, and in portions of the People's Liberation Army (PLA). Pursuit of power involved building a career within one of these organizations. The rules governing mobility within these organizations, in effect, became the code governing the behaviour of power-seekers.

Several aspects of mobility in the CCP and PLA were of particular importance. Lateral mobility into these organizations at higher echelons was almost nonexistent. In many societies, men may climb wealth or knowledge hierarchies, and at a later date use their wealth or knowledge to acquire political power. In China, political power had to be pursued within the organization possessing it.

Class background and seniority were important factors affecting mobility in the CCP and PLA. Promotions were granted more readily to people from worker and lower-class backgrounds and from families which participated in the revolution. People from bourgeois, landlord, and capitalist families were viewed with considerable suspicion. Consequently, it was more difficult for such people to enter the Party and the PLA. Because of the problems they faced, many from these backgrounds chose not to pursue political power.

As to seniority, the key positions of power were monopolized by the generation of cadres who had joined the CCP before 1949; people who had joined the CCP after 1949 often found their Party seniority insufficient to win rapid promotions, particularly in such powerful departments as the Organization Department and the secretariats. Young men eager for advancement sometimes wished to enter less powerful CCP departments, such as Finance and Trade, simply because the chances for upward mobility were greater.

The pursuit of power involved different considerations in urban and rural areas. There are a number of indications that in comparison to rural dwellers, urban residents found it somewhat easier to pursue political power. The percentage of the population who were Party members was considerably higher in urban areas than in rural areas. Urban officials seemed to have had higher rates of upward mobility than rural officials, because they had the opportunities to develop the widespread personal contacts which facilitated upward mobility. Assignment to the countryside frequently signified a severe setback in an official's career. And it appears that women were more able to pursue power in urban areas than in the countryside. (The Chinese press frequently complained of prejudice against admitting women into the CCP among rural Party committees.)

While urban dwellers probably enjoyed some advantages in the pursuit of power, they seemed less likely to compete for it. They had more opportunity to achieve goals independent of political power. Urbanites for example had a chance to get comparatively high incomes and welfare benefits by becoming technicians or permanently employed factory workers. Obtaining such employment was somewhat divorced from the pursuit of power. For the peasant, on the other hand, the limited political power vested in lower level governmental positions appeared the best way to achieve good wages and knowledge. The only way to acquire a guaranteed wage and social security benefits in the countryside was to become a state cadre. Similarly, the security, the educational opportunities, and the chances for upward mobility found in the PLA help explain the enthusiastic response to conscription in the countryside. In short, the pursuit of power was more intimately interwined in rural areas with the attainment of security, high income, and knowledge than in cities.[1]

Further, access to political power and its relationship to other goals varied with the fluctuations in public policy. In crude terms, the political system in China prior to the Cultural Revolution oscillated between two distinct phases. The "mobilization phase" occurred when the CCP's salient goals were to change attitudes and mobilize the masses. This phase was ascendant during the collectivization of agriculture and the socialist transformation of industry in 1955–6, the Great Leap Forward of 1958–60, and the socialist education campaign of 1963–4. The "consolidation phase" occurred when the salient goals were to stimulate commerce and consolidate the previous gains in achieving social change. Such phases occurred during the economic relaxations of 1954, 1956–7, and 1961–2.[2]

Political mobility increased during the mobilization phases, which usually involved CCP recruitment drives to provide opportunities for "activists" to become Party members. Further, the purges of Party officials during these periods opened up positions at higher levels. But at the same time, the intense pressures generated by mobilization, the calls for retrenchment in organizations, and the dispatching of large numbers of cadres to lower levels meant that some power-holders awaited campaigns with apprehension.

During the consolidation phase, class background became less

[1] A similar pattern existed in the Soviet Union. See Alex Inkeles and Raymond Bauer, *The Soviet Citizen* (New York: Atheneum, 1968), pp. 94–5.

[2] For a sophisticated analysis of the oscillation in policy, see G. William Skinner, "Compliance and Leadership in Rural Communist China", paper read to the 1965 meeting of the American Political Science Association.

important in the attainment of power, and entry into powerful organizations was granted to people with higher educational attainment. For example, in 1956–7, many bourgeois intellectuals were invited to join the Party, while in 1965, youths from upper and middle class backgrounds were assured explicitly that their rights to join the Communist Youth League (CYL) were guaranteed.

While it appears that class backgrounds were less important during consolidation the differences between urban and rural areas became more noticeable. The hallmarks of consolidation were free markets and bureaucratic routine—both urban phenomena. The locus of power was primarily in urban areas. But an often-stated purpose of the mobilization phase was to shift power to the country-side. The shift often was symbolized by the moving of the head-quarters of the *hsien* (county) CCP committees to rural areas. With the disruption of bureaucratic promotion channels, during the mobilization phase people in rural areas apparently enjoyed greater opportunity to pursue power.

The relationship between power and income differed during the mobilization and consolidation phases. During mobilization, political power became instrumental to the pursuit of almost any goal. During consolidation, however, politics did not intrude so relentlessly into all sectors of society. The spread of free markets and the increased importance of pay scales and piece-rate wage systems during these phases meant that high income could be pursued apart from political power.

High income

A goal openly pursued in many parts of the world, high income or material well being, could be pursued only surreptitiously in China. Pursuit of money in China did not involve the private accumulation of income-producing property, for that was impossible. Land reform and nationalization of industrial enterprises ended large private wealth. Although some former capitalists continued to live in luxury, their funds were impounded by state-owned banks. The state tolerated income-producing private property, such as apartment houses in urban areas or small vegetable plots in the country-side, but these were not sources of really high income.

Rather, material well being was to be found in secure, high-wage positions. During periods of economic relaxation, large earnings were also obtained through shady activities which the state found difficult to control, such as black marketing and illegal entrepreneurship. In general, though, increased income could be obtained only as a byproduct of advancement in the power or skill hierarchies. Those with power had access to state property, which could be used for personal enjoyment. Those with scientific and technical skills earned comparatively high wages and held relatively secure jobs. The rules governing the pursuit of material well being, in short, were intertwined with the rules either for the pursuit of power or of scientific and technical skills.

Justice and equity

Mao attempted to structure Chinese society so that the altruist would find it easy to act upon his unselfish concerns. In democratic societies, the altruist must select the cause to which he dedicates himself. The very necessity of choice, however, causes the altruistic act to have overtones of selfishness, for one must decide what *he* desires to do for society, rather than having society tell him what it demands from him. In addition, in democratic societies, someone seeking to build a more just society often needs other resources, such as wealth, power, or knowledge, in order to make an effective contribution. The altruist may be forced to pursue these goals before he can make a significant contribution to society, and in the pursuit of these instrumental goals, he easily forgets his initial objectives.

Prior to the mid-1960's, Mao apparently believed that he had solved these problems. He claimed that in Communist China, the unselfish man needed no prerequisites, such as power, wealth, or knowledge, before he could make his contribution, nor did the altruist need to ask himself what was to be done. All the unselfish person needed to do, Mao said, was to surrender his life to the CCP; in its infinite wisdom, Mao believed, the CCP would use the altruist in the way that would most benefit mankind. According to Mao, the altruist would become a willing cog for the CCP and Chairman Mao. And if a Chinese wished to donate only part of his time to a greater cause, he had ample opportunity to participate in the movements continually under way: reading to illiterates, eliminating pests, collecting scrap metal, and so on. In sum, Mao believed that he had harnessed and given direction to altruistic impulses. Moreover, his intensive ideological efforts were intended to awaken and intensify the people's desires to participate in selfless activities.

But the available evidence suggests that some Chinese altruists came to doubt the validity of Mao's appeal. They raised these questions: When Mao appealed to the unselfish instincts of many urban youths, asking them to volunteer to go to remote, rural areas of China, was he using their talents in the most constructive way possible? While Mao asked others to serve the people and become cogs in his service, was it not possible that Mao himself was motivated in part by considerations of power and glory? Had not the pressure upon the populace to be unselfish, to serve, to volunteer become so great that supposedly "unselfish" acts really were acts of desperate self-preservation? Among the youth, were not some who "enthusiastically" responded to Mao's appeal only trying to attain a "progressive" or "activist" label? And were not the naive but true disciples of Mao often victimized by the more cunning, false "activists"?

The answers to these questions and the opportunities which were perceived to create a more just society ultimately depended upon attitudes towards the Maoist vision. Those who trusted in Mao responded to his appeals for self-sacrifice, which he enunciated most strongly during the mobilization phase. To the dedicated Maoist, the consolidation phase was a period in which the populace began to indulge itself in the pursuit of selfish pleasures. For the altruist distrustful of Mao, however, the consolidation phase, with its limited freedom and security, provided the best opportunity to improve the society and to acquire the skills that would contribute to China's development. Such a man, after living through several mobilization phases, perceived them as something to endure, a period when self-preservation had to become his paramount concern.

Respect

To have a good reputation and be admired by peers are goals pursued by many. No uniform code governed the behaviour of those desiring the respect of their peers, for there were differences in the values of various reference groups in China. To oversimplify, one can classify Chinese peer groups into two categories—those that were imbued with the Maoist ethic and those that were not.

To be sure, Mao seems to have been particularly successful in structuring the peer groups to which many Chinese referred for guidance and respect. He was more successful among the young than among the old, and among the urban populace than among the country folk; his success reached its peak during the mobilization phase and diminished during the consolidation phase. But in varying degrees throughout the society, Mao succeeded in building new peer groups and infusing them with new values, thereby influencing the behaviour of the groups' members. These groups—the most important being the small study group—frequently cut across naturally cohesive groups to facilitate external control of them. Through the CCP's monopoly of the mass media and the manipulation of the topics discussed in these groups, Mao desired to control people's perceptions of the dominant values of the group. He hoped that individuals, seeking the respect of the group, would act upon and internalize the perceived values.

The extent of Mao's success, particularly among urban youth, is reflected in this verbatim transcript of an interview of a young ex-resident of Amoy. Asked about the reasons for student activism, the informant underlined the importance of peer group pressure and the desire for respect:

Interviewer: A number of factors probably prompted someone to be an activist. Which factors were commonplace? Which were unusual?

Informant: The most important reason is that most youth want to be known as "progressive" [*chin pu*], not backward [*lo hou*]. The CYL is the organization of progressives, and those who want to be recognized as having a "progressive attitude" therefore want to join.

Interviewer: What indicates a "progressive attitude?"

Informant: Actively to participate in the motherland's construction.

Interviewer: Let me draw an analogy here. The messages of the CCP and the CYL, such as "actively to participate in the motherland's construction", can be likened to a seed, while the recipient's mind can be likened to the soil. In some, the seed takes root and grows. In others, there is no reaction. Why?

Informant: The CYL is usually able to get a response because it has been preparing the soil, so to speak, for a long time through its ideological education programme. The programme is everywhere; everyone places a high value upon being progressive. Thus, when the call comes to be "progressive," most people react...

Interviewer: Are there other reasons for being progressive?

Informant: Yes, people don't want to be left behind. There is an old Amoy saying, "One transports men, but not the battlefield" [*shu jen, pu shu chen*]. This means that if one man leaps ahead of the group, the rest of the group need not be embarrassed. But if the group moves ahead, and you are left behind, then you must move ahead to be with them. Chinese people like to be with the group. The saying describes this phenomenon. If you are behind, everyone can ridicule and laugh at you...

Interviewer: When the government tells someone to do something, why does he do it?

Informant: Two particular penalties are the most operative sanctions— criticism (which leads to struggle) and labour reform [*lao kai*]. People fear labour reform, which is very difficult and bitter. People wish to avoid criticism and struggle for many reasons, but one reason is that it results in one's friends having to criticize you. This is unpleasant, and it breaks the solidarity [or unity, *t'uan chieh*] that exists among one's friendship group.

The informant mentioned other considerations in becoming a "progressive", such as enhancing career opportunities. But the informant clearly indicated that the fear of isolation and the desire to be accepted by the group were important goals for many Chinese. His testimony suggests that many youths, to achieve these goals, responded to Mao's appeal to become "progressive".

Many Chinese, however, sought the respect of peer groups dominated by other values. Among older people in rural areas, for instance, Mao's ethic had not penetrated so deeply, and the values of peer groups there were more likely to consist of pre-Communist belief patterns. Particularly during the consolidation phase, organizational identity was given to traditional groups, such as the family. (Production teams in Kwangtung in the early 1960's, for example, were often based on sub-lineages [*fang*].) Winning the approval of such a peer group tended to involve conforming to the norms of the old society, and if one were a cadre, seeking the approval of the group and defending its interest against the demands from the outside.

A more scientifically oriented ethic was gaining adherents among engineers and technicians. This ethic stressed professional competence, analytical rigour, and the role of technical expertise, and questioned the wisdom of some of Mao's approaches to economic development.

While groups with non-Maoist values persisted into the mid-1960's, the artificially constructed peer groups controlled by the CCP had begun to lose their efficacy. Initially, the control techniques in these groups were extremely successful. Gradually, however, the members of the group came to realize that the other members often spoke insincerely. Each, fearful of the criticism of the group, expressed sentiments he did not believe. As the group became aware of the sham, the process became a ritual performed to satisfy the CCP representative in the group. Instead of becoming a "progressive" to win the group's approval, one acted progressively to meet the minimum demands of the CCP representative.

Many adult Chinese, familiar with the system, perceived the hypocrisy and duplicity of a large proportion of the populace. While no one admitted pursuing material pleasures, clearly many people did seek high incomes. People acted "unselfishly" or "progressively", so they could further their careers. And so on. In a tense environment, where discrepancies between thoughts, words and deeds were frequent, men able to retain their integrity became much admired. So too, those able to beat the system or to make the system work for them, were admired by some. Ironically, the very pressure that Mao exerted to change the values of the society and to involve the populace in affairs of state both enhanced the traditional virtues of sincerity, loyalty and rectitude, and encouraged people to avoid rather than participate in public affairs. Particularly under the pressure of the mobilization phase, men remaining true to themselves and sincere to their friends earned the respect of their peers. But to remain uncorrupted required limiting political commitment and involvement. For many, the pursuit of power and wealth appear to have become antithetical to the pursuit of respect.

Emotional security and quietude

The incessant demands which the government made upon their lives led many Chinese to place a high premium upon security and quietude. To enjoy the warmth of the hearth, to escape the unpleasant political pressures exerted by the CCP, to enjoy those limited pleasures which entailed low risk of criticism—these became the main goals of many.

The high priority attached to these goals throughout society was a reflection of Mao's failure to sustain the earlier mobilization of the Chinese people. In the early days of the Chinese People's Republic, the leaders actively involved the aroused masses in the implementation of policy. Mao and his associates desired to eliminate the traditional attitude of distrust towards the arbitrary world of politics and power which was held by perhaps the majority of the population. This distrust traditionally had led many Chinese to isolate themselves, as much as possible, from the political system. The Chinese Communists sought to involve the masses in the affairs of state, to destroy the barriers between officials and the masses, and thereby to tap an eager reservoir of human energy and talents for industrialization purposes. But the way the Chinese Communists involved the people, particularly during the mobilization phase, tended to confirm the view of many that the political world indeed was harsh, arbitrary and somehow unfair. Mao's vigorous attempt to shatter the value placed upon the family and other ascriptive bonds, in fact, intensified the desire for the security derived from them.

It appears that the quest for security and quietude covaried with their deprivation. In other words, at those times, in those places, and among those classes able to achieve some security and quietude, there apparently was a greater propensity to pursue other goals.[1]

[1] The one major exception to this generalization seems to be related to sex differences. Females, who had greater opportunity to attain security and quietude than males, did not display a greater propensity to pursue other goals. This no doubt was related to different socialization experiences of males and females.

Hence, during the consolidation phases, in the countryside, or among the poorer classes—all of which tended to offer more security and quietude than their opposites, the mobilization phase, the urban areas, or the wealthier classes—deliberate attempts to withdraw from the political system were less noticeable.

FACTORS AFFECTING ATTAINMENT OF GOALS

The analysis of various goals which people pursued suggests that the most salient characteristic of each was its relationship to the political system. Moreover, the goals clustered into two sets—those that were found outside the political system, and those that had to be pursued within it. Security and quietude, the respect of peer groups whose values were more traditionally or scientifically oriented, the non-Maoist visions of an equitable and just society—all these goals had to be pursued independently of the political system. On the other hand, values such as political power, the respect of peer groups imbued with the Maoist ethic, or the just society envisioned by Mao were inextricably intertwined with the political system.

The key determinants affecting the opportunity to attain these goals, then, were related to the unequal penetration of the political system into different sectors of society. At those times, in those places, and among those classes, age groups, and organizations where the political system was most assertive, the chances to achieve the goals offered by the system were enhanced. For example, since the range of human activities falling within the political domain reached its zenith during the mobilization phases, those were the times when the goals of power, respect from Maoist peer groups, and Maoist justice were more easily realized. The consolidation phase made it somewhat less difficult to attain goals that had to be pursued outside the political arena, when the area of human affairs directly affected by the political system diminished.

The impact of the Communist government was less intensely felt in rural areas than in urban areas. Hence, it was somewhat easier to pursue such goals as emotional security and quietude or the respect of traditional peer groups in the countryside. Though the goals associated with the political system were less attainable in the countryside, this did not mean that the competition for these goals was any less fierce than in the cities. On the contrary, there was intense competition among rural youth for entry into the Army or among rural middle school graduates for employment by the state. Those rural youths who were attracted by urban life, standing only a remote chance of realizing their dreams, knew that power and the respect of Maoist peer groups were the principal instruments for the achievement of their goal, and that the PLA and the government bureaucracy were their main avenues to power.

The political system also differed in the way it impinged upon people from different class backgrounds. People from wealthier economic backgrounds found the pursuit of political power risky. Since they tended to be under constant political pressure, moreover, they longed for, but were denied, security and quietude. With the status reversals that occurred during the Communist revolution, they almost had become the outcasts of society. People with a revolutionary background (i.e., those who had joined the CCP and PLA prior to 1949 and their children), on the other hand, were the privileged members of society, and found it easier to achieve their goals.

As the discussion of career stages suggested, age also apparently was a factor influencing the way people related to the political system. It seemed that the older the individual, the more likely he was to seek those goals found outside the political system. Three hypotheses, not mutually exclusive, may help to explain this phenomenon. First, older people, socialized during the pre-Communist period, may have tended to find less convergence between their goals and those of the political rulers. Second, older people had more experience with the political system, and particularly as a result of the unfulfilled expectations carried over from the campaign phases, may have been more reluctant to become involved in political affairs. Third, it may be that as one aged, the demands made by the government gradually diminished and one's skill in evading the demands increased; as a result, as one grew older, one was more able to pursue goals not related to politics.

Perhaps in part since it was run by men, the political system appears to have been more open to, but also made greater demands upon, males. Not surprisingly, given their different childhood training and adult responsibilities, females seem to have been more inclined to pursue the non-political goals, and certainly were more able to attain these goals.

Finally, political pressure from the centre was applied unevenly within the bureaucracy. That is, some institutions were under tighter control than others, and the officials in the less politically sensitive posts were more able to pursue goals outside the system. As a rule of thumb, government agencies tended to be less politicized than Party agencies; economic agencies tended to be less politicized than propaganda or coercive agencies; and lower level units tended to be less politicized than higher level units.

In sum, it appears that by 1965 the key factors affecting career opportunities included the broad policy of the moment, and the person's geographical location, class background, age, sex, and organizational affiliation. (Obviously, the ability to master particular skills—discussed below—also affected one's chances.)

On the basis of the available data, however, I am unable to establish precisely the importance of each factor or their interrelationships.[1] The well-defined cases were those in which all the variables were working in the same direction. Thus, during the mobilization phase, young urban male CYL members had relatively good opportunities to attain such goals as power and the respect of Maoist reference groups. Or, during the consolidation phase, elderly rural females were in a strong position to enjoy security, quietude, and the respect of a traditionally oriented reference group. But in many instances, the determinants did not converge so neatly. Precisely what, for example, were the chances that, during the consolidation phase, a rural youth from a middle peasant family could enhance his power position? Or, during the mobilization phase, that an urban, middle-aged woman married to an industrial labourer could have some peace and quiet? It is by no means clear in such

---

[1] An example of such an interrelationship was that the career implications of sex differences was greater in the countryside than in the urban areas. But on the other hand, it is not clear whether class backgrounds were more salient in rural or urban areas.

instances which were the more powerful operative factors. To repeat, a complete understanding of the factors governing career mobility and the attainment of specific goals awaits better data.

Nonetheless, the general effects of several key variables have been identified. Moreover, it does seem that by 1965 the self-conscious careerist roughly could calculate his chances for achieving any particular set of goals, given the broad policies of the moment, and his station in life. The careerist then could select his response to his opportunities, cognizant of the risks he faced. The system had fixed the odds, and they were usually not attractive, but the participants were free to make their wagers.

SKILLS

Achievement of particular goals depended not only upon one's station, but also upon the ability to master specific skills which, for convenience, can be subdivided into two categories: (1) those that enabled withstanding the inescapable demands of the political system and advancing in the system; and (2) those that enabled pursuit of goals found outside the system. The politically relevant skills included being familiar with political affairs, being good in interpersonal relations, and being effective in communication and persuasion. Skills that enabled one to be less dependent upon the political world and to pursue the goals which were less intertwined with politics included technical skills, commercial skills, and knowledge of the arts and humanities. Let us examine each of these skills at greater depth.

Political skills: familiarity with political affairs

No matter whether the goals pursued were inside or outside the political system, Chinese had to develop skills for coping with governmental demands. For example, effective criticism and self-criticism in small group and self-evaluation activities, routine parts of life particularly in urban areas, required familiarity with current policies. And, at all times, citizens were well advised to know what behaviour was considered deviant, what classes were in disfavour, and what beliefs were discredited.

The ability to understand policy depended in part upon correctly interpreting the press, a skill which arose from a sound knowledge of Marxist–Leninist doctrine, the writings of Mao Tse-tung, the history of the world Communist movement, CCP history, and Chinese history and traditions. For examples, a *Red Flag* article commenting on the Boxer Rebellion, appearing when students were surrounding foreign embassies in Peking in early 1967, was a tacit way of informing the students how they should behave towards foreigners residing in the capital.[1] Authoritative analyses in *People's Daily* during 1966 on the CCP's 1929 Kut'ien Conference probably related to the current policy on Party–PLA relations. Discussion in the Peking press in the early 1960's on the Ming imperial adviser Hai Jui actually referred to the 1959 removal of Minister of Defence P'eng Te-huai. In 1955–6, the analyses of Stalin's 1927–8 collectivization drive shed light upon the CCP's own policy in the countryside. The tendency to cloak intense policy debates in historical allegories, in short, meant that policy sometimes could be deciphered only with a thorough knowledge of the past.

In addition, to interpret the press correctly required familiarity with Communist jargon and the slogans used in the mass media. One had to understand the significance of policies which had been encapsulated in such slogans as the "three red banners", "the four goods", "the three-eight work style", "the three guarantees", "the twenty-three points", "the sixteen points", "the eight-point charter", "red and expert", adventurism, and so on. Similarly, it was useful to be able to relate the importance to one's own life of a passage in a speech by a Politburo member, such as, "We must recognize our shortcomings...At the present time, it is important to oppose both conservatism and dogmatism", or "Let us not forget the three red banners". The former phrase could signal a shift to a consolidation phase; the latter, a shift to a bureaucratic phase.

The cues hinting at major policy shifts were particularly important. If someone detected a shift from, say, the consolidation to the mobilization phase about two weeks before it occurred, he was in an

[1] See Ch'i Pen-yü, "Ai kuo chu i hai shih mai kuo chu i?" [Patriotism or Traitorousness?], *Hung ch'i* [Red Flag], No. 5 (1967), pp. 9–24, esp. pp. 14–15.

excellent position to attain his goals. A classic case in this regard was the ability of some to decipher articles in *People's Daily* in late May 1957 in the light of the CCP's mode of operation.¹ These people realized that the Hundred Flowers movement, in which Chinese were encouraged to criticize the CCP, was going to be terminated, and that the critics would be subject to condemnations. They therefore refused to participate in the criticism of the Party. In June, when the Hundred Flowers did give way to the anti-rightist campaign, those who had interpreted the press correctly were able to join the chorus of condemnations against the "rightists". Similarly, in 1961, when the mobilization phase gave way to the consolidation phase, some students detected early signs of the shift, and seized the moment to pursue their studies diligently—without, of course, insulting their Party superiors, for they knew another mobilization phase would come eventually.²

Political skills: managing interpersonal relations

Requisite skills for political survival and advancement also involved being able to conduct oneself appropriately with superiors, equals, and subordinates. By 1965, unwritten rules of proper conduct had evolved which generally worked to reduce the tensions and provide limited freedoms in a political system of high pressure and pervasive controls. Ezra Vogel's masterful descriptions of these rules need not be repeated here, but some additional observations should be made.

Particularly relevant to the theme of this paper is that different codes governed the behaviour of people pursuing different goals. To cite a specific instance, the ritual in small group criticism meetings of college students prescribed different roles for leaders, for activists who were looking for opportunities to enhance their political standing, for people wanting to avoid trouble, and for people wishing to display their sympathy for the criticized member of the group. As unobtrusively as possible, the leader had to encourage the group to criticize the person under attack; he had to persuade rather

¹ See Robert Loh, *Escape from Red China* (New York: Coward McCann, 1962), chap. XII.

² See Tung Chi-p'ing, *The Thought Revolution* (New York: Coward McCann, 1966), chap. IX.

than coerce. An activist usually spoke early in the meeting, enthusiastically, and at length, but he did not go beyond the confines of criticism set by the leader, lest he raise the leader's ire. The "trouble avoider" talked in the middle of the session, offering the minimum comments he thought were expected of him. The "sympathetic critic" often spoke towards the end of the session—although this entailed personal risk—and while criticizing the person, might say a few words on his behalf, such as: "Although he has improved, it is clear he has not improved enough." The available evidence suggests that many Chinese, particularly college students, chose their roles quite deliberately and were aware of the skills required to perform these roles well.

Among the many skills in interpersonal relations, two seem to have been paramount, the abilities to avoid making enemies and to bargain effectively. Enemies were more harmful than friends were helpful. In fact, as Vogel has suggested, friendships were not easily exploited for personal gain, and often entailed unpleasant political risk. Many Chinese were not particularly eager to know the inner feelings of persons they cared about, for fear that they might have to divulge the information in criticism meetings. The only people who gained from friendships, in short, were those who sought the respect, emotional security, and quietude which friendship offered, and these gains were severely circumscribed, particularly in urban areas, by the risks attached to friendships.

On the other hand, most Chinese realized that criticism by a single enemy during the annual year-end evaluation or during a search for a suitable target in a campaign could ruin their life. Or, an enemy might one day control their career. For example, one of my informants had been an employee in a provincial Department of Chemical Industries. A new personnel officer assigned to this Department turned out to be a former schoolmate whom my informant had criticized several years previously for being a "false activist". Soon thereafter, my informant was sent to the countryside to work on his department's state farm. He thought the personnel officer used the first opportunity to even the score and to remove someone who might damage his promising career in organization and personnel work.

Chinese avoided creating enemies by not initiating criticisms of anyone, doing what was demanded by the group leader, and not undertaking something that might reflect ill upon their whole group. Escaping troublesome situations was the key.

But if someone's goal was power, then he had to risk creating enemies, such as by initiating criticism to prove his activism, accusing his leader of malpractices in hopes of removing him, or pledging that his group could achieve a difficult task. In such an instance, a power-seeker often selected persons to criticize who were or would be rendered harmless by the charges (and who therefore would be unable to gain revenge) or undertook activities that led to a rapid promotion, thereby enabling him to escape the repercussions.

To pursue power while keeping enemies at a minimum required deviousness and a sense of timing. If someone else could be manipulated into doing the dirty work—such as initiating criticism— then a power-seeker could assume the guise of behaving enthusiastically without appearing overly ambitious. Or, fewer enemies were created by cloaking acts with the virtue of necessity. People tended to excuse behaviour if they thought it was necessary to avoid political trouble.

In addition to avoiding enmity, the ability to bargain effectively was important in interpersonal relations. One of the most common relationships involved a superior giving orders to a subordinate. Although power in this relationship was unevenly distributed, superior and subordinate each depended upon the other. The superior depended upon his subordinate to respond immediately and enthusiastically, thereby enabling the superior to demonstrate his leadership capacities. The subordinate depended upon his superior for good work assignments, allocation of resources to complete these assignments, and favourable recommendations. The superior sought compliance with a minimum expenditure of resources; the subordinate often sought to modify instructions and to obtain the greatest reward in exchange for his compliance.

Though constantly vulnerable to severe sanctions, a skilled subordinate was able to enhance his bargaining position by hoarding his resources and increasing his superior's dependence upon and confidence in him, while keeping his superior from viewing him as a threat. In very subtle ways, the subordinate might also remind his superior of any common ties they had, such as common provincial origins or common revolutionary experience. Although in some instances, the bargaining process could become explicit, such as over the targets in production plans or even the wording in the annual individual evaluations, for the most part the process was implicit, with both superior and subordinate probing and sensing how far each was able to go.

The bargaining process between superior and subordinate was complicated by the fact that any particular relationship was part of a long chain of command. The room for manoeuvre was limited, so that, for the average official, bargaining skills enabled him mainly to reconcile or at least reduce the conflicting demands coming from above and below. Consider the unenviable task faced by both the county leaders and their subordinate commune and brigade leaders at a county meeting convened to set targets in a water conservancy campaign.

The county leaders typically had obligated their county to supply the province and special district (*chuan ch'ü*) with a certain number of corvee labourers for irrigation projects financed and directed by these higher level units. In addition, the county leaders usually had pledged that within their county a certain number of new wells would be sunk, new irrigation ditches and ponds would be dug, and so on. They had obligated themselves to targets they thought would both satisfy their superiors and could be fulfilled by the communes and production brigades in their county; they convened the meeting of commune and brigade leaders to subdivide the man-power and construction tasks. The county leaders then had to elicit a hopefully voluntary response from their subordinates, each of whom were asked to contract for a portion of the county-wide obligations.

The county leaders had limited material rewards to give to more responsive subordinates. They also could promote or damage the careers of their subordinates. Further, they could manipulate symbols and exercise propagandistic appeals to secure compliance. In addition to these standard remunerative, coercive, and normative sanctions, and perhaps even more important, was the superior's ability to keep the subordinate off balance psychologically. The superior often intimated, sometimes correctly, that he had secret information which, if divulged, would convince the subordinate that he should comply. Moreover, sometimes by advance consultations with his more loyal and trustworthy subordinates, the superior attempted to create a "band wagon" effect; resistance, objections and passivity were perceived by subordinates as futile.

At the county meeting, the commune or brigade official had to be sensitive to the pressures of the moment concerning how hard he could bargain for low figures without being labelled a "rightist" who "underestimated the labouring enthusiasm of the masses". He had to know what political arguments were effective at the particular moment, as he sought to protect his unit from excessive demands. If the official wanted to become known for his activism and loyalty to the regime, he contracted for high targets. But in the back of his mind, the commune or brigade official recognized that ultimately he had to live with his obligations; he had to be able to return to his village and elicit the required response from his team leaders and team members to fulfil the targets. The commune or brigade leader who held his position for a long time undoubtedly had the talent for consistently meeting at least the minimum expectations of his superiors while not arousing the enmity of his subordinates. Throughout the society, similar bargaining skills were required for political advancement or survival.

Political skills—communication and persuasion

To write well, to articulate thoughts effectively, to persuade others in face-to-face encounters, to summarize complex ideas so that uneducated people could understand them—all these skills greatly aided those pursuing power. The curriculum in cadre training schools included a number of courses in how to deliver reports, how to summarize, how to help the masses analyse problems, and so on. Interviews with former cadres suggest that many learned their lessons well, for they tended to give articulate, well organized, and insightful answers to difficult questions.

The example of the tasks of commune and production brigade officials during a water conservancy campaign illuminates the importance of these skills. After the officials had obligated their units to contribute manpower and undertake specific tasks at the county meeting, their main burden was to convince their team leaders and villagers that the targets were reasonable and attainable. Though the threat of coercion always lurked in the background, their task essentially was a persuasive one—to entice, cajole, arouse, incite, or shame their audience into action. A high premium was placed upon securing volunteers rather than assigning people to specific tasks. A verbatim passage from one of my interviews further emphasizes the importance of well-developed persuasive skills in such a situation:

Interviewer: How were the shock brigades [*t'u chi tui*, e.g., the leading work teams] formed in water conservancy work?

Informant: Usually, they were composed of volunteers.

Interviewer: What are the good and bad points of a brigade composed of volunteers?

Informant: If the brigade was composed of volunteers, it means that spirits [*ch'ing hsü*] were high. But if the incentive was not there, there may not have been any volunteers. Whether people volunteered or not really depended upon the leader [*ling tao jen*].

Interviewer: What did that involve?

Informant: If in the meeting, the leader judged the "spirit" to be high, he let volunteers apply, and set up the "shock brigade" that way. But if he judged enthusiasm to be low, he assigned [*fen p'ei*] people to the brigade. If the leader misjudged, and called for volunteers but none came forward, then he suffered a defeat. In such a case, it was evident to the leader that the people looked down upon him [*k'an pu ch'i*]. And then it would be a real pity.

The importance of the communicative skills, particularly in the pursuit of power, appeared to be equally important in urban and rural areas and during the consolidation and mobilization phases. One hypothesis, however, is that different types of persuasive skills proved more valuable in the countryside or during the mobilization phase, when face-to-face communications seemed to be more predominant. In urban areas and during the consolidation phase, on the other hand, there seemed to be increased reliance upon such impersonal forms of communications as the mass media and, within the bureaucracy, written instructions.

Skills for non-political goals

In addition to the skills which facilitated the pursuit of goals within the political system, a number of skills enhanced a person's ability to remain somewhat independent from and have some interests outside of the political system. These included scientific and technical skills, commercial skills, and knowledge of the arts and humanities.

Scientific and technical skills enabled one to compete for positions having good incomes and a degree of security. Chemists, physicists, biologists, metallurgists and engineers were able to enjoy some immunity from the incessant demands of the political system. Others, such as agronomists, hydrologists, linguists and medical doctors, were more susceptible to political pressures, but they too enjoyed some privileges not available to unskilled workers or peasants.

The chance to develop and use these skills, however, varied according to class, place and time. Children from upper and middle class families were raised in an environment which prepared them for the rigours of formal education; further, acquisition of technical skills was their best hope for attaining good incomes, respect and security. Since urban school systems tended to be better than rural ones, urban youths were better equipped to acquire technical skills. Finally, people were more able to exploit their technical skills during the consolidation phase; during the mobilization phase, with its emphasis upon egalitarian values and reliance upon the labouring power of the masses, people with technical skills often were assigned to menial tasks and forced to spend much time in political study.

Remarkably little is known about careers open to people with commercial skills: entrepreneurial talents, knowledge about marketing, or even the ability to use an abacus and keep a ledger. Not surprisingly, interviews with peasant emigrés suggest that in rural Kwangtung, at least, economic planners and accountants in communes and brigades, and managers of credit cooperatives and supply and marketing cooperatives tended to be people with commercial skills. Not a few accountants, children of ex-merchants, won their jobs simply because their parents had taught them how to use the abacus. And many who gave advice on planting of cash crops were elder peasants whose knowledge of price fluctuations and marketing practices ante-dated Communist rule.

It appears that such people came to the fore in the consolidation phase, particularly during times of economic crisis such as from 1960 to 1962. At those times, free markets flourished, and in order to restore the economy, people with commercial skills were not discouraged from undertaking black market activities and establishing all sorts of contacts throughout the country. For example, one informant, a young "wheeler-dealer" type, after obtaining a truck in Canton in 1961-2, made several trips to southern Hunan, where he sold manufactured items and bought lumber to be sold on the Canton market. He profited handsomely during this time, but then was sentenced to labour reform during the Socialist Education Campaign.

In many societies, people cultivate knowledge of music, literature, art, history, or handicrafts as an avocation. In China, little solace was found in such hobbies, for they made one vulnerable to charges of "individualism" (implying selfishness) and "bourgeois conservatism". Some people were deeply committed to and continued in the pursuit of the literary and artistic skills deprecated by the rulers, but they paid a high toll, especially during the mobilization phase, for their persistence.

Summary

Almost everyone needed to develop some minimum skills in interpreting political affairs and managing interpersonal relations, no matter what goals they wished to attain. In addition, if one wished to pursue political power, manipulative skills were important. Technical skills acquired in the regular educational system increased the chance of leading a secure life; this route to success was often pursued by children of urban, middle class families. Commercial skills yielded wealth during the consolidation phase, but at a high risk of criticism during the mobilization phase.

GENERAL STRATEGIES: "THE FIVE DO'S AND FOUR DO NOT'S"

In emulation of the Chinese penchant to reduce such matters to numerical slogans, the strategies which enabled skills to be used effectively might be labelled "The Five Do's and Four Do Not's". These strategies deserve lengthier study. They were the basic operational code for political survival and advancement, and are described only superficially below. Those already discussed in this article are only summarized.

The First Do: Be aware of the general policy line, know it by heart, and know its implications. The policy line always called for displaying some enthusiasm, especially in campaigns, and for avoiding the label of a "passive" or "backward" element.

The Second Do: Hoard resources; do not squander them. Resources included knowledge, influence, and personal obligations owed by others, as well as material goods. These vital resources enabled the meeting of sudden demands coming from above or below. The retention of vital information by lower level bureaucrats and the accumulation of excessive inventories by factory managers, both frequently condemned practices on the mainland, were examples of such strategy.

The Third Do: Cultivate good relations with the immediate superior, especially the small group or team leader, without becoming totally "his man". A leader could cause enormous difficulties unless relations with him were satisfactory. In the countryside, a peasant's wages depended upon favourable assignments from the production team leader. Within small study groups, Chinese were vulnerable to persecution by a hostile group leader. Moreover, the small team or production group leader provided an essential recommendation for those wishing membership in the CCP.

Good relations with a superior were cultivated primarily by agreeing with him. In a sense, to challenge a superior amounted to challenging the immediate representative of the CCP. Moreover, a display of excessive initiative led people to think that one was trying to win promotions and to curry favour with higher level personnel. This made one a potential target in a campaign.

While cultivating good relations with his superior, most Chinese appeared reluctant to become "his man". That is, Chinese tended to avoid becoming so closely identified with their superior that their fate became intertwined with his. If the superior fell, then they would fall with him. Further, too close a relationship with a superior reduced the opportunities of subordinates to move ahead of him; they became reluctant to criticize him or to face him after a promotion. Subordinates were wise, in short, to retain some flexibility by having connections (*kuan hsi*) with other than the immediate superior.

The Fourth Do: Master the "three learns" of responding correctly to the important political aspects of life in China: (1) to behave correctly in small group activities; (2) to live with campaigns; and (3) to balance conflicting obligations. Proper conduct in small group activities involved the ritualized responses already described.

To learn to take the disruptions of campaigns in one's stride and to safeguard personal interests in the midst of the turmoil involved a number of routine responses, particularly on such matters as volunteering, criticism and meeting campaign targets. The organizational techniques of a campaign were generally the same. Typical campaign devices included Peking's designating the campaign goal to be the key indicator for evaluating the performance of bureaucrats, establishing a special CCP committee on each governmental level empowered to circumvent normal bureaucratic channels and responsible for directing the campaign, convening lower level officials to allocate work tasks, and mounting a feverish propaganda effort. In addition, higher level authorities usually dispatched work teams (*kung tso tui*) to the local levels to perform guidance and supervision functions.[1] Campaigns also resulted in a reallocation of funds and manpower to the crash programme from previously planned activities. More specifically, then, learning to cope with the campaign involved mastering such lessons as how to respond to the work team dispatched to one's unit, to judge correctly which associates were likely to be attacked during the campaign and to react accordingly

[1] For a detailed account of the work teams in action, and indeed the way an ideological campaign was run in the Kweichow Department of Machine Building Industries in June, 1966, see Kweiyang Radio, April 26, 1967. Previously unavailable in the mainland press, the account is particularly valuable because it confirms the details about ideological campaigns provided by emigrants.

The steps of a campaign are described in greater detail in A. Doak Barnett with Ezra Vogel, *Cadres, Bureaucracy, and Political Power in Communist China* (New York: Columbia Univ. Press, 1967), and Thomas P. Bernstein, "Leadership and Mass Mobilization in the Soviet and Chinese Collectivization Campaigns," *The China Quarterly*, No. 31 (July–September, 1967), pp. 1–47.

(such as by disassociating from the targets), to give immediate verbal support to the purposes of the campaign, and to admit to previous minor errors in the area being attacked in the campgain. For example, in a campaign against wastage of grain, it was wise to admit to a lack of frugality in the past, or in a campaign against bourgeois thought, it might sometimes be proper to admit to an excessive concern with clothes. Such admissions reduced the chances of being criticized for major errors, and indicated to peers and superiors that the campaign was having its intended effect.

The third "learn", to balance conflicting obligations, was perhaps an impossible lesson to master, for the obligations were often irreconcilable. The most keenly felt tension was between the obligations to politicized reference groups, such as co-workers or student groups, and the obligations to less politicized groups, such as the family or village. The balance struck between the time, effort and loyalty given to these groups depended not only upon one's values, but also upon government policy. During the mobilization phase, Chinese tended to place increased emphasis upon obligations to politicized groups. On the other hand, during consolidation phases, they were more able to fulfil obligations to the less politicized groups. Family outings, for example, were more prevalent during those times.

The Fifth Do: Set goals commensurate with one's talents and "virtues". This was essential for a happy life. Careers rested upon the Party's evaluations of talents and "virtues", with "virtue" including such factors as one's socio-economic background. For example, few choices in China invited frustration more readily than the decision by children from bourgeois or landlord background to pursue political goals.

The First Do Not: Avoid associations with "the five elements". By 1965, the rulers had designated five undesirable types of people: landlords, rich peasants, counter-revolutionaries, rightists, and bad elements. Individuals who were one of the five elements, were clearly marked and known to all. No matter what the goals, a career was jeopardized by associating too closely with any of them.

One informant stated that this rule extended to work assignments within the bureaucracy. Employment in the CCP United Front

Department, the Party organ handling religious and minority groups, was shunned in part because Party workers in this agency had to come into contact with less desirable elements in society.

Moreover, because people were judged by the company they kept, politically ambitious people tended not only to avoid dealing with the "five elements", but also to shun anyone whose political reliability was less than theirs. As a result, "activists" tended to associate with each other; they wanted nothing to do with "passive" or "wavering" elements. Party members with little seniority tended to stick together; they were reluctant to associate with activists who were not yet Party members. And senior Party members tended to feel most comfortable with one another; they were reluctant to welcome junior Party members into their midst.

The Second Do Not: Neither purchase luxury items nor engage in conspicuous consumption. The acquisition of expensive or superfluous items made Chinese vulnerable to charges of "bourgeois thought". A frugal existence was more in accord with the ethic encouraged by the regime. While this particular rule of conduct was frequently ignored by many people who spent their money on nice clothes, hair fashions, or art work—particularly in urban areas during bureaucratic phases—it is equally clear that such behaviour consistently invited criticism.

The Third Do Not: Avoid associating with foreigners or adopting foreign ideas.

The Fourth Do Not: Never utter remarks critical of the regime and particularly of Mao Tse-tung. The slogan of the United States Senate was applicable to China: "Them that goes along gets along." Remarks critical of the regime often were entered in one's dossier. Since the dossier was a constant companion, it was advisable to keep it as clean as possible.

While easily stated, the "Four Do Not's" were not easily obeyed. Particularly during the consolidation phase, many were tempted to purchase a rather expensive item or utter a disparaging remark about the government or strike up an acquaintanceship with a less desirable element In the subsequent mobilization phase, these actions frequently were recalled and diminished the chances of achieving one's goals.

IMPLICATIONS: THE LADDER OF SUCCESS
AND THE COMMUNIST REVOLUTION

If a revolutionary society is marked by rapid, violent social change, in which uncertainty and instability are the order of the day, then by 1965, China was no longer a revolutionary society. Life had become somewhat predictable. The life stages and the specific career options which Chinese faced had become set: first, the initial contact with the political system; then the selection of education and occupation; next, the pursuit of ambition; and, finally, the increased desire for security. The qualities surrounding such goals as political power, high income, respect, equity and justice, and security and quietude had become well defined. These goals tended to cluster into two groups—those which required extensive participation in politics, and those which were found outside the political system. Moreover, by the mid-sixties, the factors determining the chances of realizing career goals had become identifiable. Similarly, the skills required to survive or advance politically in China were clear—to be familiar with political affairs, to manage interpersonal relations well, and to be able to communicate effectively. Though the requisites for pursuing goals outside the political system were less clear, they appear to have involved acquiring technical or commercial skills. Finally, the strategies for success, which we have labelled the "Five Do's and Four Do Not's", were understood and practised by many. A ladder of success had emerged.

Unanswerable questions

Naturally, the impressionistic data employed for this exploratory study only enable a crude presentation. Many important questions simply must go unanswered at this stage of research. The operational code guiding behaviour of people working in different organizations or on different levels of the political hierarchy probably varied, but the precise variations remain elusive. Also exactly what explains the variation among individuals in their drive for power, wealth or respect necessitates further work on child rearing and educational experiences. Precisely what factors, in other words, determine an individual's response to the Chinese system and precisely what personality types were more likely to be blocked as they attempted to mount the hierarchy? Until research on these topics can be undertaken, we will not be able to say much more than has been said here about the personalities and backgrounds of those who pursued power in Communist China.

At best, the available information produces tantalizing ideas which can not be developed without additional data. One such idea results from noting that the relative importance of each of the "five do's and four do not's" varied through time. For instance, at times, pursuing material pleasures was the main object of attack, while at other times associating with foreigners was singled out as particularly vile behaviour. Since different "do's and do not's" were emphasized in each mobilization phase and since people were recruited into the political system during each mobilization phase, it is possible that people recruited during each mobilization phase had different strategic orientations.[1] Indeed, this idea may help to explain the apparent cohesiveness among people recruited during the same time span. Not only were they unified by their common experiences and equal seniority, but also by their similar operational codes. They understood each other. This hypothesis also may partly explain tensions among age cohorts in the CCP; each cohort may have had somewhat different strategic orientations. But considerably more and systematic interviewing is necessary before these observations can be fully developed.

In addition, the data do not permit a rigorous charting of trends. Indeed, though this article describes the ladder of success of the mid-1960's, many of the same phenomena were observable in the mid-fifties. The basic structure of opportunities and many of the "rules of the game", in fact, had taken shape by 1956–7.

Trends

Nonetheless, though hard to document, changes did occur from the mid-fifties to the mid-sixties. For example, the perceived value of particular goals appears to have changed through time. Apparently, the entire populace gradually became more aware that the pursuit of

---

[1] Credit for this important insight belongs to John Lewis.

power exacted a high toll, and by 1964–5, it had become a less attractive goal. (A case in point, the Lien-chiang documents contain reports of the reluctance of youths to become local cadres, fearing the trouble involved.) Moreover, it became more difficult to attain political power; at least, many observers of the Chinese politics have noted decreasing rates of upward mobility through time.[1] The difficulties associated with the pursuit of power may have encouraged more Chinese to opt for other goals.

Another likely trend seems to have been that with the stricter controls imposed upon migration to urban areas in 1956–7 and the reduction in middle school enrolments following the Great Leap, the PLA became an even more important avenue for mobility out of the countryside in the early 1960's than it was from 1955 to 1957.

The available information leaves the impression that perhaps the most important trend was the growing awareness throughout society of how to use the ladder of success for personal ends. With the widespread acquisition of the requisite skills for political survival and the "five do's and four do not's" becoming planted in mind, Chinese became increasingly conscious that they had to play one of four career games: (1) advance towards one's goals during the consolidation phase and try to hang on during the mobilization phase, a strategy played by those with technical and commercial skills and/or with the goals of knowledge, respect of non-Maoist peer groups and non-Maoist concepts of justice and equity; (2) attain goals during the mobilization phase and endure the consolidation phase, the strategy of those with political skills and/or with the goals of political power and construction of the Maoist society; (3) mount the ladder of success during both mobilization and consolidation phases, a dangerous game played by opportunists; and (4) retire, isolating oneself from the fluctuations in policy, a strategy played by those pursuing security and quietude. In extremely oversimplified terms, by the mid and late 1950's, the populace was learning the first gambit, although they had not yet mastered the

[1] See in particular A. Doak Barnett, *China after Mao*, (Princeton: Princeton University Press, 1967), pp. 70–1, 81–3, and *passim*; and John W. Lewis, "Political Aspects of Mobility in China's Urban Development", *The American Political Science Review*, LX (December, 1966), pp. 899–912.

techniques for hanging on during the mobilization phase. Many learned the second gambit during the Great Leap Forward. After the drastic swing in policy in 1957 and the disasters of the Great Leap Forward, increasing numbers were opting for the fourth ploy. And as the rules of the game became ever clearer, a few were even trying the third gambit.

The key factor enabling Chinese to develop life plans was the routinization of campaigns and small group activities. The Chinese populace, unaccustomed to the scope and intensity of these control techniques, did not know how to handle them in the early and mid 1950's. But gradually, many Chinese learned to cope with first the small group and then the campaigns. As already noted, since campaigns were conducted in similar ways, the populace learned to anticipate the steps of a campaign, and took appropriate countermeasures. Further, while Party bureaucrats initially appreciated the campaign for the increased power it gave them over remnant KMT government bureaucrats and the general populace, the Party bureaucrats gradually came to dislike the campaign for the disruptions and increased pressures it brought to their lives. Especially as a result of the Great Leap Forward campaign and its disastrous aftermath, through a variety of techniques, these bureaucrats attempted to subvert and delay campaign efforts. The Socialist Education Campaign of 1963–4 can be viewed as an effort by Mao and his associates to reinvigorate society and polity through another campaign, only to find that this technique had lost its effectiveness.[1] People had planned their lives to include the mobilization phase and the temporary reversals it might bring; moreover they had learned to keep these reversals to a minimum. (From this perspective, then, the Cultural Revolution can be seen as Mao's attempt to design a new organizational weapon to replace the no longer effective regular campaign.)

[1] For preliminary discussions, see Charles Neuhauser, "The Chinese Communist Party in the 1960's: Prelude to the Cultural Revolution", *The China Quarterly*, No. 32 (October–December, 1967), pp. 3–36; Richard Baum and Frederick C. Teiwes, *Ssu-ch'ing: The Socialist Education Movement of 1962–1966* (Berkeley; Centre for Chinese Studies, University of California, 1968); and my "Communist China: A Quiet Crisis in Revolution", in Franz Schurmann and Orville Schell, *The China Reader* (New York: Random House, 1967), III, 388–400.

Implications

The chief consequence of these trends was that the totalitarian regime, born in revolution, had begun to lose some of its capacity to mobilize the populace. Nor is this surprising. Karl Deutsch, for example, foresaw the process involved.[1] Deutsch said: "To elicit full identification and loyalty, a government must be to a considerable extent accessible and predictable." Moreover, he continued, "Predictability, in turn, implies the commitment of manpower and resources to the repetition of previous patterns of behavior which now have become expected, or to the carrying out of policies which have been previously promised." Deutsch concluded that: "the more predictable and expectable a government becomes, the less totalitarian it is likely to remain", for "as soon as the new commitments of resources mobilized by totalitarianism tend to become permanent, these resources are no longer completely available to the totalitarian regime".

In the case of China by the mid-sixties, then, the new network of customs and established expectations increasingly limited the range of decisions still open to totalitarian command. More specifically, the leaders of the CCP attempted to recruit dedicated members, enforce discipline, and direct an organization capable of fostering change, but for several reasons their task proved impossible. The Party, representing the best avenue for upward mobility, attracted opportunists. Younger idealists, imbued with the Maoist vision, often found themselves shunted aside, unable to make the contributions they wanted to make.

Further, CCP members had acquired a vested interest in the evolving system. Their life's plans rested upon the system's predictability. Far from being enthusiastic agents of social change, many CCP members could be expected to use their political skills and limited power to defend the system against radical efforts to change it. And as many CCP members aged and opted for the goals found outside the political system, the Party inevitably lost its revolutionary dynamism.

[1] Karl Deutsch, "Cracks in the Monolith: Possibilities and Patterns of Disintegration in Totalitarian Systems", in Carl J. Friedrich, ed., *Totalitarianism* (New York: Grosset & Dunlap, University Library Edition, 1964), pp. 308–33.

Moreover, though the Party varied in the degree of its penetration into different sectors of society, it is clear that the CCP's influence was felt by all Chinese. But as the CCP extended its network and became deeply embedded in Chinese society, its parts came to represent particular interests. For example, the rural CCP cadres to some extent voiced the interests of their local constituents. Or CCP cadres involved in directing heavy industries began to perceive that their interests coincided with the interests of their subordinates, upon whose performance their own leadership skills would be judged. The CCP was becoming a complex bureaucracy, with diverse constituencies and supporters, rather than a community composed of like-minded members whose interests coincided with those of the top leader.

Finally, as more people became aware of the unwritten "rules of the game", it became increasingly difficult for the rulers to elicit an immediate response from their subordinates and the populace. The rules were there, to be used by both superiors and subordinates. As subordinates became skilled in exploiting their meagre resources, the organizations which the rulers had structured to control society were being used as protection against the rulers' incessant demands. The organizational weapons were being turned against those who forged them.

The implications of these developments should be put in perspective. In 1949, a unified China emerged under one party rule; the Party was dedicated to mobilize the nation's resources for achieving rapid economic and social change. Fifteen years later, the single Party still had a monopoly of power. But in part due to the emergence of a stable, non-revolutionary society, with routine career patterns, the Party's capacity to mobilize the nation's resources appears to have diminished. The Chinese case suggests that a one-party regime cannot retain its capacity to mobilize the resources unless it deliberately fosters an unstable, revolutionary atmosphere.

347

PART IV

THE NEW VIEW OF POWER IN THE CULTURAL REVOLUTION

THE STATE OF COUNCIL AND THE CULTURAL REVOLUTION

DONALD W. KLEIN

This paper attempts to explore the status of the leading personnel in the State Council since the advent of the Cultural Revolution.[1] The State Council, of course, contains some of Peking's most famous personalities—such as Chou En-lai and Lin Piao—but my purpose here is to ignore for the most part the famed leaders and, rather, to dwell on a quantitative assessment of the entire body of 366 persons who were (in 1966) ministers and vice-ministers and chairmen and vice-chairmen of China's 49 ministries and commissions.[2] One might also describe this as a study of the focal point of "experts" in China, even though it is clear that the State Council does not have a monopoly on China's "expert" talents.[3]

The role of the State Council is too obvious to dwell upon at length, but a few remarks may be of use to give this paper its proper setting. Established in the autumn of 1949, the State Council[4] has met more regularly and more "publicly" than any other body in China. To be more exact, the Council met 385 times between 1949 and March, 1966, after which meetings were no longer announced (if, indeed, they have been held). Not surprisingly, it met more

[1] The date for the launching of the Cultural Revolution is a matter of dispute. For the purposes of this paper I have used the late spring of 1966 when large numbers of leaders fell from power, disappeared from the public scene, etc. The cut-off date for the study presented here is February 1968.

[2] For the sake of simplicity the term "ministry" is used below to refer to both the State Council ministries *and* commissions. Similarly, the terms "minister" and "vice-minister" include also the commission chairmen and vice-chairmen.

[3] It would have been useful to include the Academy of Sciences in this study, but a preliminary check revealed that there was too little biographic data about Academy personnel to draw meaningful conclusions.

[4] The Chinese cabinet was known as the Government Administration Council from 1949 to 1954, and since then as the State Council. I have used the latter term throughout the paper for the sake of simplicity.

frequently in the take-over and consolidation years. Thus, from 1949 to 1954 sessions were held on an average of almost one a week, but since 1954 they have been convened slightly more than once a month. The overall average (1949–66) works out to almost exactly twice a month. As might be expected, the Council agenda items, numbering roughly 850, cover virtually every topic imaginable. They also reflect a preponderant concern with domestic affairs over foreign affairs (running roughly at 80% vs. 20%). The State Council is perhaps unique among Chinese institutions in that its results, usually tersely stated, have been largely devoid of polemical or ideological content. The complete text of a hypothetical session would read as follows: "The State Council held its XXXth meeting today. Vice-Minister Li Li-li gave a report on coal production in the first half of the year, and after hearing a report by Vice-Minister Wang Wang-wang on the Sino-Soviet trade agreement for 1957, the agreement was ratified. The meeting also passed upon a number of appointments and dismissals." Taken individually, such information is of little value, but in aggregate terms it provides a considerable body of knowledge about the State Council and the specialities of the many ministers and vice-ministers.

The State Council is unique in another respect, and one which is pertinent to the methodology employed in this paper. It is the only institution that has regularly announced the appointment and dismissal of its subordinate personnel. While the record is not perfect, it approached the 99% mark until 1966—a fact which stands in contrast to the nightmarish problems of keeping abreast of personnel changes in the Chinese Communist Party (CCP), the People's Liberation Army (PLA), and many of the mass organizations. Thus it is possible to have a virtually perfect record of the State Council's ministers and vice-ministers at the outset of the Cultural Revolution.

As suggested by the types of subjects dealt with, the subordinate organs of the State Council have a preponderant orientation toward economic issues, and thus some three-quarters of the ministries and commissions are directly concerned with economic questions. This was true when the Council was established in 1949, and it remains true today. The ministries have doubled since 1949 (from

24 to 49), but the total number of ministers and vice-ministers has increased fivefold from 76 to 366.

By and large, the State Council has been marked by a rather high degree of continuity in terms of its personnel. Of the initial 76 ministers and vice-ministers, nine have died, but in 1966, 13 were still serving in the identical posts they held in 1949 and another 16 were ministers or vice-ministers in another ministry. In other words, 17 years after 1949 exactly half the original appointees were still senior officials in the Council's ministries. It should not be assumed that the other half had fallen from political power; on the contrary, aside from a few isolated purges, most of the remainder had advanced by 1966 to more senior posts in other political institutions, or, in the fashion of Premier Chou En-lai, had merely relinquished a concurrent ministerial portfolio (as Foreign Minister). This continuity of personnel, combined with the fact that the overwhelming majority of the appointees to State Council posts since 1949 gained on-the-job training in their special fields prior to their appointments, provides the rationale for regarding this institution as one of the focal points for "expert" talent in China.

Turning to the impact of the Cultural Revolution on the State Council, a few remarks must be made about methodological problems. This paper, which attempts to assess the status of the 366 ministers and vice-ministers, is based primarily on the author's own files which have been richly supplemented by the biographic files of the American Consulate General in Hong Kong, a collection of data on some 30,000 Chinese leaders. If the Chinese press in the post-1966 period had been as "open" as in the mid-fifties, one could assume a very high degree of accuracy for the figures cited in the following tables. Similarly, it will be apparent to all readers that our knowledge of the activities of ministers is considerably more detailed than our knowledge of vice-ministers. And there is, of course, far more information available about some ministries than others (e.g., the Foreign Ministry in contrast to one of the Machine Building ministries engaged in military production). Nonetheless, because virtually all ministers and vice-ministers work in Peking, we do not face the serious methodological problems encountered, for example, in attempting to assess the status of personnel in the provinces. In brief, although the numerous tables below tend to exude an air of statistical accuracy, it should be kept in mind that *they are at best approximations.*

One note on terminology should also be mentioned. I have used the word "criticized" to embrace all forms of accusations and the few cases where such criticism apparently ended in death or suicide. I have also used the word "rehabilitated" to cover the numerous situations where a man has been criticized but reappeared at a later date as a participant in the political processes. In a number of instances "rehabilitation" is clearly an exaggerated term, but I have used it consistently throughout this paper in an attempt to capture some degrees of statistical accuracy regarding the many cases where careers have fluctuated quite wildly through the stages of the Cultural Revolution.

ATTACKS ON STATE COUNCIL PERSONNEL—HOW WIDESPREAD?

We might begin the substance of this paper with a consideration of the level of criticisms directed against the 366 ministers and vice-ministers. Through mid-February 1968, the aggregate figures are as follows:

Table 1

Number of men	Criticized	Criticized but rehabilitated	Not criticized
366	152	30	214

Combining the last two figures, it would appear that two-thirds of the ministers and vice-ministers are still working at their posts. In fact, however, this is almost certainly a distorted presentation—first, because data on criticisms are certainly not complete and, secondly, because excessive periods of time have passed since the final appearance of many of the allegedly "uncriticized" and "rehabilitated" ministers and vice-ministers. Further refinements

354

of these figures should reflect a more accurate picture of the current viability of the State Council. Table II, which gives the dates of the *final* appearances of the 49 ministers, is structured by time periods to reflect the various stages of the Cultural Revolution.

Table II. *Final appearances of the 49 ministers*

1965 (Jan.–June)	1965 (July–Dec.)	1966 (Jan.–May)	1966 (June–Dec.)	1967 (Jan. June)	1967–8 –(July, 1967– Feb., 1968)
2 (4%)	1 (2%)	3 (6%)	17 (35%)	7 (14%)	19 (39%)

Thus nearly half of the ministers—a group of men who normally receive a great deal of attention in the press—have not been identified in public since the end of 1966. Moreover, and more important, some of the ministers who appeared in public *after* 1966 have been subsequently attacked (e.g. the Minister of the 7th Ministry of Machine Building). Therefore, it would be well to restructure these materials in the fashion set out in table III.

In other words, nearly half of the State Council's ministries are without a politically active minister.

We can move to another level of refinement by considering the entire universe of 366 ministers *and* vice-ministers, although it is completely evident that vice-ministers, even in the best of times, receive less attention in the press than the ministers. Because 58 (16%) of the vice-ministers have not appeared in public since 1964 or before, I have eliminated them from table IV on the grounds that their long absence from the public scene may be the result of illness, lack of data, etc.

The above modified sample demonstrates that roughly half of the ministers *and* vice-ministers have been missing from the public scene for about two years (i.e., since the late spring of 1966). It would be tempting to conclude that the 30% who have not appeared since the end of 1965 provides us with a retrospective "signal" that the Cultural Revolution was in the offing. Lo Jui-ch'ing

Table III. *Ministers (arranged by ministries)*

Uncriticized	Criticized but later "Rehabilitated"	Criticized but not "Rehabilitated"
Aquatic Products	Finance	Agriculture
Chemical Industry	Foreign Affairs	Allocation of Materials
Food	6th Ministry of	Building Construction
Foreign Trade	Machine Building	Building Materials
Forestry	8th Ministry of	Coal Industry
Geology	Machine Building	Commerce
Internal Affairs	National Defence	Communications
1st Ministry of	Petroleum Industry	Culture
Machine Building	Public Security	Education
2nd Ministry of	State Farms and Land	Higher Education
Machine Building	Reclamation	Labour
5th Ministry of	Commission for	2nd Ministry of Light
Machine Building	Economic Relations	Industry
Posts and	with Foreign	3rd Ministry of
Telecommunications	Countries	Machine Building
Textile Industry	Scientific and Techno-	4th Ministry of
Water Conservancy	logical Commission	Machine Building
Commission for	State Planning	7th Ministry of
Cultural Relations with	Commission	Machine Building*
Foreign Countries	Overseas Chinese	Metallurgical Industry
1st Ministry of	Affairs Commission*	Public Health
Light Industry		Railways
		Nationalities Affairs
		Commission
		Physical Education and
		Sports Commission
		State Capital Construc-
		tion Commission
		State Economic
		Commission
TOTALS: 15	12	22

* Based on information after February 1968, the Overseas Chinese Affairs Commission should be placed in the third column and the 7th Ministry of Machine Building should be placed in the second column. Thus, the totals remain the same.

is a case in point. But I would caution against such a conclusion and would suggest instead that the 30% figure results in the main from the weakness of our data.

Table IV. *Final appearance of 49 ministers and 259 vice-ministers (308 Men)*

1965 (Jan.– June)	1965 (July– Dec.)	1966 (Jan.– May)	1966 (June– Dec.)	1967 (Jan.– June)	1967–2 (July 1967– Feb. 1968)
42 (14%)	48 (16%)	49 (16%)	77 (25%)	31 (10%)	61 (20%)

Reorganizing the above materials, table V provides the final public appearance of *any* minister *or* vice-minister within a given ministry. It is, of course, virtually impossible to devise any chart that properly reflects the many complexities of the Cultural Revolution, and the following compilation is no exception. Therefore, it is important to make some qualifying remarks. No reader will be surprised to see that the Ministry of Education seems to be out of business as a political institution. On the other hand, whereas one of the vice-ministers of Public Health appeared in public as late as May, 1967, neither the minister nor the five other vice-ministers has appeared since November, 1966. Similarly, one of the vice-ministers of Culture appeared as late as October, 1967, but the last appearance of *any* of the other 10 officials is December, 1966.

We might make yet another attempt to gain insight into the viability of the 49 ministries by restructuring the material in still another manner. Table VI is designed to answer the question: In which of the ministries have half or more of the personnel (i.e., the minister and vice-ministers) become inactive because of Cultural Revolution-generated attacks? (Counting both the minister and vice-ministers, each ministry has an average of nearly eight men.)

Combining the two columns in table VI, it seems evident that a number of vice-ministers were caught in the politically awkward position of serving as principal targets of the Cultural Revolution. This is particularly pointed in the Ministry of Culture (headed by Lu Ting-i), the State Economic Commission (chaired by Po I-po) the Nationalities Affairs Commission (chaired by Ulanfu), the Physical Culture and Sports Commission (chaired by Ho Lung).

357

Table v. Last public appearances (ministers or vice-ministers) by ministries

1965	1966	1967 (Jan.–June)	1967 (July–Dec.)	1968
Aug.: Labour	*Oct.:* Education	*May:* Commerce, 1st Ministry of Machine Building, 5th Ministry of Machine Building, 7th Ministry of Machine Building, Public Health, Nationalities Affairs Commission, State Capital Construction Commission	*July:* 4th Ministry of Machine Building, 6th Ministry of Machine Building, Textiles Industry	*February:* Foreign Trade, Finance, Foreign Affairs, National Defence, Petroleum Industry, Posts and Telecommunications, Public Security, Commission for Cultural Relations with Foreign Countries
	Nov.: Higher Education, Allocation of Materials, Building Materials, 1st Ministry of Light Industry, 2nd Ministry of Light Industry, 2nd Ministry of Machine Building		*August:* Metallurgical Industry, State Economic Commission	
			September: Railways	
			October:	

3rd Ministry of
Machine Building

June:
Agriculture
Building Construction

Aquatic Products
Coal Industry
Culture
Food
Forestry
Internal Affairs
8th Ministry of Machine Building
State Farms and Land
Reclamation
Water Conservancy
Overseas Chinese Affairs
Commission

November:
Chemical Industry

December:
Communications
Geology
Physical Culture and Sports
Commission

Commission for
Economic Relations
with Foreign
Countries
Scientific and Techno-
logical Commission
State Planning
Commission

Table VI[1]

Ministries in which more than half of the personnel have been attacked	Ministries in which exactly half of the personnel have been attacked
Culture	Building Materials
Education	Coal Industry
Labour	Higher Education
3rd Ministry of Machine Building	2nd Ministry of Light Industry
Public Health	
State Economic Commission	
Scientific and Technological Commission	
Nationalities Affairs Commission	
Physical Culture and Sports Commission	

Lu's Ministry reveals 9 of his 10 vice-ministers as "victims"; the figures for Po's Commission are 7 out of 12; in Ulanfu's Commission they read 3 out of 6; and in Ho Lung's Commission there are 4 out of 7 vice-ministers out of operation. This correlation, however, breaks down in Nieh Jung-chen's Scientific and Technological Commission. Nieh has been under fire a number of times, but a strong case can be made that he has emerged during the Cultural Revolution in a political position of greater strength than before it began. Nonetheless his Commission has been one of the most severely hit, with seven of his nine deputies no longer in action. It is less easy to link ministers and vice-ministers in the other ministries included on table VI, but in some cases (e.g., the Ministries of Education and Higher Education) it seems evident that the institution rather than the man is under attack. On the more positive side, it appears that over half of the ministers/vice-ministers are politically active in about 32 ministries (i.e., about 65% of all the ministries).

It should be clear, then, that a large number of men have been under fire because of their affiliation with the leading "victims" of the Cultural Revolution, and that another significant group has fallen because of its affiliation with "institutions" that have been under heavy attack—particularly those associated with culture

[1] Because the 2nd and 7th Ministries of Machine Building had no vice-ministers as of 1966, they have been excluded from table VI.

and education. Turning the question around, we might ask if any cluster of ministries has been "protected" during the Cultural Revolution. Efforts to manipulate the data have been uniformly uninstructive in this regard. For example, one might hypothesize that the defence-related ministries were shielded. Assuming that 12 ministries represent the hard core of defence-related ministries (Chemical Industry, the eight Machine Building Ministries, Metallurgical Industry, Petroleum Industry, and the Railways ministry), we find about three-quarters of the ministers and vice-ministers still active in contrast to about two-thirds for the entire sample. In view of the fact that we have always had less data about defence-related ministries, I would assume that this rather slight statistical variation is without real meaning.

It would be particularly useful if we could draw correlations based on policy considerations, e.g. emphases on heavy vs. light industry, the allocation of resources, agriculture vs. industry. There have, in fact, been some interesting suggestions in selected fields. For instance, in the culture–education sphere there was apparently a major debate centring around the issue of vocational schools (the "Red vs. expert" question). However, using our aggregate cases for the entire State Council, the attacks on the vast majority of the personnel are phrased in such polemical terms that it has not been possible to draw any correlations of significance. One presumes that a more detailed study of Red Guard materials in this connection may result in important findings.

Summarizing the comments and tables thus far, we might make these generalizations. Something upwards of one-half of the State Council's ministers and vice-ministers seem to be politically active, although as time passes these figures will probably require revisions unless a genuine stability returns to the PRC. It is more difficult to make generalizations about the ministries, but one might hazard the opinion that at least a half a dozen are defunct and perhaps another dozen or so are perilously close to being inoperative or at least are severely lacking in day-to-day leadership.

I stated at the outset that it was not my purpose to dwell upon the more famed leaders who work in the State Council. However, it might be useful at this juncture to take note of the fact that Party

Central Committee members and alternates in the State Council have fared somewhat less well than their non-Central Committee colleagues. It appears that only five out of 47 have escaped criticism. Sixteen more were criticized but later "rehabilitated". Most important, however, is the fact that over half of them (26 out of 47) were criticized and have subsequently disappeared from the public scene.

From this point we can move to a series of other considerations that will hopefully cast some light on the workings of the State Council since the Cultural Revolution began.

PARTY VS. NON-PARTY PERSONNEL

It is well known that the original (1949) Chinese cabinet contained a high percentage of non-Communists—presumably to demonstrate a United Front posture and to draw on some highly qualified expert talent. Perhaps less well known, though hardly surprising, is the fact that after the consolidation years the number of non-Communists in the State Council dwindled sharply. Thus, in 1949, 58% of the ministers and vice-ministers were Communists, and 42% were non-Party persons. But in 1966 these figures read 87% and 13% for those on whom we have information about Party affiliation. (Inferential evidence suggests that the CCP percentage would be considerably higher if we had complete information.) Nonetheless, one of the most easily documented (and perhaps most ironic) facts about the Cultural Revolution is that the non-Party ministers and vice-ministers have come through the turmoil almost unscathed. To be exact, of the 38 men in question, only two of them have been criticized and one of these was "rehabilitated" thereafter. In a period of such great strains and stresses, I would find it difficult to accept the notion that the powers-that-be would concern themselves with the niceties of maintaining the United Front posture. Rather, it was probably a fairly easy solution to short-term problems to maintain the talents of a group of men who did not aspire to political power (as opposed to administrative authority) and who, in any event, were quite elderly. In any case, it is evident that the non-Party "democrats" have fared remarkably well.

THE MILITARY ELEMENT IN THE STATE COUNCIL

In view of the vastly increased authority of the PLA, it is relevant to ask if this could have been anticipated by examining State Council appointments made on the eve of the Cultural Revolution. This is also prompted by the many raised eyebrows in the spring of 1965 when some military men were appointed to the Ministry of Culture. Or, to put this question in its bluntest form: is there any evidence suggesting that Lin Piao was able to "pack" the State Council? To test this proposition the careers were examined of the 60 men newly appointed as ministers or vice-ministers from January, 1965 to March, 1966.[1] Only five of these 60 men had been transferred from a military assignment to the State Council, whereas the balance (i.e. 90%) could be described as normal career advances. Even among the five military men, common sense seemed to dictate the appointment in certain cases; thus Wang Ping-chang, an Air Force deputy commander, was made Minister of the 7th Ministry of Machine Building which is responsible for the manufacture of aircraft. Moreover, at least three of the five "new" military men have already fallen victim to the Cultural Revolution. In short, there is strikingly little evidence to suggest that the PLA tried or was successful in infusing a significant element of military personnel into the State Council on the eve or in the earliest phases of the Cultural Revolution. In this respect the State Council stands in very sharp contrast to the provincial "revolutionary committees" which contain a very high percentage of career military officers. Or, to cast this in another fashion: Even though something on the order of half of the State Council's ministers and vice-ministers have become victims of the Cultural Revolution, there is little evidence to suggest that the PLA has served as a reservoir of personnel to *replace* the fallen ministers and vice-ministers.

REGIONALISM AND THE STATE COUNCIL

Because of the degree of "regionalism" that is now apparent, it may also be relevant to test this proposition in terms of the

[1] No appointments have been made since the State Council held its last "formal" meeting on March 9, 1966.

State Council. Regionalism, of course, can take many forms, but the purpose here is to test the proposition that one or more of the key regional leaders in the take-over period (e.g., Teng Hsiao-p'ing in the Southwest or Li Hsien-nien in Central-South China) was able to "pack" the State Council following his transfer to Peking. The first step was to ascertain the working locale of the 366 ministers and vice-ministers (information being available for 80% of the sample). Dividing China into the six administrative units that existed in the early years of the People's Republic, in addition to a category for those who worked in the central organs in Peking, we find the percentages shown in table VII:

Table VII. *Working locale of the 366 ministers and vice-ministers in the early fifties (percentages)*

Centre	East China	Central-South	Northeast	North China	Southwest	Northwest
37	16	14	11	10	7	6

None of these figures seems to suggest that a regional leader was able to place a disproportionate share of "his men" in Chou En-lai's State Council. Rather, they seem to reflect the spread of China's population density, as well as the presumed fact that a fairly significant number of men were assigned to Peking on the basis of the technical experience they gained in East and Central-South China (e.g., Shanghai, Wuhan and Canton). Turning this proposition around, we might ask if there were significant figures revealed by an examination of those "criticized" during the Cultural Revolution who were not later "rehabilitated". The first row of table VIII repeats the percentages of table VII, below which are placed the percentages of those criticized.

These percentages are so remarkably similar that they should lay to rest any notion that one particular group of regional leaders bore the brunt of the criticisms and purges resulting from the Cultural Revolution. One hastens to add, of course, that these figures are confined to the State Council, and consequently tell us nothing about possible regional factors in play in other key organs of power.

Table VIII. *Working locale of the 366 ministers and vice-ministers compared with those criticized during the Cultural Revolution (percentages)*

Centre	East China	Central-South	Northeast	North China	Southwest	Northwest
37	16	14	11	10	7	6
31	17	11	13	13	7	9

THE "DECEMBER 9TH CLIQUE"

Amidst the numerous charges and countercharges, "criticisms" and "rehabilitations", it is not easy to identify specific groups that have been singled out as prime targets of the Cultural Revoluttion. There is, however, one very notable exception: the "December 9th Clique". A few words of explanation are required. On December 9, 1935, large numbers of students in Peking (at Peking University, Tsinghua, etc.) staged massive demonstrations against the steady Japanese encroachments upon Chinese sovereignty. From this date until the outbreak of war in mid-1937, the students formed a number of highly active organizations. Although the Communists almost certainly played no role in the initial demonstrations in 1935, they quickly moved in to rally the students to their cause. Among the key Party figures involved in the recruiting and the guidance of these students were P'eng Chen and Liu Shao-ch'i. When war erupted scores of the "December 9th" students went to Yenan, and in the early years of the People's Republic of China they more or less dominated the key organs of the New Democratic Youth League (later the Communist Youth League). Then, by the mid-1950's, presumably because they were among the best educated of the Communist leaders, many of these men (then in their early forties) were transferred to State Council. They also made progress in Party channels, and by 1958 six of their numbers were full or alternate members of the Party Central Committee.

For obvious reasons we do not know the complete "membership" of the "December 9th" group, but nonetheless about sixty have been identified as politically active since 1949. Their inability to survive the turmoil of the Cultural Revolution is striking. In general, the "December 9th" cadres have worked principally in technically oriented or educational posts. In view of the fact that practically all educational institutions have come under severe attack, it is not surprising that these former North China students have suffered politically. Perhaps more surprising, particularly in light of the widely held notion that science and technology have been largely shielded from the Cultural Revolution purges, a significant number of the "December 9th" group holding technically oriented posts have been attacked.

Turning in more specific terms to the State Council, at the outset of the Cultural Revolution 18 members of the "December 9th" clique were ministers or vice-ministers in the State Council. Thirteen of the 18 have been sharply criticized, and three of the other five have not made public appearances since the launching of the Cultural Revolution. A simple listing of the posts held by the 13 presumably purged should suffice to indicate their importance:

Ministers	Vice-ministers
Higher Education	Petroleum Industry
1st Ministry of Machine Building	Scientific and Technological Commission (2 men)
Commerce	Public Health
	State Economic Commission (2 men, one of whom is concurrently a vice-minister of the Ministry for the Allocation of Materials)
	Higher Education
	Aquatic Products
	Commission for Cultural Relations with Foreign Countries
	Physical Culture and Sports Commission

It might be noted in passing that four of the above were Party Central Committee alternate members, and assuming their removal, the "December 9th" group had lost *all* its seats on the Central Committee. It is also of interest that another dozen men (who did not work in the State Council) have been specifically criticized, and not a single one has reappeared. Among them is Lu P'ing, who came into instant fame in the late spring of 1966 as the President of Peking University, one of the chief targets of the Cultural Revolution. Moreover, with a few exceptions, another 30-odd men, although not specifically attacked, have disappeared from the public scene. Because of ties with Liu Shao-ch'i and P'eng Chen stretching back three decades, it is not surprising that many of the charges made against the "December 9th" group were directly linked to Liu and P'eng. In short, it appears that one of the most able and well-educated groups within the Chinese Communist leadership has suffered a severe blow.

FOREIGN AFFAIRS

Because foreign affairs are the responsibility of the State Council in the most formal sense, we might examine briefly the impact of the Cultural Revolution on the Foreign Ministry. Foreign Minister Ch'en I has been under fire on numerous occasions, but he seems to have survived politically in spite of these attacks. One can make a persuasive case that Peking's foreign relations are in shambles, but the case is more complex than that. In early 1966, on the eve of the Cultural Revolution, the Chinese had embassies in 48 nations. In terms of personalities, there were three vacant ambassadorial posts, 40 ambassadors abroad, and five chargés d'affaires abroad.[1] The recall of ambassadors (which must be distinguished from the formal removal of the ambassadors from their posts) coincides tidily with the various crucial stages of the Cultural Revolution. Thus, about twenty ambassadors returned home in the latter part of 1966, about ten more returned in early 1967, and another handful

[1] Three chargés d'affaires a.i. were in the U.S.S.R., Yugoslavia, and India; it is clear, however, that the absence of an ambassador is the result of Peking's diplomatic "warfare" with these three nations over the past several years. For the purposes of this paper I have regarded these three men as "ambassadors". Similarly, I have regarded the two men who head the "offices of the chargé d'affaires" (in England and Netherlands) as ambassadorial equivalents.

returned in the spring and summer of 1967. In short, by the early autumn of 1967 Peking had its ambassadors in only two countries— the United Arab Republic and India. (This situation had not changed by early 1968.) With the recall of ambassadors from all but two countries, we obviously cannot draw any conclusions in terms of policy considerations *vis-à-vis* any grouping of nations. The withdrawals were clearly based on domestic considerations. Since their return to Peking, 10 of the 45 ambassadors have appeared in public—normally described simply as the ambassador to "X" country (and usually in connection with the visit to China of important leaders from that country). One might suppose that in the months to come more of these "ex-ambassadors" will again emerge, but as of early 1968 the situation is inconclusive.

It may be more pertinent to ask if China's missions abroad are still operative—particularly in view of the many suggestions in the press (usually implicit rather than explicit) that a number of embassies have been closed. Here the answer is an unqualified "yes". With the exceptions of Ghana and Tunisia, both of which severed diplomatic ties with Peking, the Chinese have maintained their embassies in all other nations. They have, to be sure, cut their personnel to an apparent bare minimum, but in all cases their diplomats continue to operate. In this regard it is interesting to note that the quasi-official missions in Japan, Italy, and Chile (devoted mainly to promoting trade) are also still operating. Parenthetically, it should be noted that the Ministry of Foreign Trade, which organizationally has fared reasonably well during the Cultural Revolution, has continued to conduct trade negotiations and has sent some of its vice-ministers abroad to conclude trade agreements. Obviously, however, this work has been impeded in a number of ways.

In the meantime, the Foreign Ministry in Peking has witnessed troubled days, particularly in the summer of 1967 when for a few days it appeared that some overzealous Red Guards were in almost complete control of the ministry. Within a few days this chaotic situation was remedied (however imperfectly), and as of early 1968 the Foreign Ministry was operating with some degree of normality. Returning to our consideration of ministers and vice-ministers, we have already taken note of Ch'en I's status. Of Ch'en's 10 vice-ministers, three have apparently escaped criticism, and another three have been criticized but have subsequently returned to the political scene. Of interest in this connection is the fact that Chang Han-fu, one of Chou En-lai's oldest colleagues, has fallen victim to the Cultural Revolution.

The viability of Peking's foreign relations, as examined in the light of other State Council-controlled mechanisms, can be tested in still another manner. First, a word of explanation. Beginning in 1952 the Chinese began establishing bilateral scientific and technological committees with the other Communist nations. The committee sessions have alternated between Peking and the foreign capitals concerned, and they have normally met every six to twelve months. Each side has a chairman for its "group", and in the Chinese case this post has almost invariably been held by one of the vice-ministers of the State Council. As might be expected from the nature of the work (the exchange of technical personnel, blueprints, etc.), the ministries concerned have had a strongly technical orientation (e.g. Petroleum Industry). In view of the seemingly chaotic state of Chinese Communist foreign relations, it would not be unreasonable to assume that these joint committees had ceased to function since the start of the Cultural Revolution. In fact, however, no less than 14 sessions have been convened (some in Peking, some abroad) with 10 Communist nations.[1] Moreover, the time lapse since the previous meetings has been only slightly longer than normal. In all but one instance the Chinese chairman has been "predictable", i.e., a vice-minister from one of the technically oriented ministries. Even the exception, Miss Chang Pen, has had technically oriented experience, having served in the early and mid-fifties as deputy director of the East China Textile Administration Bureau.[2]

CONCLUSION

Because the Cultural Revolution remains in progress, no one can

[1] Mongolia is the only Communist nation that has not held a meeting with the Chinese since the inauguration of the Cultural Revolution.
[2] I am indebted to Heath Chamberlain who brought Chang's earlier career to my attention.

predict the ultimate fate of the Chinese cabinet. It is possible that the campaign might peter out in the near future, followed by a return to relative normality by the State Council. Another possibility would be further upheavals, coupled with a transfer of State Council authority to other more "revolutionary" organs. A third possibility might be a continued "limping along" upon the present lines, with the avenues of authority ill-defined and with some tasks usurped by other institutions.

In considering these possibilities, we might focus on two major considerations, one of them in terms of personalities and the other in terms of institutions and some tenets of political modernization. The personality consideration naturally centres on Chou En-lai who for nineteen long years has headed the Chinese civil bureaucracy. Now in his seventieth year, Chou has already managed to survive a succession of crises. If we can believe the numerous Red Guard accounts of his actions over the past two years, he has felt compelled to "defend" many of his key subordinates on countless occasions. But there is little to suggest that he has attempted (or perhaps dared) to defend those of his subordinates working in the critical "soft spot" of the State Council—the educational and cultural spheres. One might even speculate that as part of a bargain with the Mao–Lin elements, Chou was forced to sacrifice his educational–cultural specialists in favour of some degree of protection for his host of other specialists. But if the sanctity of the State Council rests upon the political agility of one man, then it is indeed in far greater trouble than any of the data suggest.

Turning to institutional considerations, we can note that the State Council continued to issue directives, usually in conjunction with the CCP Central Committee and the Party's Military Affairs Committee. But it is difficult to know, in fact, if this is an indication of institutional viability or the personification of the dominant personalities of Mao Tse-tung, Lin Piao, and Chou En-lai. It also appears that the State Council continued to hold meetings, but these were certainly less routinized than in the pre-1966 period, and we have virtually no idea of the specific agenda items. In terms of personnel, at the minister/vice-minister level the State Council is "frozen". As already noted, Chou En-lai seems to have been able to prevent the intrusion of new personnel from other organs of power, but there are absolutely no signs that he has been able to promote personnel within his own organ of power. This is best illustrated by the unprecedented delay in filling three ministerial vacancies (which presently exist in the Ministries of Foreign Trade and Textile Industry, and the 3rd Ministry of Machine Building).

At a broader level, we might begin with the proposition (however unlikely) that China could exist without a Communist Party, but it could not exist without a central civil bureaucracy. This, of course, is a very un-Maoist thought and the very antithesis of the spirit of the Cultural Revolution. Yet even Maoists must rely on more than the Little Red Book if they are to pursue the admittedly ill-defined goals generally subsumed under the concept of "modernization". David Apter's comments, though somewhat out of context here, seem highly relevant: "Civil servants, through their expertise and the modes of organization, comprise the single most important group for the translation of government policy into social practice. But they are a difficult group for political leaders to deal with or assimilate because...they are generally better educated than the politicians...and...have a greater security of tenure, which creates a totally different outlook."[1] Apter also writes that: "Ultimately, the modernizing elites must accept an ideology of science (whether or not they accept nationalism or socialism at the same time). This type of ideology is based on the need for information, verification, experimentation and empiricism. Modernizing elites must also accept rules of eligibility based on technical expertise."[2] If one accepts these propositions, then one must also grant that the Chinese cabinet represents a permanent "opposition" group as opposed to an institutionalized "political opposition". In using these terms I rely on the subtle but highly useful distinctions drawn by Ionescu in his study of the European Communist states, as well as those discussed by Franz Schurmann. Ionescu's broad definition is sub-divided into the "conflict of interest which originates from the friction and rivalry between groups within the community" and the "conflict of values,

[1] David E. Apter, *The Politics of Modernization* (Chicago: Univ. of Chicago Press, 1965), p. 167.
[2] *Ibid.* p. 175.

...which originates logically from the incompatibility of opinions, outlook and beliefs among people of different allegiances and mentalities..." These are differentiated from "political opposition" which is "institutionalized, recognized and legitimate".[1] In a similar vein Schurmann distinguished between Kao Kang-type "factionalism" as opposed to "opinion groups" held by such alleged economic "conservatives" as Ch'en Yün.[2]

In assessing the future of the Chinese civil bureaucracy, these are useful tools of analysis. At a minimum they should be more fruitful than past analyses which have simply viewed the State Council as one of the major elements in the "power structure" or as the personification of Chou En-lai's role in Chinese Communist history. Returning to Apter's propositions, one might argue that the Chinese Communists could disband the central civil bureaucracy. But this would jeopardize many modernization goals, and sooner or later some sort of "civil servant" institutionalization would certainly reappear, whatever its nomenclature. Therefore, we can assume a basic continuation of an institution that will be characterized as a focal point of "expert" talent and will in varying degrees continue to express differing interests and values.

[1] Ghita Ionescu, *The Politics of the European Communist States* (New York: Praeger, 1967), pp. 2–3.

[2] Franz Schurmann, *Ideology and Organization in Communist China* (Berkeley and Los Angeles: Univ. of California Press, 1966), p. 56.

ARMY–PARTY RELATIONS IN THE LIGHT OF THE CULTURAL REVOLUTION

JOHN GITTINGS

Most students of Chinese affairs would probably agree that the Cultural Revolution has administered a salutary shock to them, forcing a reappraisal of both their basic assumptions and the conclusions which they have thereby reached. Those who study Chinese military affairs have been as much affected as anyone else. The dismissal of Marshal P'eng Te-huai in 1959, and subsequent attempts to "reverse the verdict" against him, constitute a sort of *Leitmotif* to which the Cultural Revolutionary orchestra constantly returned, and it led to a very comprehensive exposé in the Chinese press of his "criminal activities" extending back over many decades (and also of the crimes of ex-Chief of Staff Lo Jui-ch'ing and of a number of other prominent military leaders). These revelations, if taken at face value, are so far-reaching as to suggest the necessity for a reversal of our own verdicts on much of the history of the People's Liberation Army (PLA).

In point of fact, when we allow for the degree of bias and distortion contained in these revelations, they do not appear to affect the basic validity of the more important conclusions generally reached about the PLA. While some of these conclusions may appear slightly eccentric in the light of what has happened since 1966, this is largely explained by the very eccentric course which the Cultural Revolution itself has followed. But it is probably true that hitherto, through lack of information and also through lack of primary research, we have tended to look at the role of the PLA very much from a macroscopic view, perhaps emphasizing those aspects of the system making for general unity and harmony, while paying insufficient attention to the localized points within the system at which disunity and discord may have been generated. The evidence provided by the polemics of the Cultural Revolution obviously goes to the other extreme, but it does give us the chance to use, if not a microscope, at least a magnifying lens in order to focus in greater detail upon the PLA and its relations with the Chinese Communist Party (CCP).

Yet before attempting to bring this relationship into sharper focus, it is incumbent upon us to ask what it actually consists of—a question which is not as easy to answer as it sounds. For the Army–Party relationship assumes so many different facets, depending on which way we look at it, that it may rapidly transport us into the realm of metaphysics. At its simplest level, the relationship may be viewed as one between two discrete but interlocking systems, which can be portrayed without too much difficulty in diagrammatic form. Thus it can be established that the Chinese Communists have used and adapted a pattern of political control over their armed forces which originated with that of the Soviet Union after the 1917 Revolution, and which in turn was heavily copied by the Chinese Nationalists in the 1920's (when the Communists derived their first-hand experience of it).

The bare bones of this relationship, however, still need to be fleshed out by a number of less tangible variables, stemming both from the changes in role and responsibility of both Party and Army over a period of four decades, and also from the impact of individuals within the systems, and their own assessments of what roles they should play and what allegiances they should owe.

A static view, in other words, of the relationship between Party and Army, whether it is seen as one of essential harmony or rather as one of continuing rivalry and contest for power, is far from sufficient for our purposes. Changes in the balance between these two systems may be dictated to some extent by whatever happened to be the dominant political or military priority of the moment. Thus during the Korean War, the PLA enjoyed considerable latitude and freedom from political demands under the slogan of "Everything for the Front". After the war came to an end, and the nation returned to the task of peace-time rehabilitation, the PLA's privileged status was progressively whittled away.

The allegiance of individuals within either system was also likely to vary according to the particular responsibilities which they held at the time. As will be shown later on, it is extremely hard to identify the majority of officials either in the PLA or in the Party as being immutably committed to either system. During the Revolution, such people often alternated their service between one policy area and the other; or held positions which might involve concurrent responsibility for military, political and government affairs. By the mid-1950's, the roles of most officials had become more narrowly defined and specialized, but up to the present day a degree of interchangeability has persisted between these three major spheres of power. The case of each individual, strictly speaking, has to be considered on its merits, and we are often obliged to fall back on guesswork in seeking to establish which weighs most in his mind, his past affiliations and personal connections, or his current responsibilities in what may be a very different field from the one to which he was accustomed. A further variable—and one which has come to the fore in the Cultural Revolution—is the degree to which an individual's loyalty to the "centre" in Peking may override his more personal allegiances or even, perhaps, his own better judgement as to what the "correct" policy in his area of responsibility may be.

These complex considerations should be borne in mind in any two-dimensional discussion of the relationship between "Party" and "Army", although it would be impossible—for reasons of space alone—to invoke them in this paper at every stage of the argument. The main questions which will be discussed in these pages relate, rather, to additional areas of complexity which have been underlined, revealed, or hinted at, during the course of the Cultural Revolution, and which present at least a *prima facie* case for "reversing the verdicts" on some of the somewhat bland assumptions often held by outside observers—including this writer—in the past about the state of Army–Party relations.

Most serious writing on the PLA in recent years has portrayed its role in the Chinese revolution and post-Liberation as one which is basically harmonious with the ruling Communist Party and well-adjusted within itself.[1] While this does not exclude the existence at

[1] I am limiting my discussion of the revolutionary period in this paper to the years of the anti-Japanese and civil wars, after the Long March. This was the formative period of the PLA as we know it; it is also the period on which the historical myth of "Army–Party unity" is based.

various times in the PLA's history of sources of tension and conflict, and even of a continuing contradiction between the rival demands of military and political priorities, it is generally agreed that the conflict has been minimized with remarkable success for the most part, and that the contradiction has usually been kept on a "non-antagonistic" level, with rare exceptions. Certainly by comparison with what might have happened, one is impressed by a high degree of stability and continuity in this relationship. The following three features have been frequently commented upon:

1. The overall continuity of military leadership and a low level of discord between it and the Party leadership.

2. At lower levels (i.e. regional and below) a lack of separatism and autonomism of the kind associated with the "warlord" period, and even with the period under Kuomintang (KMT) rule, and a low incidence of friction between military and party/government organs.

3. The success with which official policies have been imposed or impressed upon the PLA by means of the system of political indoctrination and control. Here a greater variety of conflicting opinions between the military and political viewpoints is admitted, but it is usually thought to have been kept within tolerable limits.

The question now arises as to how far these formulations stand up to the evidence revealed by the Cultural Revolution, and if they are still correct, whether they still hold true for the actual period of the Cultural Revolution itself. In other words, have we been deluded by the picture, so consistently projected by the Chinese for decades, of an all-pervasive "Army–Party unity", and if not, what has caused this unity to break down during the Cultural Revolution?

ARMY–PARTY LEADERSHIPS

Personal relations

For years the Chinese have been saying that their army is not an army of the bourgeoisie but an army of the proletariat, that it does not represent the old militaristic traditions of the warlords and of the KMT, but the new revolutionary traditions of socialism, that it does not therefore, nor can it in the future, pose a threat to the leading role of the Communist Party. The epithet "warlord", when it has been used in connection with the army, refers to relatively minor manifestations of anti-social behaviour, not to the much more serious crime of military separatism. There have only been two occasions in the history of the CCP since the Tsunyi Conference of 1935 when first echelon leaders have been accused of genuine warlordism—of seeking to establish their own "independent kingdom". Both cases, those of Chang Kuo-t'ao and Kao Kang, fall far short of what is usually meant by the term.

Now, perhaps somewhat to our surprise, all those military leaders who have come unstuck in the Cultural Revolution are being accused of precisely those attributes which were previously said to be un-thinkable in a people's army—personal ambition, fostering of cliques, arrogance and a penchant for fame and publicity, disdain for central and political authority, and "warlordism" itself.

Thus Chu Te, the father of the Red Army, is now described as "a big warlord who has wormed his way into the Party", and is accused of having had commissioned a laudatory biography of himself, in order "to take the merit that belonged to Heaven as his own", and to advertise himself as "the founder of the Red Army" and as "the great leader of the Chinese people".[1]

Ho Lung has similarly been denounced for having always been "extremely arrogant", and for having "stuck to the reactionary stand of feudal landlords and harboured and encouraged bad men".[2] A string of charges has been levelled against P'eng Te-huai's revolutionary career, a great number of which accuse him of engag-ing in foolhardy and adventuristic military campaigns (including the Hundred Regiments campaign of the winter of 1940) in order to satisfy his "individual ambitions" and to increase his "personal

[1] "Confession of Chu Te, Man of Vaulting Ambition to Usurp the Party and the Army", *Hsin Pei ta* [New Peking University], No. 39, February 16, 1967, *Current Background*, No. 822. The same magazine condemned Chu for having displayed feudal filial piety in mourning the death of his mother in 1944. Contemporary issues of the Yenan *Chieh fang jih pao* [Liberation Daily] carried several eulogies, now said to have been commissioned by Chu, in memory of "Mother Chu".

[2] "Towering Crimes of Ho Lung, Anti-Party Element and Army Usurper", *T'i yu chan hsien* [Sporting Front] (Peking) January 28, 1967, in *SCMP*, No. 3912.

influence".[1] It has been claimed that Lo Jui-ch'ing's "world out-look" was one of "bourgeois extreme individualism", and that "In pursuit of personal gain and power and position, he unscrupulously did all wicked things..."[2] Finally Yang Ch'eng-wu, who succeeded Lo as Acting Chief of Staff and was dismissed in March, 1968, was accused by Lin Piao in person of "mountain-stronghold mentality", and was alleged to have "ousted or removed" three-quarters of his colleagues in the Chin-Ch'a-Chi border region during the civil war.[3]

Perhaps the most interesting feature about these charges is the simple fact that they are made; that the sins of these disgraced military leaders should be described in language which so strongly reminds one of the standard denunciations of would-be "usurpers" in dynastic China. Another aspect of this with similar historical overtones is the alleged attempt at self-glorification by means of tampering with written documents or fabrication of plays, films and novels portraying the chief protagonist in a flattering light. P'eng Te-huai is described as having encouraged the publication of a novel on the North-West campaign in the civil war which "distorted historical facts", in order to "shamelessly glorify" him as a "talented strategist" and "supreme commander".[4]

There are a number of obvious reasons why we should not accept at face value this kind of retrospective evidence which has been thrown up by the Cultural Revolutionary polemics. Much of its credibility is destroyed by the indiscriminate way in which the charges are levelled. Each military leader who comes under attack

[1] "The Wicked History of Big Conspirator, Big Ambitionist, Big Warlord P'eng Te-huai," unidentified Red Guard source, n.p., *Current Background*, No. 851.

[2] "Lo Jui-ch'ing Deserves to Die 10,000 Times for His Crimes", *Ching kang shan* [Chingkang Mountains] and *Kuang tung wen i chan pao* [Kwangtung Literary and Combat Bulletin] (Canton), Nos. 7–8 (September 5, 1967), in *Survey of China Mainland Press* [*SCMP*], No. 4046.

[3] Lin Piao, speech at reception of army cadres, March 25, 1968, *Kung lien* [Workers' United Headquarters] (Canton), April, 1968, in *SCMP*, No. 4173.

[4] Wen Hung-chun and others, "The Novel 'Defend Yenan'—a Vivid Example of Opposing the Party through Novels", *Jen min jih pao* [People's Daily], November 12, 1967, in British Broadcasting Corporation, *Summary of World Broadcasts, Part III: Far East* [*FE*], No. 2635.

had his name linked to those who have already been denounced, and his name in turn joins the foot of the list to await the next target for attack. The Chinese indeed seem to go in for the same kind of guilt by retrospective association as some China Watchers do. Once the dismissal of a particular leader has been decided upon, meetings are held from Central Committee level downwards at which all those present are obliged to scrutinize their relationship with the accused and to "expose his crimes".[1] The charge sheet which eventually emerges may have little to do with the actual offences which led to his dismissal. The whole process is further encouraged by the importance always attached to rewriting the historical record in Communist China (and for that matter in dynastic China).

But the rapidity and ease with which these polemics have degenerated to the level of personal abuse, and the wealth of evidence in this vein which they purport to offer, does require some speculative consideration.

In the first place, it is reasonable to make an assumption that has in the past been too often ignored—that the Chinese Communist leaders are human beings like anyone else. They are equally likely to have been motivated, to some degree, by personal ambitions, friendships and dislikes, as by any more high-minded considerations for the "good of the Party" or "loyalty to the centre".

But in view of the remarkably low level of dissidence within the Party leadership in the past, it is also reasonable to assume that these personal emotions were, for the most part, subsumed or kept in check by the strong sense of discipline and cohesion which is one of the chief characteristics of Party life. Especially during the revolutionary periods, this sense of solidarity would have been reinforced by the objective situation in which disunity would have spelt political or military disaster for the Communist movement. As we shall see, a degree of local autonomy was in fact encouraged at various times, and decentralization of command stemmed naturally

[1] Three Central Committee meetings were held to discuss the dismissal of PLA Acting Chief of Staff Yang Cheng-wu in March, 1968, as a result of which a ragbag collection of his "crimes" was produced. Commenting on these, K'ang Sheng told a meeting on March 27 that "These are only what is already known to us...In the future, when our comrades will continue to expose him, I believe that more serious problems will be found." As no doubt they will.

from the scattered and geographically self-contained nature of the Communist-controlled areas, but these autonomist tendencies did not necessarily conflict with an over-all and mutually shared assumption of unified leadership.

After 1949, however, as the leadership expanded in size and in its functions, and as the pressure upon it for unity grew less under peacetime conditions, one may also assume that personal motives became more pronounced, and were less easily contained by abstract considerations of loyalty and discipline. Yet they were still kept within reasonable bounds so long as they were not unduly exacerbated by any major disagreement over national policy. But the Great Leap Forward—and here one may accept at least part of the retrospective version of events served up in the Cultural Revolution—constituted the first policy issue since 1949 on which differences of opinion within the leadership could no longer be contained by an appeal to inner-party solidarity. The repercussions of the dismissal of P'eng Te-huai in 1959, and of the continuing post-mortem on the failure of the Great Leap, can be traced as a continuous thread in the course of internal politics since then. The Leap acted as a catalyst upon the latent antipathies or rivalries within the leadership, and as time went on these became more pronounced, until the Cultural Revolution exposed them to public view.

If one distinguishes, moreover, between the façade of monolithic unity traditionally adopted by the Chinese Communist leadership, and the tolerance for free debate and disagreement which was sanctioned—as long as it was conducted behind closed doors—according to the principle of "inner-party democracy", one cannot rule out *a priori* the possibility that some of the revelations of the Cultural Revolution contain a measure of truth. Each case has therefore to be considered on its own merits, taking into account as far as possible such contemporary evidence as can be gleaned from the open press.

Nor is it even implausible that some of the anecdotes alleging disrespect for Chairman Mao on the part of his close colleagues may contain a grain of truth. While he may be a man possessing an unusually compelling "charisma", he also seems to have become—especially in recent years—a very difficult man to work with. Besides, the closer they were to him, the less they would be overawed by the charisma, and some may even have been wryly amused—if not irritated—by his latter-day deification. Thus Ho Lung, addressing members of the Hunan provincial CCP committee, is alleged to have commented that "Hunan is the home of our Emperor. It won't do to bungle things here."[1] As far as the PLA was concerned, its loss of influence and prestige after the Korean War, and its lower position in the scale of national priorities, may also have helped to sharpen old personal antagonisms. P'eng Te-huai, according to his wife, frequently complained after 1953 that he was old and unwanted, disliked by the Chairman, and that he was reluctant to be in the same place as Mao.[2]

The revolutionary period

It has often been shown that the Army and Party leaderships in the revolutionary period were virtually interchangeable, and that this symbiotic relationship minimized the opportunities for conflict. It was not so much a case of the Party being "in command of the gun", as of the Party holding the weapons in its own hands. After the Central Committee moved from Shanghai to the Kiangsi Soviet, the Communist movement never again suffered from the kind of divided leadership—urban-based political direction linked to rural-based military operations—which has been characteristic of many other insurgent movements, e.g. the Algerian FLN and until recently most of the South American movements.

Against this evident unity between the two leaderships, we should perhaps attach more weight to the pull of autonomous action and decision-making which was allowed or tolerated at various times during the revolution, although, as has already been shown, this was not necessarily in conflict with the over-all demands of unity. But at times it did give rise, as Mao himself admitted, to "certain phenomena of indiscipline and anarchy, localism and guerrilla-ism", although at other times it encouraged local commanders "to bring their initiative and enthusiasm into play and to come through long

---

[1] "Towering Crimes of Ho Lung...", see p. 377, footnote 2.
[2] Judge's note on the trial of P'u An-hsiu, *Ta p'i p'an t'ung hsün* [Great criticism bulletin], October 5, 1967, in *SCMP*, No. 4124.

periods of grave difficulties".[1] The phenomenon of localism was regarded as desirable or undesirable according to the military situation at that time. When the PLA was on the defensive, and local initiative at a premium, decentralization of command was actively encouraged, as in the lean years of 1942–3, and during the winter of 1947–8. But the stages of offensive expansion which followed both these periods called for a much greater degree of centralized direction, and for the elimination of these so-called "harmful" tendencies.

Even the greater autonomy allowed to local leadership in 1942–3 was qualified by the insistence that the highest source of authority at the local level should be concentrated in the Party rather than in the Army. The area "political and military committees" which had often been dominated by the Army forces in control, were to be abolished and replaced by "unified leadership" in the hands of the civilian Party committee.[2] The civilian Party secretary was to serve concurrently as political commissar of military units at the same level, and Army political departments were to become subdepartments of the Party committee.[3] Among the examples of "discord" given as the reason for these changes was the fact that ". . . the Army shows a lack of respect for local Party units and local government authority". In the future, it was stipulated, the regular armed forces should "carry out the decisions and resolutions of Party committees at all levels and the laws of all levels of government", only reserving for itself the right to initiate on strictly military and security matters —such as military movements, troop deployment, and martial law.[4]

[1] Mao, *Selected Works* (Peking: Foreign Languages Press, 1961–5), IV, 273. Mao was discussing here plans to strengthen collective, centralized, leadership on the eve of the major offensives of autumn–winter 1948. A similar critique of localism and guerrilla-ism was made by T'an Cheng in 1944, on the eve of the Communist forces' massive expansion in the last year of the anti-Japanese war.

[2] Note the parallel between the "political and military committees" and the "military and administrative committees" set up after 1949 to enforce military control over the newly liberated areas.

[3] Note also the parallel with the move after 1958 to place the regional or provincial PLA political commissarship in the hands of the first Party secretary of the same level (see below).

[4] "Central Committee Resolution on the Unification of Leadership in the Anti-Japanese War Bases", passed by the Politburo, September 1, 1942, trans.

The leadership since 1949

Although leadership nexus within the PLA can be identified dating back to the Kiangsi Soviet period, sometimes occupying the same field of responsibility, or geographical area, for decades on end, it is extremely hard to find any evidence that this had led to factional rivalry. The ease with which these groupings were dispersed in the early years of the People's Republic (or in some cases allowed to continue without apparent harmful results), has tended to support the hypothesis that any inclination towards centrifugal factionalism was counterbalanced by the tradition of loyalty to the "centre" and of deference to the Party's political control.

The crucial period is generally admitted to be that of 1950–4, in the course of which the organs of military control (the local military control committees and the regional military and administrative committees) were phased out, the six major military regions (coinciding with administrative regions) were replaced by thirteen smaller regions without administrative responsibility, and the regional military leadership "promoted upstairs", either to the rapidly expanding PLA General Headquarters in Peking, or to non-military Party or government office, or to the newly created and specialized service arms. It has also been taken as a sign of the absence of factionalism that these forms of promotion were extended, without favouritism or discrimination, to approximately equal numbers of leading officers from the commands of all four field armies. The fact that some military groupings were allowed to persist (especially in the remoter provinces) was also taken to indicate that the regime had no reason to fear that such groupings might in the future pose a factional threat to central stability.

But the avoidance of factionalism within the military leadership until the Cultural Revolution no longer seems quite so effortless or ineluctable. It begins to look less like an inherent characteristic of the system, and more like the product of a set of partly fortuitous circumstances (although the importance of the tradition of loyalty to the Party should still not be discounted). In the first place, the

in Boyd Compton, ed., *Mao's China, Party Reform Documents, 1942–44* (Seattle: Univ. of Washington Press, 1952), pp. 161–76.

Korean War provided an opportunity to break up the existing field army commands with the minimum of dissent, offering those who might otherwise feel aggrieved the chance to win their spurs once again on a different battlefield. Secondly, the large-scale transfer of PLA leaders to Party or government posts in the transition period of 1950–4 also helped to emasculate the field armies, while providing those thus transferred with the opportunity for advancement in a new field, again minimizing discord. Thirdly, the modernization of the PLA generated new jobs, higher status, and professional opportunities which would attract the genuine careerists in the PLA and compensate them for losing some of the perquisites of active command. Transfer to the rapidly expanding PLA General Headquarters in Peking was also probably regarded as a prestigious form of promotion. Meanwhile, the general move upwards in all these fields created space further down the ladder for promotion of lower-ranking officers. It was mainly this second echelon category of PLA leadership which, after 1954, was left undisturbed in the same areas where it had been active since before the Liberation, and in view of their relatively low status, it is unlikely that they were thought capable of posing any kind of threat to the centre.

But there was a small group of high-ranking Party leaders, also entrusted with concurrent military responsibility, who were not affected by this game of general post, such as Wang En-mao in Sinkiang, Ulanfu in Inner Mongolia, and Chang Kuo-hua in Tibet. It can be argued that the fact of them being left *in situ* indicates a lack of fear of military regionalism on the part of the centre, even in these traditionally separatist provinces. Yet the truth may not be quite so simple. Were they left undisturbed because they posed no threat, or because attempts to move them might generate a threat? Certainly the behaviour of all three of the leaders mentioned above during the Cultural Revolution, and the opposition displayed in their provinces, does suggest the possibility that their relationship with the centre may always have been more "autonomous" than that of the less remote provinces (although again with the proviso that local autonomy and de-centralization of responsibility from Peking may not have been frowned on, especially if it made for greater efficiency at the provincial level).

ARMY–PARTY SYSTEMS

The relationship between the Army and Party as *systems* also requires much closer investigation in the light of the Cultural Revolution. After the reorganization of 1954, the Army system of provincial military districts was matched by a similar system of provincial civilian Party committees and people's governments. Five of the 13 military regions (those of them which only covered one province) also had their Party and governmental counterparts. After 1960, the military regions were also ranged against the six much larger Party regional bureaux which had been reconstituted in that year.

A dual system also existed at the central level in Peking, where the Party Military Affairs Committee (MAC) was matched by the Ministry of Defence and its General Headquarters. Each side of this duality also possessed its own potential contradictions—between the MAC and the Central Committee (CC) to which it was technically subordinate, and between the MAC and its chain of lower level Party committees within the PLA on the one hand, and the General Political Department (GPD) and its chain of lower level political departments or bureaux on the other. Although the MAC–GPD relationship is strictly intra-Army, the MAC has sometimes appeared to be more "Party"-oriented, while the GPD tends to be more "professionally" inclined.[1]

National level

At the central level in Peking there has been no perceptible evidence of discord between the MAC and the CC (or rather the CC's Politburo which exercises effective power). The *ex officio* Chairman of the MAC's Standing Committee is probably Mao himself, and before the Cultural Revolution four of the Standing Committee members were also Politburo members, while all belonged to the CC. During the period covered by the secret Army documents (*Kung tso t'ung hsün*, 1961) the MAC seems to have had the freedom to

---

[1] Other points of possible intra-army systems friction, outside the scope of this study, but deserving closer attention, include the relationships between Military Region and Military District commands, between both of these and the Garrison Commands of major cities, between front-line troops and regional forces, and between the different service arms (army, navy, air-force, etc.).

initiate major acts of military policy with only formal approval by the CC.[1]

But the relationship between the Party/MAC and the MND/GHQ seems to have been considerably more complex. As far as we can tell, the years 1950–4 saw a steady growth in the responsibilities of the General Headquarters, which continued after the reorganization of 1954 and the creation of the Ministry of Defence, until by 1957 or thereabouts the MAC had virtually taken a back seat in military decision-making. (This was the period of leadership by P'eng Te-huai as Minister.) The years 1958–9 saw a reassertion of the powers of the MAC, probably inspired by Mao with the support of Lin Piao (elevated to the Politburo Standing Committee in May, 1958— the same month in which the MAC met to initiate radical changes in military policy). This led to the dismissal of the Minister and of the three GHQ heads (Chief of Staff, Directors of the Political and Rear Services Departments) in 1959. Under the new leadership of Lin Piao, the MAC continued to play the dominant role. A better working relationship with the MND/GHQ seems to have been established, but in the Cultural Revolution the new Chief of Staff and the Director of the Political Department again came unstuck (Lo Jui-ch'ing and Hsiao Hua).

Such friction as was generated by this relationship appears to have become most intense at the leadership levels of Minister of Defence and of the three GHQ heads (and among these three, particularly at that of Chief of Staff). It was at this level of leadership, occupying the key positions on the policy-transmission belt between the political centre and the military machine, that the conflicting pressures from above and below, and between political and military priorities, seems to have been most concentrated.

Both P'eng Te-huai and his successor, Lin Piao, were concurrently Minister of Defence and first Vice-Chairman of the MAC, but while P'eng seems to have preferred his ministerial hat, Lin has distinguished himself in his MAC capacity. Lo Jui-ch'ing, as Lin's new Chief of Staff, managed to maintain a delicate balancing act between the political and military aspects of his job for several

[1] Ralph L. Powell, *Politico-Military Relationships in Communist China* (Washington: Department of State, 1963), pp. 4–7.

years, but by 1964-5 (according to later charges against him), he had become alarmed that the extreme degree of politicization of the PLA now being advocated in Lin's name, and attempted to suggest tactfully that Lin "should not take charge of matters about the armed forces more than necessary".[1]

P'eng Te-huai has been accused of having sought to "liquidate" the MAC and to set up his own "military commission" (presumably based on the MND),[2] of having "failed to seek instructions beforehand or reported afterwards",[3] and of having placed his own nominees in the key leadership posts of the GHQ.[4] It is possible that P'eng's responsibilities for military policy-making had already begun to be curtailed in 1958-9, before his dismissal, when the MAC's role was reasserted.[5]

Local level

At the provincial level and below, local military commands have at various times been enjoined to accept the "supervision" of local Party, government and mass organizations. In January, 1954, the GPD instructed Army commands to delegate representatives to serve on local Party committees and to exchange information with them. At the Eighth Party Congress in September, 1956, T'an Cheng, Deputy Director of the GPD, emphasized that the PLA must not reject such supervision "on the plea of centralization of

[1] "Lo Jui-ch'ing Deserves to Die 10,000 Times for His Crimes", see p. 378, footnote 2.

[2] Li Hsin-kung, "Settle Account with P'eng Teh-huai for his Heinous Crimes of Usurping Army Leadership and Opposing the Party", *Peking Review*, No. 36 (September 1, 1967).

[3] "Principal Crimes of P'eng Te-huai, Big Ambitionist and Schemer," *Ching kang shan* [Chingkang Mountains] and *Kuang tung wen i chan pao* [Kwangtung Literary and Combat Bulletin] (Canton), Nos. 7-8 (September 5, 1967), in *SCMP*, No. 4046.

[4] "The wicked history of...P'eng Te-huai," see p. 378, footnote 1.

[5] This is implied in a remark alleged to have been made by P'eng during his self-criticism at the Eighth Plenum. "I am unwilling to serve as Minister of Defence and to take charge of routine work in the Military Commission. [He had been advised by his Chief of Staff, Huang K'o-ch'eng, that]...since the Central Committee had already made a decision on the matter, it was better for me not to bring it up again" (source as preceding footnote).

command".[1] On the eve of the Cultural Revolution, in his report to the PLA Political Work Conference of January, 1966, Hsiao Hua, the GPD Director, stated unequivocally that "The system of dual leadership by the military command and the local Party committees, under the unified leadership of the Party's Central Committee, must be enforced."[2]

What precisely is meant by "supervision", and how would local military commanders react to such a requirement? There are two well-defined areas where the PLA accepts advice from local authorities, in organizing and training the militia, and in establishing quotas for the annual conscription.[3] There is a wide variety of other issues where, in the interests of good public relations and of "Army-people unity", the local authorities should be consulted (e.g. requisition of land or housing, grain procurement, conduct of military manoeuvres, etc.). Considerable efforts were made in 1956–8 to strengthen this form of consultation, in order to dissipate popular grievances which had arisen because "some units...do not maintain the same close connections with local Party and government organs as in the past".[4] Local PLA commanders and commissars are encouraged to maintian close liaison with key local leaders, and on occasion they are invited to "sit in" at meetings of local Party committees.[5]

But the question becomes more delicate if it is a matter not merely of "supervision" by Party authorities on issues where heavy-handed military action might harm civil relations, but also of—as Hsiao Hua implied—"leadership". In 1949–54 most leadership that was exercised had operated in the reverse direction, with the PLA dominating two, and prominent on two others, of the six military and administrative Committees, as well as a number of provincial

[1] T'an Cheng, "Questions of Political Work at the New Stage of Army Building", report to the Eighth CCP National Congress, September 18, 1956, trans. in *Current Background*, No. 422.

[2] *New China News Agency* [*NCNA*], January 24, 1966, in *SCMP*, No. 3627. The context makes it clear that the reference here is not to Party committees *within* the PLA, but to civilian Party committees of the same level.

[3] A. Doak Barnett, *Cadres, Bureaucracy, and Political Power in Communist China* (New York: Columbia Univ. Press, 1957), pp. 242–9.

[4] *Jen min jih pao*, January 17, 1957, in *SCMP*, No. 1459.

[5] Barnett, *Cadres, Bureaucracy*..., p. 249.

and municipal governments.[1] But this was not entirely a one-way affair. It has been noted that, in the early 1950's, the top post of PLA political commissar in the provincial military districts was usually held by a Party veteran who often doubled as provincial Party secretary.[2] After 1954, the separation between military and Party/civilian leaderships was almost complete (with a few special exceptions, e.g. Inner Mongolia and Sinkiang). While the military were excluded from local Party and government organs, their own political commissars were always PLA men rather than political importees. The military commander frequently doubled as political commissar of the same unit.[3]

But after 1958, as Party control of the PLA was again reasserted, the post of first political commissar in the Military Regions and Districts came increasingly under the control of the senior ranking Party official—again usually the first secretary of the provincial Party committee (or, after 1960, of the regional Party bureau). Most of these appointments date from the time of Lin Piao's succession to P'eng Te-huai or later, but they were not necessarily Lin's men. As Professor Powell has suggested, they may have been installed by the Party apparatus in order to provide a counterbalance to Lin's growing influence. (The great majority of them have in fact been unseated in the Cultural Revolution—commissars of nine military regions have been dismissed, as against only one commander from the same regions, and the casualty rate of commissars as against commanders in military districts has also been much higher.)[4]

Perhaps by way of compensation, there was later a discernible trend in the opposite direction, with some regional or provincial military commanders being awarded a concurrent position on the

[1] Gittings, *The Role of the Chinese Army* (London: Oxford Univ. Press, 1967), pp. 268–71. The two regions under extensive PLA control were the Northwest and Southwest. There was a sizable PLA presence on the Central-South and East MAC's, but only a small representation in North and Northeast China.

[2] Donald W. Klein, "The 'Next Generation' of Chinese Communist Leaders", *The China Quarterly*, No. 12 (October–December, 1962).

[3] Over-all PLA influence in the upper ranks of the Party declined during the same period. See calculations in Klein, "The 'Next Generation'".

[4] R. L. and H. F. Powell, "Continuity and Purge in the PLA", *Marine Corps Gazette*, LXII, No. 2 (February, 1968).

corresponding civilian Party committee, but the numbers and the positions involved were less significant.

One would therefore suspect that, since 1958, the relationship between local Party and Army systems has involved a good deal of balancing and compromise, and has on occasion given rise to a degree of friction. One Cultural Revolution document gives, in dramatized form, some idea of the sources of tension.

In an attack on Ou-yang Ch'in and Li Fan-wu, first and second secretaries of the Heilungkiang provincial Party committee, it is claimed that

In order to set up an "independent kingdom" in the province, they employed every conceivable means to oppose the leadership of the Party Central Committee and the Military Affairs Committee [operating through] the Military Affairs Committee in the Heilungkiang Provincial Military District, saying, with ulterior motives, that the Provincial Military District was not a part of the national defence army or the regular army, and that its task was mainly concerned with the localities and its principal leadership was the Provincial CCP Committee... The Political Commissar they planted in the Heilungkiang Provincial Military District never concerned himself with the problem of militia organization, but on the contrary, belittled the important role played by the people's militia in defending the dictatorship of the proletariat, and strangled militia work in the province.[1]

This passage suggests (a) resistance by the local Party to MAC control overithe provincial forces, (b) some disagreement as to how far provincial troops came under the same jurisdiction as regional forces, (c) control by the Party authorities of the Military District, through their own appointee as political commissar.

[1] Lung Wei-tung, "Repudiate the Towering Crimes of Ou-yang Ch'in and Li Fan-wu in Opposing Chairman Mao's Military-Thinking", Harbin Radio, October 6, 1967, in *FE*, No. 2632.

A similar charge was levelled against Ulanfu in Inner Mongolia. He was alleged to have sought "to build a national army in a vain attempt to separate the units of Inner Mongolia from the PLA system", and to have "clamoured that he and the Central Authorities should assume dual leadership in the Inner Mongolia Military Region", basing his argument on such pretexts as "the special nature of Inner Mongolia" and "the problems of the nationalities", Huhehot Radio, July 26, 1968, in *FE*, No. 2838.

Militia and regional forces

Differences of opinion over the importance to be attached to the militia and to the "regional forces" (second-line troops) may also have political overtones, since both bodies—corresponding to the militia and the guerrilla forces of the revolutionary period—were in varying degrees "not divorced from production", confined to their own locality, and therefore more subject to civilian/Party than to military control.

P'eng Te-huai has been accused of deciding, in April, 1953, to cut the militia by 10–30%, and of having ruled that "from now on no more emphasis should be laid on the universal application of the militia system".[1] It is alleged that the "people in authority taking the capitalist road" were always opposed to militia expansion. "They regarded the people's militia...as a great hindrance for them in usurping the Party, military and political power...They either directly opposed the arming of the masses and the organizing of contingents of the people's militia on a big scale, or advocated the purely military viewpoint in the course of militia building."[2]

These charges are quite consistent with the contemporary record of militia policy. In November, 1950 a directive on "strengthening militia building"—which P'eng is now said to have reversed in 1953, set the target for militia expansion at 5% of the total population, or 23,700,000, to be achieved within three years.[3] Less than half of the target was ever achieved, and the militia system was entirely eclipsed in 1954, when conscription was introduced, and an entirely separate reserve system—not including the militia—set up.

The militia was revived in 1957, when it was merged with the reserve system, and received a massive stimulus to growth in the "everyone a soldier" movement of 1958 which accompanied the

[1] "The Wicked History Of...P'eng Te-huai," see p. 378, footnote 1. The same document relates how "In June through December 1953, traitor P'eng Te-huai arbitrarily decided to 'replace the militia with the reserve service, abolish the militia and recall the arms issued to guard against the rise of problems.' This brought heavy losses and confusion to militia work from 1954 through 1956."

[2] *Chieh fang chün pao* [Liberation Army Daily], editorial, August 6, 1967, in *FE*, No. 2537.

[3] Chang Ching-wu, "Strengthening our Militia Work", *NCNA*, November 21, 1950.

Great Leap Forward. At the time this was admitted to have met with
opposition in the PLA, on the grounds that "fighting is the business
of the army, and the masses must not be mobilized and relied upon".[1]
P'eng is also accused of opposing this move, arguing in August, 1958
that "Regarding the extensive establishment of militia divisions and
people's communes, my view is that one of them will crumble one
day."[2] The militia was cut back in 1960, when it became clear that
the campaign had got out of hand, but expansion was again urged
from 1962 onwards. Lo Jui-ch'ing, by then Chief of Staff, is said to
have obstructed this move, and a number of provincial leaders
followed his suit.[3]

The history of the so-called "regional forces" is more obscure.
At the time of the Korean War, there was a distinction between the
first-line field armies, and the second-line "regional independent
armies" (*chün ch'u tu li shih*), the latter at a lower state of readiness
and capability, serving as garrison troops, and also providing manpower to replenish the field armies at the Korean front. The regional
armies in turn were replenished from the militia, and the whole
tripartite system was a close copy of that in force during the revolutionary period.

With the introduction of conscription in 1954, the regional forces
as well as the militia, appear to have been allowed to lapse into
obscurity, although Mao is said to have "repeatedly" argued in
favour of their expansion from 1949 onwards.[4] The question was

[1] Liu Hsien-sheng, "Let the Whole People be Armed to Defend the Homeland", *Kiang su ch'ün chung* [Kiangsu Masses], October 1, 1958, in *Extracts from
China Mainland Magazines*, No. 150.

[2] As p. 391, footnote 1.

[3] Yen Hung-yen, Party secretary and military political commissar of Yunnan
province, "obstructed the exchange of experiences in the study and application
of Mao's works among the militia and he exerted pressure on the Armed Forces
Department, demanding that their cadres concentrate on production and construction work and neglect Armed Forces work". Yen also failed to convey an
important report of Lin Piao on militia policy in 1962 (Kunming Radio,
August 23, 1967, in *FE*, No. 2556). T'ao Chu is said to have advised, "Don't
get too many [militia]. For a brigade, some 10 militiamen are enough. For a
commune, two basic backbone militia squads are enough" (Nanning Radio,
August 21, 1967).

[4] "Basic differences between the proletarian and bourgeois military lines",
Jen min jih pao, September 7, 1967, trans. in *Peking Review*, No. 48 (November
24, 1967), p. 14.

revived in 1960, when Mao directed that "a certain number of divisions should be selected from the main forces and sent to the coastal provinces to serve as backbone for the local armed forces". Lo Jui-ch'ing opposed siphoning off front-line forces in this way, allegedly with Liu Shao-ch'i's backing, and shelved Mao's directive for nearly five years; or so we are told.[1]

Apart from the political overtones, some of the objections to the expansion of the militia and of the regional forces were undoubtedly purely strategic, and were part of the continuing debate as to whether Mao's revolutionary strategy was still relevant for the purposes of national defence with a modernized army. It is noteworthy that an important textbook on national defence published in 1956 failed even to mention either the militia or the regional forces, and the emphasis on them from the Great Leap Forward onwards may derive largely from a renewed preoccupation on Mao's part with military affairs.[2]

PLA Party membership

The Army has in the past been one of the main sources for recruitment of Party members, both because it was felt desirable to strengthen the political loyalties of its own personnel by enrolling them in the Party, and because—at most times in its history—its recruits were chosen selectively and constituted an elite of sorts by comparison with the civilian population.

Although we lack precise figures, it seems likely that throughout the anti-Japanese and civil wars, the military proportion of total Party membership was in the region of 20%, and at times probably much more.[3] In 1950, there were some 1¼ million Party members in the PLA, out of a total Party strength of approximately 5,800,000.

[1] "Lo Jui-ch'ing Deserves to Die...", *ibid.*

[2] Shang Ta, *Chung kuo kuo fang shuang shu* (Peking: n.p., 1956), V, Part I, trans. as "The Strengthening of National Defence and Socialist Construction", by *Joint Publications Research Service*, No. 22,800 (January 20, 1964).

[3] In writings before the Long March, Mao had suggested an optimum ratio of 1–1 or 1–2 Party members in the Army. By 1950, this ratio had declined to slightly less than 1–4, John Gittings, *The Role of the Chinese Army*, pp. 110–11. Assuming that the lower ratio was operative during the period of 1937–49, and comparing the figures thus obtained with known Party membership in these years, we arrive at a fairly constant ratio for the whole period of 1–5 military members in the Party at large.

The next six years saw an expansion of the Party by almost 100%, but there was no corresponding recruitment programme in the PLA.

Liu Shao-ch'i has now been accused of deliberately halting Party recruitment in many Army units after 1949, while An Tzu-wen, director of the Party's Organization Department, has also been charged with discouraging Army membership after 1954. Both appear to have felt that PLA Party membership should be confined to reliable revolutionary veterans, and that new Party recruits should be sought in civilian society.[1]

Soon after Lin Piao took charge of military policy in 1959, renewed attention was paid to Party recruitment in the Army, which was admitted to have been seriously neglected in the past. By April, 1961, it was reported that 229,000 new Party members had been recruited in the past year, and frequent emphasis has been placed since then on the need to maintain this momentum, in order to counteract attrition through demobilization and retirement.[2] Thus it

[1] According to an article written by the "proletarian revolutionary committee" of the Central Committee Organization Department, "Liu Shao-ch'i...vainly attempted to have our Party surrender its Army and dissolve the Party organization in the Army. Shortly after the liberation of the entire country, he issued a black order that 'all those units not composed of combat troops should stop increasing their Party membership and re-organise; a decision will be made when it is necessary to increase Party membership again in those units'...An Tzu-wen said: 'As a result of the current peaceful circumstances and the enforcement of the compulsory service system, it is not necessary to enlist too many Party members from among the fighters who have generally not undergone the test of war'," Anhwei Radio, May 12, 1968, in *FE*, No. 2772.

A similar charge was made in Yu Chih-tien, "Party organisation must be composed of advanced elements of the proletariat", *Kuang ming jih pao* [Bright Daily], October 22, 1968, in *SCMP*, No. 4296, and on Anhwei Radio, October 18, 1968, summarized in *China News Analysis* (Hong Kong), No. 736 (November 8, 1968), p. 4.

[2] See *Kung tso t'ung hsün* [Bulletin of Activities], No. 23 (June 13, 1961). In his report of February 2, 1963 to the PLA Political Work Conference (*SCMP*, No. 2971), Hsiao Hua, Director of the General Political Department, observed that "because every year there are large numbers of old warriors retiring from the Army and new ones joining it the Party branches must constantly and carefully do the work of recruiting Party members. The requirement that every platoon have a small group of Party members and every section have some Party members, which is laid down in the resolution of the enlarged session of the Military [Affairs] Committee [of September–October, 1960], is suited to the conditions inside the forces and must be complied with."

was reported in 1965 that "hundreds of thousands" of young officers and fighters had joined the Party, while "several hundred thousand distinguished youths" had joined the Communist Youth League.

This revival of interest in PLA Party recruitment can be explained simply enough by the need, felt to be urgent after P'eng Te-huai's dismissal, to strengthen Party control over the Army. There was also a general expansion of (civilian) Party strength in these years.[1] But one wonders just how anxious the Party bureaucracy may have been to see their ranks swelled by novitiates from an Army which itself was becoming increasingly "Maoified" under Lin Piao.

Some concern may also have been caused by the new political departments set up during the "Learn from the PLA" campaign of 1964 in civilian industrial and commercial organs on a nationwide basis. These were directly modelled on the example of the PLA's political department structure, and they were staffed by Army cadres who had been detached from active service for this purpose. Both Liu and Teng Hsiao-p'ing have been charged with opposing this move, on the grounds—as Teng allegedly put it—that "factories must produce, schools must run their classes, and commercial firms have their business to do—they are different from the PLA". Liu Shao-ch'i is said to have insisted that the new departments should be "put under the control of economic departments of equivalent level" (i.e. not under military control), to have closed down "learn from the PLA" political training courses, and to have forbidden Party cadres to attend study classes at PLA political institutes.[2]

POLITICAL INDOCTRINATION AND CONTROL

Programmes of political indoctrination in the PLA—whether by

[1] See Table 2, in John W. Lewis, *Leadership in Communist China* (Ithaca: Cornell Univ. Press, 1963), pp. 110–11.

[2] Article by Ku Tien of the Political Department, of the Industry and Communications Centre, Peking Radio, December 16, 1967, in *FE*, No. 2650. Yü Ch'iu-li, Minister of Petroleum, is also said to have resisted the placing of PLA men in 1964 in his Ministry's political departments. Lo Jui-ch'ing supposedly objected to the placement of PLA cadres in national defence industries on the grounds that this policy was "an expression of distrust for the Party and the masses".

study or through such "therapeutic" practices as sending officers to the ranks or soldiers to work in the field—have, as might be expected, fluctuated according to the ebb and flow of actual political control. There is a close correlation since 1949 between the following four factors—(i) Party occupancy of military political commissarship, (ii) relative importance of the political and military chains of command within the Army, (iii) time devoted by Army units to political study, and (iv) PLA participation in the kind of "revolutionary" practices suggested above. A rough graph would show a strong political "presence" immediately after Liberation, with the Army and Party components of leadership still hard to distinguish, the company commissar system still going strong (as was evident in the early phase of the Korean War), and—until the Korean War began—a diminution of the PLA's relative status, with beginnings made in programmes for large-scale demobilization and diversion of Army units to production work.

The Korean War and the "modernization and regularization" trend of 1952 onwards saw a predictable decline in the political presence. "Weapons" became more important than "the human factor", the political system was allowed to fall into disrepair, political officers adjured to "pay more attention to military matters" and to defer to the military commander, the MAC surrendering much of its responsibilities to the MND and the PLA GHQ. The years 1956-9 manifested a new upsurge in attempts to restore "revolutionary" practices, now resisted by the emerging professional class. These attempts were characterized by a certain crudity and indiscriminate application of such practices (e.g., a massive economy campaign, inflated targets for PLA production work, etc.) without much regard for their relevance under changed peacetime conditions. In all probability, these efforts were largely counter-productive, arousing or intensifying the very non- or anti-political tendencies which they were designed to check, and leading to a crisis of confidence in 1958-9 and to the dismissal of P'eng Te-huai and the top GHQ leadership.

Under Lin Piao from 1959 onwards, a much more rational approach was adopted towards politicization of the PLA, in which many of the more dramatic "revolutionary" policies were quietly downgraded, while an intensive effort was made to instil political values and Party control at basic PLA levels, especially focused on the company level. A high point was reached in 1964, with the "learn from the PLA" campaign, when the PLA's techniques of political work were offered as a model for the entire nation.

In 1965, however, immediately before the Cultural Revolution, the balance which had been maintained—with some degree of success—between military and political priorities under Lin Piao's leadership began to break down. New and more extreme measures of politicization (increased Mao-study, abolition of ranks and titles, etc.) may have had the same counter-productive effect which had been brought about in 1958–9 by the "revolutionary" excesses of that time. It is at this point that Chief of Staff Lo Jui-ch'ing appears to have parted company with Lin Piao.

The evidence revealed by the Cultural Revolution on the alleged opposition by P'eng, Lo and others to political control and indoctrination of the PLA tends to support the conclusions which have been previously reached on the basis of pre-Cultural Revolutionary charges against unnamed "persons" who resisted "Chairman Mao's military line". Although P'eng and Lo are now accused of outright opposition to politicization of the PLA as such, the evidence suggests, on the face of it, that they were opposed not to the principle but to the degree of politicization.

Both P'eng and Lo are quoted as acknowledging that political work was essential, but that it was no substitute for military technique. As Lo is supposed to have said, "If political work is not well done, the soldiers will retreat in battle. But if soldiers have no military skill and their shooting is inaccurate, when the enemy rushes them in battle, will the soldiers not then retreat?"[1] This view that "Redness" and "expertise" should be regarded as mutually complementary, has in fact been standard doctrine for most of the post-1949 period, and has only been overtly disowned during the Cultural Revolution (and previously, although to a lesser extent, during the Great Leap Forward).

Whether or not all the charges against P'eng, Lo, *et al.* can be regarded as accurate if applied to them personally, they reflect

[1] *Chieh fang jih pao*, August 30, 1967, in *FE*, No. 2557.

trends of dissent over military policy which could be deduced before the Cultural Revolution. The issues involved include (i) attitude towards political work, (ii) the relative importance of military train-training, (iii) military implications of the Sino–Soviet split, and (iv) contingency planning for national defence.[1]

[1] The terms of debate, as expounded during the Cultural Revolution, on these issues have been fully analysed elsewhere, and a few examples will suffice. On military training, Lo argued that "to be prepared against war, good military training is still the most important and most basic from the standpoint of the military" (*NCNA*, August 25, 1967). Lo has been sharply criticized for organizing a national "military tournament" in 1964, on the theory that "when military skills are good, politics will naturally be good", and that "politics is the primary thing, but it won't do if we do not fight well." P'eng believed that "The achievement of our armed forces on military training and the mastery of military techniques...are the basic criteria for judging [its] fighting power today and in the future." *Hung ch'i* [Red Flag], Army Day editorial, No. 12 (August 1, 1967).

Precise attitudes towards Sino–Soviet relations are more difficult to pinpoint. P'eng was involved in the abortive negotiations on nuclear sharing of 1958–9, and his tour of Eastern Europe immediately preceded his downfall. He is now accused of having had "illicit relations with foreign countries" (*ibid.*). Some analysts have argued that Lo favoured a more positive commitment to Vietnam in 1965, coupled with a limited degree of "united action" with the Soviet Union. Liu Shao-ch'i himself is said to have advocated "the dependence of China's national defences on Soviet atomic bombs" and to have obstructed China's nuclear weapons programme (*Jen min jih pao*, October 1, 1967, in *FE* 2585). It is suggested that some leaders objected to the expense of this programme and the resources which it consumed, arguing that "scientific research is for production and must suit its needs" (*NCNA*, August 27, 1967, in *FE*, No. 2554).

The debate over strategy centred on the correct national defence posture to be adopted in the face of possible invasion by the U.S.A.—basically, on whether Mao's revolutionary strategy was still relevant, or whether, as P'eng Te-huai is supposed to have said, "Mao Tse-tung's military thinking is out of date and no longer applicable". Mao's strategy envisaged, in case of invasion, a close quarters war of a semi-guerrilla type, relying equally upon the Army, the regional forces and the militia, in which the enemy would be lured into Chinese territory, and then annihilated. The military revisionists are supposed to have advocated a policy of passive rather than of active defence, in which a regular modernized army would hold the enemy "outside the gates" (i.e., on China's frontiers), with "the building of defensive works everywhere and wide dispersal of forces to man them" ("Basic Differences between the Proletarian and Bourgeois Military Lines," *Jen min jih pao*, September 7, 1967, in *SCMP*, No. 4028). Mao's more militant strategy leads, paradoxically, to the placing of a lower priority on military preparedness and to greater caution in foreign–military policy, since while it emphasizes defence rather than offence, the means of defence are primarily ideological (the masses mobilized by the thought of Mao)

It may be doubted, however, whether these disputes over policy, important as the issues are, would have sufficed in themselves to provoke the cleavages which are revealed by the evidence which has surfaced in the Cultural Revolution—even after allowing for polemical exaggerations. The purpose of this paper is simply to suggest that the frictions generated by personal leadership rivalries, and by the duality of Army and Party control systems, may have played a larger part than the pre-Cultural Revolutionary picture led us to believe. Exactly how much weight should be attached to these factors is a question which can only be answered after a much closer investigation than has been attempted here.

THE PLA AND THE CULTURAL REVOLUTION

If, as this paper argues, much more attention should now be paid to the discordant rather than to the unifying features of the traditional PLA–Party relationship (although without going to the other extreme and detecting conflict in every nook and cranny), the PLA's role in the Cultural Revolution may come into clearer focus. For the most impressive aspect of the PLA's behaviour since the Cultural Revolution began has been its ambiguity, and its failure to side unequivocally with either of the main contending powers.

On balance it may still be argued that the PLA has taken the "Maoist" side, at least in the negative sense of failing to adopt any form of organized action to thwart even those aspects of the Cultural Revolution which were against its own interests. Loyalty may be too strong a word for the PLA's attitude towards the Maoist centre in Peking, but it can certainly be credited with self-restraint, especially when one considers the extent of provocation, of the purge

rather than military (weapons and defence installations). The exception is nuclear defence, apparently valued by Mao as much for its psychological as for its deterrent benefits.

Once again it should be emphasized that all of these retrospective charges, served up with the full flavour of the Cultural Revolution polemics, should be treated with suspicion, in so far as they purport to describe specific events or individuals. But it is a fact that the issues to which they refer are ones which, according to pre-Cultural Revolution evidence, have been subjects for debate and disagreement within the Chinese leadership.

of high-ranking officers, and of the indignities which have been inflicted upon the PLA during the Cultural Revolution.

There have been isolated instances in the provinces where the PLA, or some segment of it, has adopted a position which is clearly "anti-Maoist", but in general there is little specific evidence to show that the Army has been actively disloyal, and it has been considerably more docile than the Party apparatus, as the leaders of the Cultural Revolution have frequently pointed out.[1] Far less has the PLA shown any intention of "taking over" the country, despite the impressive amount of actual political power placed in its hands, as a less well indoctrinated or more ambitious army might have done long before.

At the same time we must acknowledge that the PLA's sympathy —albeit reluctant—for the Cultural Revolution has been retained by a number of significant concessions, whereby the authorities in Peking implicitly acknowledged that there were finite limits to its obedience. At the start of the Cultural Revolution, it was virtually granted exemption from the movement in the 16-Point Decision of the Central Committee Eleventh Plenum of August, 1966. Subsequently, every attempt by the radical faction in Peking to promote "revolution" within the PLA, or to "drag out the capitalist-roaders" from within its ranks, led to a renewed emphasis upon the PLA's prestigious and relatively privileged role. By 1968, the view that "there should be a Cultural Revolution in the PLA" was officially regarded as a heresy of an ultra-leftist variety.

Moreover, in spite of the lack of overt opposition on the part of the PLA, one may still detect its restraining influence in the more

[1] Thus Chou En-lai, in a speech of April 21, 1968: "Capitalist-roaders are of course found in individual army units; we cannot say that all army units are without capitalist-roaders. But such units are few and isolated. This is because there are two different traditions. Despite the trouble made by P'eng Te-huai, the army is under the direct control of Chairman Mao at the highest level, and that is why he could not change in a short period the traditions of more than 40 years. But capitalist-roaders infiltrated Party and government organs and so there are relatively more capitalist-roaders there", *Hung ch'i t'ung hsün* [Red Flag Dispatches] (Canton), June, 1968, in *SCMP*, No. 4218. See also similar remarks made by Chou En-lai and K'ang Sheng at a reception on June 12, 1968, for military leaders from Wuhan, trans. in *Selections from China Mainland Magazines*, No. 622.

moderate policies which, after two years of Cultural Revolution, were eventually adopted. To this extent the ultra-leftists had a point when they argued that the new revolutionary committees were simply a perpetuation of military and Party "bourgeois rule", in direct opposition to the true spirit of the Cultural Revolution. It seems plausible to suppose that the Maoist leadership in Peking was to some extent uncertain of the extent to which it could rely upon the PLA's loyalty, if pushed too far, and that the PLA's dominant role in most of the revolutionary committees was a tacit acknowledgement of the leadership's uncertainty. When one examines the actual performance of the PLA in individual provinces, it becomes even more difficult to characterize it as "pro-Mao". For the PLA almost invariably sided with, and sometimes even gave financial and material support to, the less radical "rebel" groups, while seeking to restrain (although usually with circumspection out of fear that it would be criticized) the more revolutionary and truly Maoist factions.

Finally, we can hardly regard as trivial the very extensive changes which have taken place within the uppermost echelon of military leadership in China, and the lack of vocal support for the Cultural Revolution from all but a minute fraction of this leadership.

But if the PLA cannot be regarded as unequivocally on the side of the Maoist angels during the Cultural Revolution, far less can it be cast into outer darkness among the oppositionist "ghosts and monsters". The mere attempt to choose between the two sides placed the PLA on the horns of an impossible dilemma. For the PLA, just as the rest of Chinese society, was deprived of the vital moral prop which sustained it in the past—the belief that there existed a unitary source of political authority as embodied in the Party. Now there existed two rival sources of authority—the Party bureaucracy on the one hand and the Maoist theocracy on the other.

Assuming that the record of PLA–Party relations in the past was more chequered than appeared on the surface, we can more easily understand why the Army failed to rally to the side of the anti-Mao Party and government opposition. For this was the side which previously counterbalanced the PLA at national and local levels, perhaps on occasion being seen more as rivals than as partners.

The Maoist faction, on the other hand, had since 1959 sought to build up the PLA's status and prestige at the expense of the established Party and government machine. Yet in so doing, it had advocated "revolutionary" policies which were directly opposed to the orthodox goals of the PLA, and the prestigious role of the PLA which the Maoist faction endorsed involves an unremitting participation in revolutionary politics at the expense of military technique and preparedness.

The bilateral relationship between the PLA and Party, with all its sources of potential friction should by the time of the Cultural Revolution in fact more properly be described in terms of a triangular relationship between, the PLA, the Party and the Maoists. For while the PLA and the Party as power systems and leadership groupings may have come into conflict in the past, the general military policies to which the PLA had taken exception tended to emanate more from the revolutionary Maoists. Some sections of the PLA—those for whom its revolutionary traditions were still vivid—may have had more temperamentally in common with the Maoists, but many others among the younger professional generation may have felt closer to the orthodox Party.

As the Cultural Revolution increasingly gave flesh and body to factional inclinations, this triangular relationship probably became even more confused. Alliances of convenience seem to have been formed between those elements which might on the face of it seem to have least in common. A veteran revolutionary provincial commander might join forces with his bureaucratic Party counterpart (whom he had clashed with in the past) against the Maoist centre, in order to keep the local revolutionaries from throwing his area of command into chaos. A "professional" service arm commander, on the other hand, who was totally opposed to Maoist strategy, might still choose the Maoist side, in the belief that it was more likely to favour a dominant role for the PLA in China's future political make-up. Many other permutations between unlikely partners could be imagined. Perhaps it was this sense of confusion and uncertainty as to what its role should be, as much as its much-vaunted selflessness and respect for central authority, which led the PLA to "stand idly by" in the Cultural Revolution, refraining from simply "taking over" the country in the interests of law and order as most self-respecting armies in a similar situation would have done long before. Whether a breaking-point in the PLA's loyalty to the centre might have been reached, if the Cultural Revolution had proceeded indefinitely, has become at the time of writing an academic question. The decisive shift back to more moderate policies in the autumn of 1968, in which the PLA has played a dominant part, and the tough measures adopted against the Red Guards and "rebels", cannot fail to be welcomed by China's military establishment. But was this shift itself dictated to some extent by the centre's fears that the PLA's patience had been tried too sorely and for too long?

Many observers would still discount the possibility that such a threat was a significant factor in the deliberations of Peking. The fact that the question should be raised at all is a reflection of the more critical approach which—in the light of the Cultural Revolution—must now be adopt towards the role of the PLA in China. The case for a massive "reversal of verdicts" on the PLA as seen from outside is not proven, but it has acquired a somewhat less virtuous—although at the same time more human—dimension, which in time may lead us to a more balanced view of its relationship with the Party.

CONTRIBUTORS

THOMAS P. BERNSTEIN is a lecturer in the Department of Political Science at Yale and a Ph.D. candidate at Columbia. He has taught at Indiana University and is working on a comparative analysis of collectivization of agriculture in China and Russia.

PHILIP BRIDGHAM, a research analyst at the Central Intelligence Agency, received his Ph.D. from the Fletcher School of Law and Diplomacy in 1951 and has taught political science at the University of Hawaii, the Massachusetts Institute of Technology and Dickinson College. His recent publications have focused on the origin and development of the Cultural Revolution.

WILLIAM F. DORRILL is Associate Director of the Center for International Studies at the University of Pittsburgh and Chairman of the Asian Studies Program. After doing graduate work at Virginia, The Australian National University and Harvard, he served successively in the U.S. Government, the RAND Corporation, and the Research Analysis Corporation. His research interests include the politics of Contemporary China and the history of the Chinese Communist Party.

JOHN GITTINGS, a Research Fellow at the Centre for International Studies, London School of Economics, was previously China Editor of the *Far Eastern Economic Review*, Hongkong. He is the author of books on the Chinese People's Liberation Army and on the Sino-Soviet dispute.

MERLE GOLDMAN is a Research Associate of the East Asian Research Center at Harvard where she received her Ph.D. in 1964. She has written a book on literary dissent in Communist China and currently is working on the conflict between the intellectuals and the Maoists from the early sixties through the Cultural Revolution.

DONALD W. KLEIN is a Research Associate at the East Asian Institute Columbia University. His research interests are focused on the Chinese Communist bureaucracy, with particular emphasis on elite studies.

JOHN WILSON LEWIS, Professor of Political Science and Director of the Center for East Asian Studies at Stanford University, received his doctorate from the University of California, Los Angeles, in 1962. He taught at Cornell University for seven years, and his publications include books and articles on Communist China as well as on U.S. policy in Vietnam. He is currently working on a study of the North China coal-mining city of Tangshan.

MICHEL OKSENBERG is Assistant Professor of Political Science and Research Associate at the East Asian Institute at Columbia University. He has taught at Stanford University where he will assume a position in 1970. His research interests are focused on contemporary Chinese government and politics.

LEONARD BERTRAM SCHAPIRO, Professor of Political Science with Special Reference to Russian Studies at the University of London (London School of Economics and Political Science), studied law at University College, London and was called to the Bar by Gray's Inn. Before joining the Government Department of the London School of Economics and Political Science in 1955 he practised at the Bar in London. His research and publications until recently were mainly focused on the Russian revolutionary movement and on the Communist Party of the Soviet Union. He is now mainly devoting himself to work on the history of political thought in Russia.

STUART R. SCHRAM is Professor of Politics with Reference to China in the University of London and Head of the Contemporary China Institute of the School of Oriental and African Studies. He received his doctorate from Columbia University in 1954, and thereafter carried out research for 13 years at the Fondation Nationale des Sciences Politiques in Paris before moving to London in 1967. He has written on the life and thought of Mao Tse-tung, and on the Asian metamorphoses of Marxism–Leninism.

BENJAMIN I. SCHWARTZ, Professor of History and Government and a member of the research staff of the East Asian Research Center at Harvard University, received his Ph.D. from Harvard in 1950. His publications include work on the intellectual history of modern China, the history of Chinese communism, and Chinese Communist ideology.

C. MARTIN WILBUR is George Sansom Professor of Chinese History at Columbia University where he received his Ph.D. in 1941. He was formerly Director of the East Asian Institute, Columbia University, and is the author of various monographs and articles on the history of the Chinese Communist movement.

INDEX